Class Warfare in Black Atlanta

Justice, Power, and Politics
Heather Ann Thompson and Rhonda Y. Williams, editors

EDITORIAL ADVISORY BOARD
Dan Berger   Barbara Ransby
Peniel E. Joseph Vicki L. Ruiz
Daryl Maeda   Marc Stein

The Justice, Power, and Politics series publishes new works in history that explore the myriad struggles for justice, battles for power, and shifts in politics that have shaped the United States over time. Through the lenses of justice, power, and politics, the series seeks to broaden scholarly debates about America's past as well as to inform public discussions about its future.

A complete list of books published in Justice, Power, and Politics is available at https://uncpress.org/series/justice-power-politics.

Class Warfare in Black Atlanta

Grassroots Struggles, Power, and Repression under Gentrification

Augustus Wood

The University of North Carolina Press
CHAPEL HILL

© 2025 Augustus Wood
All rights reserved
Designed and set in Arno Pro and The Sans by Rebecca Evans
Manufactured in the United States of America

Cover art: Black Atlantans swell downtown to protest the police murder of Andre Moore, 1970. Photo by Tom Coffin. Courtesy of Atlanta Progressive Media Foundation / Georgia State University Library Special Collections and Archives.

Library of Congress Cataloging-in-Publication Data
Names: Wood, Augustus, 1985– author.
Title: Class warfare in Black Atlanta : grassroots struggles, power, and repression under gentrification / Augustus Wood.
Other titles: Justice, power, and politics.
Description: Chapel Hill : The University of North Carolina Press, [2025] | Series: Justice, power, and politics | Includes bibliographical references and index.
Identifiers: LCCN 2024061740 | ISBN 9781469685670 (cloth ; alk. paper) | ISBN 9781469685687 (paperback ; alk. paper) | ISBN 9781469685694 (epub) | ISBN 9781469685700 (pdf)
Subjects: LCSH: African Americans—Georgia—Atlanta. | Gentrification—Georgia—Atlanta. | Social classes—Georgia—Atlanta. | African Americans—Political activity—Georgia—Atlanta. | Atlanta (Ga.)—Social conditions—20th century. | Atlanta (Ga.)—Social conditions—21st century. | Atlanta (Ga.)—History—20th century. | Atlanta (Ga.)—History—21st century. | BISAC: SOCIAL SCIENCE / Ethnic Studies / American / African American & Black Studies | POLITICAL SCIENCE / Labor & Industrial Relations
Classification: LCC E185.93.G4 W58 2025 | DDC 305.896/0730758231—dc23/eng/20250226
LC record available at https://lccn.loc.gov/2024061740

For product safety concerns under the European Union's General Product Safety Regulation (EU GPSR), please contact gpsr@mare-nostrum.co.uk or write to the University of North Carolina Press and Mare Nostrum Group B.V., Mauritskade 21D, 1091 GC Amsterdam, The Netherlands.

For the
Black working class
and my favorite timeless
working-class warrior,
Dorcas Wood

Contents

ix   List of Illustrations

xi   Acknowledgments

1   INTRODUCTION
Vine City as the World Trade Center

34   CHAPTER ONE
The Black Worker Struck First
Black Power, Protonationalism, and the Working-Class Offensive

86   CHAPTER TWO
The Black Urban Regime Strikes Back
Retrenchment, Repression, and the Roots of Gentrification in Atlanta

132   CHAPTER THREE
The Spoils of Class War
Neoliberalization and the Fragmentation of Black Working-Class Atlanta

168   CHAPTER FOUR
Don't Work Yourself into a Shoot, Brother!
The New Nadir and New Tools of Class War in Olympic-Era Atlanta

207 CHAPTER FIVE
The Final Bite of the Apple
Nonprofits and Petty Bourgeois "Activism" in Post-Olympic Atlanta

241 CHAPTER SIX
Robbing Peter to Pay Paul
Suburbanization and Subproletarianization of the Black Working Class

278 EPILOGUE
The Black Worker
What Is to Be Done?

289 Notes
319 Bibliography
333 Index

Illustrations

Maps

Map of gentrification in Atlanta, 1949–2013   5

Map of Atlanta neighborhoods, 1970   40

Map of the Atlanta metropolitan region, 2015   260

Figures

Mechanicsville Community Freedom Center, 1972   49

Black Power protests by Black high schoolers in Atlanta Public Schools, 1973   62

Community picket against Azar's Store, 1970   65

Black women workers on strike at Howard Johnson's restaurant, 1970   69

Black Atlantans protesting the murder of Andre Moore by police, 1970   112

Atlanta Anti-Repression Coalition, 1974   121

Bedford Pine neighborhood, 1971   140

Tables

Table 2.1. Sources of sales tax revenue in Georgia, 1978   98

Table 2.2. Income subject to sales tax   99

Table 2.3. Property tax rollbacks for Atlanta's largest businesses   99

Table 6.1. Largest employers in the Atlanta metro area, 2015   249

Table 6.2. Average costs by category, Atlanta, 2015   261

Acknowledgments

I am immensely indebted to several family members, comrades, and others who made this book possible. Primarily I am indebted to Sundiata Keita Cha-Jua, my adviser, friend, and brother, whose immediate kinship from the moment I arrived from Atlanta for graduate school changed my life forever. Sundiata challenged, supported, trained, and embraced me intellectually and as family. His guidance through all phases of this research—including reading at least a dozen drafts of this project over the years, providing succinct comments, and encouraging me to dig deeper than others had before—transformed the trajectory and stakes of this project. Most crucially, Sundiata deepened my historiographical and theoretical knowledge while also championing my leadership of multiple grassroots and labor union organizations. Lastly, he always led by example through his rigorous scholarship and empowerment of his students. Thank you, Sundiata, for your loyalty, trust, guidance, and love.

The support and intellectual prowess I received from Lou Turner also played a pivotal role in the evolution of this research. The conversations and generosity of brother Lou in sharing his comments on my project provided conciseness and context for my research goals. Stephanie Fortado also contributed critical insight into this book while also becoming one of my closest friends in labor struggle spaces. We bonded sharing our scholarship and watching movies in between having hearty debates on capitalism. Her husband, Justus, also balanced my long days of research with horror movies and football Sundays. Helen Neville also gave her time, energy, and home to build community and a sense of belonging for me. This helped invigorate my activist and academic work and often highlighted how those two worlds are inseparable. Antoinette Burton acted as a warrior and friend for me and my research from the beginning. Her consistent no-nonsense approach and encouragement throughout this process were invaluable. Thank you, Antoinette, for supporting me in every way possible. To Ashley Howard, who gave her time and intellectual rigor to challenge me in my frameworks and methodology, I thank you for your valuable friendship and leadership. To the last dope intellectual, Charisse Burden-Stelly, thank you for being a key inspiration. Your genuine theoretical depth and critique challenged me in more ways than you can imagine. Your friendship was pivotal in my love of political economy. Other valuable colleagues throughout the process include Terri Barnes, Rana Hogarth, Ruby Mendenhall, Edward Onaci, Stephanie Evans, Leon Dash, Emily Twarog, Bob Bruno, Marcellus Barksdale, Samuel Livingston, and Dan Gilbert. Thank you to Joe Trotter for your kind words when I chose to reinvigorate your proletarianization thesis in my study of the Black worker. To my favorite dogs in the world, Zeke and Anita (R.I.P.), for their fun mischief through the challenging times in writing.

I am thankful to the University of North Carolina Press, who embraced me, my ideas, and this project from day one. Thank you to the UNC Board of Governors, the Justice, Power, and Politics series editors, and the editorial advisory board members for their wonderful support and promotion of this book. Thank you to Brandon Proia, for his dedicated pursuit of my project. To my editor, Dawn Durante, who exhibited the greatest professional expertise in helping me shape my project into this book—thank you for your guidance and enthusiasm for this research. You are truly one of a kind. Thank you to my readers, whose comments greatly improved my writing and the power of my arguments. Lastly, thank you to Erin Granville and Iza Wojciechowska for their hard work in prepping the manuscript for release.

I owe a significant debt to the activists and workers who directly or indirectly informed this study. To the thousands of Black working-class people who line the pages of this work, I thank you for your struggle. Thank you to Alice and Richard Kent and Denise and Michael Broward for everything. To the Atlanta Progressive Media Foundation, primarily the founders, journalists, and activists who operated the *Great Speckled Bird* in Atlanta, thank you for your excellent work with the Black working class and your enthusiastic support and endorsement of this book. Thanks to the staff of the Robert Woodruff Archives at the Atlanta University Center, who guided and supported this project since its beginning in 2013. Thank you to the Auburn Avenue Research Library for your amazing service and care for African American archival materials that were invaluable to my study.

Finally, to my amazing family: Augustus Wood II and Dorcas Wood, who raised my sister and me to adore working people from below, thank you for all the encouragement, support, and love over the decades. Thank you to my sister, Allyson, whose passionate devotion to work inspired me and passed to me. To my extended family and kin, Antonio Harris, Anthony Anderson, Ryan Gibson, John McKenzie, Antwan Summerour: I left Atlanta and you all after thirty years to pursue a project this crucial for our people. Thank you, and I miss you all dearly. Thank you, Britney Anderson, for your unconditional support during the grueling final stages of this manuscript.

To my dearest friends who have passed on—particularly Alton Hornsby Jr., whom I thank for introducing me to archival research and a love for African American history, and Kathy Oberdeck, who enthusiastically helped develop my project over the years and set the perfect example of humanism—I am forever indebted to you.

Class Warfare in Black Atlanta

INTRODUCTION

Vine City as the World Trade Center

> All of history is the history of the struggle for freedom. If, as a theoretician, one's ears are attuned to the new impulse from the workers, new "categories" will be created, a new way of thinking, a new step forward in philosophic cognition.
> —RAYA DUNAYEVSKAYA, 1958

> It seems that no matter how brutal and vicious the oppressor is, he has always had certain members of the oppressed to help carry out his policies of oppression, brutality, and racism.
> —MICHAEL ABNEY, African American Atlanta resident, 1974

The week after Thanksgiving 2002, African American community leader Colette Ward, alongside a dozen low-income Black Vine City neighbors in southeast Atlanta, stormed a city council meeting to fight the bulldozing of their neighborhood by the National Guard—ordered by African American mayor Shirley Franklin and her majority Black city council. Ward understood all too well that the uniformed soldiers, bulldozers, and dump trucks invading their backyards signaled their forced displacement from the city, following in the footsteps of thousands of her family members, friends, and neighbors who had been exiled from Vine City over the decades. "I do not want to start over," Ward told the council. "I'm not going anywhere. I'm going to fight.... I can't afford to move."[1]

As in other assaults on Vine City, the Atlanta Chamber of Commerce (ACOC) and the Atlanta city government exploited the residents' locational advantage to launch their next pro-growth craving: this time, it was a new deep-tunnel water sewer pipeline twenty-six feet in diameter and a twelve-acre park. Black Mechanicsville activist Dwanda Farmer's assertion that "the mayor and the council are hell-bent on urban removal" was not hyperbole but the reality for working-class Black residents. In fact, between 1992 and

2002, Atlanta officials demolished 2,179 homes in working-class neighborhoods across Atlanta, "enough to replace the entire city of Austell [Georgia]."[2]

This "long-term booking" approach to gentrification complicated the residents' capacity to gain leverage against the city through sustained protest. Atlanta officials strategically cleansed a few Black working-class streets at a time in the Black Belt—inside Vine City, alongside English Avenue, or throughout the neighborhoods of Mechanicsville or Pittsburgh, for example. As a result, protest capacity stretched thin; displaced residents lost strong kinship networks and physical and social institutions for planning and training. Other challengers to the Black working class—such as anticrime activists and Black middle-class leadership in nonprofit organizations like community development corporations—took control of the meager resources that Black workers struggled to wield. By directing the National Guard's occupation of Vine City, Atlanta's Black leadership ensured that their working-class counterparts lost their power to fight for their right to the city. "The demolition we've had done has not been in conjunction with a plan to rebuild," stated Harold Beckham, African American pastor of New Jerusalem Baptist Church and president of the English Avenue Civic Association.[3]

In selling this military operation to the media, Ivory Young, an African American Vine City district city councilman and the prime sponsor for the project, downplayed any outcry and condescended to the protesting residents: "What we are talking about is trained engineers and contractors who happen to wear fatigues to provide this free service. . . . What we are doing is establishing a contractual relationship with the National Guard to do demolition."[4] This relationship, however, was colonial in nature. Black working-class people, under constant siege throughout the central city—that is, within Atlanta's official city limits, though the metropolitan area extends far beyond them—proved expendable in the political, economic, social, and cultural sense to the pro-growth power bloc directing Atlanta's privatization and internationalization. "Under the guise of progress, these neighborhoods suffered," remarked an African American Atlantan named Janice.[5]

"The Inequality of Condition"

The stakes in the battle over Vine City were clear. For working-class Atlantans, their neighborhoods held tremendous locational advantage. Vine City was bounded by Simpson Road (currently Joseph E. Boone Boulevard), the English Avenue neighborhood, Northside Drive, and downtown Atlanta and was in proximity to historic Black churches—Wheat Street, Ebenezer, and

Friendship Baptist—and the Atlanta University Center. These areas provided Black Vine City residents the resources necessary to establish and sustain agency-laden institutions: proximity to blue-collar, living-wage jobs with neighbors; kinship networks with fellow workers and Black college students; physical and social spaces like public schools, recreation centers, and churches for organizing protests, training leaders, housing funds and materials, and delivering political education; and access to downtown Atlanta for social and cultural fulfillment. More clearly, the locational power of Vine City supplied residents with the weapons necessary to reduce the sharpening of class contradictions and challenge the city's domination of their people. Thus, capital's creeping encroachment over the years forced Black working-class urbanites to constantly confront the negation of their humanity and very survival.

For Atlanta leadership, however, Vine City's spatial configuration offered new streams of capital accumulation and a bourgeois liberal "justification" for reimaging a city without poor Black people. The Georgia Stadium Corporation, comprising secret private donors who refused to reveal their investors, strategically positioned the Georgia Dome stadium in the 1990s and the subsequent Mercedes-Benz Stadium in the 2010s to facilitate a differential rent advantage—that is, surplus profits made from exploiting locational advantage and renovations—as a cluster hub in the area for tourists and upper-class residents. Unsurprisingly, this also served as a locational *disadvantage* to Vine City residents. The simultaneous construction of new avenues for surplus profits and destruction of social tangibles to African American working-class power, such as stable labor and community organizations, bolstered the anti-working-class agenda of revitalizing "Black" Atlanta. As it stands today, Mercedes-Benz Stadium serves as the core of the convention and entertainment district in the city, as it provides access to the Georgia World Congress Center, State Farm Arena, the CNN Center, Centennial Olympic Park, the College Football Hall of Fame, the World of Coca-Cola, the National Center for Civil and Human Rights, the Georgia Aquarium, and finally, the Central Business District on Trinity and North Avenues. The stadium's location prevents Martin Luther King Jr. Drive from running through downtown to the end of the city at Fulton Industrial Boulevard, thus cutting the impoverished Vine City residents off from the Central Business District and the remaining Black churches. In this context, longtime Vine City community leader Mae Wofford's analysis of the city's domination of working-class Black bodies and spaces perfectly lays out the residents' perspective on the class war raging through Black Atlanta: "If your car breaks down, you replace your car. Well, my grandmother's house is broke down and we need it replaced. . . . What they say is fair market value is not fair to us, and if you've got heart you [will] be with us. Because if you don't, we're gonna consider you as Osama bin Laden and Vine City as the World Trade Center."[6]

This proclamation revealed the experiences of a class of political actors living with unprecedented violence, both direct and structural, struggling to build, sustain, and control the social institutions that impacted their daily lives. For the postwar Black urban working classes, the city and those who commanded its vast resources underscored a path to vanquishing racial oppression. As Black working-class people challenged Atlanta leadership's pro-growth colonization of their bodies, neighborhoods, and social institutions, new political economic alignments ripped the city's geographical, social, and economic landscape apart: ACOC's captaincy in restructuring new streams of capital accumulation, tourism development, and stadium construction; unaffordable housing construction; the combination of police repression and local anti-poor laws; and most crucial, the replacement of productive, livable-wage labor sites with low-wage, service-sector *subproletarian* labor offerings. Consequently, this relatively new racial class formation restitched Atlanta and the urban market to benefit those on top as those at the bottom plummeted through the gaping hole in the municipal safety net.

On a macro scale, this structural violence against working-class actors is unprecedented in contemporary urban centers. By the beginning of the 2010s, Atlanta's Black petty bourgeoisie, as the junior partners of capital, authorized the demolition of all 14,000 of the city's federally subsidized housing units, exposing close to 100,000 people each year to housing insecurity and resettling hundreds of thousands of predominantly low-income Black families into hypersegregated, resource-deprived, far-flung suburbs surrounding the core city. The website Governing, which collects data on census tracts with median household income, exposed the deliberate destruction of Black working-class Atlanta. Between 1990 and 2000, Governing classified thirteen of the seventy-eight eligible tracts—out of 127 total tracts—as gentrifying. Of these, most were clustered in the historically Black working-class downtown neighborhoods often referred to as the Black Belt of Atlanta, which would transform into the Turner Field area over the decades. This included Summerhill, Techwood Homes, Capitol Homes, Mechanicsville, and Peoplestown. However, the same measurement between 2000 and 2010 shows that the number of gentrifying tracts increased to thirty out of a total sixty-five eligible tracts; thus, the percentage of gentrified tracts almost *tripled*, going from 16 percent to 46 percent. The number of tracts not eligible to gentrify also increased from 49 to 62, meaning that by 2015, ninety-two out of a total 127 tracts, or

Atlanta gentrification maps and data. Retrieved April 20, 2016, aerial photograph courtesy of Georgia State University Library blog.

72 percent of tracts in the city of Atlanta, were classified as gentrifying.[7] These newly gentrified tracts were locationally advantageous for the Atlanta Beltline Construction Project, a twenty-two-mile multiuse repurposed train railway that transports individuals around upgraded tourist sites in the southwest, southeast, and west corridors of the city.

This political economic shift worked as a dialectic; it not only established new sites of accumulation via finance, information, tourism, and real estate, but it did so predominantly as a counter to Black working-class community demands for power and self-determination. Thus, these clashing forces not only defined the making of the financial capital urban site but did so by deepening *intraracial* class conflicts. To understand the "progress" of Atlanta's development as an epicenter for global financialized capital, one must see that poor Black bodies and spaces served as expendable commodities for these urban market exchange value interests. Other cities followed suit, like New Orleans, Oakland, New York City, and more recently Chicago, but Atlanta possessed the three components that allowed it to establish the model for disciplining the Black worker through neoliberalization, gentrification, and subproletarianization: those components were a distribution-based economy, an international airport, and a flood of Black working-class rebels who challenged Atlanta's power brokers over control of the city.

The history of Atlanta has been typically narrated without mentioning the two engines shaping the social process of urbanization: the Black working class and the capitalist structure. Therefore, this book serves as a critique of the history and political economy of Black Atlanta, meaning that it analyzes intraracial class warfare from below: Black working-class Atlantans battling the city's main bourgeois and petty bourgeois power brokers over land, labor, access to public resources, and control of the region. Concurrently, capital's deliberate fragmentation of Black working-class sectors as a response to the Black worker's collectivized protest was central to the reconfiguration of accumulation in metropolitan centers in the final quarter of the twentieth century. As scholar Lou Turner suggests, studies of Black urban history and communities have "barely scratched the surface of what exactly is at stake in what makes Black working class urban struggles, the forms they take, and their contradictory development with urban space such radical expressions of power and resistance that they evoke the full force of state and private repression." This violence, both direct and indirect, on Black bodies and spaces exposes the transactional relationship at the center of urban regions; the modernization and revitalization of cities owes their origins "not to the equality, but the *inequality* of condition."[8]

Centering the perspectives, voices, and experiences of Black working-class people illuminates how Black grassroots struggles over the political, economic, social, cultural, and spatial institutions that directly affect their day-to-day lives produced an anti-working-class, neocolonial redevelopment that diminished the lives and resistance capacities of these overlooked protagonists. Beginning in the late 1960s, Atlanta's elites—comprising white and Black capitalists, elected officials, former civil rights leaders, and institutions like the ACOC, Coca-Cola, the Georgia Stadium Corporation, and nonprofit corporations—responded to grassroots rebellions by waging pogrom-like war against the majority Black residents. In transforming Atlanta into one of the most strategic networks for global capital accumulation and circulation, these pro-growth forces implemented policies and programs that battered and bloodied the demands and capacity of their working-class counterparts to obtain quality goods and services, livable-wage labor, affordable housing, physical movement, social organizations for community and cultural power, and social movements against labor exploitation and gentrification.

Class Warfare in Black Atlanta investigates the political, economic, and social implications of gentrification and urban revitalization from a historical materialist perspective, an intervention that remedies other works that neglect to understand the complex process from below. In both popular and scholarly arenas, gentrification and urban redevelopment are generally defined by singular, top-down processes controlled mostly by real estate interests. The sociohistorical record, however, tells a different story. I trace how gentrification in contemporary urban centers in America operates as a vessel to subproletarianize the Black worker and other working classes in non-Black spaces. Gentrification through the lens of real estate narrows the multifaceted process of reshaping the social relations and social dislocation of working-class actors; rather, gentrification intentionally moves working-class urbanites from stability to instability, primarily via labor. The affordable-housing crisis at the center of gentrification is determined by the twin oppressive forces in capital, rent and interest, which need their third sibling in exploitation—labor—to violently extract comprehensive productive forces from a colonized group. More clearly, an internal neocolonial framework displays two central components of gentrification that are often overlooked. First, capital must dismantle livable-wage labor in targeted areas as part of its strategy to cheapen land and property and discipline the worker. This repression accomplishes two objectives for stakeholders: (1) the extermination of vital neighborhood resources disrupts the necessary process of social development for the masses, which leads to (2) the dehumanization of the Black worker. Second, the African American middle-class leadership that supervised capital's dominance and transformation in the 1970s consciously administered the subproletarianization of their working-class counterparts through dispossession, resource deprivation, state-sponsored violence, and exile.

Drawing from a range of Black working-class voices, too often left out of their own history, this book contributes to the growing scholarship on working-class agency by rematerializing blue-collar Black urbanites as a politically conscious collective that strategically challenged the class interests of their affluent counterparts. Black working-class Atlantans' objective to seize power over their own destinies through the control of their own social institutions threatened urban revitalization and the establishment of new sites of accumulation. Atlanta power brokers commenced the subproletarianization of the Black worker in three interlocking ways.

First, intraracial class warfare over the conflicting ideologies and implementation of Black Power—that is, determining which class of Black people controlled the political, economic, social, and cultural direction of African Americans—reshaped urban racial oppression into an internal neocolonial structure. This dialectic of colonial domination and resistance defined Atlanta's transformation into a strategic site of global financial capital production, circulation, and consumption. As the growing Black working-class majority flooded the central city in the 1960s, they enthusiastically launched their vision for Black Power. They wielded revolutionary protonationalism, a class- and community-based strategy to possess autonomy over the productive forces of their development: labor, social institutions, and neighborhood social movement capacity. They organized protest activity primarily at the point of production—erupting labor strikes and independent Black unions in the public and private sectors of Atlanta. Labor struggles allowed Black workers to marshal their revolutionary nationalist ideological base, resources, structure and discipline, and collective kinship networks to address community concerns like inhumane housing, police violence and surveillance, and lack of community control over Black neighborhood institutions like schools, community centers, grocery stores, and hospitals. These grassroots efforts not only reconstituted many of the productive, necessary material resources from bourgeois domination—in effect disciplining the affluent classes—but also disrupted the city's "progressive" public reputation and endangered redevelopment plans for the Atlanta metropolitan region. In other words, Black working-class urbanites eschewed integration for power through a mostly class-based revolutionary nationalism via their neighborhoods. Thus, this book moves the boundary line for Black Power in the United States beyond the North and the West Coast. Not only did Black Power flourish in southern urban centers like Atlanta, but it also reconstructed the interaction between the material and human environment that allowed the circulation of capital in urban space. In other words, Atlanta whites, more than any others in the United States at the time, shared capital and the direction of accumulation with Black decision-makers.

This power bloc responded to grassroots insurgency by disciplining the Black worker on multiple fronts. A coordinated effort between white and Black business leaders remade class within Black Atlanta. It did so by incentivizing the growing Black professional and managerial classes, promoting bourgeois ethics of possessive individualism and personal ambition to align with Black capitalists and against their working-class counterparts. This sharpened the contradictions of class struggle within Black Atlanta. It created a new public-private partnership on which the Black petty bourgeoisie—middle-class leaders and management—facilitated the displacement of Black labor and opened new routes to profit accumulation. They did so through a structurally violent paradigm that denied resources to poor Black urbanites. Consequently, this power bloc purposely attacked the working class at the point of production. It destroyed labor's organizing capacity and militancy, thus effectively removing a potent weapon for reinforcing social institutions and working-class agency. In other words, this book demonstrates that by their self-activity and self-organization, Black working-class Atlantans' resistance set in motion a dialectic in which Atlanta's capitalist class and Black leadership class restructured the metropolitan region's political economy into an anti-working-class framework.

This new Black petty bourgeoisie—molded from previous civil rights leadership, middle-class administrators, real estate moguls, legal service providers, and members of the nonprofit industry—oversaw neoliberalization and shifted federal, state, and local public funds and resources away from working-class needs to bolster profiteering for gentrification. Therefore, this project makes clear that the betrayal of the Black worker manufactured the glossy, tourist-driven, international Atlanta. Like in other majority-Black urban regions, Atlanta's pivot away from its working-class constituencies and toward bourgeois internationalism and finance was a deliberate retrenchment —a political response to the colonized subjects' rebellion.

Second, this relatively new racial formation shaped class structures, and in turn, classes attempted to shape the political economy for their own benefits. Atlanta's Black workers represented one example of a decade flooded with African American urbanites in Detroit, Philadelphia, and other Black municipalities, attacking the point of production and disrupting wide swaths of capital. Capital was forced to respond violently by restrategizing class structure and accumulation around the subproletarianization of the Black worker. Not only did capital shift its dominant mode of production toward financialized global markets, but it did so by reorganizing the division of labor into a *direct production* model—unskilled/semiskilled, subproletarian labor typically reserved for Black, women, and immigrant workers. This political economy displaced Black labor at a mass level as technological advancements left behind those most exploited by direct production. Subsequently, Black workers lost significant capacity to organize at the point of production and, as a result, lost resources typically used to address other crises in Black communities. More clearly, *Class Warfare in Black Atlanta* demonstrates that capital's fragmentation of African American working-class neighborhoods in Atlanta functioned as a negation of their humanity by propagandizing to the world—through grand larceny of survival needs—that low-income African Americans were not deserving of power.

What makes Atlanta so critical in this watershed moment is that the city's leadership understood the potential in the precedent-setting history of the neocolonial situation. The pursuit of the 1996 Olympic Games expedited an already in-motion process to repress the capacity of the Black worker to self-sustain. The Olympic Games hurried Atlanta to achieve its neoliberal, anti-working-class dreams faster than any other urban region. In his celebration of his quarterbacking Atlanta's ruling class toward its anti-working-class Super Bowl of surplus profits, African American mayor and former civil rights activist Andrew Young famously stated, "Atlanta has no identity. We are now creating one."[9]

Third, the loss of public resources and, in turn, local movement centers in Black working-class neighborhoods reshaped the understanding and capacity for resistance in far-reaching ways. First, the newly made Black petty bourgeoisie purposely exacerbated and exploited mass Black unemployment and underemployment at the end of the 1970s and early 1980s to repurpose working-class anger toward growing immediate threats. Black local officials dismantled the critique of capital and class struggle in the Black grass roots through a "Black united front" discourse to fight crime. In other words, as class antagonism between Black Atlantans sharpened, the Black bourgeoisie and petty bourgeoisie weakened, muted, and folded grassroots outrage into a homogenic shell. They promoted bourgeois Black nationalist solidarity as a response to growing crime to gain support for their "revitalization" and urban "progress" agenda. Thus, working-class opponents held few resources to impede gentrification and the violent displacement of millions of Black poor people. The Black leadership classes chose to annihilate the lives of Black workers as a palatable and "progressive" political solution. The homogenization of the Black community and the ideology of bourgeois nationalist solidarity served to weaken the political, economic, social, and cultural position of the African American working classes. Consequently, nonprofits supplanted grassroots social movements. They presented themselves as the "rational" or neoliberal solution to urban poverty. However, they propped up the Black bourgeoisie's bureaucratization of the urban structure.

Thus, this book offers an alternative analysis to the often-triumphant perspective of African American agency in much of the scholarship today. A critique of the political economy demonstrates the dialectic of Black resistance to racial oppression: it often produces severe consequences on the subjugated people from the dominant classes for challenging internal neocolonialism. Thus, this book builds on historian Winston Grady-Willis's conceptualization of Atlanta as having an apartheid structure.[10] Here, I extract the class eruptions that soldered the central city into the neocolonial position it holds today. In other words, my critique of the political economy of Black Atlanta's revitalization of the last forty years through neoliberalization, internationalization, and gentrification situates subproletarianization as the newest position of the African American majority under the contemporary neoapartheid urban structure. *Class Warfare in Black Atlanta* contradicts the cultural or pathological argument of Black "damage" or "broken" Black people to explain the worsening position of the African American masses in society; rather, I stress the material and social dislocation at the center of racial oppression.

Gentrification, the major weapon of neoliberalization, is central to internal neocolonialism in Black urban centers like Atlanta because it reorganizes the majority of the African American working classes into a subproletariat—defined primarily by their proximity to mostly unstable, low-wage, unskilled labor prospects and a lack of access outside the metro suburbs to the core city. Gentrification, regardless of form or function, is structural violence against low-income urbanites. It disrupts the working poor's capacity for day-to-day survival, working, caring for family and kin, and allocating neighborhood resources for the collective good of the people. By deliberately targeting and eliminating materials that contribute to the *use value* of working-class neighborhoods, the bourgeoisie and petty bourgeoisie subtract mechanisms of hope from the Black worker that assist in developing a vision for liberation.

Gentrification is also violent because its intended goal is always to cleanse a targeted space of an "undesired group." As urban geographer Neil Smith notes, gentrification serves solely as activism *against* the working class.[11]

Class Warfare in Black Atlanta insists that scholars have underestimated or mischaracterized the relationships of race, class, and capital that shaped the political, economic, and social construction of Atlanta. It was the conflict between the Black working-class communities and Atlanta's Black and white elites that informed the physical and social shape of the city, namely the distribution of people, the allocation of resources, and the ways space and place were built, transformed, and disrupted. Atlanta leadership's pursuit of international finance and tourist capital produced a net loss for working-class Blacks' prospects for achieving self-determination and strengthening the power of their communities. This book makes clear that it is difficult to understand the complexities of Atlanta or contemporary urban space without cementing class struggle and the subjugation of working-class resistance and survival as the defining social processes of the urban engine.

As a result, *Class Warfare in Black Atlanta* challenges urban studies scholarship's propensity to homogenize Black city dwellers—either into one group or to view the perspective of the lower classes through the lens of their elite counterparts. By highlighting how Black Atlantans split predominantly along class lines, this conflict, more than a struggle over who would control public resources, was a war for the core city itself. To this end, Black Atlanta's uneven development helped construct bridges between the Black professional and managerial classes and the Atlanta capitalist class. At the behest of pro-business/pro-growth/nonprofit community development corporations like the ACOC, Central Atlanta Progress, Summerhill Neighborhood Incorporated, the Atlanta Committee for the Olympic Games, and the Edison Project, the municipality funneled resources, primarily public funding, out of working-class neighborhoods and into locationally advantageous residential and commercial properties. Real estate firms also worked closely with the Atlanta City Council and legal firms to organize exclusionary zoning to develop affluent neighborhoods like the Black upper-class "Gold Coast," where building height limits, school district lines, zoning, and tax increment financing policies increased property values and concentrated low-income Black families in poverty enclaves in the surrounding metropolitan region.

By understanding Atlanta as a site of intraracial class warfare, this book writes fluid racial class positions into Black neighborhoods. Although Black leadership consistently operated against most survival needs of their Black working-class constituency, they successfully procured their votes and support by propagandizing their individual "bootstrap" ascension to political power as "race leaders." Popular Black leaders like Maynard Jackson selected strategic moments, particularly those of anti-Black police violence or anti-poverty discourse, for performative and superficial declarations of a "Black united front" to mute class antagonisms while exacerbating them. More clearly, Black elites, through the control of private media, cunningly sought to blur the class lines in Black Atlanta when it benefited their class interests. Gentrification captured the public by erasing class critique by homogenizing and subsequently dehumanizing all low-income urban dwellers as too unstable and unfit to reside in a revitalized city. Thus, *Class Warfare in Black Atlanta* traces the white supremacist underpinnings in the discourse used by the bourgeois media, the local government, and the Atlanta police in justifying the subproletarianization of the Black working class.

Subproletarianization by way of gentrification thereby complicates extant narratives of Atlanta's urban structure by focusing attention on the nature of class in determining racial oppression and internal neocolonialism. Unlike any other study of contemporary cities, this book demonstrates how race and political economy are entangled and that only by moving between the scales —from the streets to the boardrooms, from the neighborhoods to global politics—can we properly historicize what happened in Atlanta and other urban centers in the United States. By examining Atlanta's gentrification as a new model for twenty-first-century urban apartheid, this book requires scholars to examine intraracial class struggle as an indispensable lens for understanding contemporary Black urban life and its racial formations throughout urban America and beyond.[12]

"Duality of the Mir": Critical Interventions in Black Studies and History Scholarship

Although the focus on agency and resistance of a united people has carried African American history scholarship in rich directions since the post–civil rights period, it has also often overlooked the clearly defined yet fluid class positions that fueled the social processes of the African American sociohistorical experience. Therefore, a historical materialist critique of the political economy of Black Atlanta offers the most succinct framework for class struggle from below. In other words, *Class Warfare in Black Atlanta* showcases how the warring contradiction of the vying classes within a society must be at the heart of any analysis of political economic development of space. For Atlanta and other major metropolitan centers in the United States, the Black working class dictated the restructuring of capital more so than any other social force in the city. Therefore, Black working-class people must function as the central protagonists in the history of modern Atlanta.

In 1881, Karl Marx corresponded with Russian Marxist Vera Zasulich on the revolutionary potential of the *obshchina* (the mir), or the Russian peasantry. Marx, who spent years learning Russian and researching the political economic developments in Russia over the previous two decades, chose not to give a definitive position on whether the mir was "capable of developing socialist direction" or "destined to perish." Rather, he argued that the "historical context in which it [the mir peasantry] is situated" would shift their duality toward either a proprietary or a collective, revolutionary tendency. More clearly, Marx correctly predicted that the heterogenic class interests within the mir—some owned large swaths of land while others ranked among the poorest residents—sharpened the contradictions of the political economy of the time: "Now the question is: can the Russian obschchina, though greatly undermined, yet a form of primeval common ownership of land, pass directly to the higher form of Communist common ownership? Or, to the contrary, must it first pass through the same process of dissolution such as constitutes the historical evolution of the West?"[13]

This anecdote highlights the contradiction in the formation of the new Black petty bourgeoisie in neoliberal urban centers like Atlanta. Because some upper-level members of the Black working class held proximity to the direction of capital—and, therefore, aspirations to share the capitalist pie—they consciously betrayed their class brethren to ally with their oppressors. This book traces this duality and subsequent dissolution of the post–civil rights era African American majority, whose professional and managerial elite —under the restructuring of global capital and its need for indirect rulership of the oppressed—fortified the barrier between the Black worker and self-determination. Thus, the proprietary potential of the control of resources tore apart Black urban communities. The Black petty bourgeoisie concretized the exchange value of their working-class counterparts' lives, labor, place, and space as their core principles under this new racial formation. More explicitly, the class contradictions in the political economy of Black Atlanta's gentrification set working-class Atlantans on a path of warfare against their own racial class conspirators.

A historical materialist framework exposes these contradictions and allows us to conceptualize Atlanta and other metropolitan centers in an internal neocolonial framework. Historical materialism concretizes *labor* and the *laborer* as the basis for productive forces in society. Most gentrification studies focus solely on two specific forms of surplus value—interest and rent—without the third piece, labor. However, *Class Warfare in Black Atlanta* clarifies the necessity of labor in the trinity. Therefore, all three forms of surplus value worked in tandem to expel the Black working class out of Atlanta. By destroying access to the point of production by demolishing living-wage job sites, union density, and other social movements in the city, the petty bourgeois Black leadership class exacerbated the precarity of the working masses through rent manipulation and skyrocketing interest rates that became unaffordable. Thus, historical materialist methodology provides the analytic tools to see the African American working class as a colonized enclave.

Additionally, historical materialism does not restrict us to a singular social process or one set of individuals. Rather, historical materialism allows us to investigate how both macrolevel and microlevel social processes work together to sharpen class contradictions—how wealth is produced and distributed, how products are produced and exchanged, and how labor and the *laborer* incite the dialectic and cause capital to discipline the worker through repressive direct and indirect structural violence. More clearly, it offers us the chance to fully dissect the social organization of the Black Atlanta working class under attack by pro-growth forces. For example, when capital gentrifies poor Black urbanites out of the central city, it reorganizes them into a subproletariat in metro Atlanta counties like Douglas, DeKalb, Cobb, Gwinnett, and Clayton. Thus, the lives and resistance of poor urbanites did not stop at displacement, as most gentrification studies display. Rather, the Black worker sought new strategies for building social institutions and kinship networks and pooling resources, such as jobs, extended-stay motels, carpool clubs, and makeshift food banks. Historical materialism secures the agency of the Black working class by centralizing their fight against oppression as the primary engine of the political economy.

The Black worker has typically resided on the fringes of Atlanta and African American urban history. Although noted scholars like Alton Hornsby Jr. crafted important studies of African American leaders in Atlanta, scholars did not concretize class in Atlanta until political scientist Mack Jones's critique of the city's political structure. More explicitly, Jones successfully challenged scholars to excavate the contradictions within what former mayor Ivan T. Allen dubbed the "city too busy to hate."[14]

Political scientist Clarence Stone's urban regime theory attempted to problematize the race-centered analyses of Atlanta. However, as political scientists

Neil Kraus and Adolph Reed Jr. noted, Stone's description of interracial alliances in the governing of Atlanta overlooked the regime's dialectical relationship to its Black working-class constituents.[15] Stone's regime politics closely mirrored other scholarship that promoted the popular ghettoization thesis at that time, where mostly white elites held such supreme power over the voiceless, agency-less, institution-less African American masses that they served as lambs to the slaughter. Historian Kevin Kruse, geographer Larry Keating, and anthropologist Charles Rutheiser continued in this tradition by depicting modern Atlanta as a predominantly white supremacist project victimizing Black urbanites. However, this book challenges the ghettoization model by probing intensely at the dialectics of political economy and racial oppression—where African American working-class people built autonomous social institutions and collectively resisted racial oppression.[16]

As historian Joe W. Trotter has noted, the problem with the ghettoization thesis is that it overshadows the consciousness and political focus of insurgent activity among a subjugated urban population. Centering the African American majority class in the study illuminates how Black working-class people navigated their colonized position and strategized their social movements toward collective goals and actions often outside of or in opposition to the dominant structure. My focus on the changing day-to-day material realities of Black working-class Atlantans clarifies how revitalization and gentrification destabilized and further alienated them from their *Gattungswesen*—their very capacity to build kinship bonds within proximity to each other, establish social institutions for community power, and exercise collective agency.[17]

Thus, *Class Warfare in Black Atlanta* provides a pragmatic depiction of how grassroots struggles rise, function, succeed, and fail: despite the heroic and brave sacrifices made by these working-class movement actors, there is little triumphalism in the domination of a people. Their rebellion against apartheid often set in motion a violent response with two interlocking goals: to accumulate capital and to reduce the rebels' very capacity to continue their struggle against domination. The ghettoization model contradicts these historical truths because it presents the ghetto inhabitants in a homogeneous context and often nullifies any relationship between capital accumulation and the organization and subsequent fragmentation of poor Black people.

More clearly, at the core of typical ghettoization studies is a homogenization of African American urbanites. Consequently, this erases class struggle from the concrete center of the social processes in urbanization. Apart from Trotter and Sundiata Cha-Jua—whose study of Afro-Brooklynites in Illinois expanded the proletarianization thesis—urban scholarship and African American urban history has not fully investigated the intraracial class struggle that fragments the Black working class over material interests throughout American history. Particularly in relation to the development of modern urban regions, this study of Atlanta—a city distinct from other urban spaces because of its relatively robust Black capitalist class, spatial configuration, and hosting of the Olympic Games—reflects the intertwined nature of class warfare and urbanization.

The lack of class struggle in ghettoization studies contributes to the problematic "underclass" concept. As sociologist John Arena has posited, this liberal paradigm camouflages "the ways contemporary neoliberal, capitalist restructuring is worsening the material conditions of all segments of the working class." Without a conscious and collective body of subjugated masses responding to assaults on their capacity to live or obtain power, urban structural analyses give way to scholarship that considers "the declining significance of race."[18] Consequently, this misconception informs mainstream debates on the question of racial oppression. For some, poverty operates at an individual level because, in their view, capital's disciplining of the collective power of labor by repressing the *laborer*—through deindustrialization, underemployment, the annexation of public resources, and heightened state-sponsored and private anti-Black-working-class violence—is not the main reason for racial oppression. This argument concludes that poor African Americans are not poor because of the restructuring of production; they are poor because of how they consume on an individual basis, which opens the door for "bootstrap" narratives. Consequently, racial oppression with a critique of capitalism at its core evaded the mainstream consciousness, opening a void filled by racial colorblindness frameworks that further muted racial class domination and racial distinctions in the nation's consciousness.

The proletarianization model, introduced by Trotter in 1985 and reignited by Cha-Jua in 2000, upends much of this problematic trend because it considers the class position of the worker as the most foundational characteristic of the sociohistorical experience of the African American majority. As Trotter has successfully argued, African American urbanites, proletarianized in substandard labor throughout urban ghettos, "expressed their class interests in explicitly racial terms."[19] Unlike ghettoization, which considers interracial relations as the sole determinant of the Black worker, proletarianization and subsequent subproletarianization clarifies the dialectic of the political economy and racial oppression by considering how the Black worker's interracial *and* intraracial relations impacted their labor position, housing, resistance, community and institution building, and politics. In other words, my research into Black Atlanta requires the complex, microstructural community study that the proletarianization model provides.

Centralizing the voices, struggles, and relationship to the political economy of the Black working class in urban studies informs the transformation of urban space. Therefore, the Black worker is a necessary analytical weapon to develop a more legitimate analysis of urban history. More clearly, the Black worker further enriches our understanding of the complex class structure by conceptualizing the workers who represent the lowest sector of the working class: the subproletariat. Originally conceptualized by revolutionary scholars C. L. R. James and Raya Dunayevskaya in the 1940s and reintroduced by sociologist Martin Oppenheimer in 1974, the concept of subproletarianization is defined as "dirty work," or labor with the five following characteristics: (1) unskilled; (2) often physically demanding, exhausting, uncomfortable to perform, or "regarded by that particular society at that particular moment as the least desirable, the dirtiest"; (3) offering wages that are likely too low to offset rising costs of living and/or inflation; (4) typically created, maintained, and manipulated via the mode of the political economy—because these workers act as a reserve army of labor during labor surpluses, as history demonstrates, they sometimes replace unionized or stable blue-collar labor; and (5) tending to be "performed by dark skinned people."[20]

Historically, the labor typically performed by Black workers in the United States can be classified as subproletarian work. Following slavery, Jim Crow sharecropping provided the most astute example of "dirty work." Black tobacco workers took home between four and ten dollars less per week than white workers. When Black workers migrated to urban cities during and after World War I, they typically labored in the most intensive (and often hottest) sections in food-processing, tobacco, textile, iron, glass, paper, and steel factories. As Trotter noted, "African Americans . . . worked in the most difficult, dangerous, dirty, low-paying categories of industrial work. . . . Their jobs entailed disproportionate exposure to debilitating heat, deadly fumes, disabling injuries, and even death." However, in contrast to white proletarianization, Black proletarianization during the 1910s generally represented upward mobility. Cha-Jua added that proletarianization was fluid, with African Americans going from wage raises in industrial capitalism to being sentenced to the lowest sectors of the factory. Indeed, Trotter and Cha-Jua highlighted how the white ruling class subproletarianized African Americans as a political response to Black demands for decision-making power.[21]

Once we juxtapose this with the racial formation of the late 1970s—using Cha-Jua's Black racial formation and transformation theory—we can fully conceptualize subproletarianization as the intended consequence for the Black working class under internal neocolonialism. After working-class labor rebellions and nationalist social movements in the 1960s and 1970s threatened capital's domination over labor, the bourgeoisie constructed a new professional class of administrative, indirect rulers to function as supervisory broker chiefs and shift the mode of production from the industrial to the service sector. As a result, extractive, labor-intensive work expanded while the conditions of work for the masses did not improve. Low interest rates and concessions on investment expenditures (like low taxes) encouraged the import of capital-intensive investment, as did the private demand of local elites and the needs of international investors.[22]

Subproletarianization derives from this structure. Automation cheapened the value of the laborer, thus reducing the demand for skilled labor, and increased surplus profits. As Oppenheimer noted, "The urban poor throughout the capitalist world are likely to find themselves the more or less permanent objects of technological and sociopolitical forces over which they have no control as the result of the twin forces of labor.... Black slaves become sharecroppers and sharecroppers become unskilled laborers and urban service workers ... without changing their bottom-dog status, because upward mobility is blocked by the nature of modern technology."[23]

This highlights the dialectic of subproletarianization under an internal neocolony like the United States. There tend to be more Black lower-income and less-skilled workers across the United States relative to their proportion of the population. Black people tend to live in homogenous spatial relationships, the result of apartheid policies and practices in labor and housing at the federal, state, and local levels. This racial formation creates two prominent features in the subproletariat. First, it results in a nationalist sentiment among the group. This informs individuals' capacity to organize collective social movements against oppression, because they develop kinship bonds over shared values, cultures, ideas, and struggles. Second, this racial formation creates an ethnic differentiation that allows the dominant group (the white bourgeoisie and petty bourgeoisie) to identify and propagandize low-income Black workers as the "appropriate" subproletariat in the United States. Particularly in a shift to a low-wage, unskilled, service-sector economy, the demand for a subproletariat in the United States is higher than ever. Because of the historical colonial domination of Black people, a sizable portion of them continue to serve as a reserve army of labor, moving in and out of the proletariat. More clearly, the dialectical nature of subproletarianization created two opposing microstructures: one white and technologically advanced and one darker and unskilled.[24]

This book also asserts that progress for the city of Atlanta meant retrenchment for the African American majority. Black working-class activists never abandoned their antiracist class struggle; rather, the possession of movement resources proved key. The violent usurpation of the day-to-day survival needs reduced the materials to build and sustain social movement organizing against neoliberalization and gentrification. However, despite the dismantling of Black working-class institutions, labor, and housing, Black workers continued to pool resources and form informal support networks to improve the collective use value of their living and social spaces.

Therefore, a critique of the political economy illuminates the Black worker's move from proletariat to subproletariat and situates low-income African Americans as the primary social force in urbanization. Recent scholarship on Atlanta that highlighted class as a point of contestation in the post–civil rights era underplayed the macrostructural and microstructural violence in the planned displacement of the Black majority. Historian Maurice Hobson's *Legend of the Black Mecca* successfully complicated the political maneuvering within the African American polity that cast low-income African American Atlantans in a disparate position in the last three decades of the twentieth century.[25] However, Hobson's top-down approach to examining the making of class in Atlanta shielded the multilevel interactions between the Black majority class and the capitalists and Black leadership directing the social forces within a revitalizing Atlanta.

Class Warfare in Black Atlanta, however, highlights the class *fluidity* that Black elites like Maynard Jackson, Andrew Young, Coretta Scott King, and Hosea Williams navigated throughout their complex careers. As sociologist Erik Olin Wright posited, class position is determined generally by the lived experiences of people. More clearly, Marxist scholar E. P. Thompson stated that class can also mean "when some men, as a result of common experiences (inherited or shared), feel and articulate the [position] of their interests as between themselves and as against those whose interests are different from (and usually opposed to) theirs."[26] Thus, as Wright and Thompson contended, the individual's location within the capitalist structure is only one mechanism that generates class position—it is not intrinsically more important than community or social relations in developing class consciousness. This compels individuals to confront class *identity*, or the ways people place themselves into different systems of class formation at different points in their lives.[27] This returns us to the duality of the Black petty bourgeoisie and their subsequent betrayal of the Black working class. In terms of Jackson, the shrewd politician took power at a time when capital sought new sites of accumulation, which required a repurposed set of administrators from Black Atlanta with ideological commitment to privatization. His social interaction with the ruling elite of Atlanta, who secured his power in the city, informed his fluid movement along class lines. However, from the dialectic, those same elites needed Jackson to deliver the Black majority votes. Therefore, as *Class Warfare in Black Atlanta* highlights, Jackson's vision for a privatized future led him to express minor firm positions that improved the conditions of the Black working class from a *material* sense. But he often spoke on working-class crises from a *superficial* sense. For instance, he publicly condemned police brutality often. Yet Jackson supported and protected a police chief who enacted violent programs against poor Black urbanites. He also appropriated the wages and benefits demanded by his working-class constituencies such as public-sector workers for police militarization. For Coretta Scott King, class fluidity allowed her to amass great wealth under the guise of freedom fighting for an equitable future for all. Her highly publicized role in struggles against racism domestically and overseas shrouded her powerful land grabs and her leadership in the razing of Black working-class Auburn Avenue. Therefore, as Wright concluded, "consciousness of class interests ... is oriented toward the future ... reflecting the time horizons in terms of which individuals understand their relationship to the class structure."[28] The fluidity of class for African American elites often reflected the power of Black workers and their response to the political economy.

This study of Atlanta from below functions primarily through the alienation of the Black worker. Therefore, I complicate frameworks on African American agency and resistance by conceptualizing movement capacity as the key variable in urbanization and gentrification. As sociologist Aldon Morris contended, the capacity for local Black activists to challenge inequality relied on their development of "agency-laden institution[s]," or "local movement centers." Morris posited that local movement centers are "developed by a dominated group to produce, organize, coordinate, finance, and sustain social protest" and "house movement resources, train leadership, solidify mission, vision, strategy, and tactics of the movement." As Morris highlighted, "Movements are deliberately organized and developed by activists who seize and create opportunities for protest."[29] Thus, the Black working class and their fight over control of their resources and their right to the city was not only to access survival needs. As this book demonstrates, local movement actors in Atlanta also strategically repurposed neighborhood resources through local movement centers to define their collective understanding of community control.

The Black working-class tendency to construct agency-laden institutions offered several tactical innovations that strengthened movement capacity. First, it fortified protest activity under a formal, disciplined structure of shared goals, accountability, and consistency. Black radical unions took action, like the Mead Caucus of Rank-and-File Workers, which built an escalating strike against the Mead bottling company in 1972 through consistent commitment, political education, debate, and training through a local movement center. Second, local movement centers crystallized an indigenous collective outcry, or what Black studies scholar Robin D. G. Kelley identified as *infrapolitics*, into a concise, objective-based social movement. Kelley's framework for infrapolitics lays a useful foundation for examining how working-class urbanites used jokes, anger, folklore, and other cultural practices to construct social bonds. However, *Class Warfare in Black Atlanta* expands this framework by presenting infrapolitics as the key phase that transforms a protest moment into a social movement. The social bonds developed between oppressed people contribute to neighborhood social movement capacity by tightening kinship networks, building community, and sharing movement resources. In other words, this project shows how infrapolitics were used primarily in building and sustaining social bonds within social movements in Black working-class Atlanta.

This book also grounds gentrification in a historical materialist framework to better accentuate how structural violence devastates multiple aspects of those most affected by it. Scholarship on gentrification has typically bolstered capital's political objectives. As capital introduced gentrification as its dominant tool in class warfare, the earliest scholars and policy officials sought to depoliticize the phenomenon. Late 1970s and 1980s researchers rationalized what they deemed to be the organic nature of US gentrification. More clearly, they argued it occurred naturally from individuals arriving in and leaving neighborhoods. This trend attempted to justify a "positive" effect of neoliberalization's free market ideology.[30]

The 1980s neoconservative movement in academia pounced on this consumption-side propaganda. Many conservative scholars doubled down on what they deemed to be an "insignificant" moment of postindustrial society, where middle-class people, they argued, could finally feel free and safe enough to gradually return to the city.[31] These writings offered justification to bourgeois liberal politicians who wanted to "wash away the ghetto slums" via displacement and justify the cultural pathological argument. Essentially, this depoliticized the structural and material underpinnings of gentrification.

Marxist scholars soon built a viable counter to the consumption-based gentrification narrative. Beginning with geographer Neil Smith, these researchers framed gentrification as an inorganic, structurally based, uneven development that resulted from a shift in productive forces in the 1980s. More clearly, they posited that gentrification served as a combination of capital—that is, material and social conditions—and cultural factors that caused hegemonic forces to displace the working classes.[32] While the studies contributed a necessary critique of the political economy of neoliberalization, they often did so from a macrostructural and predominantly theoretical standpoint. In other words, these scholars mainly framed gentrification via a ghettoization conceptualization, where brutal ruling-class forces moved faceless and voiceless working-class people without resistance. I seek to expand the production-side argument by starting from a point of alienation: tracing the microstructural forces, including Black working-class institution building, internal resource mobilization and social movements, and resistance as the central feature of gentrification. This book illustrates how gentrification served capital in more ways than merely by rearranging the structures of accumulation. It also depowered and destabilized the collective struggle of working-class people spatially as well as socially.

Thus, *Class Warfare in Black Atlanta* politicizes both gentrification and resistance as sites of struggle that inform the social processes of the urban engine. A dissection of gentrification cannot occur without the focus on the working classes, their land, labor, and built environment. Therefore, the stakes of this research prove crucial in reestablishing the oppressed at the center of a radical struggle against gentrification and other forms of racial oppression in Atlanta.

Within this framework, neoliberalization and gentrification are best understood as structural forms of violence against poor urban dwellers. They operate to a certain extent like anti-Jewish pogroms, with the planned destruction or removal of a massive portion of a specifically defined group from a space. As historian Charles Lumpkins accomplished in his pathbreaking study of the anti-Black pogrom in 1917 East St. Louis, I examine the long-term, *deliberate* process of structural violence at the macro and micro levels.[33] I expand Lumpkins's thesis in two ways. First, I contend that anti-working-class pogroms like gentrification do not necessarily have to be explicitly violent or riotous to accomplish the goal of destroying or cleansing a group or space. A *structural violence* framework illuminates the organized, macrolevel planning apparatus of the cleansing while also showcasing how violence against oppressed groups can be structural. As scholar Johan Galtung argued, violence as a somatic incapacitation—or "the deprivation of health" predominantly through "killing at the hands of an actor who intends this to be the consequence" or as "an overt form of coercion such as warfare, suppression of dissent by government forces, or physical assault"—is too narrow of a concept.[34] To fully understand the complex dynamics of violence against oppressed groups and individuals in an internal neocolonial structure, scholars must expand the pogrom framework to incorporate class struggle and social movement capacity as motivations for cleansing.

In fact, Galtung's approach to violence accentuates why subproletarianization, urban renewal, and gentrification are best defined as structural violence against poor urban dwellers. Galtung defines violence as "the cause of the difference between the potential and the actual, between what could have been and what is." More clearly, Galtung suggests that violence is that which *decreases* the distance between a potential and the actual. For example, if a person succumbed to dysentery in the seventeenth century, it cannot be conceived as violence because the lack of knowledge regarding the disease at that time made the death almost unavoidable. However, if a person died from it today, despite all the medical resources that make death from dysentery avoidable, then violence is present.[35] Expanding Galtung's framework, I contend that when a dominant group purposely deprives both material and nonmaterial sources from a subordinate group in an effort to reduce their capacity to build institutions that both strengthen and improve the quality of their living and social spaces, those policies, even if indirect in nature, must be considered violent. From a dialectical perspective, Galtung's theory of violence works in similar ways: "The potential level of realization is that which is possible with a given level of insight and resources. If insight and/or resources are monopolized by a group or class or are used for other purposes, then the actual level falls below the potential level, and violence is present in the system."[36]

Therefore, Galtung's theory is a framework for subproletarianization—through gentrification—qualifying as *indirect* violence against oppressed groups because "insight and resources are channeled away from constructive efforts to bring the actual closer to the potential."[37] In other words, as scholar Mary Anglin posited, violence also assumes the form of the expropriation of vital political, economic, and social resources that subvert the capacity for the oppressed to construct and sustain social movements. By experiencing structurally violent acts like neoliberalization and gentrification, individuals may be destroyed or maimed with direct violence. However, they, alongside institutions, neighborhoods, and resources that inform the use value of living and social spaces, are also manipulated by a *structure* that contains actors, social organizations, and political regimes responsible for the violence. In fact, under structural violence like gentrification, there is usually not one specific entity who directly harms the oppressed group. The violence is built into the process and manifests as inequality, usually as racial oppression, intraracial class warfare, and inequality in life opportunities.[38] Kwame Ture (formerly Stokely Carmichael) and Charles Hamilton expressed in their seminal work, *Black Power*, how structural violence erases the individuality in racial class struggles because it is "less overt, far more subtle, less identifiable in terms of specific individuals . . . but is no less destructive of human life." In its long-term meticulousness, structural cleansing "is more the overall operation of established and respected forces in the society and thus does not receive the condemnation" that direct violence and explicit killing receive. However, groups under assault from indirect violence are politically, socially, and economically marginalized in ways that simultaneously deny them physical, psychological, and emotional well-being and heighten their exposure to social problems, such as housing insecurity, underemployment, and mass incarceration, that disproportionately elevate the risk of sickness and death.[39] Thus, *Class Warfare in Black Atlanta* centers Black working-class people as community heroes seeking resources for one another. The fight for resources that impact the use value of neighborhoods also bolsters neighborhood social movement capacity.

Last, this book centers the nonprofit-industrial complex as a critical arm in the pro-growth assault on Black working-class people. As neoliberalization looted funds from public spaces and redistributed it to the private sector, nonprofits filled the void quickly, thanks in large part to the decreasing fight by the American labor movement at the point of production. More clearly, the lack of a radical critique of political economy after the end of Black Power and the commencement of the New Nadir—the lowest point of socioeconomic conditions for African Americans—removed the necessary framing to question the legitimacy and motives of nonprofit organizations. Sociologist John Arena provided a powerful framework for understanding the intersection of the neoliberal character of nonprofits and urban revitalization in his work *Driven from New Orleans*. Because nonprofits are nongovernmental private institutions that promote the ruling-class program without use of force, they are often seen as palatable and relatable solutions to the uneven development of urban capital. The most critical subsection of these organizations, Arena contended, is "the religious, charitable, scientific, and educational subset" that registers as 501(c)(3) tax-exempt organizations with tax-deductible status for donors.[40]

These nonprofits, Arena explained, typically function in two ways for capitalism: they assume the service role originally controlled by the state, and they purposely undermine the development or maintenance of grassroots social movements—*rational* solutions to oppression. Particularly as they gained immense power in the 1990s and 2000s, nonprofits primarily targeted the Black petty bourgeoisie, typically college-educated individuals who had a notable reputation in working-class communities and were willing to concede their radicalism or progressivism for either monetary rewards or alignment with antipoverty or social change organizations. Thus, as Arena concluded, the purpose of nonprofits generally is to turn "threatening" movement actors and organizations into "non-threatening" appendages of pro-growth programs. Finally, to appear "down" for the cause, these co-opted agents instead push bourgeois liberal identity politics that conspicuously erase the class contradictions and the critique of capitalism from the analysis.[41] Meanwhile, community development corporations coordinate with banks to purchase cheap land and properties and cleanse them of "undesirable" populations. Thus, nonprofits recognize poverty as a manageable asset for big business and thereby refuse to erase it. Community development corporations like Summerhill Neighborhood Incorporated and its proprietor Douglas Dean sold the working-class Summerhill residents to the Olympic Stadium wolves in the 1990s, with other organizations following suit.

The Dynamics of Class Struggle in Black Atlanta

For the purposes of this project, I define the "Black working class" as the racial class of workers who typically do not possess the capacity to own the means of production, their own labor, or land. My conceptualization of "working class" aligns with the original Marxist paradigm of class position: proximity to decision-making power and control of capital. Additionally, these workers' socialization among their neighborhood peers—discussed in chapter 1—aligns their class interests with the working class. Therefore, blue-collar and service-sector workers are typically considered working class. However, teachers and nonadministrative school staff, for example, must be considered working class as well because they do not hold decision-making power over their labor. Additionally, I separate administrative, professional, and managerial workers and political officials into a distinct racial class: the petty bourgeoisie. This group also does not own the means of production; however, its members have a closer proximity to capital because they possess decision-making power for, influence over, and stakes in the direction, accumulation, consumption, and circulation of capital. Additionally, the petty bourgeoisie act in the interests of the bourgeoisie. Particularly in Atlanta more than in other Black-majority cities, the Black capitalist class maintains the capacity to purchase a sizable portion of the labor power of workers. Although this class is still relatively small in actual wealth in comparison to its white counterpart, it is relatively much larger and wealthier than it has been in previous periods and other spaces. Therefore, their control of the administrative, professional, and managerial class of workers is much mightier than in most other US urban spaces and thus a crucial component to their domination of the metropolitan region's working classes. More clearly, Atlanta's petty bourgeoisie is one of the most influential and powerful in the world.

I do not characterize income level as a determinant of class position; instead, I use the terms "Black working class," "low-income Blacks," "poor Black urbanites, " and "the Black worker" interchangeably. I prescribe that job type is the best indicator of class position for many reasons. First, income does not necessarily determine class interests. Veteran steel factory workers can generate higher incomes than human resources officers or fast-food restaurant managers. Yet the former possess no control over their labor, while the latter two professions wield decision-making power over business operations. Second, working-class laborers, especially in economically volatile times, move frequently between blue-collar livable-wage labor and service-sector minimum-wage labor. Third, my period of study muddies the waters on the correlation between income and class level. My research shows that by the mid-1970s, real wage growth in the form of purchasing power for Black workers began a steep decline and has yet to recover. Consequently, by the mid-1980s, wage growth did not catch the increasing cost of living. Thus, it is safe to conclude that wages for all working-class individuals were low enough that the noticeable differences between "low-wage" and "high-wage" working-class individuals became nearly indistinguishable. As Cha-Jua's New Nadir framework demonstrates, this trend worsened in the twenty-first century. However, I do not attempt to simplify or collapse the working classes into one another. There are subtle differences I discuss throughout this study between low-wage Black workers and livable-wage Black workers.[42]

The best means to investigate the complex nature of class warfare in Black Atlanta is through a predominantly Black working-class resource base. I foreground existing, previously disregarded Black working-class and non-elite archives, particularly the *Atlanta Voice*. Founded by African Americans Ed Clayton and J. Lowell Ware in 1966, the newspaper challenged Atlanta's white and Black bourgeois conservative media like the *Atlanta Daily World* by employing a more left-leaning perspective with working-class and radical columnists. Under the slogan "A People without a Voice Cannot Be Heard," the *Atlanta Voice* provided full, alternative coverage of political, economic, social, and cultural issues affecting grassroots Black Atlantans that mainstream publications like the *Atlanta Journal, Atlanta Constitution*, and *Atlanta Daily World* refused to cover. This included the civil rights and Black Power movements, white supremacist and police violence, housing and labor struggles, radical student movements, and neighborhood destabilization from the perspective of the residents.

I also depart from dominant methodological strategies in the discipline of African American and urban history by allowing working-class-specific documents (letters and correspondence), oral interviews, and other unorthodox sources like neighborhood organization meeting minutes and speeches, public-access media, and left-leaning policy research to support the critique of the political economy of Black Atlanta. Some of my sources, particularly documents from the Southern Center for the Study of Public Policy at Clark Atlanta University and *Endarch*, a Black leftist political science journal, are Black intellectual sources, yet they provide the most critical studies of the African American working-class experience at the time. Black theorists like Mack Jones, who contributed to both archives, centralized social crises in the Black communities in his assessment of Atlanta's political structure.[43] Scholars have overlooked these sources as evidence of the centrality of the African American working class in Atlanta's history. To be clearer, individuals who passed over these sources generally did not consider working-class voices and viewpoints to be valuable to their historical perspective.

This project also foregrounds previously disregarded radical print archives that further expose the class warfare in Atlanta. The *Great Speckled Bird*, which was published from 1968 to 1976 (with a very brief resurrection in 1984), operated as the only underground, alternative periodical out of 800 newspapers in Atlanta at the time. Because of its devotion to the daily lives of oppressed communities, it maintained the third highest circulation of any media outlet in the city! A multiracial collective of Marxist-Leninists, anarchists, and antiwar pacifists published the *Bird*. It sustained its popularity in Black working-class Atlanta by both critiquing racial oppression as a colonial structure and directly challenging local institutional powers like the ACOC, Atlanta city hall, Atlanta Police Department, and Georgia governor's office.

The *Bird*'s greatest impact was that it consistently recorded and foregrounded the voices of the oppressed locally, nationwide, and globally. This successfully linked the colonial struggle of Black Atlanta workers to other dark-skinned peoples' fight for liberation across spaces. The periodical also printed hours' worth of interview transcripts, community organization posters, demands, and action calls. It covered labor and rent strikes daily, the anti–Vietnam War movement, and self-defense training exercises, exposed exploitation of all kinds, and publicized the daily struggles of working people. Therefore, the *Bird* was not simply a periodical. It functioned as a crucial weapon for oppressed Atlantans in their fight for liberation. The *Bird* headquarters and its journalists were pivotal local movement resources for grassroots struggles until financial trouble shut down the paper in 1976. Although the *Bird* attempted resurrection in 1984, it never operated fully again. With its demise, oppressed groups lost a crucial weapon in their neighborhood movements.

Mapping Class Warfare

In his opening verse on Atlanta hip-hop group Goodie Mob's 2006 song "Hold On," rapper Big Gipp illustrated the alienation of the Black worker navigating the growing anti-working-class character of his hometown in the present day:

> Every day my city seems to grow, and grow . . .
> Prices going up, people giving in . . .
> By the city to be toxic, but ain't nothing said
> Always on the down low, never in the mainstream.[44]

The lyrics paint a harrowing reality of a city ravaged by decades of malignant neglect, uneven development, and repression of its largest population base. As Big Gipp alluded, the modern Atlanta political economy reshaped the political, economic, social, and spatial prospects of hundreds of thousands of Black working-class lives—the vast majority locked into an ever-increasing subproletarian class position.

Class Warfare in Black Atlanta pinpoints the 1966 Summerhill rebellion as the rupture in racial class formation and capital accumulation in Atlanta. More clearly, this Black working-class uprising was the result of Atlanta capitalists expediting the general law of accumulation by constructing Atlanta Stadium (later renamed Atlanta–Fulton County Stadium) on top of Black Summerhill. The very act of the general law of accumulation, meaning "revitalizing" urban space, produced the misery and alienation in the Black worker that generated the conditions for collective rebellion. Therefore, urban rebellions like that in Summerhill provided the most succinct episodes demonstrating workers challenging capital to remake class in their interests—by targeting institutions of their oppression and igniting an offensive struggle for autonomy.

The Summerhill rebellion also highlighted the recalibrated class divisions within the Black Power movement in Atlanta, as the ever-increasing number of Black working-class residents declared war against all institutions and policies that threatened the use value of their neighborhoods. Beginning our analysis at this moment concretizes the role of Black working-class collective resistance in the shaping of the social processes of Atlanta's transformation. Conservative and liberal Black Power leaders, seeking new structures of accumulation in the city, viewed Black working-class neighborhoods through an exchange value lens. Consequently, by 1970, class warfare erupted across the city over who controlled those very institutions. These battles played out over stadium construction gentrification, labor exploitation, police violence and surveillance, the dismantling of Black public schools, deplorable grocery store conditions, and fair housing.

These working-class expressions of revolutionary nationalism caused the power bloc between capital and petty bourgeois leadership to foreground their pro-growth goals by promoting an anti-working-class agenda. Throughout the 1970s and 1980s, both the Maynard Jackson administration and the Andrew Young administration worked hand in hand with groups like the ACOC and middle-class leaders to discipline the Black worker. This public-private partnership dismantled the bargaining power of the city's unions, targeted lower-income residents with a regressive tax, and abandoned Black children during a murder crisis. Last, the Black petty bourgeoisie leadership militarized and expanded the Atlanta police to the point where it operated as an occupying force. This crushed all opposition to pro-growth ideas by targeting and incarcerating known Black community leaders and destroying public local movement centers like the Black Panther Party headquarters and the *Great Speckled Bird* offices.

This repression induced severe consequences for Black working-class Atlantans. First, the combination of antilabor federal policy, technological outsourcing, and the constant threat of Black rebellion at the point of production and beyond in Atlanta and other urban cities forced capital to expend the Black worker from the labor sector. This neoliberalization process drastically undercut the working class's bargaining power and disproportionately destabilized the Black working class's social conditions and resources necessary to strengthen the use value of their neighborhoods. The city's power brokers exploited the destabilization of the neighborhoods to initiate full-scale gentrification, beginning with the construction of the Georgia World Congress Center, an international airport, and the Omni Hotel. With these three new beacons of international finance capital, Atlanta leadership provided a sales pitch to international capital that the city operated under a neoliberalization framework. Both Jackson's and Young's Black urban regimes traveled to multiple nations selling the land and labor power of Black working-class Atlantans to the highest bidder. Beginning with Jackson's administration, every Black urban regime in Atlanta's history wielded the police as a mechanism to cheapen the land and property value of targeted neighborhoods. Without the neighborhood organizations and resources to fight gentrification and other immediate threats to the use value of working-class Atlanta, Black residents faced growing concentrations of poverty and violence from the underground economy. Atlanta police did not stop violent crime and the drug trade; rather, it concentrated these activities in specific enclaves, which drove down the price of the land and property over time.

Second, ACOC's Central Atlanta Progress, the citywide planning apparatus of the organization, invoked tax increment financing, zoning policies, federal housing funding (enterprise zones), and coordination with nonprofit organizations to privatize sizable portions of working-class public spaces. The goal for capital and its junior partners was not simply to obtain the Olympic Games in 1996. Rather, they sought to use the Olympic Games to further weaken the working-class voice and presence in the central city. Jackson's third administration as well as Bill Campbell's introduced harsher penalties on poorer Atlantans to counter the resurgence of Black working-class social movement A'NUFF (Atlanta Neighborhoods United for Fairness). Because the Olympics threatened to drop the second stadium on Black Atlanta in less than three decades, A'NUFF organized substantial leverage against the games. Unfortunately, the combination of the rising nonprofit sector, the conservative media, and the lack of movement resources proved too much for A'NUFF.

The Olympics provided rationale for Atlanta's power brokers to fully assault the Black working class. The games offered a vision of Atlanta without the Black worker and poor people in general. Therefore, Mayor Shirley Franklin's Black urban regime led the post-Olympics destruction of viable labor and public housing in the central city. With the most crucial necessities out of reach of the Black masses in the city, the skyrocketing housing prices pushed a sizable portion of Black Atlantans into the metro region suburbs. To ensure that Black workers could not afford to resettle inside the city for the foreseeable future, city leadership recruited cheap, nonunion, subproletarian labor providers like Walmart to build multiple supercenters in the city. Labor available for the Black working class in metro counties like DeKalb, Douglas, Cobb, Clayton, and Gwinnett amounted to restaurant jobs, janitorial service, sweated warehouse work, and gig economy services like Uber and Grubhub.

The study of the Black worker in Atlanta concludes where it began: Black working-class Atlantans fighting stadium construction in their backyards. In the 2010s, capital preyed on Vine City again after decades of pecking away at the area's use value. After Atlanta–Fulton County Stadium and the Olympic Stadium were built, the Mercedes-Benz Stadium leveraged the class war in Black Atlanta in favor of the power brokers. While many of the remaining African American workers moved into extended-stay motels, some remained in tiny clusters in the city, cut off from the booming new bourgeois tourist and banking culture. No longer a majority Black city, Atlanta now resembles the real American Dream: an abstract tapestry of wealth, privilege, and violence against those who dare challenge the power.

Class Warfare in Black Atlanta is neither a triumphant nor a pessimistic study of Black struggle. Rather, it situates the fight for power in urban space as a dialectic, influenced primarily by the sociohistorical experiences of working-class urbanites. However, this book, as a critique of the political economy of Black Atlanta, is an indictment of pro-growth urban revitalization. Since the creation of the United States, capital has thrived and reconstituted its accumulation power through the usurpation of poor Black bodies and spaces. My study is by no means a personal attack on any individual actor or organization. Rather, it seeks to establish a historical truth regarding the centrality of class conflict in contemporary racial oppression and the complicated nature of human agency. Thus, Black working-class actors are not "heroes" because they won. Black working-class actors are not "losers" because they failed to halt gentrification and subproletarianization. Instead, *Class Warfare in Black Atlanta* demonstrates that despite the sheer brutality of the bourgeois and petty bourgeois forces, Black working-class urbanites are heroes because they continue to fight for themselves, their families, their neighborhoods, and their kin. Gentrification and subproletarianization are their processes—they generate them by challenging capital at all levels of society. The ruling classes therefore are required via their class position to discipline them for being willing to battle for Black Atlanta. This book charts a model for other urban studies of grassroots actors who have found increasingly creative and sometimes difficult ways to build collective resistance to racial capitalism. My study concludes with the objective truth that no matter how disruptive the political economy, subjugated peoples' philosophy of liberation always remains collective.

CHAPTER ONE

The Black Worker Struck First
Black Power, Protonationalism, and the Working-Class Offensive

> Black people will not be oppressed, repressed, or depressed. We produce the wealth, and they take the wealth. People who produce the wealth should get it.
> —SHERMAN MILLER, African American chairman of the Mead Caucus of Rank-and-File Workers and member of the Atlanta chapter of the October League, 1972

> Why do they have the gold,
> Why do they have all the power,
> Why do they have friends at the top, why do they have
>   jobs at the top.
> We've got nothing, always had nothing,
> Nothing but Holes and Millions of Them.
> Living in Holes,
> Dying in Holes,
> Holes in Our Bellies,
> And Holes in Our Clothes.
> Marat we're poor and the poor stay poor,
> Marat don't make us wait any more.
> We Want out rights and we don't care how, We want
>   our Revolution NOW!
> —PETER WEISS, *The Persecution and Assassination of Jean-Paul Marat*, 1963

On Tuesday, March 17, 1970, after ten years on the job, African American garbageman Gene Truelove joined over 2,500 predominantly Black city workers in a thirty-six-day strike, the largest public-sector work stoppage in the city's history at the time. The revolt began as a one-day solidarity "holiday" but soon escalated into an open-ended strike after the Atlanta City Council spent the workers' promised pay raises on enticing new streams of capital to the area, namely for a new sports coliseum, highway expansion, and police pay raises.[1] Strikers, however, framed the work stoppage as a betrayal of *their* community interests. More clearly, the rebels invoked the revolutionary nationalist tenet of Black Power that swept through urban neighborhoods at the time. Flyers, chants, and speeches spoke to demands for Atlanta to reorganize city revenue toward the material needs of Black workers. "If the city can find money for a coliseum," Black labor organizer Jesse Epps said, "it can find money for a wage increase." "They spend OUR money and buy ammunition to kill OUR boys, but there's no money for bread," declared Ethel Mae Matthews. Indeed, many in this garbage strike movement contextualized the episode as a struggle over power relations in Atlanta. "Like the fingers on the hand, we are united into a fist against oppression," neighborhood activist Linda Jenness stated.[2]

The coordination between the strikers and the neighborhood activists gridlocked Atlanta and expanded the strike beyond the point of production. Once the strike spread past the large sewage plants on Hill Street in southeast Atlanta and beyond the city disposal sites and incinerator on Jonesboro Road and Magnolia Street, strikers halted expressway maintenance and construction throughout the southwest area. Morehouse College, Spelman College, Morris Brown College, Clark College, and Atlanta University students coordinated travel to and from locations to leave donations and strike supplies. Strikers' wives, sisters, and mothers organized other Black neighborhood residents to build local movement centers for strike support near their homes. They chose the Butler Street YMCA in southwest Atlanta as the official strike headquarters and Mount Moriah Baptist Church, West Hunter Baptist Church, and the Electric Plaza Building across the street from Atlanta Stadium as strategic resource points to house strike materials, serve food to families, distribute strike funds, print flyers, hold tactical meetings, and train picketers and speakers. Neighborhood volunteers leafleted education materials at city events, including at a screening of the leftist film Z. These support systems not only strengthened the strikers' will in the fight but also helped bond the community to the strike by establishing kinship through shared work, resources, communication, and celebration. At the height of the strike, some demonstrations had over 1,000 supporters across the city.[3]

Despite this leverage against the city, Atlanta exploited the tense class fractures in the Black Belt to weaken the strike. By April 20, Black leaders, including state senator Leroy Johnson, insurance capitalist Jesse Hill Jr., Rev. Martin

Luther King Sr., and Rev. Sam Williams, had met with city hall without consent of the strikers and pressured picketers to concede and return to work. After securing a tentative agreement with the city that offered only a one-step pay raise, these individuals splintered support for the strike as resources dried up. When strikers returned to work, supervisors retaliated against them, harassed them, cut their pay, extended layoffs, or fired them outright without the slightest resistance from the Black leaders.[4]

In a letter addressed to African American vice mayor Maynard Jackson, Kelley Kidd, a resident of the Summerhill neighborhood, summed up the underlying fissures in Black Atlanta: "Ultimately, this strike raises the fundamental question of our time: shall we perpetuate gross inequality of wealth, income, and power or shall we move towards a more democratic society?"[5] More clearly, Kidd's question highlighted the struggle over Black Power and who held the power to define and direct it in urban spaces. When Black workers became the dominant populace in Atlanta at the end of the 1960s, their demands for community control of social institutions flew in the face of their middle-class and upper-class counterparts, who were committed to carving out a piece of the capitalist pie. This war erupted along racial class lines, through the lens of vying ideologies of Black Power, and on multiple fronts, particularly in schools, neighborhood stores, housing, and most crucially, labor.

This chapter explores how political actors within the Black working class organized a multipronged offensive front to capture control of social institutions and the levers of power in the central city. These grassroots social movements increased the use value of Black working-class communities by securing resources that solidified their daily routines, strengthened kinship bonds, and formalized structure, trust, and commitment to sustained social movements. This revolutionary protonationalism challenged the other vying strata of Black Power in Atlanta: liberal pluralism (electoral politics) and conservative nationalism (Black capitalism). Consequently, Atlanta elites promoted grassroots leaders from Black Atlanta to command these strata and move the Black worker away from collective grassroots protest. This new racial formation, foundationally about how to restructure capital to maximize profits at the expense of the colonized Black majority, also sought to minimize the power of Black working-class residents. Both sides in the war over Atlanta chose Black Power as the vehicle to challenge the opposing vision and to seize control of the political economy of the Atlanta metropolitan region in their interests.

Black working-class Atlantans placed primacy on organizing at the point of production and recognized it as the crucial space for sustaining and expanding resources for resistance. The petty bourgeoisie and bourgeoisie reacted by sending city leaders to co-opt movements and redirect goals toward profit-generating schemes. Between 1967 and 1977, labor strikes engulfed much of the city. Additionally, labor organizing produced resources and trained leadership for other working-class neighborhood movements. Thus, during the Black Power era, low-income Black urbanites constructed their vision of self-determination based on their material needs, which directly conflicted with the vision of Black and white Atlanta elites. This chapter demonstrates that the transformation of modern Atlanta into an international powerhouse for the circulation and distribution of capital can be understood through the war fought over who wields and who benefits from Black Power. Within this paradigm, urban expansion can be conceptualized as a protest against the autonomy and self-determination of working-class Black dwellers. In Atlanta and other urban sites like Detroit, Philadelphia, and Newark, the Black worker struck first, struck often, and channeled revolutionary protonationalism as the vehicle toward liberation.

"You Ain't Going to Hurt Him No More": The Roots of Black Power in Atlanta

By the summer of 1966, thirteen-year-old African American Elotse Daniel was sharing an uninhabitable room at the Markham Street Hotel with her forty-five-year-old father, George; her forty-year-old mother, Grace; her fifteen-year-old sister, Linda; and her eight-year-old brother, Mark. Because George only earned forty dollars a week, the family received $79.80 a month in welfare, not even close to enough to rent a decent apartment in the city. Their one-room hotel had a useless wooden heater, an unsanitary bathroom without running water, and no icebox or cupboard for food. The Daniels, alongside a family of six living in the adjacent room, battled a horde of ants, roaches, and rats that came for the exposed food, some that Elotse noted were "bigger than my doll." She often woke after rats had chewed parts of her ear in the night.[6]

A block away from the Daniel family resided forty-year-old part-time construction worker Willie Williams with his forty-seven-year-old wife, Lisa, and their three children, five-year-old Willie Jr., two-year-old Renay, and thirteen-month-old Sammy. Like the Daniels, Willie had no plumbing, holes in the wall for rain and wind to blast through, and falling plaster. His neighbor, twenty-three-year-old Robert Lee Edwards, lived with his three sisters, nineteen-year-old Mary Alice, eight-year-old Pamela Denise, and six-year-old Christine, and his mother, Georgia. Their rooms were so cold in the winter that they had to wear coats all day and night. Like Elotse, they shared their unsanitary bathroom with roaches and rats and all other residents on the first floor of the apartment building. The rotting floor was falling through along with the windows, and the front door was broken to the point that residents could not close it.[7]

Down the street from Willie and Robert lived seventeen-year-old single mother Jaqueline Louise Dewberry, who raised her eighteen-month-old son, David Bernard Dewberry, in a run-down, twenty-five-dollar-a-month apartment without plumbing on Foundry Street. Her attempt to find viable work in the city failed. Therefore, she requested welfare but only received one check, for $8.45. The money was not enough to fill in the holes in her walls and windows or to secure her newborn proper health care. Two days after Christmas that year, David succumbed to the harsh winter winds circulating throughout the apartment before his second birthday.[8]

These episodes only scratch the surface of the extent of domination endangering Black workers in the city in the late 1960s. Slumlord Joe Shaffer, who owned each property discussed above, controlled multiple avenues of resources necessary for Black Atlantans to thrive in the city. Besides being the owner, Shaffer served as employer, grocer, creditor, sheriff, judge, and jury over the residents of Markham Street. According to the residents, Shaffer offered unemployed residents part-time manual-labor work at below minimum wage, lent them money at 50 percent interest, stole their welfare checks, and used the threat of taking their job away or throwing them off his property as leverage to make them do whatever he asked of them.[9] Shaffer exemplified the dependent relationship that the Atlanta bourgeoisie exploited over poor Black urbanites. Black workers throughout the city had no room to breathe, and the detonation was near.

In the afternoon hours of Tuesday, September 6, 1966, the Summerhill neighborhood exploded when Atlanta police officers R. H. Kerr and Lamar Harris shot twenty-five-year-old African American Harold Louis Prather in the back as he ran for his life to his mother's house. At the intersection of Capitol Avenue and Ormond Street, hundreds of Black residents converged in anger, aired their grievances at police and city leadership, and quickly turned to confront the growing number of riot squad and shotgun-wielding police.

Once Atlanta mayor Ivan Allen Jr. ordered the tear-gassing of residents, chaos ensued: Black rebels fought back against police with rocks and glass bottles and shattered windows in white-owned grocery stores and cars. Fires carried the rebellion into the evening hours as chants of "Black Power" swelled amid the fury of the crowds. The rebellion carried over to the Boulevard neighborhood a few days later but did not elicit as large of a demonstration. By the end of the week, the police had arrested twenty-nine Black rebels, fourteen of them identified as activists. Marjorie Prather's decree to the police as her son lay at her feet drowning in blood echoed the radical wave charging through the Summerhill and Peoplestown communities: "You ain't going to hurt him no more. There used to be days in slavery times when they killed people like dogs, but this is another day. If you live and he lives, you'll pay for this!"[10]

Although Harold Prather's murder sparked the Summerhill uprising, this violent demonstration indicated that a radical tide had turned in the consciousness and political economy of African American Atlantans. The lack of material gains in the civil rights movement meant that the thousands of Black workers newly arriving to Atlanta found little to no access to social needs in a city unprepared and unwilling to support them. The Atlanta bourgeoisie proletarianized these new Black workers into the lowest sectors of labor possible in the city at the time. By 1966, the 186,051 African Americans in Atlanta resided predominantly in the bottom three income brackets (with an annual family income between $0 and $4,000). In fact, only 1,046 Black families earned over $10,000 a year in 1966, compared to 17,894 white families. Unsurprisingly, the central city employed 69 percent of Black men in factory work, in service work (hotels), and as laborers, while only 3 percent were employed in middle-class professions. Black working women fared much worse. Eighty percent of Black Atlanta women toiled in private domestic household work, while only 4 percent worked in professional fields.[11]

Between 1966 and 1970, the African American population in the central city exploded from 186,051 to 255,000 (38 percent and 51 percent, respectively, of the total population), giving Atlanta a Black majority for the first time in the city's history. In relative terms, the Black population in Atlanta rose by 17.5 percent between 1950 and 1960, whereas in the four-year period between 1966 and 1970 it rose by 13 percent. With Auburn Avenue's bifurcation via the highway and parts of low-income Black Atlanta dissected by the new Atlanta Braves stadium, Black working-class migrants arrived to dwindling social conditions. Atlanta's postwar urban renewal proletarianized working-class migrants by concentrating most of these Black urbanites in low-wage, blue-

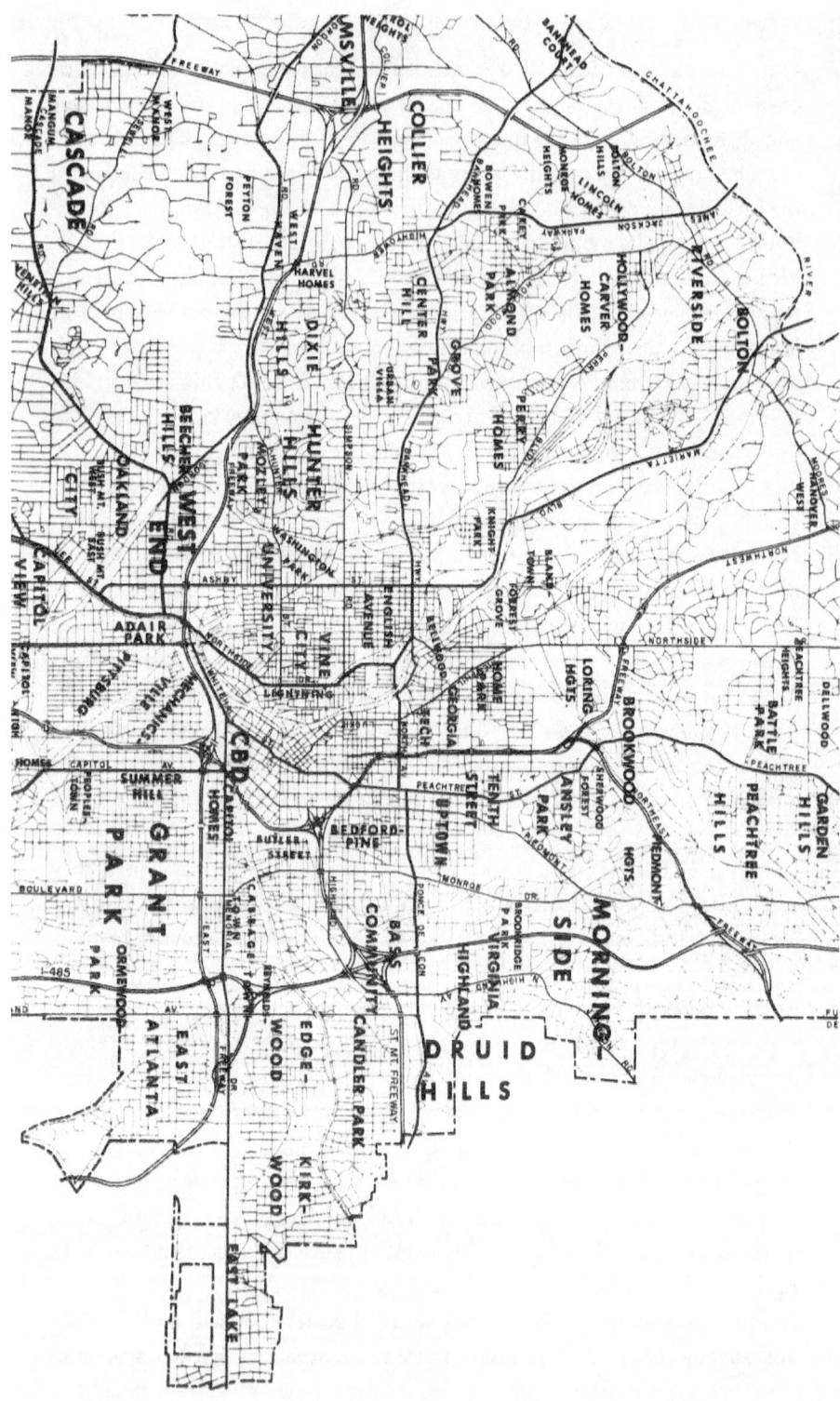

Map of city of central Atlanta neighborhoods, 1970. Courtesy of Community Council of the Atlanta Area, Grace Towns Hamilton Papers, Woodruff Library of the Atlanta University Center, Atlanta.

collar labor and in the oldest housing stock in neighborhoods surrounding the Central Business District: Summerhill, Peoplestown, Pittsburgh, Mechanicsville, Bedford Pine, and Vine City.[12]

In the decades before 1970, slum clearance programs targeted these areas, but the city tore down just over 40 percent of the poorest housing (an estimated 22,000 units) and never replaced it. In fact, the Atlanta Housing Authority (AHA), the federally subsidized housing agency for low-income people, sold most land cleared of blighted housing to the highest private bidder. As a result, low-income housing in the 1960s was scarce, and the percentage of housing deemed "unrepairable" had increased by 23 percent by 1970. Activist David Morath of the antislumlord organization Emmaus House explained that new Black working-class residents faced a dilemma in organizing fair housing movements: "The buildings are too worthless to be fixed, but if they're condemned—well it's just that much more crowding."[13]

Over 1 million white residents fled the city during these years and flooded the five suburban counties surrounding the city limits (where only 311,000 Black suburbanites lived). Much of the economic activity left the newly majority Black inner city and traveled to the northern metropolitan area, including Gwinnett, Cobb, and Cherokee Counties and northern parts of Fulton and DeKalb Counties. Black working-class spaces shed industrial, retail, and high-paying service-sector jobs. Banks, law firms, real estate developers, stockbrokers, accounting firms, and retail stores all fled north. Industrial labor, which had always been decentralized in the city, dispersed farther from Atlanta's core after a highway expansion, when the major means of transporting goods shifted from trains to trucks.

Evidence suggests that Atlanta's postwar power base coordinated poor Black colonial enclaves in designated areas of the central city. Community eligibility provision areas are spaces where families are three times more likely to have inadequate incomes than families in other parts of the city. In 1970 Atlanta, 25.7 percent of all families in community eligibility provision areas lived below the poverty line, while another 8.7 percent of all families in other parts of the city experienced similar economic constraints. Additionally, 45 percent of Black Atlantans living in poverty resided in the community eligibility provision portion, which contained over 35 percent of all Black people in the central city. The greatest proportion of poverty-stricken families of any category were African Americans, with seven or more family members living in the community eligibility provision portion. Over 50 percent of these families fell below the poverty level that year. Ethel Mae Matthews described her precarious economic stability: "I have a 13-year-old daughter to support.

I also receive disability social security so that I'm not getting any more than if I didn't get it. Also, recipients get no money for telephone or insurance. People can get free clothing if their case workers writes them a note. . . . Not many recipients are told that."[14]

African Americans who looked to the state government to generate livable income faced mounting barriers, especially underemployment. Those Black workers who drew state payroll checks did so around the bottom rungs of the hierarchy. Georgia's Department of Health, the largest state agency in 1972, had 12,238 employees, of whom only 29 percent were Black. Over two-thirds of that Black workforce was classified as "auxiliary" or "custodial." In fact, 84 percent of all Black state employees in 1972 were auxiliary, clerical, or custodial workers.[15]

City hiring data at that time revealed an employment ceiling in Atlanta for most African Americans. The Atlanta Community Relations Commission released a fifty-five-page report in August 1970 stating that 70 percent of African Americans in the city were clustered in the lowest sector of labor while only 14 percent of whites were similarly employed. What is most striking in the report is that of the twenty-eight city departments, only five employed African Americans outside of the dirtiest jobs.[16]

Inflation served as a dialectical catalyst for Black workers. First, inflation eroded wages. This, combined with discriminatory hiring and pay, prompted a higher surge of Black labor strikes. However, many of those gains were wiped out by more inflation, higher taxes, and shorter workweeks. Atlanta factory production workers' purchasing power dropped 5 to 6 percent during the first quarter of 1970. This meant a decline in gross average weekly earnings from $137.23 in December 1969 to $129.26 in March 1970. Take-home pay for a worker with three dependents dropped from average weekly earnings of $117.44 in December to $112.36 in March. This proved disastrous for Black households, as the income disparity gap widened between the races to record levels. In 1970, the Black median household income was $5,710, to whites' $12,146.[17] Business owners, however, felt little to no effect from inflation. That same month, Coca-Cola reported that its net earnings for the first quarter of 1970 set a record high of $26.9 million, up from $23.9 million in the first quarter of 1969.[18]

Investigative journalist Boyd Lewis compared Atlanta labor to "serfdom" for Blacks. He reported that many "unemployable" Black men performed heavy manual labor for one-tenth the federal minimum wage and were "compelled by unimaginable poverty to live little better than animals." As a result, Black physical and mental health deteriorated and jeopardized people's lives as well as their capacity to establish beneficial daily routines and local movement centers.

For example, African Americans Charles Williams and David Scrivens brought home thirty-six dollars a month, thus earning seventeen cents per hour each as full-time maintenance men for the Juniper Street apartments in 1971. They were on call twenty-four hours a day, seven days a week, cleaning and repairing apartments. The owner of the apartments, Brewer-Head Realty Company, offered the two workers two basement rooms the men described as "filthy, adjoining the boiler room with no toilet nor bathtub and swarming with roaches." In early 1971, Williams was carrying full trash cans down four flights of stairs when he suffered a hernia attack. Following his operation, Williams, suffering from the pain and possible side effects of medicine, set fire to their twenty-dollar-a-month shack. Police jailed him for criminal trespassing and brandishing a pistol. With his monthly income cut, Scrivens was forced to move to a house in Mechanicsville without running water, gas, or electricity. Williams remained in jail with no guarantee of a psychological evaluation.[19]

Wage theft also afflicted the Black worker. In 1970, the Wage and Hours Board of the US Department of Labor revealed that Atlanta-area businesses were responsible for stealing approximately $1.12 million from employees over the previous fiscal year. Almost 1,000 Atlanta companies paid an estimated 4,768 laborers wages lower than those permitted by the Fair Labor and Standards Act. However, these federal protections excluded all hotel, motel, restaurant, and agricultural employees because these sectors had high numbers of low-wage Black workers. Because African American women represented a high proportion of such employees, it is appropriate to conclude that they suffered wage theft at a disproportionately higher rate than Black men and white men and women. Considering employers' historical tendency to discriminate and steal wages from African American workers in general, it is also safe to assume that many of the affected Atlanta workers were Black.[20]

Georgia state revenue problems trickled down to Black Atlanta's pockets. At the beginning of January 1972, the recession forced more people to use Medicaid while medical costs rose, resulting in the state paying more for welfare programs ($33 million in 1971). Consequently, Georgia sought a sales tax increase of 4 percent to grow the state's revenue. Because the sales taxes levied survival items at the same rate that they taxed luxury goods, they were regressive: poor people who spent most of their money on necessities paid a larger portion of their income in taxes than did members of the affluent classes. Concurrently, almost $6 billion worth of property in Georgia, most of it improved and highly valuable, went untaxed every year.[21]

The federal government dealt Black Atlantans another blow when it came to housing. Only three years after the Fair Housing Act of 1968, the Supreme Court upheld a California law that the people in a community could call for a referendum to decide whether they would permit low-income housing units to be built in their community.[22] Although defining "community" was a legal snafu, not only did the landmark legislation cut off large swaths of available land for public housing; it also assisted urban communities like Atlanta in constructing colonial boundaries for future middle- and upper-income residential housing and commercial development. As later chapters discuss, the Atlanta Chamber of Commerce took advantage of this market-rate housing development decision by building more housing units adjacent to low-income units in southwest Atlanta in the late 1970s and southeast Atlanta in the late 1980s. This facilitated early gentrification efforts in Atlanta by increasing rents and displacing the Black poor.

These social conditions informed Black working-class Atlantans' embrace of grassroots revolutionary nationalism as a strategy to liberate themselves from racial oppression. As Amilcar Cabral argued, this domestic, imperial domination of subjugated people "by the means of violent usurpation of the freedom of development" produced a tendency toward nationalism.[23] The colonial power, or the bourgeoisie, alongside the managers and administrators of capital, or the petty bourgeoisie, restricted the material, spatial, and social resources to the point that it negated the very historical process and personality of the Black working class. Therefore, nationalism—demonstrated through what power brokers deemed to be "irrational tactics" like violence, via urban rebellion or self-help defense, and social movements driven by protonationalism—offers "the regaining of the historical personality of the people, its return to history through the destruction of the imperialist domination to which it was subjected."[24]

For instance, as historian Ashley Howard argued, civil disorder provided these "nontraditional political actors"—Black working-class urbanites—the capacity to shift "the political contest outside of established spheres of power" and launch an offensive that "operated on parallel footing with the state, albeit temporarily."[25] Thus, political actors operating under the notion that they are in a nationalist struggle with a colonial power recognize that violence must both answer the brutality of the oppressor and ensure the might of the social movement. Kwame Ture, who participated in the 1966 Summerhill rebellion, said about the violent response: "The revolt was, and is, against the *bestiality* of a racist mayor and a corrupt police department. . . . Mayor Allen has refused to deal with the rats, roaches, and unemployment in the Black community."[26] Ture drew a comparison between the direct violence being done to African Americans' bodies and the structural violence that diminished the social conditions of Black workers. To add insult to injury, the petty bourgeoisie is the first to shield the state and the ruling class from the type of critique that violent protest produces. As historian Winston Grady-Willis noted in his rich study of the Summerhill rebellion, Mayor Ivan Allen Jr.'s condescending words to the rebels, as well as his demeanor, exposed the reputed "paternalistic plantation owner who suddenly found himself in the midst of an uprising by field workers" and crippled his power to govern the city streets.[27]

Most crucially, Black working-class Atlantans seized control of their own struggle by recalibrating their ideology and objectives outside of Atlanta's petty bourgeois leadership. Throughout the Summerhill rebellion, Black rebels screamed for "Black Power," wore African garb and jewelry, and raised posters with images of jet-black panthers.[28] The sheer magnitude of this new formation broke the petty bourgeois leadership into pieces. When Southern Christian Leadership Conference (SCLC) Atlanta chapter representative Hosea Williams announced his intent to take lead of the crisis by leading "all-out" SCLC protests against the "bestiality and brutality" of Atlanta police, Rev. Samuel Williams, the national vice president of the SCLC and co-chairman of the Metropolitan Atlanta Summit Leadership Conference, denounced any SCLC-led protest against the police, refused to request that Martin Luther King Jr. come to Atlanta, and publicly ridiculed Hosea Williams as nothing more than a "hired hand" who "does not set SCLC policy."[29] This internal struggle within the SCLC foreboded a fracture over class interests and Hosea Willliams's tendency toward labor struggles.

City stakeholders reached similar conclusions in the early moments of the Black Power movement in Atlanta: do everything to move away from the slogan and denounce it as often as possible. Mayor Allen quickly jumped to nationwide television to create and control the narrative, condemning Black Power as "violence" that has "upset the status quo." This rupture from the civil rights movement launched the Black Power movement—and class warfare over control of the central city—throughout the neighborhoods.

Additionally, the Student Nonviolent Coordinating Committee (SNCC) planted crucial seeds for Black Power in the city through its Vine City Atlanta Project. Headquartered on Raymond Street in northwest Atlanta, SNCC's Atlanta Project functioned foremost as an agency-laden institution: "To stimulate people to talk about issues and problems, and to organize themselves around these issues."[30] Although the Vine City project initially tied itself to opposing SNCC representative Julian Bond's unseating in the Georgia House of Representatives, it also challenged slumlords over inhumane housing conditions. For instance, SNCC allied with the grassroots organization Vine City Council to distribute blankets and other warm objects to residents neglected by Joe Shaffer. This action, combined with political education sessions, ignited an organizing light in the residents, and they began to meet nightly to plan a rent strike against Shaffer.[31]

Although this is merely one small example of the influence of SNCC's Vine City Atlanta Project on the city's Black working class, it highlights two important points for how working-class urbanites adopted a mostly class-based revolutionary nationalism as their ideological position in their fight for self-determination.[32] First, their struggle remained indigenous. SNCC provided the lighter fluid, but the residents lit the fire and carried it through the city. Second, it shaped the minds of other oppressed Atlantans seeking to liberate their neighborhoods. In effect, Black Power was the chapter in the city's history in which the African American majority recognized their colonized position, worked furiously to raise the consciousness of wide sectors of their base, and opened new avenues of resistance.

The Power of Place: Neighborhood Use Value and Black Social Movement Capacity

At the heart of Black working-class Atlanta's day-to-day struggle was the inherent contradiction with the city over the desire to control their social institutions. Thus, Black workers attempted to obtain the political, economic, cultural, and spatial resources that both satisfy essential needs and strengthen community. Concurrently, capital sought to maximize the profit potential in the exploitation of Black workers, their labor, and their space. As urban geographers John Logan and Harvey Molotch posited, the city's pursuit of *exchange value* presented a simultaneous push for both goals by two distinct groups as "a continuing source of tension, conflict, and irrational settlements." Sociologist Ruby Mendenhall added that this special intensity constructs an asymmetrical market relation between buyers and sellers where landlords determine property prices not by worth but by how much the residents *value* the distinctive locational benefits. This market, Karl Marx contended, structures urban phenomena and determines the experiences and relationships of city dwellers.[33]

Black urbanites conceived of maximizing their *use value* of place as indispensable to their social objectives: they recognized that they could survive in less desirable places, but their *quality* of place determined their political, economic, social, and cultural power. This struggle for place, inherent in most Black urban spaces, generates and possibly sustains access to resources that enhance neighborhood social movement capacity (NSMC), including access to work, community oversight of public education institutions, kinship networks, family, and proximity to survival-needs shops (primarily grocery stores). From a conceptual sense, how working-class actors developed and organized their "home" informed their capacity to resist racial oppression. "Home," as sociologist Kevin R. Cox conceptualized, is a vested network—meaning that oppressed people's relationship to place has extremely high stakes and carries intense feelings and commitments related to long-term and complex social, material, and emotional attachments. Access to these benefits is so important to residents that they are willing to employ organized protests, social movements, violent insurrections, or political regulation to procure stability in their living and work spaces.[34]

Logan and Molotch's use value framework provides a succinct measure to examine how Black working-class Atlantans constructed a viable resource base to sustain NSMC in their war against Atlanta power brokers. In fact, the Black community's interpretation of use value provides crucial insight into how they employed protonationalism. First, the *daily round* is how residents learn about and make conscious decisions to adapt facilities, locations, and offerings to their day-to-day routines and to the benefit of their community. In other words, the daily round is how residents adopt a consistent movement throughout the day that minimizes their time and resources for both future individual and community benefit. Aspects that affect the daily round include labor within relative proximity to home; transportation between home, work, school, and social spaces; food security (relative proximity to grocery stores and quality fruit, vegetables, meat, and dairy); amenities (electricity and gas/heat for the winter); and childcare services.[35]

The daily round allowed Black Atlantans to develop integrated mechanisms for dealing with multiple social problems in their neighborhoods. In July 1970, the Pittsburgh community in southeast Atlanta conducted door-to-door "rat surveys" to determine why more vermin were populating their homes, playgrounds, and community center. The survey concluded that improper storage for loose and damaged garbage cans (provided by the city) not only caused a boom in the rat population but also contributed to a host of other problems that impaired the daily round. Pittsburgh resident Beatrice Garland teamed up with residents in the Citizens Neighborhood Advisory Council of Summerhill and Pittsburgh and built new garbage can racks, repaired damaged garbage cans, and scheduled mandatory block area cleanups.

The racks also decreased pollution, limited stray dogs roaming the streets, and made the neighborhood more attractive.[36] These upgrades, completed by residents themselves, did not cost the neighborhood, as renovations typically raise prices under an exchange value model. Rather, they redirected residents' time and energy from those problems toward other family and community needs.

Apartheid is a crucial determinant in the daily round. Racial oppression exposes the daily round as vulnerable, because if residents lose one of the elements in the routine or their original residential place, the value is either penalized or outright erased. For instance, in January 1970, the Atlanta Aldermanic Zoning Committee voted 3–1 to rezone a southwest Atlanta residential area for the development of an additional 600 apartment units on Sewell Road—making a total of 2,000 apartments (housing 6,000 people) concentrated in a three-to-four-mile radius over a three-year span. With approximately 9,000 people consolidated in a compact space and beset with subpar labor and services, new residents struggled to establish a daily routine while established residents reported a disruption in their public services. For both sets of dwellers, an increase in population without attention to improving labor options and services undermined the daily round. Labor became scarce while city services were depleted under the weight of more consumers. Consequently, poor residents traveled beyond their schedule to search for a short supply of jobs, thereby jeopardizing other segments of their routines. In November of that same year, the Atlanta Transit System cut bus lines across the city. The most impactful line cut was the No. 35 Decatur Street–Grady Hospital (down twenty runs per week), which forced hospital workers to alter their schedules and find a new way to get to work every day.[37]

Time is also a significant variable in the daily round. The bus line cuts resulted in longer travel times by an average of twenty-six minutes for each bus line. Thus, residents like Shelby Cullom lost a consistent travel practice for both family and community care, having to change when to drop children off at day care, when to schedule (or cancel) community organization meetings and events, and when to go to sleep and wake up for work. Money also determines the daily round. An August 1969 bus fare hike from twenty-five cents to thirty-five cents cash or thirty cents token priced many Black workers out of public transportation and pressured them to disrupt their daily round to preserve their financial budgets. Eighteen months after the fare hike, Atlanta Transit System secretary-treasurer Henry Taylor noted that the number of bus riders had decreased 8 percent.[38]

Mechanicsville Community Freedom Center. The *Great Speckled Bird*, December 25, 1972. Courtesy of the Atlanta Progressive Media Foundation / Georgia State University Library Special Collections and Archives.

Next, residents maximize an informal "marketplace" through an *informal support network*, a loose organization of individuals who provide life-sustaining goods and services to the neighborhood via a reciprocal bartering system. Examples of such network actions in Black urban working-class communities include loaning food to neighbors, babysitting children for friends and acquaintances who offer aid like electricity sharing when a neighbor cannot afford to pay their bills, instituting a carpool service (e.g., in response to the Atlanta Transit System bus line cut discussed above), or providing referrals for jobs. When Willie Williams fixed the plumbing in his run-down Markham Street apartment, neighbors in the low-income area took turns carrying pails of water to other neighbors daily.[39]

Informal support networks also help colonized groups build and sustain physical and social spaces. Whether they become functioning local movement centers or not, these neighborhood centers stabilize the overall structure, health, and reciprocal bartering in working-class communities. In 1969, low-income residents across the Black Belt established the Atlanta Consumer

Food Project co-op in a downtown warehouse with a locational advantage to all the working-class neighborhoods. However, budgetary issues forced the enterprise to close after two years. Black Mechanicsville and Summerhill community members decided to pool their remaining funds from the co-op and create a neighborhood buying club. Located on Georgia Avenue, the Sum-Mec buying club provided residents volunteer opportunities in exchange for hardship items like food, clothing, or small loans. In fact, African American Harriet Darnell, who had helped operate the co-op, stated that Summerhill and Mechanicsville residents coordinated a fundraiser for the club that raised more than $500. Food distribution circulated resources, volunteer time, and communication across the two neighborhoods. These efforts proved so successful that Mechanicsville residents opened a second space, the Mechanicsville Freedom Center, to further circulate survival needs like clothing in a thrift shop, education on family budgeting, and other community services.[40]

Most critical to Black Mechanicsville residents was that the Freedom Center operated solely on the funds collected, raised, and disbursed by residents only. They refused to accept any federal or outside grants and alluded to the fact that external support dampens the value of the members accountable to the institution.[41] In other words, the informal support network bonds together oppressed people as kin—collectivizing their struggle toward goals and responsibilities for empowering the use value of the neighborhood. When anthropologist Carol Stack conceptualized these "kinship networks" as conventional, reactionary consequences of racial oppression, she overlooked their dynamism in activating the consciousness of collective struggle in working-class urbanites. Although Stack is correct in that kinship networks generate stability and function in a dysfunctional environment, they also serve as proactive bonds that help Black working-class neighborhoods and social organizations thrive to a point beyond precarity. As a result, the community's objectives move toward securing autonomy.[42]

The resourcefulness and resiliency of neighborhood informal networks amid perpetual urban decay do not compensate for or perpetuate the poverty cycle; rather, they represent a crucial resource made possible only by *community*. These networks solidify the bonds people build that enable them to rely on one another when capital threatens to smash them and their neighborhoods into pieces. Community establishes the fourth variable for the use value of a neighborhood, *security and trust*, because it provides residents with a sense of shared cultural symbols, values, and kinship ties. Colonized urbanites channel these elements in the development of their consciousness during the stages of a social movement. Beginning in the infrapolitical phase, community members complained loudly, told jokes, and created songs and jingles to align their frustrations with their social conditions on the same collective page. Denise Broward spoke of impromptu jingles about "honkys and crackers" and of her and friends making "oink" noises when police drove past her Eleanor Terrace subdivision. According to Broward, "It was what we did. We thought you were cool and with us if you laughed at the inside jokes like that."[43]

As a result, residents developed and maintained a distinction between community member and outsider that informed their trust and organizing strategy for future movement action.[44] Signs of commonality (skin color, clothing, diction, and participation and attendance in Black social institutions) serve as a means for categorizing members and nonmembers of neighborhoods and social movements. This "categoric knowing" is reinforced through shared aid in the daily round, such as carpooling during the Atlanta Transit System fare hikes or building a new neighborhood garbage collection system.[45]

Neighborhoods also provide residents with a significant spatial as well as social demarcation that strengthens the linkage people establish between their locational advantage and their racial class position. *Identity*, in the form of class, is the fifth asset for a neighborhood's use value and informs the sixth and seventh resources, *agglomeration* and *ethnicity*. The status of a neighborhood's residents as a Black working-class community negates the neighborhood's identity as simply a "collection of houses"; rather, it establishes an enclave of complementary benefits where the concentration of many similar people—informed by the variables that strengthen use value—stimulates the development of NSMC.[46] The neighborhood's shared ethnicity serves as a summary characterization of all the overlapping benefits of the resources for NSMC. Most residents in a neighborhood have similar daily rounds, represent a shared lifestyle, and have similar social boundaries for sustaining interpersonal support.

This struggle works both ways. As Black urban space is consistently in play for fragmentation and exchange value interests, residents often face displacement, eviction, or some type of disruption to place or to the use value of neighborhoods and NSMC. Black studies scholar Lou Turner notes that for capitalists, the use value of the Black community as a neighborhood asset "is no more than a commodity with an exchangeable market value for development and finance capital in the same way that a corporation or factory with financial vulnerability is a purchasable asset for private equity firms."[47]

Thus, capitalists categorize afflicted Black neighborhoods as mere fodder whose planned depreciation puts them on the market to be bought and sold, recycled, and reinvested. In 1970s Atlanta, this emerging struggle between Black working-class residents and pro-growth, bourgeois reformists became a struggle over the value of Black lives, space, and place in the city.

"The City Is the Black Man's Land": The Debate over Black Power in Atlanta

In May 1970, African American teenager Beverley A. Matthews submitted a letter to the editor of the *Atlanta Voice* in which she exuberantly described the political and cultural shift occurring in Atlanta: "I am a 17-year-old, who is very glad this self-awakening is happening to Afro-Americans. It is long overdue. If we make a big deal out of our 'Blackness' these days, it's because we are no longer ashamed of ourselves. . . . Not all Negroes are Black. . . . You had better get hip to the word because 'Black' is where it's at."[48] Indeed, all four streams of Black Power—revolutionary nationalism/radicalism, cultural nationalism, liberal pluralism, and conservative nationalism—crashed into the city at once, overlapping and contradicting one another around class. Although all proponents of Black Power believed it to be a vehicle for some form of self-determination for people of African descent, the question of *who* wields the autonomy drove the development of grassroots rebellion, municipal power, and subsequently, the disciplining of the working class in Black urban centers.

The conflict over Black Power in Atlanta challenges existing Black Power studies by highlighting the complexity of contesting Black Power's ideological strands in the transformation of capital and southern urban space. This research forces us to rethink the "declension" narrative of Black Power and its periphery shots at working-class collective social movements as "unorganized." Clayborne Carson's analysis of SNCC charged Black Power with failing "to provide a coherent and radical set of ideas for future Black struggles." Carson concluded that Black Power also precipitated the destruction of SNCC and the civil rights movement.[49] Carson's argument overlooked the political realities of indigenous Black people. In fact, local community studies in Black urban neighborhoods demonstrated that Black people across the class spectrum charted a path outside of the civil rights movement for the most strategic and transferrable program to the masses for social change. As a result, the four fully developed and strategic strands of Black Power operated in conflicting terms with one another, typically over the issue of *class*. Despite these distinctions, the study of the Black worker and Black Power disrupts the long civil rights movement thesis. Black working-class urbanites who demanded to control the organizations and institutions that affected Black people demonstrated that Black Power was not civil rights. Black Power was, in part, a rejection of the goals, discourse, strategies, tactics, symbols, leadership, and ideology of civil rights.[50]

In general, each stream of Black Power diverged equally on ideology and strategy alike. The Black working class tended to align with revolutionary nationalism because of its emphasis on autonomy. Revolutionary nationalists typically argued that people of African descent were colonized as an oppressed working class who must unite, locally, nationally, and in some cases internationally, for their own self-interests. According to organizations like the Republic of New Afrika, revolutionary protonationalism is grounded in anticapitalism, anti-imperialism, collective self-determination, community control, and redistribution of land and resources for colonized peoples. As historian Edward Onaci demonstrates, the revolutionary nationalist slogan "FREE THE LAND!" outlined the goal of Black people controlling their own destiny by sojourning to their very own resources needed to build their own society.[51]

Cultural nationalists, on the other hand, were stigmatized as "reactionary nationalists" who desired to adopt African culture as the means to liberation. Evidence suggests that their position in Atlanta's Black Power era was more fluid than fixed: they did not assume a significant organizational or movement presence, but they individually participated in political actions for both neighborhood and Black petty bourgeois groups. Therefore, as scholar Algernon Austin implied, cultural nationalists were much more political than their historical reputation suggests.[52]

Atlanta liberal pluralists like Julian Bond and Maynard Jackson believed that Black Power was simply "a natural extension of the Civil Rights Movement." Therefore, many of them, like the remaining members of the SCLC and other civil rights organizations, attempted to affix liberal integrationist ideals and strategies onto Black Power movements. Liberal pluralists promoted pro-growth reformism and believed Black Power derived from electoral representation. Conservative nationalists, on the other hand, argued that profit is the true measure of equality. Therefore, these Black capitalists sought to align with sympathetic white business leaders and government figures like Richard Nixon to compete for capital and sit alongside the ruling class. Floyd McKissick and Atlanta's Andrew Young argued that Black Power meant getting a fair share of capital and that militancy must give way to free enterprise and private wealth.[53]

Bourgeois and petty bourgeois African Americans tended to believe that Black capitalism especially offered a framework to guide the newly arrived Black majority in Atlanta toward hard work and constructive competitiveness. Black construction corporatist Jesse Hill Jr. believed that access to profit accumulation was the answer to the ills of Black Atlanta. Atlanta's Black chairman of Grassroots Exposition, Jackson R. Champion, stated that "Black Capitalism is necessary to sustain minority communities and eventually blend Blacks into the mainstream of the American economy." New World Developers, one of the largest Black business organizations in 1970s Atlanta, built the first Black-owned "superstore" in working-class Kirkwood, on the corner of Howard Street and Boulevard Drive. According to Rev. Joel West Marshall, the president of the New World Developers board of directors and stockholders, this was the "first time in the history of the state where nearly one thousand Black people have pooled their money and other resources together to prove to the world that Black people can organize and develop business enterprises in their own community." The corporation added that "the Black man will never be recognized, respected, nor appreciated regardless of his educational status until he decides within himself that he must own and control some of the business enterprises and some of the wealth of this nation." However, New World Developers, like most Black capitalist ventures, was not operable solely through Black funds; it was dependent on white financial institutions. At the groundbreaking ceremony, Marshall told interested parties that he and his board of directors "are going to file their application with all the banks ... and the cooperation of responsible Blacks and whites."[54]

What is often neglected in thinking about the framework for Black capitalism is that it opposed cooperative economics—known as "communality" during the Black Power era—because it advocated public and *shared* power. African American venture capitalist Richard Clark delivered this message to Atlanta businessmen, adamantly opposing cooperation with the Black working class, Black small business owners, and the government. "A communal kibbutz for American Blacks is lunacy," Clark told a group of over 100 Black college graduates and Atlanta business firms in March 1970. "Community economic effort runs contrary to the American ideal.... Black people are motivated by the same degree of individual success as whites. It's an ego thing." When asked to consider Black community agency and control over public resources, Clark stated, "Group reaction to oppression isn't like pooling pennies to build a 10-cent store in a shopping center."⁵⁵ Clark's philosophy underscored the lack of respect for the Black worker under conservative nationalist ideology. The war for Atlanta was not one-sided and launched through only working-class social movements. Conservative nationalism, at its core, sought to concentrate all African American power, wealth, and agency in a tiny segment of its richest members. Thus, Black capitalism operated the same as white capitalism in the 1970s—disciplining the worker, subjugating the activist, and repressing the resistance.

Black revolutionary nationalists publicized their disdain for Black capitalism frequently as Black and white media wrestled over what to do with Black Power. *Atlanta Voice* columnist F. C. C. Campbell likened conservative nationalism to abstract idealism and alienation:

> The essential misconception held by members of the Negro-American Liberal Establishment is that [capitalism] is expanding a vital, powerful, manner.... If we clear away the mysticism surrounding [capitalism], we can see the reality.... We can see unemployment among young and old ... intensifying layoffs ... lousy welfare ... confused integration schemes ... death and misery in Vietnam ... alienation.... Hence, if you decide to follow Mr. Roy Wilkins['s] advice and join the System, you should at least be cynically aware that you are with a losing cause, though there is wealth to be made at the trough for the short run.⁵⁶

Black liberation theologian Rev. Isaac Richmond struck back at Richard Clark's philosophy by outlining the contradiction between exploitation and autonomy:

> The myth that Blacks can be like whites (meaning big capitalists, big bankers, international financiers) is nonsense.... Wealth was not built on genius and hard work, it was built on slave labor. Anybody trying to imitate white capitalism will find themselves using slave labor—and exploiting....
>
> Black leadership, then, instead of holding out an impossible capitalist development to the black masses, must offer viable alternative systems and economics ... and this cannot be done until more black leaders study and come to understand the inherent slavery [in] a capitalist society, instead of screaming about enlarging the cesspool.⁵⁷

Richmond's assessment exposed the stark reality of African American attempts to grasp a piece of the capitalist pie. Even at its peak in 1972, Black business ownership barely scratched the day-to-day lives of the African American masses. The US Department of Commerce reported that the 195,000 Black-owned businesses that operated in 1972 were overwhelmingly small-scale retail and service centers like grocery store franchises, dry cleaners, and barbershops. Less than 20 percent of these businesses paid employees, meaning that they were more than likely family businesses. In fact, Black businesses that year—which conservative nationalists argued could uplift the hard-working job seekers out of the ghetto—employed less than 250,000 of the estimated 4 million unemployed African Americans in the United States at the time.[58]

This, too, points back to the dialectic of the Black political economy. Because African Americans' low purchasing power—combined with declining bargaining power toward the end of the Black Power era—Black-owned businesses had little chance of moving Black customers away from white businesses. Therefore, even large Black banks like the Citizens Trust Company had to accept stock and bond purchases by the Ford Foundation. Those businesses that did not receive white capitalist support did not possess the capital to survive economic instability and as a result offered little opportunity to the Black working classes.[59] As has been the case with Black capitalism since its inception, it provided the perfect allegory for the problem of Atlanta, its "Black Mecca" myth, and urban space in America. The engine functioned on a monolithic dream of abstract idealism more than on material benefits for the Black masses. The isolated episodes of personal gain for a select few African Americans offered little aspiration in the social realities of the Black worker in Atlanta and the United States.

Ideological conflicts over Black Power spilled over into informed neighborhood movement actions in Atlanta. In the summer of 1970, revolutionary nationalists residing in the Vine City slums conducted a door-to-door survey asking residents a two-part question: What do they need, and how do they expect to get it? Vine City African Americans overwhelmingly chose resources for children, protection from police, and community control of schools. As a result, neighborhood activist Tim Hayes created the Georgia Black Liberation Front (GBLF), with a vision of "self-reliance based on social practice." It quickly established a free breakfast program for children that became so popular among the neighborhoods that when police questionably arrested and jailed GBLF members, Vine City residents raised funds to bail them out.[60]

With its reputation growing in the Black Belt, the GBLF assisted in the struggle of Atlanta University Center students fighting racist attacks on college campuses that same year. Class conflicts quickly drove wedges through the solidarity efforts, however. Black college students and the GBLF threatened a boycott of all universities and demanded that the Morehouse College, Spelman College, Morris Brown College, and Atlanta University administrations pass resolutions to suspend all academic activities and hold political education sessions in response to recent racist violence against Blacks in nearby Augusta and at Jackson State University. According to Tim Hayes, while Atlanta University and Morris Brown passed the resolutions, Morehouse and Spelman called Atlanta SCLC president Hosea Williams and Jesse Jackson to "suppress the voice of the people." Hayes issued a statement accusing Williams and the SCLC of making "fund-raising campaign rallies for their own glorification, forcing students to participate in their march, and drawing attention away from the students demands."[61]

In their most incendiary accusation, the GBLF stated that the SCLC "destroyed all political aspects of the students' efforts, and staged a pop festival starring LeRoi Jones, Andrew Young, and an almost complete roster of CIA-paid bullshitters that hit the campus so hard that it would take the political organizers on campus a week to recover." The GBLF ended by telling the crowd that the "CIA pays groups such as US and SCLC to 'cool you down' when you get hot." The Atlanta Revolutionary Youth Movement joined in condemning the SCLC's actions that day. It accused the SCLC of telling marchers to stop chanting "Black Power" slogans.[62]

Both the GBLF and the Revolutionary Youth Movement conveyed SCLC's ideology, strategy, and tactics as being detrimental to insurgent Black protest actions erupting across the city. It did not help the SCLC's reputation that it allowed white Atlanta mayor Sam Massell—who held a problematic reputation among working-class Black Atlantans over rampant police brutality and labor exploitation—to lead the March Against Repression on the Morehouse College campus only a few months after he attempted to crush the 1970 sanitation strike. Black spectators like Barbara Joye reported that Black Atlantans despised Massell's presence and booed him.[63]

"It's a War Now": Protonationalism in Practice in Black Atlanta Neighborhoods

Revolutionary nationalists in working-class neighborhoods fought to wrestle control of social institutions away from bourgeois and petty bourgeois leaders. For low-income Blacks, institutions that directly impacted the use value of their neighborhoods, including schools, grocery stores, and social services like fire stations, were viable weapons against racial oppression if controlled by local neighborhood actors. Accordingly, Black working-class movement actors wielded protonationalism as their choice of weapon for survival, building and sustaining NSMC, and moving closer to autonomy and liberation.

Although Black workers took pride in local public schools, federal desegregation legislation recalibrated their mission to seizing control over administration, curriculum development, and delivery in a revolutionary nationalist sense. The Nixon administration's policies in the South resulted in the consolidation of schools and mass firings and demotions of Black teachers and principals. This brought about dire consequences for Black students, including heightened discrimination and mass closings of Black schools; the latter severely impacted the daily routine of working-class Atlantans as they had to restructure transportation and security and trust networks outside of their communities.

The threat to Black neighborhood control over public schools moved faster than expected. According to a study conducted by the Race Relations Information Center, by 1971 Black teachers and principals faced extinction in the South. In Atlanta specifically, the numbers were alarming: in 1970, the number of white teachers rose by 615 while the number of Black teachers decreased by 923! Another report, *The Status of School Desegregation in the South, 1970*, posited that school systems were circumnavigating the issue of discriminatory firing by forcing Black teachers to instruct courses for which they had no knowledge or training. The report listed examples of gym teachers assigned to biology or English courses and vice versa. Then, the school system fired them for "incompetency." In 1970, 235 African American schools in the South closed, with 57 percent of them less than twenty years old. Officials converted closed school buildings to administrative offices or sold them to private interests. Newly desegregated schools overcrowded Black students into small-capacity classrooms and barred them from social activities. School dances and other extracurricular activities were moved to all-white community centers or country clubs to restrict Black student access.[64]

Consequently, Black students and parents vowed to keep their schools open and under their own decision-making. When the all-white Fulton County school board selected the Black Eva Thomas High School to close in 1969, Black students organized so quickly that they caught their opposition on their heels. "We've got to show them now that they can't close Black schools and get away with it," proclaimed African American student Jessica Allen. Once the school closed, students held pickets at the Fulton County Board of Education, occupied the school building illegally, and held freedom classes that focused on Black Power and African American history. When

Black students refused to attend the all-white schools, they forced the courts to reopen Eva Thomas High, securing a strong victory for Black working-class Atlantans. Although this invigorated other Black communities to defend their public schools, judges put nine other all-Black schools in Fulton County metro Atlanta under court order with the possibility of closure.[65]

Conceptualizing Black working-class Atlantans as an internal colony offers key insight as to why they designated public schools as indispensable to revolutionary nationalism. The domination of the Black masses through political subjugation, economic exploitation, and social humiliation requires a fifth column of effectively trained individuals to eradicate every element of the African American experience—particularly those that challenge the authoritarian, technocratic, profit-driven power structure. Schools, more than media and religious spaces, set the terms for Black culture, socialization, history, and empowerment. Thus, the Black masses recognized schools as local movement centers where they could disrupt white supremacy via liberation-themed curriculum, leadership training, and resource circulation with the community. Instead of docile workers committed to the American system, Black workers sought to produce rebels committed to increasing the viability of revolutionary nationalism and Black pride. F. C. C. Campbell summed up the Black worker's attitude best: "There must be absolute community control over Black schools by local boards working in concert around a common educational program . . . responsive to grass roots people."[66]

The Emory University Black Student Alliance expressed this desire for revolutionary nationalist control over education during their march and information picket on May 25, 1969. They stated that in launching their movement against the racist administration at Emory,

> Black students demand a change through an Afro-American Studies program which will not praise the good white fathers of this racist society, but will tell of how the good white fathers created this racist society—through the Black man's sweat and blood! . . . Black Power was expressed by the Black students who were standing up against a system . . . which, if not changed, will have to be destroyed and replaced with another. . . . Black students at Emory will not allow Black workers' needs and rights to go unheeded. . . . Whitey, watch out. Black Power is gonna git yo mama![67]

Liberation community schools became viable institutions throughout Black Belt Atlanta. The earliest Black community school in Atlanta opened in April 1970. The Atlanta Center for the Black Arts was housed on Gordon

Street in southwest Atlanta and promoted the Pan-Africanist concept of "a United struggle of all African peoples and seeks to develop a local nucleus of community people for that struggle." It offered courses to Black children aged twelve to twenty in African and African American history, politics, culture, and dancing. Many of the teachers, like Larry Rushing, Kofi X, Babtunde, and Karen Spellman, were active in community struggles and catered their teachings to a shared value system. Consequently, the center provided tenets of cultural nationalism as well.[68]

Despite successful community school centers, Black workers also launched multiple offensives to take control of Black public schools. On July 2, 1970, Bankhead Courts parents held a massive protest in the streets promising to "shut down" Mayson Elementary School over the removal of a popular principal. According to the parents, Atlanta Public Schools transferred Principal Otie Mabry as political retaliation against her active role in the Bolton Garden public housing tenants' rent strike earlier that year. The school board superintendent told the parents that Mabry, a six-year veteran principal, was being moved because she was "physically incapable of running the overcrowded Mayson school because of foot ailments." Parents reported that area superintendent Cecil Thornton had stated that "Negro children are harder to teach." Mabry refuted this and honored the community pickets alongside a dozen Mayson teachers. Armed police detectives soon arrived to "monitor the protest" but incited violence when residents reported that officers drove their vehicle through a line of picketers without sounding the horn. The vehicle nearly struck two picketing children. A swarm of Black parents surrounded the car, and the detective told them, "I'll do it again."[69]

The movement escalated from defending Mabry to attacking the system. Community members soon demanded that Thornton resign as superintendent to further ensure leverage for Mabry. A week after the first pickets, Black parents and teachers, organized by Black neighborhood stalwarts Louise Whatley and John Shabazz, stormed Thornton's office at the Area IV school district headquarters but were stopped by locked doors. The parents banged so loudly on the office windows and doors that they tripped the security alarm, prompting police, television reporters, and newspapers to arrive on the scene. When Thornton finally appeared, one parent told him, "I don't see why you don't retire if you find it so hard to get along with Black people!" Whatley added, "Transfer yourself, a Black man will replace you."[70]

Atlanta leadership moved quickly to suppress the rapidly growing rebellion. The Atlanta Community Relations Commission (CRC), housed in the office of the mayor, called a meeting with the Bankhead Courts parents,

Area IV administration, and Mayor Massell for a cooldown session. Movement actors, however, used the leverage they obtained in meeting with Atlanta leadership to address the long-standing housing crisis in West Adamsville. Bankhead Courts residents spoke of caved-in apartment ceilings, windows so weak that rain poured into their apartments, maggot- and rat-infested garbage cans, and poor drainage that caused swimming pool–sized flooding during rainstorms.[71] Their escalation tactics had positioned Black working-class activists to expend resources on other campaigns and other local movement centers in the Black Belt.

The forty-plus protesters at the meeting warned Atlanta leadership that violence was possible if Thornton remained in power and Bankhead Courts continued to deteriorate. "We will declare war on Atlanta," Whatley stated to the CRC. "Until our problems are solved, we're going to hit the streets. Some of us may get hurt, some may get killed. But it's a war now." "There's going to be riots and burning if nobody listens to us. We're being treated like nobodies ... but we are somebody," Lilia Kapers, mother of eight children, told the CRC. "We asked Mayor Massell and the alderman to do something, but they didn't ... and we don't want to have anymore [Black] politicians at Bankhead Courts asking for our votes and making promises but who go downtown to sit with the white man." When asked what would happen if any residents were unjustly evicted for their role in this protest, Kapers concluded with a threat that the entire neighborhood stood behind: "We'll kill the man who touches our furniture and puts us out. We'll kill him and be the pallbearers and flowergirls."[72]

Shabazz spoke next, reiterating the movement's time frame for action and putting the next crucial move on the Atlanta leadership. "In September, if Mrs. Nelson [one of the protesting parents] says the school won't open without Mrs. Mabry, it won't open," Shabazz promised. The protesters gave the city thirty days to produce an action plan, or "it might be so hot out here that you won't be able to get close.... There might be bonfires from here out to Chappell Road."[73]

At a press conference the next week, residents, parents, and teachers joined in condemning Thornton for being "insensitive to the needs of our community and children" and noting that the Mabry crisis was a microcosm of a larger problem of lack of community power in Atlanta Public Schools. Harold Huggins, a teacher at West Manor Elementary School, told the *Atlanta Voice* that the school system suffers from intense overcrowding, faulty curriculum, and inadequate buildings and materials. Benjamin E. Mays, the African American chairman of the Atlanta Board of Education, former president of

Black students storm Atlanta Public Schools headquarters for Black Power. The *Great Speckled Bird*, February 19, 1973. Courtesy of the Atlanta Progressive Media Foundation / Georgia State University Library Special Collections and Archives.

Morehouse College, and major figure in the Atlanta middle class, opposed the Bankhead Courts movement and contextualized the residents' protests as disruptive and "structurally out of order" with the policies of Atlanta schools: "The board's policy ... is an administrative function.... I don't think the administration could function very well if parents had to be consulted on every appointment."[74]

The summer of escalating actions by Bankhead Courts residents pressured the Atlanta leadership to reconsider Mabry's transfer in August. Besides achieving this victory, this movement activated other Black workers to seize control of their public schools. In March 1971, Marietta closed two all-Black schools, Central School and Marietta Junior High School. African American parent Walter Moon led a walkout of over seventy-eight Black parents at a school board meeting, telling the board, "You may save a dime here and a dime there, but it'll disrupt the ... community.... As God as my witness, we are determined that we are not going to sit by and continue to be ridiculed by the white people!" After numerous community protests, the school board buckled and reopened Marietta Junior High School within three months.[75]

The school control movement sprinted through southwest Atlanta. On April 8, 1971, Black parents from West Manor Elementary School organized a boycott to protest overcrowding and lack of communication with the community. Over 90 percent of the students enrolled did not cross the picket line: only seventy of the 642 students attended school that day.

After the school day ended, the parents set up a motorcade and disrupted an Atlanta Board of Education briefing session to air their grievances. In their comments to the board, residents like Henrietta Canty made it clear that their school's deterioration was not because it was fully Black now; rather, it was because city services had cut the funding and resources *now that* the school was fully Black: "We find classes being held in the principal's office; classes being held in the book room.... We find no difficulty in taking whatever action necessary to bring this racially tinted treatment to an immediate halt."[76]

The protonationalist movement reached beyond grade schools and into universities across the city. In March 1971, the DeKalb County Board of Education denounced as "separatist" Black college students' request to institute a Black studies program. The students responded by organizing the Black Life at Core Curriculum (BLACC) to combat the "typical power structure's attitude towards the Black man." BLACC's secretary Beverly Stewart refused to concede to an administration-approved book list that forced instructors to teach Black history as a subsection of previously existing western civilization and US history courses: "Our history is different. You just can't teach it like that." Instead, BLACC demanded a full Black studies curriculum that offered courses in African American history, literature, contemporary drama, and jazz. BLACC also hoped that the Black studies program would open the door for more Black teachers at DeKalb College.[77] Thus, not only did BLACC seek control over the school curriculum, but it also attempted to increase the wages and job types in the community and reverse the declining number of Black teachers in the city.

Black working-class Atlantans also targeted grocery stores for community control. The neighborhood grocery store provided three essential variables to low-income urban dwellers: (1) locational advantage for Black working-class people who lack transportation, (2) food, and in many cases (3) job opportunities. However, whites who did not reside in those communities owned and operated most neighborhood groceries in 1970s Atlanta.

One significant episode occurred at the turn of the decade in Summerhill. Azar's liquor and grocery stores sat right across the street from Atlanta Stadium on the corner of Fraser Street and Georgia Avenue and served the entire Black Belt. The owner, Donald Azar, had a long history of conflict with the Black residents. One anonymous youth told the *Great Speckled Bird* newspaper that Azar had been in Summerhill for over fifteen years and owned a lot of property in the area, including more liquor stores, a pawn shop, and a washateria. Summerhill residents also noted that Azar was notorious for physically attacking Black residents, and in the previous year he allegedly ordered a policeman to shoot a child in the leg for petty theft. Aside from his racist violence, Summerhill residents also objected to Azar economically exploiting the neighborhoods. Azar's store prices were sometimes fifty cents higher than in other stores in the city.[78]

Azar's racism came to a violent climax one day when he struck African American Miriam Smith, an employee of his who earned seventy-seven cents an hour. According to eyewitnesses, she and Azar began arguing when Azar hit her, causing her to grab the store gun and shoot at him. Azar subdued her, took the gun, and held her at gunpoint until the police arrived. Police charged her on three counts and bound her to the state prison. Once word reached Summerhill, over two dozen residents set up a picket at Azar's with signs reading, "Azar must go! White go cheat each other and stay away from us! Black people are the backbone of the world!," "Azar—you have hit a woman for the last time. Get out, " and "For blacks to have our way, [first] we must send the white away."[79]

As the picket continued daily, Summerhill residents escalated and sued Azar for violating their rights while also using his own strikebreaking tactics against him. Azar attempted to bribe many of the teenage picketers with free liquor to leave the protest, something he tried in previous boycotts of his store. This time, Summerhill was prepared. They trained the teenagers to take the liquor, keep picketing, wait for the police, and then start drinking in front of the police. When the police asked where they got it, the Black youth told officers that Azar sold it to them. Police then arrested Azar and charged him with distributing alcohol to minors. This resulted in the aldermanic committee challenging his liquor license and closing the store.[80]

Black working-class Atlantans expanded this movement into a citywide campaign to either take control over white-owned neighborhood stores or close them completely. Angier Avenue residents followed suit in 1971 and shut down their white-owned neighborhood grocery, Whiteman's, after a pattern of sky-high price markups and employee discrimination. When the residents and employees instituted a combination strike-boycott-picket outside the store, business halted, and the owners locked the doors for good. The National Council of Distributive Workers and Operation Breadbasket —two groups comprising mainly working-class residents and radical college students—joined in support of the residents.[81]

Neighborhood activists recognized how protonationalism helped restructure their daily round by redistributing survival needs, schedules, and infor-

Community picket at Azar's Store. The *Great Speckled Bird*, February 2, 1970. Courtesy of the Atlanta Progressive Media Foundation / Georgia State University Library Special Collections and Archives.

mal kinship networks when necessary. Community leader Bob Goodman stated that if residents had to close every white-owned store in Black neighborhoods because they would not acquiesce to Black community demands, then they were prepared to organize carpools and strategic bus trips to supermarkets in white neighborhoods. Several neighborhood churches agreed to furnish buses for a group of residents in a neighborhood to buy a week's worth of groceries and distribute them to other residents.[82]

The grocery movement next targeted King's Grocery a few blocks from Whiteman's. After witnessing what happened to Whiteman's, King's Grocery quickly agreed to lower prices and increase wages for their Black employees without much fight. Boulevard residents then moved to Arlan's Supermarket on the predominantly white Ponce De Leon Avenue. The protesters threw up a picket when Arlan's refused their demands to empower Black employees. When word reached the national vice president of Arlan's chain of stores in New York, he immediately called Operation Breadbasket's Rev. Carl Dorsey and conceded to raise the pay of Black employees and give them back pay. Ed's Superette on Fairburn Road in southwest Atlanta served Black Adamsville and Bowen Homes residents. The supermarket had a reputation for discriminatory practices against Black employees. For instance, Elonora Phillips cashiered for five years and made only $1.70 an hour with no lunch or rest breaks. Additionally, armed security followed Black customers, and management forced humiliating bag searches for Black customers only. Residents enacted a combination strike-boycott-picket that proved so effective that only three white customers crossed the picket line in the first week! According to Metropolitan Atlanta Summit Leadership Conference's Rev. Joseph E. Boone, "We calculate Ed's Superette takes in from $15[,000]–$17,000 a week, the majority of that from Black people. Now the flow of customers has been slowed to a trickle." One of the former grocery employees, Richard Nelson, summed up the protonationalist and class consciousness in the Boulevard movement: "No white man—or Black man either, if isn't concerned with us—can come in there and scoop up the profits." Reverend Dorsey added, "If we find one [store] owned by a Black person doing the same things [as white-owned stores], he'll be the first to go."[83] Thus, the grocery store movement understood economic exploitation as a central obstacle to Black control of social institutions in the city.

Black working-class movements against inadequate-quality grocery stores sometimes highlighted the class fluidity in Black Atlanta. Many neighborhood leaders sought money, meeting space, and other resources on the grounds that movement actors maintain decision-making power. More clearly, even though working-class Black nationalists typically disagreed with petty bourgeois leaders over the goals and ideology of liberation for the Black masses, they sometimes found common ground on immediate threats to the wider community. For grassroots movements, which often experienced resource and financial scarcity, civil rights groups like SCLC, Metropolitan Atlanta Summit Leadership Conference, and on rare occasions the Community Relations Commission offered funding, meeting spaces like churches, and local and national media and business contacts. Individuals like Hosea Williams, in stark contrast to his fellow SCLC colleagues like Andrew Young, often allied with Black Belt labor movements—but on their own terms.

In fact, labor served as a primary space for Black working-class Atlantans to assemble informal network systems that housed, distributed, and circulated both survival needs and movement resources. Historically, organizing at the point of production offered the tangible structure, discipline, tactics, trainings, education, and stakes to build and sustain NSMC. Black labor organizing during the Black Power movement proved to be much different than typical white-dominated labor strikes and grievances. Rather, Black workers desired decision-making power in the operation of a company or city in order to allocate resources—including profit sharing, jobs, holidays, and donations to organizations—to their communities. Black workers' critiques of capitalism did not rest solely on exploitation; rather, Black labor strikes often demanded concessions outside the contract that impeded capital's fragmentation of their communities. Also, white unions in the American labor movement often refused to recognize and grieve racism at the work site and within union ranks. Therefore, Black workers understood that their interests held weight in their own independent unions.[84]

Atlanta's Black firefighters attempted to wrestle control away from a white supremacist administration after years of demanding intervention by city officials. Instead, in the spring of 1969, several dozen Black firefighters, led by William Hamer, formed Brothers Combined in opposition to a growing number of oppressive measures levied against them. Brothers Combined listed the following grievances against the city of Atlanta: (1) supervisors and captains called them "nigger" and "boy" and ordered them to shine their shoes; (2) Black workers were restricted to the dirtiest jobs with no chance of promotion (in 1970, the Atlanta Fire Department had 234 white officers and no Black officers); and (3) apartheid diminished their access to safety equipment, beds, and shift assignments. The fire department also used a mental ability test that 82 percent of Black workers failed, compared to 48 percent of whites. However, when Hamer conducted a study of the prep classes for the exam, he found that Black firemen were given practice tests three times a week and made high marks; but when they asked for a promotion, they failed the official exam. Concurrently, Hamer reported, whites from outside the city limits who performed lower than Black people on the exams were promoted to the highest positions in the fire department.[85]

Racial animosities against Black firefighters were as detrimental to the Black working-class neighborhoods as they were to the firefighters themselves. Because Black firefighters had their shift assignments reduced, white firefighters either delayed traveling to fires in low-income Black neighborhoods or, as reported by F. C. C. Campbell, went beyond putting out the blaze and destroyed Black property. Campbell noted that a Black woman called the fire department and the all-white team "busted up the entire apartment, sprayed water everywhere," and stole items from her.[86] Thus, labor exploitation and racial oppression destabilized the use value of working-class neighborhoods.

Initially, Brothers Combined leveraged enough pressure on Atlanta officials to secure a grievance procedure and promotions for Black workers. When white supervisors and white firemen discriminated against firefighters, especially drivers, for filing racism charges against their superior officers, this grievance committee victory protected Black workers from retaliation. Brothers Combined secured a much-needed component of protonationalism that guaranteed them some leverage to push further for decision-making power against the city.

"They Trapped Me with Chain and Gun": Gender and Black Women's Labor Struggles

In early June 1970, fifteen African American female workers walked off their jobs at Howard Johnson's on Washington Street in southwest Atlanta. The restaurant held significant locational advantage for the city: it was one of the most popular restaurants in Atlanta and hosted crowds of sport enthusiasts coming and leaving Atlanta Stadium. However, as the working women described it, Howard Johnson's resembled a southern plantation. When the workers began signing union cards, manager John Manion verbally abused the "agitators" and even fired a few workers.[87]

Most of the strikers were waitresses who brought home sixty-five cents an hour as part-time workers, seventy-five cents an hour as day shift regulars, or one dollar per hour as night shift workers, plus tips. As a result, the restaurant possessed a locational *disadvantage* for the workers' labor stability, wages, and ultimately their daily round capacity. As one striker pointed out, customers

Black workers strike against Howard Johnson's restaurant. The *Great Speckled Bird*, June 29, 1970. Courtesy of the Atlanta Progressive Media Foundation / Georgia State University Library Special Collections and Archives.

rarely tipped the waitresses because the food prices were too high. Plus, the stadium goers often ordered their food to go. "They order a dozen hamburgers to go, and we wait on them, but they don't tip. During some ballgames, we don't even have a chance to sit down."[88] Only "regular" workers in name, waitresses were often laid off on days when there were no planned events at the stadium. Sometimes, waitresses were told to work at another Howard Johnson's for the day and expected to pay the transportation themselves to a location in Hapeville. With this instability and wage theft, waitresses often took home less than twenty dollars a week. Few men worked at this Howard Johnson's because, as one striker stated, "they don't pay enough for men."[89]

Supervisors and customers alike also subjected the waitresses to daily sexual harassment. Manion demanded that the women wear white bras, white girdles, and light pantyhose every day they came to work, speak in a "pleasant" tone, and "take it" when Manion dressed them down in front of the customers. Fed up with these conditions, the women went on strike. The restaurant attempted to replace the strikers, but the work stoppage crushed the business. One striker told Bob Goodman, "We've stopped the day shift regular customers almost completely."[90]

Resource deprivation tied to the combined forces of capitalism, racism, and sexism informed how Black women workers constructed their protest activity. White unions and women's rights organizations often neglected Black women workers. Additionally, they were excluded from legal benefits like minimum wage laws, the National Labor Relations Act, and other structural resources. White unions, already holding a discriminatory attitude toward Black women workers, designated their labor as domestic workers, waitresses, manual laborers, and clerical staff as too unstable and "unworthy" of organizing efforts. Therefore, Black working-class women's material and social conditions were treated as more superfluous than their male counterparts'. Thus, these conditions made Black working-class women more prone to protonationalist organizing at the point of production—including extralegal wildcat strikes and housing rent strikes—to procure autonomy and resources for NSMC.

In fact, Black working-class women's protonationalism challenged the rising second-wave feminist movement at the time. In their understanding of their historical role in the political economy of the United States and their superexploited status as Black women, they consciously chose not to fight in a gendered women's movement that excluded their Black male counterparts and positioned them as antagonists. Rather, despite Black male chauvinism, they sought to educate, unite, and equalize their standing among Black men to weaken capitalism exploitation and white supremacy. At the 1970 International Women's Day march in Atlanta, one of the few Black women in attendance argued that "the struggle is different for Black women [than white women]" and their objective must be to "unite with Black men in order to build a liberation army." Black Atlantan Jean Jamison added, "I fail to see the feasibility of your being liberated as a woman when you have yet to be liberated as a Black.... How can a Black Sister be liberated while her Black Brother is being oppressed and enslaved?" WAGA TV news reporter Felicia Jeter's perspective on white feminism offered insight as to why Black working-class women generally viewed the Black community as a colony: "Women's groups get upset with me because I tell them 'I'm Black before I'm a [woman] because that's the order in which I'm threatened. If you deal with the problem of being a "nigger" then the other things seem to fall into place.' I really believe that this the reason why so many Black women are not more involved in the women's movement."[91]

As historian Ashley Farmer argues, "Black women's collective, and, at times, conflicting, debates over Black womanhood show that the ... activists' idealized, public projections of Black manhood and womanhood—was a critical site of Black Power activism and theorizing." Black women especially considered Black solidarity outside of Eurocentrism to be the path to autonomy. Thus, women in the Black Power era typically understood their position or identity as political. As Farmer continues, this was a cornerstone of the Black Power era. Black working-class women sought to redirect their political position in both the movement and society.[92]

Black women workers consciously chose the point of production to achieve these goals. Fighting for better working conditions, higher wages, and agency in the work space vastly improved women's ability and positioned them closer to their male counterparts to move the neighborhoods closer—through security, trust, and identity—against those outsiders threatening them: banks, real estate agents, and elected officials. Thus, Black working-class leaders like Louise Whatley and Eva Davis recognized that organizing at the point of production offered Black working women the space and resources to equalize their standing with Black men while opposing racial exploitation.

In May 1970, Louise Whatley attempted to unionize Black women workers at Kessler's Department Store in southwest Atlanta. She organized a union card drive with the independent Black union the National Council of Distributive Workers, which she had worked closely with in supporting the sanitation strike that year. Once store owner Ed Kessler discovered this, he immediately fired Whatley. Because Whatley was as an esteemed Black Belt activist, the community quickly set up pickets at Kessler's, singing, "Ain't gonn make no money today. . . . Ain't gonna sell no records today." The Kessler's picket eventually disrupted the city's busy weekend. On Saturday of the first week, virtually all the stores in the downtown area were in a state of confusion; many stores remained empty as shoppers feared crossing the picket lines. One protester made it clear that this fight was part of a larger struggle for Black Power: "This is not a fight for Louise Whatley. It is for all Blacks and women especially in the store." After three weeks of picketing, Kessler's was closed forever.[93]

Atlanta power brokers felt the potency of Black working-class women's social movements, primarily because they secured enough leverage to disrupt multiple sectors of the urban region. One such organizer, Eva Davis, built overlapping movements across space, housing, and labor to upend the subproletarian status of African American women, both at work and in the oppressed East Lake Meadows community. Built in October 1970, East Lake Meadows public housing project in the DeKalb County section of Atlanta was criticized for its poor construction from the start. The $15 million units housed close to 5,000 residents with an estimated 8,000 additional people on the waiting list. Most of those individuals never saw the inside of an East Lake Meadows apartment, while others were displaced. The housing sat on land that was cleared for the city to build a new civic center, stadiums, insurance buildings, and banks. The twenty-five to thirty acres of land in East Lake Meadows earmarked for parks remained barren. Because East Lake had been built on country club grounds, the turf grass was removed and never replaced. Drainage was such a crisis that constant flooding produced what the residents called "red clay pools" around the project. Elderly residents lived in a high-rise section with no accessible nurses or recreational activities. Since the promised shopping center was never built, the closest stores were the high-priced Majik Market and Colonial Store on the other side of a four-lane street. Colonial Store employees especially were known to sexually harass Black female customers. As a result, Black East Lake residents were forced to constantly change their daily rounds to get to cheaper, better-quality grocery stores. The Atlanta Housing Authority and city hall often ignored residents' demands for repairs. Because of a lack of traffic lights (commonly missing from Black urban spaces), a car hit three children and killed a woman at the intersection of East Lake Boulevard and Memorial Drive. The residents also had to choose between no police presence or police harassment and abuse. When Davis organized a confrontation with the African American aldermanic police chair, Q. V. Williamson, no action was taken to assist the residents.[94]

Davis channeled East Lake Meadows' anger in early May 1972, when she gathered a dozen Black East Lake Meadows women to picket a Church's Chicken restaurant on Second Avenue. When the protesters arrived, all employees inside walked off the job and joined the picketers. The strikers delivered a massive list of demands to end their wildcat strike: the rehiring of a Black assistant manager who was fired without cause; a pay raise above their $1.60-an-hour salary; sick leave; fringe benefits; and overtime pay. Davis sought to make the restaurant chain pay for its right to reside in Black Atlanta yet no longer operate in the community's interests. "The enterprise makes over $7,000 a week in the Black neighborhood," Davis stated, "but refuses to cooperate with neighborhood projects or hire within community."[95]

By the second week of picketing, the Church's wildcat strike became a Black working-class symbol for citywide resistance and class solidarity. The East Lake Meadows restaurant closed, and the protesters moved to the Moreland Avenue location, where employees did not walk out but customers refused to cross the picket line. By the end of the second week of May, Davis had created a movement with groups scheduled at different times of the day to picket five separate Church's locations throughout the city. The strike produced a successful local movement center: protesters created pamphlets and flyers, walked door-to-door recruiting picketers and monetary donations, and set up resource centers at neighborhood churches and Davis's home. By mid-May, the movement had closed ten Church's restaurants with a plan to strike more.[96]

Much to the chagrin of Davis and her comrades, however, SCLC's Hosea Williams requested to negotiate the labor contract on behalf of the Church's Chicken workers. Williams's fluid motion through multiple Atlanta movements created a paradox for grassroots Black revolutionary nationalists. Following his call for Martin Luther King Jr. to protest the murder of African American Henry Prather that sparked the 1966 Summerhill rebellion and his support for the sanitation strikers in 1970, Williams had fallen out of favor with other SCLC leadership. Tensions boiled over after he played an active role in other labor strikes for Black hospital, steel, and factory workers. Thus, Williams held an esteemed reputation for assisting labor struggles outside of the typical SCLC agenda. On the other side, though, he had also been heavily criticized for his liberal pluralist campaigns for elected office and for conceding to city hall and downtown businesses in some labor negotiations. As a result, working-class Black Atlantans were cautious with Williams: he was the exclusive member of the Black petty bourgeoisie with a reputation for fighting for the needs of poor Black people, but he took no concrete ideological stance on Black Power. Additionally, since this was an illegal wildcat strike, the workers had no real access to legal representation. Thus, it is more than likely that Davis reluctantly agreed to allow Williams to assist for access to legal resources; however, she made it known that Williams did not speak for her or the East Lake residents: "Church's can do what they want with SCLC but they haven't settled with us."[97] In other words, Davis wanted to keep both residents' and workers' movements united while she carefully navigated Williams's arrival and his role in both struggles.

Black Atlanta grew more enraged at Church's when the company held an event in East Lake Meadows during the strike and gave 6,000 free pieces of chicken to the residents. Church's attempt to co-opt Black working-class urbanites unleashed a groundswell of community support for the strikers. Morris Brown College students organized solidarity pickets at the Markham–Northside Drive location, prompting a swarm of police to fight picketers. Officers severely beat two Black students, Andrew Mackey and Donald Denson, for their picketing. Police jailed Denson without medical care for three broken bones and eye and head injuries. When his brother stormed the jail and saw him bloodied, he mobilized 200 Morris Brown students to go to the Fulton County Jail. At the threat of possible violent rebellion, police finally released Denson and friends rushed him to Holy Family Hospital for treatment.[98]

Following this altercation, Hosea Williams ramped up negotiations and quickly announced a settlement with Church's that raised more than a few eyebrows. The employees received a ten-cent-per-hour raise and the franchise implemented a policy to retain only two part-time employees. Church's designated all other employees as "regular," meaning they were granted hospitalization, insurance, overtime pay, holiday pay, and retirement pay.[99] Williams hailed the settlement as "one of the greatest victories for the poor in the history of Atlanta," but for East Lake Meadows, it left more to be desired. Although the East Lake women were central to improving the working conditions at Church's restaurants, Williams did not bargain Davis's original demand that Church's hire from within the neighborhood and contribute funds to the community's interests. In fact, Williams negotiated demands outside of community interests, including a clause for Black firms to receive "contracts."[100] While this agreement offered Black capitalists the opportunity to invest in the restaurant chain, it typically left Black workers out in the cold.

When evaluating the East Lake Meadows strike, the incorporation of Black petty bourgeois leadership at the negotiation table subverted the movement's original protonationalist intent and reoriented it toward more conservative nationalist concessions. However, Davis and the East Lake women demonstrated that struggle inherently strengthened the use value of neighborhoods. The sheer amount of communication, coordination, picket training, political education, and resource mobilization involved in closing ten restaurants across the city bolstered their informal support networks both inside and outside the neighborhood boundaries. Their complicated experience in dealing with intraracial class conflict reinforced their security and trust values within their own neighborhood and strengthened their challenge of their affluent counterparts in Atlanta.

A month later, Davis and the East Lake activists escalated their struggle via coalition building with other Black Belt neighborhoods. They joined residents from Bankhead Courts, Carver Homes, Buttermilk Bottoms, Techwood/Clark Howell Homes, Thomasville Heights, Herndon Homes, and Bedford Pine in organizing a citywide rent strike for the 39,000 tenants living in deplorable AHA public housing. In the first week of July, over a dozen members from the tenants coalition stormed and overtook a city hall–sponsored "open house" ribbon cutting on Linden Avenue in northeast Atlanta for a new AHA project. The protesters set up an informational picket, shut down all remarks by AHA director Lester Persells, and took over the ribbon cutting, with Louise Whatley taking the scissors and proclaiming, "I'm cutting the ribbon of the model apartment—the model hell." After more speeches by other women, the police attempted arrests, but Whatley quickly shot back, "Go right ahead! Jail's not that different from public housing!"[101]

Whatley's enthusiastic and militant leadership educated and invigorated low-income residents leading up to the rent strike. Her subtle emphasis on Atlanta's treatment of poor people as apartheid galvanized the movement into a quickly expanding rebellion. For example, Whatley spoke to the AHA about using welfare to keep poor Black people powerless and dependent on the state: "Once they get you on those welfare rolls they'll never let you off. They throw you in public housing and go sky high on your rent. They don't provide any childcare, so when you get a job, you have that extra expense at the same time they take away part of your support because you are working." Also, there were locational disadvantages in AHA public housing that disrupted the residents' daily routines and kinship networks. Tenants had to mail their rent each month because the city refused to create an on-site center. Because most public housing tenants lacked checking accounts, they had to pay extra costs for stamps and money orders. This required travel to and from the AHA office on South Pryor Street downtown, which for some residents was a four-hour bus ride! Last, the rent strikers acknowledged that the political economy of public housing exposed the AHA as only one symptom of a larger federal crisis. Because the city of Atlanta allocated little to no funds to support the AHA, the institution relied on rapidly decreasing federal funds under the Nixon regime. The instability of the release of federal housing funds—which did not do long-range, comprehensive housing funding because "they make statewide grants a portion at a time completely tangled in red tape and restrictions"—kept tenants in a constant state of volatility.[102] This drastically undercut Black workers' capacity to stabilize the use value of their neighborhood and, in turn, NSMC. Thus, the strikers' major demand, besides full repairs of the housing projects, was to become voting members on the AHA Board of Commissioners. If Black working-class female tenants took control away from the five wealthy businessmen on the AHA board, they could obtain the power to control conditions in public housing across the city. In other words, protonationalism remained at the center of this social movement.[103]

The rent strike began with crucial support from several local organizations. The Georgia Tenants Association released a statement to all tenants requesting that they withhold their July rent. Additionally, leased housing residents in Betmar La Villa, Amanda Gardens, and Suburban Court refused rent payments as well. Community leaders led the pickets at each of the AHA's project management offices. The education and organizing was so effective that one AHA project manager defected to the side of the rent strikers and vowed that no staff member at his site would cross the picket line.[104]

Not all Black Atlantans sympathized with the housing woes of the Black poor. One African American AHA official told the *Atlanta Voice*, "This is uncalled for. They're blaming public housing for their uncleanliness."[105] The *Atlanta Journal* and *Constitution* refused to print tenant comments, but they eagerly ran AHA statements throughout the duration of the strike. Meanwhile, the city attempted multiple tactics to break the strike. City hall, the Economic Opportunity of Atlanta office, and the AHA conspired to send the police to intimidate picketing women and children. The AHA threatened to fire all managers, most of whom were underpaid Black women, who honored the strikers' picket line (strikers included a demand for more assistance and pay for housing project managers). The AHA also appointed a Black tenant, Susie Labord, to dissuade strikers from continuing.[106]

By the second week, the strikers had closed twelve AHA offices with sights set on the final ten. Indeed, city housing operations halted. Neighborhoods took turns hosting weekly political education sessions in community centers and in front yards on the history of housing discrimination in Atlanta. The leverage on display here rested on multiple residents from different housing projects engaged and socializing together. This dispelled the city power brokers' often-used divisive tactic to claim that each project's issues were distinct from one another.[107] Instead, political education in these local movement centers unmasked the solidarity of the rebels' interests. These sessions activated the consciousness of many residents, who pledged to donate their rent money for the duration of the strike toward housing repairs that AHA refused. In other words, the rent strike's NSMC boosted the informal support networks by increasing resident buy-in and providing potential to remain long-lasting after the rent strike.

By the third week, Persells had reached desperation levels and begged the strikers for a meeting. However, Massell did not feel enough heat to concede to the strikers, and he refused to allow the strikers into city hall, forcing them to stand in pouring rain for hours. As a result, strikers gave the AHA a deadline of August 2 to develop an action plan or they would extend the rent strike into that month. When the meeting between the two sides occurred, over 300 strikers and supporters joined Whatley at the John Chiles Community Center. Ernest Jackson, the African American director of housing for AHA and second in line to Persells, arrogantly announced that they were only willing to change their lease agreements and grievance procedure without fixing the current inhumane conditions. Lilia Kapers did not hold back when expressing her disgust to Jackson about the clear class conflict: "[You're] a Black man with a white heart.... You look on us like we're rats and roaches." Whatley added that they would continue to advocate for tenants to withhold payments under their own discretion, but the damage was clearly massive, with the city breaking out all the stops to scare the strikers into paying their rent.[108]

The long-term booking and perseverance worked for the Black rebels. By mid-October that year, the AHA had lost over $185,000 in uncollected rents. Also, because of the length of the rent strike (many tenants refused rent payments through 1973), the national media attention, and other questionable AHA practices, the US Justice Department, Internal Revenue Service, FBI, and Department of Housing and Urban Development launched a fraud and corruption probe into the AHA.[109] Although it did not yield the protonationalist results they hoped for, the Black tenants' rent strike created informal support networks across living and social spaces while also excavating hidden histories of grassroots struggles to show wider national and international audiences.

"Soul Power! Worker Power! Black Power!": Intraracial Class Struggle in the 1972 Mead Wildcat Strike

Although Atlanta's industrialized sector was small in comparison to other American urban sites, it remained a contested site for a radical conception of Black Power. The largest strike of Black workers in 1972 occurred at the Mead factory on West Marietta Street near the Central Business District. Mead served as a nationwide manufacturer of beverage and food packaging. It was one of the largest plants in the United States at the time, with about 1,200 workers, 800 of them African Americans with two-thirds men and one-third women. Per usual, the company concentrated Black workers in the most dangerous, dirty areas of the plant. One Black worker recalled the hellish conditions when he joined Mead in 1970: "There was an area that dealt with inks, and there was a vat that had acid in it, 'cause there was this solvent type ink.... Two white guys who worked in this area, they slipped and fell into the vat; and when they came back up, all you saw were their skeletons.... And after that they hired about five Blacks and put them in that area."[110]

The plant had branch administration offices, a warehouse facility, one Black foreman, and no Black supervisors. Additionally, most of the workers juggled other jobs because their wages were so low. Early rumblings had occurred two years earlier on May 25, 1970, when workers in the gluing department organized a wildcat strike for a cost-of-living raise. Within twenty-four hours, so many workers had joined the walkout that the Mead factory ceased operations. "A little money—that's basically what it's about," an anonymous worker told the *Great Speckled Bird*.[111]

Although Mead obtained a court injunction against a strike, the workers stayed out. By that Sunday, the wildcat had pressured Mead to reopen negotiations with Atlanta Printing Specialties and Paper Products Union Local 527 on their three-year contract—an unprecedented move. However, this early struggle revealed racial fractures among the Mead union. One Black worker stated that when they arrived at a union meeting, whites sat in a circle among themselves and "pushed their chairs back for fear of being too close" when Black coworkers sat next to them.

Two years later, the workers' anger boiled over after several incidents. In January 1972, workers reported that Mead unfairly fired four Black employees within weeks of one another. During the summer heat wave that year, several Black female workers fainted from heat exhaustion during forced overtime shifts. A Black female worker complained that when she asked a white worker to help her lift something, he threatened to "smack her if she didn't leave him alone." Another Black woman who suffered from anemia had a doctor's note stating that she could not work more than eight hours a day. Her white foreman, however, forced her to work twelve-hour days until she collapsed and had to be rushed to the hospital.[112]

Black workers attempted to address their grievances through the union at first; however, Local 527 neglected grievances related to Black employees. Also, the union allegedly acted as a "sweetheart" with the Mead management. Therefore, the Atlanta chapter of the October League, a Marxist-Leninist organization that grew out of the splintering of the Students for a Democratic Society and whose members worked at Mead, grabbed the initiative and organized secret meetings with workers. Their young, energetic leader, African American Marxist-Leninist Sherman Miller, acted as the main organizer at the plant.

They held their first strategy meeting on August 6, 1972, at the Mass House close to Atlanta Stadium, a prime location near many of the workers' neighborhoods. At the meetings, they formed the Mead Caucus of Rank-and-File Workers (MCRFW) organization outside of Local 527 representation. MCRFW members elected to wildcat strike outside of union jurisdiction and set in motion their organizing plan: "For three weeks we organized the plant. The committee met almost daily. We assigned people to organize areas of the plant which hadn't been represented. We developed a list of thirty demands, circulated them, started mass discussions. At a mass meeting they were debated, developed, increased to near fifty. At this mass meeting of over two hundred Mead workers, we officially became the Mead Caucus of Rank-and-File Workers, and we delivered an ultimatum to the company."[113]

On August 18, MCRFW and most Black Mead workers struck the plant under their "Black Manifesto," outlining the apartheid conditions of the Mead corporation. The manifesto contained fifty demands that empowered the Black workers to take control of the working conditions of the plant and extinguish racist and sexist discrimination. MCRFW sought preferential policies toward Black workers to overcome inequality in compensation, job type, and safety and also demanded equal pay and treatment for Black female employees. From a financial standpoint, the strikers requested fifty-cent raises and ongoing quarterly adjustments for all hourly employees. They also sought job protection for injury, bereavement, and arrest, full health-care coverage, improved ventilation and temperature controls, protective gear, and an on-site nurse. A sticking point for MCRFW was worker autonomy. The group demanded to select their own grievance and safety committees and the power to determine policies, benefits, job descriptions, and oversight of supervisory staff hiring.

The workers also wanted a Martin Luther King Jr. holiday, emergency phone call privileges, and contributions made to Black neighborhoods.[114]

Mead president R. N. O'Hara immediately sent word to MCRFW that they would negotiate only with Local 527 and declared the strike illegal. "We intend to resolve our real problems with our employees, their legally elected labor officials, and government agencies," O'Hara announced. Mead also argued that all demands in the Black Manifesto fell under the authority of the collective bargaining agreement, which contained a no-strike clause. In other words, Mead attempted to avoid conflict with MCRFW on the legal basis that they would violate a labor agreement by negotiating with a splinter group.

Management's passive-aggressive tiptoeing around the issue inflamed Mead workers. As a result, an estimated 75 percent of the workforce joined the picket lines. To their advantage, many of the strikers were highly skilled machinists, which made it incredibly difficult for management to find replacement workers with comparable training. Picket lines filled with signs reading "United We Stand, Divided We Fall," and freedom songs echoed down Marietta Street. Sherman Miller's picket line chants included "Soul power! Worker power! Black power!"[115]

MCRFW tapped into its NSMC to reinforce its strike leverage, especially regarding political education of the community:

> We had what people called mass meetings, and in these mass meetings students and people from other companies, they would come and find out what was going on. We would set up a phone tree with these people, and call them, get them to bring friends.... To really build a movement that was wider and greater than just the workers that worked at Mead 'cause this was a struggle of all the people . . . it was important to set up committees to talk to them, to go into the community . . . so that when we had these marches they would join us. And they did. And that kind of strategy worked. It really paid off.[116]

Miller likened this broad-based movement organizing to full self-determination for Black workers: "This is the kind of spirit that we will need to achieve the final liberation of Black people; this is the kind of organizing that we gonna need to achieve the final liberation of Black people.... We are gonna rally the Black community around us and show the power structure that the Black people of Atlanta and the Black people of the country will no longer be oppressed, repressed, or depressed!"[117]

Because of the strike's wildcat status, it left the MCRFW with very few resources from the union to sustain the protest. Consequently, Black supporters donated plentiful amounts of food and money and mobilized other striking workers at the Nabisco Plant and Sears Warehouse.[118] The *Great Speckled Bird* added a significant agency-laden institution to MCRFW's wildcat. The *Bird* worked with the Metro-Atlanta-DeKalb chapter of the SCLC—which provided local movement centers like Wheat Street Baptist Church to house strike resources, trainings, and meetings—to educate residents and publicize updates and support for the strike. Additionally, the SCLC issued a citywide boycott of Mead's products, including all Coca-Cola, Pepsi, Budweiser, Schlitz, Black Label, and Morton Frozen Foods products.

This shaky alliance between the MCRFW and SCLC fractured strike support over ideological clashes. The MCRFW, to their credit, looked beyond SCLC's liberal politics to build a Black united front. Miller stressed the need for neighborhood alliances with SCLC as Mead management used this fight to "take a stand against this year's wave of rank-and-file strikes." Further, he expressed to Black residents that Mead had essentially "declared war on . . . Black workers and through this action . . . declared war on all the poor working Black and white communities in the city." Regardless of the affiliation with civil rights groups and leaders, Miller expressed his aims for this Mead strike to encourage a national action against capitalist exploitation: "The final aims is to rid this country of Rockefeller. . . . Our final aim is to rid this country of them. . . . A few people like Rockefeller run this country and have a dictatorship over millions . . . of people. . . . What we are saying is that these millions of working and oppressed people should have a dictatorship over the few people. . . . Kick them out completely."[119] Miller concluded that if the company won without a struggle, it would "[open] the road to fascism."[120] As another Black protester stated, "The enemy is not the white man. It is the capitalist economic system and things are going to be turned around in this country when Black people join with poor white people." Although the majority Black strikers constantly emphasized that their fight was not against white workers, Local 527's stewards were predominantly white and ultimately sided with management. The union issued a statement declaring the walkout "illegal" and urged its members to return to work or face dismissal.[121]

Mead ramped up its offensive against the wildcat in the face of mounting financial losses. The company obtained an injunction from Fulton County Superior Court that prohibited the leaders of the movement from interfering with employees who attempted to cross the picket line. The following week, Mead filed another injunction to ban the twelve MCRFW leaders from striking and limit the number of picketers. Unsurprisingly, Fulton County Superior Court judge Elmo Holt ruled in favor of Mead and issued the following proclamations: only five picketers can be at each Mead gate; one person was allowed to move back and forth on the driveway; the others must stand two on each side of the gate; and all other picketers must be at least "a half-a-football field away" from company property. Mead then used fear and intimidation to co-opt the MCRFW leadership. They sent termination letters to the core leaders and indefinite suspension letters to the secondary leadership and threatened disciplinary action to any worker who refused to cross the picket line. Mead also attempted to red-bait strikers to "get rid of their commie leadership."[122]

Mead also attacked MCRFW's neighborhood resources, especially local movement centers. Residents near the plant had allowed picketers to use their front lawns to pass out leaflets and hold rest and food stations. However, Mead purchased those lands and restricted all strike activity on front lawns. The company also exploited the class conflicts in the strike support to turn the general public against MCRFW. Mead retained a Black public relations law firm with state representative Ben Brown as partner to purchase large amounts of advertising time on popular radio stations in the Black community, including WIGO, WXAP, and WAOK. The company issued pleas for strikers to return to work. Lastly, Mead coerced police to harass the picketers and set up traffic patrol at each gate at the opening and closing of each shift.[123]

Petty bourgeois forces worked to break the MCRFW for good. The *Atlanta Constitution* fanned anticommunist propaganda against MCRFW by suggesting that the October League had instigated the wildcat and "brainwashed" employees with the assistance of Hosea Williams. In response, Michael Klonsky, the president of the Atlanta chapter, held a press conference to make the October League's position clear: "It is not the October League which has practiced racial discrimination in their policies of hiring and promotions ... while black workers are kept in the dirtiest, lowest-paying jobs. It was Mead and not the October League who directed the Atlanta Police Department to attack the Mead workers on September 21, jailing more than 100 workers and brutally clubbing the arrested workers to the ground, possibly blinding one Black worker.... To the charges of fighting to put an end to these conditions and the oppressive system, we in the October League plead 'guilty'!"[124]

Possibly feeling his reputation in jeopardy, Hosea Williams went on the offensive against the MCRFW leadership and disassociated himself and the strike from the October League. He told the media that the league did not help organize or finance the Mead wildcat. Williams continued to denigrate the leftists in public, claiming that the October League "almost ruined it [the strike] by trying to take over the show.... They never do any work.... I don't think these folks could raise 10 people this afternoon if their lives depended on it."[125]

Williams attacked the October League and the radical roots of the wildcat because they challenged his ideological stance on Black Power and who should wield it. Williams may have wanted the workers to win the strike but not on their clearly defined, radical terms and not with their own voices and actions. Also, Williams clashed with the structure of the MCRFW, which operated with a horizontal, rank-and-file democratic decision-making process. Williams and the SCLC, on the other hand, functioned through a select few charismatic, top-down, petty bourgeois leaders. Despite his unbridled support for Black labor struggles in Atlanta, Williams maneuvered politically when Black working-class leaders like Sherman Miller or Eva Davis challenged his class position. Ultimately, like in the East Lake Meadows Church's Chicken wildcat strike, Williams would be the compromised factor for MCRFW.

On September 6, in a major victory, Mead conceded and announced that MCRFW would replace Local 527 as the recognized bargaining agent for Mead employees moving forward. However, Mead also offered a new committee of rank-and-file workers that it had selected to meet with O'Hara monthly regarding grievance issues. This undermined the previously established committee set up by the workers. The company sought to neutralize Miller and his capacity to rally the workers behind his voice and leadership.[126]

The monthlong wildcat had proved expensive and exhaustive for the strikers. By September 1972, the police jailed workers they believed to be leaders of MCRFW for contempt of court and sentenced them to ten days each. The police also arrested an estimated sixty-six picketers for "criminal trespassing," a state offense, and bound them to state court with a bond set at $500–$1,000 each. Despite these setbacks, the strike forced Mead to establish four-day workweeks. Mead offered the workers a deal to rehire about 100 employees who had been suspended or fired for the wildcat.

After two months, the city of Atlanta unleashed its Black petty bourgeois forces to extinguish the strike support. On October 3, Mead sent a settlement proposal addressed to Andrew Young, the chairman of the CRC. Young, who had a reputation of being a concession-style mediator, worked on behalf of the city to end labor disputes regardless of tangible outcomes for the workers. He agreed to step in and immediately proposed concessions for the strikers, including an end to protest activity and "improved relationship structures" between management, supervisors, and workers. In other words, Young worked to put the strikers back to work and to decrease the capacity for more action in the future. Five days later, the MCRFW struck a tentative agreement with Mead. The terms of the settlement included the following: (1) Mead promised to establish a "human relations council" for grievance procedures (it is not known who chose members of the council); (2) Mead offered $20,000 to buy additional equipment to cut down on dust in the finishing area; (3) employees would receive an increase in pay whenever they were assigned additional responsibilities; (4) the company promised to investigate and eliminate any and all acts of discrimination for reasons of race, sex, age, or national origin, including banning racial slurs; (5) the company would make one non-interest-bearing loan of $200 to any employee during a thirty-day window; (6) with the concurrence of the union, the company submitted the cases of discharged and suspended employees to a panel of arbitrators selected by a federal mediation board from a panel of arbitrators nominated by the Atlanta CRC; and (7) based on the company's future manpower requirements, qualified and interested employees, both white and Black, would be selected for presupervisory training and development and for other salaried positions.[127]

Hosea Williams spoke at the settlement press conference, claiming that "we did not gain everything sought, but we gained a whole lot more than we had when we began." The problem is that the settlement contained no real teeth regarding enforcement or preventative measures for retaliation for striking. Management's proposal offered ambiguous guarantees without structure or substance to ensure that the workers moved into a more advantageous position in the company. Therefore, Young and Williams operated as economic sponsors for a working-class movement—outside of their own personal class interests—and jeopardized the core radical principles from the beginning. The gains proposed offered little more than empty platitudes and shattered the possibility of protonationalist power at the point of production.

Within the neocolonial relationship, the petty bourgeoisie walks a very tight rope of denying genuine power to colonized people for fear of eroding their relationship to the bourgeoisie. This is mainly because the petty bourgeoisie "do not possess the economic base to guarantee power," therefore making them politically impotent outside of their relationship to the bourgeoisie in the long run. Consequently, the petty bourgeoisie is dependent on its tenuous relationship with both the bourgeoisie and the working classes and must move fluidly between both with primary loyalty belonging to the ruling class. Hosea Williams's "victory" for the Church's Chicken restaurant workers and the Mead workers offered tertiary rewards when compared with their initial demands—despite MCRFW's strong leverage for much of the strike. In fact, Andrew Young and Hosea Williams exploited the strike to construct a bureaucratic apparatus with the labor agreement to bolster their power over capital accumulation. The problems of weak wages, lack of health coverage, and concentration of Black workers in the dirtiest work, however, continued without meaningful change. In fact, numerous incidents of retaliation against strikers plagued MCRFW for months following the wildcat. As Sherman Miller noted at the strike's end, the MCRFW movement revealed the seed of intraracial class struggle that would dominate Atlanta's revitalization for decades to come: "In the course of the strike, we recognize some weaknesses of the people's struggle in Atlanta right now. . . . One of those weaknesses is the lack of an effective united front that could mobilize around the Mead strike or other workers movement. . . . The united front they've attempted so far hasn't been successful so far because they don't have workers at the center and workers leading them . . . especially Black workers."[128]

On June 23, 1973, at least 150 Black working-class community members gathered in Capitol Homes for a people's court action against Atlanta police officer J. D. Roberts. Roberts had been cleared of all charges for shooting a fourteen-year-old girl earlier that month. People's courts were popular protests in Black working-class communities because they gave a voice to those neglected by the American legal system. People's courts allowed community leaders to uphold the dignity of the neighborhood by trying the external offender with violating the safety and power of the community. When a few plainclothes police officers attempted to infiltrate the people's court, the community shouted them out of Capitol Homes. Black Belt Atlanta activists like Malcolm Suber (judge), Bobby Patterson (witness to the shooting), and others playing the parts of Roberts, the ballistics expert, and the other officer presented a detailed examination of the shooting, including admission from the accused of being a "cowardly pig." "Attorney" Sherman Miller concluded the trial by asking the crowd for a verdict, which led to a chant of "guilty!"[129]

This display of community solidarity, political education, and empowerment embodied the protonationalist spirit igniting Black working-class Atlanta. Revolutionary nationalism thrived in working-class Atlanta, and the massive offensive of protest activity symbolized the radical ideology and challenge to the subjugation of Black workers. Thus, when the Black worker struck first, it foregrounded the Black Power era in Atlanta. The city's power brokers interpreted working-class rebellion as a threat and sought to restructure the political economy to discipline, destabilize, and ultimately subproletarianize the Black worker. The Black worker struck first, but the empire struck back.

CHAPTER TWO

The Black Urban Regime Strikes Back
Retrenchment, Repression, and the Roots of Gentrification in Atlanta

> It seems that no matter how brutal and vicious the oppressor is, he has always had certain members of the oppressed to help carry out his policies of oppression, brutality, and racism.
> —MICHAEL ABNEY, African American Atlanta resident, June 8, 1974

> My Daddy told me a story about the Boll Weevil. You know the boll weevil used to keep the poor man down by eating the cotton crop. Then they came up with this spray that's kill 'em. Now all the boll weevils moved to the city and put on coats and ties.
> —FINLEY HOLMES, African American Atlanta sanitation worker, February 4, 1974

> If there was a case of hepatitis or a wide-spread epidemic, the Mayor and everybody else would be on all the tv stations saying let's get out and find out what happened, but it took Maynard Jackson from July of last year when the two boys were found at Niskey Lake to July of this year to create a task force. I know it can't be because we're Black. It is because we're poor.
> —CAMILLE BELL, African American founder of the Committee to Stop Children's Murders, August 14, 1980

On Monday afternoon, February 15, 1971, thousands of spectators watched 400 Black Atlantans clash with 150 police officers in the Central Business District on Broad Street. Eyewitnesses, mostly Black youth who waited for their buses after school, reported that the uprising erupted after African Americans stopped a white man from attacking a Black child near a bakery. Nearby police moved in and immediately handcuffed the interveners. Next the young Black witnesses recounted that someone, likely the police, shouted, "Get out-a-here, ya nigger." A fight broke out between a Black man and an officer, and police officers Burton, Spier Jr., Hollman, and Haight swarmed the area, arrested the involved Black man, and took turns beating him with clubs and pistols. Immediately, Black bystanders began yelling at the officers to stop, tossing produce from a nearby fruit stand at the police. Dozens of newly arrived police officers chased the children on foot through the Woolworth department store, blocked off Broad Street, and used their nightsticks on any Black person they apprehended.[1]

Over the next hour, the uprising grew to over 400 Black Atlantans, who strategically circled the sidewalks and streets to prevent more police from entering the area. Although the rebels physically fought back, the heavy police reinforcements—including helmeted riot teams, plainclothesmen, and Georgia Bureau of Investigation agents—overwhelmed the crowd. Police handcuffed dozens of Black rebels before clubbing them, some until they were limp or unconscious. In the aftermath, police injured dozens of citizens and arrested thirty people, all Black but one, on flimsy charges. A light rainfall in the second hour of the uprising caused the Black rebels to disperse, and police pushed the smaller group north toward Hunter Street. With the streets now clear, the white-collar workers who had watched the violence from their high-rise office windows sprinted from their buildings, quickly driving away to their secluded suburban homes.[2]

This mad dash from the cities to the suburbs captured Atlanta's power dynamics in the Black Power era. Black working-class Atlantans interpreted the Broad Street rebellion as yet another struggle against those Black Atlantans who aligned with power brokers seeking to defuse their fight for autonomy. As one rebel told a reporter when asked why they refused to stand down to the police and city officials, "Man . . . folks still refuse to realize that there ain't no more niggers in this world."[3] In other words, protonationalist struggles under Black Power not only illuminated class antagonisms in Black Atlanta but also transformed how African American Atlantans saw themselves and their capacity to disrupt city business. As previously discussed, protonationalism, especially at the point of production, provided Black Atlantans the necessary leverage to reshape power dynamics between the Black classes and to endanger the reputation of a "city too busy to hate." However, the conflict in Atlanta was deeper than the mainstream propaganda of race; it was class warfare. The rapid growth and socialization of Black working-class urbanites wounded the good ole boy regime politics that had governed Atlanta for decades.

In contrast, the middle-class Black officials and capitalist rulers perceived actions like the Broad Street rebellion as a troubling shift in the balance of power in the city. The Black majority's struggles for autonomy meant that the newly crowned Black urban regime (BUR) of elected officials, business owners, real estate entrepreneurs, and middle managers struggled to dominate the resources necessary for their revitalization plans. To satiate their senior capitalist partners, the BUR struck back at Black workers, seeking to put them down and toss them out of the Atlanta power structure for good.

This chapter explores how the combined forces of Maynard Jackson's city hall, the Atlanta Chamber of Commerce (ACOC), and the Atlanta Police Department disciplined the Black worker by delivering the decisive counterblow to rampant revolutionary Black Power in Atlanta's grass roots. It shows how the BUR strategy of economic retrenchment, union busting, police repression, and malignant neglect of low-income Black Atlantans snatched resources from Black public spaces and redistributed them for reinvestment and gentrification. Looking to the 1970s revenue crisis, the 1977 sanitation workers strike, and the Atlanta power structure's "war on crime," within the context of the Atlanta child murders, this chapter showcases how this public-private partnership sharpened the class and gender divide in Black Atlanta, destroyed the point-of-production leverage in the city, reverberated this loss throughout low-income neighborhoods, led to the loss of a radical critique/class consciousness in grassroots struggles, and set the metro region on the path toward neoliberalization, gentrification, displacement, and finally subproletarianization. The roots of gentrification in Atlanta materialized from the repression of the Black working class.

The Broad Street rebellion underscored the constant unrest in Atlanta during the Black Power era that set the stage for a new regime to take repressive control of the city. With the election of Maynard Jackson as the city's first Black mayor and the subsequent growth of Black elected officials controlling resources in the city, the capitalist class unleashed a new fifth column to develop new accumulation centers for capital and deplete the use value of Black working-class neighborhoods. In other words, the BUR aimed to maximize the exchange value potential of Black bodies and spaces by extinguishing Black working-class neighborhood social movement capacity (NSMC). The Atlanta bourgeoisie and petty bourgeoisie accomplished this by using three interlocking tactics: launching an anti-working-class campaign in the media, hijacking decisive public and financial resources from low-income urbanites and reappropriating them for militarized and occupying police, and sapping the leverage from the point of production. This would be the most crucial counterattack against the Black worker.

The Atlanta bourgeoise and petty bourgeoisie quickly encouraged conservative media giants the *Atlanta Journal*, *Atlanta Constitution*, and *Atlanta Daily World* to portray the Broad Street rebellion in a distorted, pathological narrative, aimed at Black degeneracy as the cause of urban strife. The newspapers and television stations excluded the eyewitness testimony about anti-Black violence that was provided to the *Great Speckled Bird* and the *Atlanta Voice*; instead they depicted the participants as Black rabble-rousers laying siege to the peaceful, harmonious downtown business district. The *Atlanta Daily World* fabricated a story, stating that the melee began "when several young Blacks—allegedly Black Panthers—started roughing up shoppers." Atlanta police chief Herbert Jenkins picked up this theme and emphasized the danger of "criminals" downtown who "take advantage of the crowdedness to hide themselves and their criminal activities."[4]

Atlanta mayor Sam Massell pledged city hall's undying allegiance to the city's business class by promising to reduce the power of the Black majority and reshuffle them outside of the lucrative and burgeoning downtown urban sector. "Surely whites don't have to put forth too much effort in thinking Black to understand that half the population, Blacks want half of the power," Massell told a group of white business owners. "I spoke to the Black community about the economic damage we could all suffer from our city going all Black."[5] By acting in concert, the Atlanta business class with their media and municipal allies crafted a narrative in which radicalized criminals sought to threaten innocent individuals going about their professional, consumer, and civic duties. The threat and the mission became clear for Atlanta leadership: contain Black autonomy at all costs.

Within a year of the Broad Street clash, the Atlanta Police Department, city hall, and the ACOC militarized downtown Atlanta—specifically Broad Street and the surrounding thoroughfares of Forsyth, Marietta, Alabama, Hunter, and Whitehall Streets—with specialized SWAT team weapons and tactics.[6] Redevelopment, redistricting, and heightened surveillance had significantly reduced the daily routine and organizing capacity of Black workers. Massell and Jackson elicited a whitewashing campaign for the police department to normalize police occupation in Black neighborhoods. However, the police presence did not reduce crime or protect residents; rather, it contained low-income Black people and the underground economy in designated nodes in the central city so that they did not interfere with flourishing business and revitalization plans in the new downtown sector.

The neocolonial relationship is vital to recognizing the repressive nature of the Atlanta power structure against the Black working class. As the bourgeoisie and petty bourgeoisie sharpened the contradictions between themselves and the working classes, poverty grew immensely and strengthened protonationalism.[7] More clearly, the Black working class actively countered Atlanta's ruling-class attempts at domination. This chapter also explores working-class resistance to repression, including grassroots social movements like the Committee to Stop Children's Murders (STOP). STOP built local and national networks for social, financial, and cultural power to protect Black boys during the Atlanta child murders of the late 1970s, when more than twenty children and teenagers were murdered over the course of two years—most of these murders remain unsolved. Studies of the Atlanta child murders often overlook the contradiction in public safety at the time: the BUR militarized the police more than at any other point in Atlanta's history at the time, yet the Black working class and their neighborhoods experienced more vulnerability and danger than ever before. Consequently, a critique of the political economy of Maynard Jackson's BUR fills this gap and exposes the contempt for low-income Black urbanites in the city. STOP became a necessary bastion of self-defense for the Black worker. In fact, Black urbanites adapted, altering their strategy, tactics, and messaging to face these increasing restrictions to their social movement capacity and safety. However, the BUR strategy, tied directly to the shifting political economy of the time, was bound up in a concerted effort to weaken Black organizing capacity. Therefore, the city demanded action be taken to halt Black organizing efforts immediately.

The New Black Petty Bourgeoisie: Maynard Jackson and the Black Urban Regime Strategy

Atlanta's elite recognized the changing face of the city and established a new urban political order. As political scientist Adolph Reed Jr. conceptualizes, Black elected officials (BEOs) who constitute the majority or near majority in city governments and maintain the Black working class as their main political base form BURs. A new Black capitalist class, diverted from the old Black bourgeoisie, depended to a greater extent on a Black middle class of local leadership, the corporate sector, and subsidies from the federal government. Thus, new Black capitalism was no longer closely tied to the Black masses, heightening class tensions in Black cities like Atlanta.[8]

BEOs served as the newest complementary piece to the emerging racial formation in urban space. Between 1969 and July 1977, BEOs increased threefold in the United States, from 1,185 to 4,311! Despite these statistical gains, African Americans, who comprised 11 percent of the US population in 1977, accounted for less than 1 percent of the more than 522,000 elected officials. There were only nineteen BEOs for every 100,000 African Americans, while there were approximately 282 non-Black officials for every 100,000 non-Black people. Sixty percent of all BEOs were in the South (where 53 percent of Black people resided), with Georgia ranking in the top ten states, with 225 BEOs.[9]

Reed's conception of BURs provides a useful framework to understand how the Atlanta elite correlated the disciplining of the Black worker with opening new streams of accumulation. Urban scholar Mary Patillo contended that the primary function of the brokerage between capital and the new urban petty bourgeoisie was to facilitate pro-growth agendas that widened racial class divides and deepened inequality.[10] However, Reed's framework did not fully account for the role that Black Power—particularly the failure of Black capitalism on the US economic stage—played in the development of BUR strategy. Thomas Boston succinctly posited that the Black Power movement determined "the conditions for an alteration in the internal structure of the Black capitalist class and the growth of a new Black capitalist segment." Working-class militancy in Black urban neighborhoods "provided Black entrepreneurs the opportunity to seek out access to markets, knowledge, and capital previously restricted to them."[11]

As previously discussed, larger Black businesses that operated independent of white capital did not possess the required strength to weather the turbulent cyclical recessions. According to John Gloster, who headed the Opportunity Funding Corporation, a nonprofit funding service for minority businesses, "The general concept of those who have money is that small enterprises are risky anyway, and they think they're doubling their risk when they buy into a minority company."[12] Finally, the economic downturn decimated potential customers for emerging Black businesses. Black workers' low purchasing power and increasing unemployment diminished Black businesses' market share of consumers. For instance, the "real" weekly earnings for Atlanta Black workers with at least three dependents decreased over 1977. The decline continued into 1978. Black worker earnings between December 1977 and June 1978 dropped 7.2 percent, from an average of $113.57 to $105.35.[13]

A new Black capitalist class, Boston continued, diverted from the old Black bourgeoisie by depending to a greater extent on an external white clientele, the corporate sector, and subsidies from the federal government. Thus, new Black capitalism was not tied closely to the Black masses. Consequently, Black capitalism generally weakened its connection to Black working-class neighborhoods and heightened class tensions in Black America. The bourgeoisie's complete break from its working-class counterparts made it necessary for the former's courtship with the new Black petty bourgeoisie.

Economic trends for Black business growth in the 1970s support this assertion. Black capitalism generally struggled during the Black Power movement. By early 1975, the recession decimated Black businesses at a rate three times that of white businesses.[14] The upsurge, however, occurred at the end of the Black Power movement when Black capitalists grew closer to white capital. The US Department of Commerce reported that between 1977 and 1980, Black-owned businesses increased by 47 percent. *Black Enterprise* observed that this growing business reflects "the increasingly strong desire of all Black business owners ... to expand their clientele beyond the Black market."[15]

This new Black capitalism and the coinciding declension of the Black conservative nationalist stream of Black Power contributed to the rise of BURs and the new Black middle class. As sociologist Morton Wenger posited, the disappearance of the old Black petty bourgeoise and rise of the new Black petty bourgeoisie was a direct function of the development of monopoly capital and the consequently altered relationship between the white capitalist class and the Black working classes. There was no question about it: after mass urban rebellions of the 1960s and the protonationalist movements in working-class urban spaces in the early 1970s, the US ruling class feared African American mass militancy growing to a nationwide level. The capitalist class quickly developed its justification for the creation of a new Black petty bourgeois class: they functioned as doctors, teachers, lawyers, police, merchants, elected officials, and *supervisors* of the Black masses.[16]

The net results of these new social relations proved disastrous for Black working-class urbanites. White capital undergirded Black bourgeois and petty bourgeois pro-growth ambitions. As political scientist Cedric Johnson argued, these middle-class "race leaders" opted to chase access routes to the white power structure's dollars by seizing municipal government positions and forming public-private partnerships—diluting their main electoral base's autonomy and extinguishing the chance for a united Black front across class lines in the process. "We've got to get at the heart of what America's about," stated an anonymous African American Alabama state representative, "and that's money. It's nice going down to Montgomery and sitting in a legislature, but unless Blacks get access to investment capital ... all the other stuff is illusory." For BUR members, the protonationalism and militancy characterized in the radical stream of Black Power was a barrier to "Green Power." "I'm not looking for a fight," said Richard Arrington, the first Black mayor in Alabama.

"I'm looking for results. I don't care if we reach this goal amicably.... We're going to get there."[17]

Atlanta operated in the same vein. C. A. Scott, the conservative African American publisher of the *Atlanta Daily World*, pointed out that by 1980 "Sweet" Auburn Avenue, the historical epicenter of Black business in northeast Atlanta, had lost a good portion of its Black entrepreneurs to emerging white corporations. "There are more unrented offices than there ever were in the days of the Great Depression," he stated. "A few of us are holding out, but smart young men with drive and ambition don't come here anymore. They move into skyscraper offices in Peachtree Plaza."[18] By 1974, many African Americans elites recognized that Black self-determination did not align with their bourgeois class interests. As Adolph Reed Jr. suggested, the shift to the BUR strategy was conscious. It was a calculated effort to repel the Black masses' struggles for autonomy, compartmentalize them into enclaves isolated from profit-producing spaces, and reinforce the police state with money and power. The BUR strategy publicized to financiers that their metropolitan regions were ripe for private investment.

The new Black petty bourgeois professions always existed in the Black community under this new regime; they became managers, administrators, and supervisors rather than servants of the Black masses.[19] They grew their influence by reframing racial oppression as an individual issue, supplanting civil rights discourse with the War on Poverty, and becoming spokespersons for the Black community. As Lou Turner noted, these leaders focused their critique of poverty on independent unemployment data without tying it to capital accumulation or structure. Therefore, poverty assumed a "misery" index, where masses of unemployed and underemployed Black people suffered some personal setback and the ruin of less developed sectors of a capitalist economy was the result of a social or cultural decay of values.[20]

This is fundamental in the messaging that obtains the loyalty of their working-class constituencies. BURs romanticized the decaying indigenous urban economy as a natural component of integration into the national economy. This discourse informed policy and muddled class antagonisms at the same time that underdevelopment bulldozed Black Atlanta. As a result, Turner concluded, "the destruction of the underdeveloped social and economic structures of the Black community represents its final transformation into an expanded home market for a new stage of capitalist accumulation."[21] As will be examined in detail in the next chapter, Black Atlanta power brokers quickly exploited their spoils of class warfare in building this new international home market, both domestically and overseas.

Maynard Holbrook Jackson's historic win in October 1973 not only cemented African American elites' allegiance to gentrification—and against grassroots Black Power—but also flexed the new pro-growth model between the public and private power brokers moving forward. Jackson defeated his predecessor, Sam Massell, by adopting the same populist, antiestablishment rhetoric that carried Massell to victory in 1969—championing a "new deal" for the Black masses and a "stomp out crime" plan for the professional and managerial classes. Yet multiple sources reported that white capitalists promised to deliver white votes to Jackson in return for him delivering Black support for Wade Mitchell, the white city council president and vice president of the Trust Company of Georgia. African American state representative Billy McKinney not only admitted that the closed-door deal occurred but also that Black elites—including Atlanta Life and Insurance Company president Jesse Hill Jr., MARTA official Charles Reynolds, president of the Atlanta Urban League Lyndon Wade, and construction and real estate magnate Herman J. Russell, the most influential Black capitalist at the time—helped seal the deal. The white capitalists in the deal included Richard Kattell, president of C&S Bank; J. Paul Austin, chairman of the board of Coca-Cola; and Tom Cousins, the most powerful realtor in the Atlanta metropolitan region. Atlanta Socialist Workers Party candidate for mayor Debbie Bustin summed it up best: "The white power structure has become aware that Atlanta's Black majority is likely to elect a Black mayor. Naturally they would want to exert as much control as they could over a Black mayor.... This deal makes it clear just who Maynard Jackson will be working for."[22]

Maynard Jackson, an astute and complicated politician, mastered BUR strategy by manipulating his class identity when necessary. To secure the support of the Black working classes, Jackson raised his "heritage of slavery" to correlate his struggle as a Black man in a white power structure with the social crisis plaguing the Black majority. He spoke at length about the futility of the Vietnam War. He sometimes highlighted the uneven development between lavish Lenox Square and decaying Buttermilk Bottoms in Atlanta.[23] Make no mistake about it: Jackson often spoke as a Black man when it was imperative for his grassroots support—unless it interfered with the material interests of the capitalist class. As discussed later in this chapter, he also condemned police brutality while funding the expansion and militarization of the Atlanta Police Department. He understood that the Atlanta bourgeoisie desired a revamped, technological, and aggressive police to complement their increased business investment, privatization, and tourism. Thus, to win the *hearts* of white and Black capital, Jackson berated "socially acceptable hypocrisy in the name of progress" by bourgeois liberals like Sam Massell and championed business power as the healing source for Atlanta.

The Revenue Crisis of 1974–1979

President Richard Nixon's New Majority strategy to fight inflation at the expense of the "strong American worker" reshaped global capital and facilitated the neoliberal turn in American urban centers. Atlanta fared much worse than the nation. This new economic policy devalued the dollar and established wage price controls and tax incentives for corporations. His administration designed an import surcharge to improve the foreign trade position of the United States by discouraging spending on foreign goods and promoting export sales. By 1973, profits jumped sharply and inflation stabilized. However, by the end of that year, consumer prices began increasing at a rate of nearly 10 percent a year. As deindustrialization accelerated across urban sectors, manufacturing export losses devastated the trade balance. The 1974 energy crisis compounded the problem twofold and contributed to the already-diminishing manufacturing sector in Atlanta. Multiple layoff periods hit Black Atlanta hard, beginning with the oil companies.[24] When oil companies exaggerated fuel shortages to manipulate prices, oil-exporting countries kept pushing prices, causing the government to lose control of the economic imbalances. "You know that people don't think there's a shortage at all," stated Diane, an African American Atlantan autoworker who was laid off during the energy crisis. "They think they're just doing this whole thing to raise prices, drive the small gas station owner out of business, and put us out on the street. People are pretty mad."[25] Double-digit inflation became the new norm in mid-1970s US political economy. The wholesale price index—the most significant inflation barometer the government uses—surged upward, with a jump of 19.1 percent between March 1973 and March 1974.[26]

During that same period, Atlanta's cost-of-living index rose 10.8 percent, as compared to the general rise nationally of 10.2 percent.[27] The Commerce Department also reported that Atlanta's prices rose 3.7 percent in the first quarter of 1974, the largest quarterly rise since the Korean War. Between 1973 and 1974, food prices in the Atlanta area rose 20.6 percent for the average citizen. According to Economic Opportunity of Atlanta's study of food prices, the cost of bread, eggs, milk, sugar, margarine, shortening, cornmeal, and pinto beans—nine staple items most frequently bought by poor Black folks —rose from $6.16 in 1973 to $10.84 in 1974—a whopping 75 percent increase! Economic Opportunity of Atlanta reported that if the study had included meat, fresh fruit, vegetables, and cleaning supplies, the inflation percentages would have been even higher. When we examine the value of the US dollar across a five-year period, the 1969 dollar bought one hundred cents' worth of goods and services; by August 1974, the US dollar bought only seventy-five cents' worth of goods and services. This also meant that in 1974, food for a family of four cost approximately $54.40 a week, up considerably from 1969. The price of gas and electricity rose 3.4 percent and 8.8 percent, respectively. Transportation costs rose 4.8 percent in the quarter and 9.6 percent in the year. Medical care rose 8.7 percent over the course of a year as well.[28] Needless to say, this recession represented a shock to capitalism that had not been felt since the Great Depression.

This economic crisis severely diminished Black Atlantans' purchasing power. Assistant Commerce Secretary Sidney L. Jones noted that purchasing power fell at a rate of 4.7 percent between March 1973 and March 1974. Inflation moved so fast that Americans could not keep up: the Georgia Labor Department made record unemployment payments totaling $1 million weekly to over 85,000 Georgians. To place this in proper context, in the first quarter of 1973, Georgia only paid $11.4 million, compared to $20.8 million in 1974.[29]

Atlanta city hall faced a mounting revenue crisis—although it publicized it as a "budget" crisis to move blame away from the ruling class and to invoke empathy from the working classes—as it prepared for 1975. Two days before Christmas in 1974, the city council called an emergency session issuing cutbacks to the police, mayor, and council staff, canceled equipment purchases and maintenance, declared seven mandatory furlough days for all city employees, and passed a property tax rate increase of 1.3 mills. The property tax increase particularly upset Atlanta's capitalists and placed more pressure on Maynard Jackson to appease their interests.[30]

These drastic measures failed to generate the revenue needed to alleviate the crisis, and the mitigation efforts disproportionately targeted the city's poor. The Joint Board of Tax Assessors was required by state law to keep tax assessments on property at 40 percent of the property's fair market value. Yet the city did not reappraise properties—meaning that the mill rate was applied to assessments generally below where they should be. Consequently, both the city and counties in the Atlanta metropolitan region received less from property taxes than was legally possible.

Research Atlanta excavated these troubling figures in its report *The Other Side of the Tax Problem*. Lower-middle-income property was assessed at 42 percent, while expensive property in Buckhead was assessed at only 32.4 percent. In another damning find, the organization calculated that homes worth

$10,000 or less were assessed at an average of 49 percent of their market value, while homes valued at over $100,000 were assessed an average of 32 percent of their market value. Fulton County, which collected taxes both for itself and for the city of Atlanta, brought in smaller percentages of tax revenue every year. To make matters worse, a Georgia constitutional amendment passed in 1972 exacerbated the shortfall. It declared Fulton County billing institutions (like hospitals) tax exempt.[31] Slum housing, on the other hand, experienced the inverse. The values declined and the assessments remained high, so the Joint Board of Tax Assessors overtaxed poor residents. Thus, the root of Atlanta's revenue crisis in the 1970s was a deliberate consequence of the BUR's anti-working-class policies: poorer residents paid higher regressive tax rates with decreased purchasing power—while the city granted the bourgeois class an indirect tax break.

Georgia and Atlanta doubled down on the attack on poor Black people by divesting from social welfare programs to offset the crisis. On January 1, 1975, the Georgia Department of Human Resources cut 125,000 welfare recipients' payments after removing 7,000 working mothers completely from welfare the month before. The department reduced the maximum grant for one person from forty-seven dollars to thirty-eight dollars a month. Shockingly, that amount was less than half of the $106 the Welfare Department itself computed as the need for an individual.[32] The US Bureau of Labor Statistics stated that an urban family of four required $9,200 annually to maintain a "modest standard of living." A yearly Georgia welfare check, however, only provided $5,050—far below the floor needed for survival.[33]

With property taxes failing to keep up with revenue needs, Atlanta city hall colluded with the chamber of commerce and pinned its hopes on a local option sales tax to relieve the revenue strain. In 1974, Governor Jimmy Carter vetoed Atlanta's first attempt to pass a local option sales tax. The following year, Governor George Busbee signed it, but a group of state representatives led by Democrat Cynthia McKinney overrode it.[34] In 1978, though, the interested parties shifted strategy. Southern Bell, Georgia Power, IBM, Coca-Cola, and Delta Air Lines organized a campaign to push for the local option sales tax. Maynard Jackson joined the campaign in 1979 and supported a property tax rollback that would benefit the area's largest corporations. His support laid the basis for a public-private partnership to reorganize capital in the region.[35]

The Jackson administration manipulated its working-class constituencies to secure loyalty for the sales tax. Jackson initially quarreled with the sales tax campaign because he believed that it would "place an undue tax burden on the poor." Jackson concluded that he would only support the tax

TABLE 2.1 **Sources of Sales Tax Revenue in Georgia, 1978**

GOODS	SALES TAX REVENUE PERCENTAGE
Food	21%
Automotive	18%
General merchandise	14%
Utilities	13%
Manufactures	7%
Services	6%
Lumber	6%
Miscellaneous	5%
Furniture	4%
Apparel	2%

Source: Coalition Against the Local Option Sales Tax position paper, undated, box 65, folder 8, Maynard Jackson Mayoral Records, Series B, Robert W. Woodruff Library of the Atlanta University Center, Inc., Atlanta, Georgia.

if it exempted food and drugs. But within a year, Jackson aligned with Atlanta corporations in favoring the tax; he did so without any effort for a food and drug exemption. Indeed, Jackson exceeded expectations in his defense of the capitalist class's interests. Food sales generated more taxes than any other item covered by the sales tax.

Thus, the local option sales tax campaign included food to insure the maximum property tax rollback at the expense of the region's poorest residents. Poor people who spent all their meager earnings on necessities like food and utilities ended up paying a larger portion of their income in taxes than did members of the affluent classes, making this regressive levy one of the most potentially damaging in Atlanta's history. This became especially apparent when Atlanta's Bureau of Budget and Planning did not recommend the local option sales tax as a viable course for correcting the region's revenue crisis.[36] Despite this, the Atlanta leadership pushed ahead with the campaign.

While city hall, Fulton County, and its bourgeois proponents admitted the sales tax was regressive, they did not publicize how uneven the tax burden was or how truly lucrative the rollbacks would be for Atlanta's corporations. Table 2.2 illustrates that the heaviest tax burden would fall on lower-income citizens.

TABLE 2.2 **Income Subject to Sales Tax**

GROSS INCOME	INCOME SUBJECT TO SALES TAX	% INCOME SUBJECT TO SALES TAX
$9,594	$6,546	68.2%
$15,483	$9,447	61.0%
$22,584	$13,258	58.7%

Source: Coalition Against the Local Option Sales Tax position paper, undated, box 65, folder 8, Maynard Jackson Mayoral Records, Series B, Robert W. Woodruff Library of the Atlanta University Center, Inc., Atlanta, Georgia.

TABLE 2.3 **Property Tax Rollbacks for Atlanta's Largest Businesses**

FIRM	ROLLBACK
Southern Bell	$2,190,000
Georgia Power	$960,000
IBM	$511,000
Coca-Cola	$498,000
Delta Air Lines	$469,000
Ford Motor Co.	$448,000
Hilton Hotel Co.	$434,000
Sears	$405,000
General Motors	$405,000
Prudential	$347,000
Peachtree Plaza	$306,000

Source: Coalition Against the Local Option Sales Tax position paper, undated, box 65, folder 8, Maynard Jackson Mayoral Records, Series B, Robert W. Woodruff Library of the Atlanta University Center, Inc., Atlanta, Georgia.

The Coalition Against the Local Option Sales Tax released a position paper showing that an individual who owned a home valued at $50,000 was given a $5,000 homestead tax exemption. Additionally, the coalition uncovered that commercial property holders stood to receive $9 million, or 16 percent of the anticipated property tax rollback. Table 2.3 reveals the total dollar amounts of rollbacks for largest Atlanta businesses.

Atlanta's power structure controlled the narrative throughout the campaign. The BUR determined that a referendum was the best way to push through the sales tax because low-income residents—whose financial stability would be the most affected by the law—did not historically turn out large numbers in referendums. The campaign operated mostly as a quiet, behind-the-scenes movement so as not to incite the Black majority into an antitax movement—especially being a few years removed from an upsurge of Black grassroots movements.

Not surprisingly, support for the sales tax in Black Atlanta split along class lines. Jackson and the Black city council members mobilized support among the Black bourgeoisie and petty bourgeoisie who lived in the suburbs. The local BEOs pushed the BUR strategy of a monolithic, classless, united Black community mythology. Elites served as brokers of disinformation and initiated shaming of Black workers for not uniting around a tax that would "help us all as Black people." A group of anonymous African Americans calling themselves "Black Business Leaders" released a press statement in support of the tax and admonished those who opposed it. They argued that the tax represents "the most equitable way for the City of Atlanta and Fulton County to generate badly needed new money," and they felt "disturbed" by opponents, because "as Black businessmen, we face the same problems . . . struggling to survive in America."[37] The Atlanta Board of Realtors amplified the "united front" discourse to a conservative pitch: "The sales tax is the most fair alternative and that property taxpayers should not have to continue to carry the entire burden for city and county services." Defensively the realtors concluded, "Another property tax increase would be detrimental to the quality of life and growth of our region."[38]

For the BUR strategy, "responsibility" meant submission. The Jackson administration pressured Black clergy to sell the tax to their members during Sunday services or face being declared "irresponsible" citizens. Jackson manipulated the Black worker into supporting the tax through fear, telling poor residents—particularly the elderly living on fixed incomes—that unless the referendum passes, "social programs will be discontinued and city services such as police and garbage collection will be eliminated or curtailed." Last, he attempted to sell the property tax rollback to the Black poor by claiming that businesses, where they shopped and worked, were threatening to leave the metro area if it did not pass.[39]

Jackson's duplicity in his use of scare tactics is evident for multiple reasons. First, the federal government provided the primary funding for social programs in the region. Second, no legitimate threat existed from businesses to leave Atlanta, where the city offered cheap land to investors to form new sites of accumulation. Yet the Black petty bourgeoisie continued to bully the Black working class into supporting the regressive measure, exacerbating multiple setbacks—such as fewer neighborhood resources, rising consumer prices, increasing unemployment and underemployment, and the disappearing children crisis—with little attention from the city.

On October 2, 1979, Atlantans soundly defeated the local option sales tax. In fact, the voters rejected the measure in every county in the region, shocking Jackson and the business community, who believed poor residents would sit out the vote. Both Black and white working-class voters crushed the tax referendum. According to political analysts, both groups voted 80 percent against the tax. Surprisingly, 50 percent of middle-class African Americans voted against the measure as well—possibly meaning that they were not property owners and recognized the tax as a net loss.[40]

Even as his hopes of passing the sales tax dimmed, Jackson did not take advantage of federal revenue-sharing funds to fix the Atlanta budget shortfall. The Nixon administration's revenue-sharing program was designed to replace federal block grant programs, giving cities and local governments allocations they could use at their discretion with little to no guidelines. They were initially billed as "supplemental" funds to current federal programs, but Nixon gutted federal spending for cities—especially social service programs. Thus, revenue-sharing funds allocated to Atlanta amounted to only $7.1 million, for a net loss of $13.1 million in federal monies coming to the city. Research Atlanta noted that Atlanta city hall was the sole determinant in how that $7.1 million was spent, with no input from residents.[41] Jackson's administration used the funds similarly to other urban locales: cutting taxes for the rich and increasing expenditures and pay for police departments.[42] Through the decisions he made in navigating the revenue shortfall, Jackson consolidated his BUR in relation to white-owned corporations and the propertied bourgeoisie —in the process deepening the divide between the Black working class and elites. That gulf deepened with the 1977 sanitation workers strike as Atlanta power brokers set their sights on destroying Black bargaining power across the city.

"The Airplane Can't Fly": The 1977 Sanitation Strike and the Crushing of the Black Public Sector

In early February 1974, African American city sanitation worker Finley Holmes stormed into his American Federation of State, County, and Municipal Employees (AFSCME) Local 1644 union office and released his pent-up anger. "We have complaints, problems with cans with no tops filling with water.... The city couldn't pass a law even requiring things like standard cans with tops!" Fellow sanitation worker Melvin Leeks added, "They sent this man [a city employee] in a couple of years ago.... Find out where the city could save some money.... He's the kind of man who knows an airplane can fly, and he knows you know an airplane can fly, but he can sit down with his piece of paper and pencil and show you that an airplane can't fly."[43]

"They're treated like animals," AFSCME Atlanta official Ron Reliford commented on the treatment of sanitation workers. "Right down to the fact that they have to go outside and answer roll call in any sort of weather after they've already clocked in."[44]

Holmes experienced a daily routine of pain, agony, and alienation. At one house one morning, he picked up over 300 pounds of trash filled with a garbage worker's nightmares: decaying food and heavy telephone books. Very few days passed when he did not cut himself on garbage cans, reaggravate a back injury lifting cans, or fall off the moving truck. Health insurance could have provided some relief for Holmes, but when a worker went to the hospital, no city council member, union representative, or city employee knew where to send the bill.[45]

The city docked vacation and sick leave pay from sanitation workers too injured to work. It was a "cycle of dirt and scum and maggots and rain and cold and dogs," both on the route and dealing with administration. This occupation faced tremendous rates of turnover as many workers grew frustrated, tired, or resentful of their treatment at the hands of the city. But for over fifty-two years, Holmes repeated this same monotonous circuit, collected his daily wages of nineteen dollars, returned to the barn, changed his clothes, and relaxed at a bar or at home with a drink.[46]

Black garbage workers like Holmes possessed little autonomy over their working conditions. As a result of the repetitive nature of garbage collection, Holmes found fulfillment only in activities outside of labor—among his kin and friends in the neighborhoods. Karl Marx captured this alienation, writing that the worker "only feels himself outside of work, and in his work feels outside of himself. He is at home when he is not working, and when he is working, he is not at home."[47] The Atlanta garbage workers themselves described this dissociation from their true selves in stark detail:

> When you head out on the route speed is the most important thing, speed and rhythm. And it goes like this: gun the truck, four houses to go,

down the street, up the driveway, out of the truck (watch for dogs here), find those cans, (in the garage again), a kick and a lift and a heft to the shoulders, back to the truck, little spillover there, bit more heft, damn heavy, dump it in, gun the truck, backing most important, fishtailing down those long drives, back to the street, back to the Mother Truck to lose my two-ton load.[48]

This alienation produced the conditions for Black workers to leverage the point of production as the major site of struggle for autonomy. However, in the mid-1970s, Black labor militancy became an even larger point of class contention as capitalists began their destruction of productive labor spaces. Joblessness for African Americans reached a peak of 14.5 percent in September 1975—a post–World War II high—and remained above 10 percent for the next two years. Black women's and men's unemployment rates were at 12.2 and 11.5 percent, respectively, in the first quarter of 1977. In the same period, white unemployment never rose above 4.5 percent for men and 6.3 percent for women.[49]

Thus, the precarity of bargaining power and productive labor choices influenced the Black worker's upswing in strike activity. Between 1975 and April 1977—at the height of Great Depression–level unemployment and wage cuts for Black people—municipal employees withheld labor in Atlanta forty-nine times and withdrew approximately 46,404 work hours from the city.[50] This strike fever era followed another intense period—between 1972 and 1974—when Black Atlanta workers struck over two dozen work sites, including Mead, Holy Family, South Fulton, and Atlanta hospitals, Martin Luther King Sr. Nursing Home, Greyhound, Sears, Rich's, the Nabisco factory, Pepsi, Reed's, Metropolitan Atlanta Rapid Transit Authority (MARTA), C&S Bank, Bremen and Hebbell steel factories, Penny's, JCPenney, Kress, Zayre, Red Lobster, and many more. In other words, Black workers consciously understood how wielding their strike power better exerted control over their labor.

Much of the fuel driving the workers' anger at this moment stemmed from the city's announcement that there would be no cost-of-living raises—while at the same time city hall allocated major funds to MARTA construction, Central Business District revitalization, the Georgia World Congress Center, and hotel and convention center projects. Workers considered this detrimental in two ways. First, city officials earmarked funds away from municipal employees and toward urban development projects. Second, the execution of these projects threatened to break apart Black neighborhoods even further. Atlanta denied AFSCME all its most pressing proposals: an 18 percent pay increase, cost-of-living raises for all public workers, and a guarantee of no layoffs, no cutbacks, no furlough days, and no reduction in public services.[51]

Sanitation workers went on the offensive on March 17, 1975, when 500 garbagemen stormed city council chambers to confront the administration about the recently announced furlough days. Chanting "We want more money!" and "City says cut back, we say fight back!" the workers stalled city council business for hours. City hall called the SWAT squad and African American commissioner of public safety Reginald Eaves to mediate the standoff. To add insult to injury, all 500 city workers sat in on the meeting where the city council approved a $3 million renovation to the Bobby Jones Golf Course in affluent northwest Atlanta. The following Friday, the council invited AFSCME workers, the Afro-American Patrolman's League, the Fraternal Order of Police, and the Laborers International Union as a "goodwill" gesture to hear union grievances in the city. By inviting both police unions to city hall during a highly contentious battle over control of the police, the BUR diluted the sanitation workers' time to speak on their contract negotiations. Four hundred city workers arrived but were denied the time to speak. They held an impromptu protest outside of city hall and alerted community supporters about coordinated protests in the future, including at the Atlanta School Board, Grady Hospital, and the Fulton County Commissioners Office.[52]

As the workers movement built, Jackson's BUR not only stood firm on its claim of financial strain but also initiated a public relations offensive to fracture support for city employees. In March 1976, Jackson admitted he had not requested pay raises for city employees but was happy to announce that the 1976 Atlanta City Council Appropriations Committee did provide "sufficient funds for a 4.25 percent increase for the 70 percent of city employees who are entitled to an annual one-step increment." Echoing his refusal to betray his capitalist partners in the revenue crisis, Jackson concluded here that "there was simply no source of funds which could provide sufficient money to meet that level of needs without a tax increase."[53] In other words, Jackson assured real estate developers, corporations, and homeowners that he would not place their wealth at the behest of city workers, that is, by instituting a property tax. This represented Jackson's biggest test to determine where Atlanta's future lay—with the Black majority working-class residents or with a Black bourgeois and petty bourgeois power base with affluent whites. Jackson redrew the power dynamics across race and via class in Atlanta and proved his position as the junior partner of capital by disciplining the Black worker.

The city workers, however, countered Jackson's claim with their own public political education campaign. First, they partnered with Research Atlanta and discovered that the city council had appropriated, but not spent, $2 million for purchasing new police cars, garbage trucks, bulldozers, and other construction equipment. The city defended its decision to not use the funds for public employee raises, stating that "the costs of repairing what we have now would be higher than the purchase of new items and in this case, too, Atlantans would suffer a loss of efficient service delivery."[54] Workers argued that not only had the US economy trended upward since the second quarter of 1975 but Mayor Jackson had reported false revenue figures to the public. The city workers pointed to alternative revenue sources, including an obvious option: hotels and motels. Since hotel construction was one of the largest projects in the city, an extra $300,000 could be realized through a hotel-motel tax. The employees also advocated for liquor sales on Sunday to raise another $1 million. Finally, the union claimed that the city hid approximately $900,000 in the contingency fund and $1 million in the auto fund, which could be reallocated for pay raises. For example, AFSCME reported that with a 1975 actual property tax collection of $33.6 million, a 3 percent growth rate over 1975 produced another $1 million. If the $1 million were added to the 1975 figure, the 1976 property tax collection would be $34.6 million. If the difference between the estimate and the updated budget prediction of 1976 —$1 million—was used to finance pay raises, then it would have eased the 1976 and 1977 revenue shortfall.[55] With the mayor refusing to acknowledge a reallocation of funds and the Black workers exposing city hall's neglect, both sides had drawn their battle lines for Atlanta, and both continued to escalate tensions.

In January 1977, two months before the strike, dangerous freezing temperatures struck Atlanta. Many garbage workers refused to work under those conditions, and the city denied them their wages. AFSCME filed grievances for lost pay, citing inclement weather. On February 7, Jackson issued a statement refusing the workers their wages: "The refusal of some city employees to work when properly instructed to do so and when the facts did not justify their refusal resulted in Commissioner Funnye making the decision in question. I support Commissioner Funnye's decision.... I trust that you will report back to your respective jobs ... so there will be no further loss in pay and so that the services which we are charged with providing to the taxpayers and other citizens of Atlanta can continue."[56]

By the second week of March, city workers responded by announcing their intent to strike if Jackson did not meet their demands. On March 10, the workers released their "final offer" in an addendum to their contract proposal demanding the following: (1) damages covered if an incident occurs for any union member operating a city vehicle; (2) full paid medical and dental premiums for employees and their dependents; and (3) no layoffs of AFSCME employees.[57] In the meantime, Black working-class neighborhoods whipped into an organizing frenzy to support the potential strike. Informational flyers flooded the city and the supportive local newspapers, the *Great Speckled Bird* and the *Atlanta Voice*.

Concurrently, AFSCME exposed the Atlanta labor conflict to international audiences with a *New York Times* advertisement that presented the union negotiations as a power struggle between poor residents and a business-friendly mayor who betrayed his people:

> THE FALCONS AREN'T THE ONLY LOSING TEAM IN ATLANTA. TRY CITY HALL. Atlanta has seen four years of bickering, squabbling, phonyism and cronyism at City Hall. The score: higher taxes, poorer services, boarded up schools, dirtier streets. . . . The mayor was for her [the people] then against her. She [the people] got tired of the Posturing. . . . Everybody's penalized. $18 million in taxes, most of it owed by businesses, Go uncollected. The Falcons have hired a new coach. It's time for one at City Hall.[58]

Once word reached his office about the *New York Times* ad, ACOC president Richard L. Kattell angrily corresponded with the Legislative Action Committee. He appealed for bourgeois networks to "ACT NOW" and support the City of Atlanta and Maynard Jackson against Black workers' "attempt to take over city government."[59] By this point, however, Atlanta's leadership invoked the bourgeois narrative strategy of separating the civilian workers from a "corrupt, controlling union." This antiworker propaganda represented the most bourgeois characteristic of Jackson's BUR. Promoting the idea that Black workers functioned as pawns in a power play by an outside entity stripped the agency from the very Black constituency that fought to elect Jackson and his city council in the first place. This betrayal of the Black worker in Atlanta was not the first, or last, time a BUR tossed Black workers into the scrapyard.

Rank-and-file Black workers did not practice "service model unionism" —meaning they did not believe that the workers and the union were two separate entities. Rather, they practiced an *organizing* model, where they consciously understood *themselves* as the union that worked to liberate their own labor power from racism and exploitation. What Jackson and the city power structure consciously neglected was that their propaganda was not simply antiunion; it demeaned the character, legitimacy, and agency of blue-collar

African Americans. In clearer terms, Jackson's BUR sought to delegitimize Black municipal workers' capacity to empower their class position and organizing power against racial oppression.

With negotiations at an impasse, on March 29, 1977, over 1,000 public employees walked off their jobs in an indefinite strike. This marked the second major public employee strike in Atlanta in less than a decade, following the 1970 sanitation strike. Strike support advertisements flooded the *Atlanta Voice* with directions for strike material locations, details about where to send resources, and general information. By the end of the first day, over 84 percent of the city's garbage remained uncollected, none of the twenty crews at either the Hill Street or Liddell Drive substation reported to work, and only ten total crews citywide crossed the picket line. Jackson, who followed the general company line after being struck by a union, assured the public that the strike would not affect city operations and warned that there may not be enough garbage and water work for union members to remain certified—indirectly threatening to decertify the union to scare workers into reporting to work. He finished the day promoting the chamber of commerce's idea that striking Black city workers served as "pawns" of the union to take over Atlanta.[60]

On April 1, 1977, Jackson sent the following letter by registered mail to every striker who did not report to work on March 30: "Because you have refused to comply with your superior's written order of March 30, 1977, that you report to work, prepared to perform your assigned duties as an employee of the City of Atlanta, on Friday, April 1, 1977, no later than your regularly scheduled time for reporting to work, you are hereby notified that you are terminated from employment with The City of Atlanta, effective immediately, Friday, April 1, 1977."[61]

Jackson's letter escalated his war against Black workers and elevated his standing in Atlanta's power structure. By firing the strikers, Jackson took advantage of the unstable political economy and high unemployment to entice people to cross the picket line. This not only busted the strike, but it shattered the power of Black public-sector unionism in Atlanta into pieces. By April 4, half of the garbage collection routes had resumed, and some picket lines, like the one at the Liddell Drive substation, had closed.[62] With further insult, Jackson went out of his way to personally antagonize Black workers by following up his termination notice with a bush-league letter to fired strikers—a mailed, empty job application to work for the city: "The city of Atlanta has over 1,000 applications from persons applying for your former job. These new applicants are being put to work each day. It was unfortunate that you, along with many other employees, were dismissed. . . . We wish to invite you to fill out the attached application.... The city cannot give a pay raise this year.... It is unfortunate that they [strikers/union] ignored this and advised you to abandon your job."⁶³

Jackson's hard-nose union-busting approach produced desirable results for his BUR strategy. The strike weakened as the days rolled by, and Atlanta's white and Black power structures showered him with congratulations and praise. Vice president of the chamber of commerce Thomas K. Hamall, president of Central Atlanta Progress Dan Sweat, executive director of the Atlanta Urban League Lyndon Wade, executive director of the Atlanta Business League Franklin O'Neal, chairperson of the Citywide Advisory Council on Public Housing Rebecca English, vice president of Atlanta Baptist Ministers Union Rev. Howard Creecy, and Rev. Martin Luther King Sr.—who himself was personally responsible for weakening the 1970 sanitation strike—united in a solidarity press release to praise Jackson's union busting: "We are here together today to express our mutual and deep concern for this city and its workers and to express our support for Mayor Maynard Jackson in his dealings with Local 1644.... We deplore the tactics of this union which purports to represent some city workers, while using these same workers in a cynical power play aimed at taking over city government in Atlanta and a campaign to discredit Atlanta generally and Mayor Jackson in particular. They have made their point and it is time for city services to return to normal."⁶⁴

In a cruel twist of history, after Martin Luther King Jr. had sacrificed his life organizing with Black workers in the 1968 Memphis sanitation strike, his father, King Sr., aligned with the Atlanta corporate elite and busted the majority Black public-sector union. In one of the only articles praising Jackson in the publication's history, the *Atlanta Journal*—which had spent the entirety of Jackson's tenure vilifying him and other BEOs—under the questionable heading "Covers Dixie Like the Dew," thanked the mayor for putting Black militancy in its place. According to the paper, Jackson "stood firm despite a smear campaign that has hurled all manner of invective against him.... AFSCME sought to use city employees as pawns in a power struggle. And Mayor Jackson would have none of it."⁶⁵ Apparently, class and antiunionism overrode white supremacists' hatred for the Black leaders in Atlanta.

Black working-class neighborhoods and supporters regrouped and responded strongly. Black working-class neighborhood leaders Ethel Mae Matthews, Eva Davis, Gene Ferguson, Gene Guerrero, and Marian Green kept the strike alive with community rallies, political education information sessions, picket sign-ups, and strike supply collections.⁶⁶

Black political scientist Mack H. Jones rallied the Black radical scholars in the Atlanta University Center and released the most inflammatory statement—highlighting the class characteristics of the Atlanta power structure's subjugation of Black workers and equating Jackson's regime with the racist violence that sieged Memphis sanitation strikers in 1968:

> It is indeed tragically ironic that on the ninth anniversary of the assassination of Dr. Martin Luther King, Jr. who was felled by assassin's bullets when he was in Memphis to support the strike of that city's predominantly black sanitation workers, the black mayor of Atlanta announced that he was firing some one thousand low paid and predominantly black workers who were on strike seeking a wage increase and humane working conditions.... The tragedy and irony were heightened by the fact that a group of self-styled leaders led by Reverend Martin Luther King, Sr., and orchestrated by the Atlanta Chamber of Commerce met in the opulent quarters of the Chamber [to] endorse the mayor's firing of the workers and to complain that the union's tactics were damaging the city's image.[67]

Jones concluded his statement by pointing out that "just as the City finds the money to pay fat salaries to the Mayor, Commissions, and Department heads, restore old civil war paintings, and other matters of high priority it can and must find the money to pay city workers livable wages."[68] A group of unidentified college professors united to not only condemn Jackson but to also elicit unconditional support via collecting supplies and documenting city hall's actions during the labor strike. Additionally, the professors called out the union-busting orientation of the mayor, decrying him as being on an "anti-worker, anti-union crusade."[69]

The Ad Hoc Committee in Support of Striking Sanitation Workers sharpened the radical perspective of the strike, condemning Jackson and the Atlanta power structure and illuminating the alienation in sanitation work:

> We have assembled here today to declare and to demonstrate our support of the striking sanitation workers who, with their arms, their legs, their backs, perform the filthiest, most backbreaking work in the city. We condemn Mayor Maynard Jackson for his ruthlessness. Mayor Jackson, who won his election because of the support given to him by unions, is now engaging in anti-union activity. Mayor Jackson, be it known, is a strike breaker, a union buster. We recognize, however, that

the struggle of these workers is not against Maynard Jackson as an individual. This struggle is against the state, against the government, against the powerful business interests of this city who Maynard represents.[70]

William Lucy, former chairman of the Coalition of Black Trade Unionists, criticized Jackson's "hypocritical character"—citing the mayor's background in labor law: "[He] understands labor, one who has practiced at the trade, one who has given all the slogans . . . about the rights of working people and, at the same time, when a confrontation occurs . . . takes the ultimate action of firing employees. . . . [That] is absolutely unforgivable."[71]

Despite rallying support for the Black workers, the strike fizzled out by the first week of May. Many new hires replaced the terminated strikers, and all the city's garbage collection had resumed. With the high rate of unemployment at the time, the mayor's declaration to consider rehiring fired workers seemed futile for many Black residents. Concurrently, Jackson sent word to the few workers still on strike that his terms for ending the impasse were for AFSCME to sign a no-strike clause and to accept no pay raises. By the end of May, all positions were filled. Strike leaders who attempted to reapply for their jobs were told "they are no longer wanted."[72]

This devastating loss, combined with increased police power and the attack on neighborhood activists and radicals, crushed much of Black Atlanta's organizing capacity. This extreme response to the revolutionary nationalism of Black Power was meant to discipline and destabilize the Black worker. With organizing at the point of production weakened, the radical critique of racial class exploitation dissipated. Concurrently, city power brokers set their sights on neighborhoods. Police repression, through the manipulation of the political economy of crime, further threatened Black working-class neighborhood social movement capacity. The Atlanta child murders further exposed the malignant neglect of the Black worker.

Police Repression

In mid-March 1973, six DeKalb County police officers armed with sawed-off shotguns and pistols stormed the East Lake Meadows apartment complex serving welfare fraud warrants. They first kicked in Mattie Dennis's apartment door while she was at work that night. After searching the apartment, the officers next entered Mildred Pless's residence without knocking and shoved her young son out of the way to look around. The officers then burst into Pless's seventy-three-year-old bedridden mother's space, searched the room, and left. Joe Bembry, another tenant in East Lake Meadows, met the officers at the door of his mother's apartment and blocked their entrance. The police arrested him for obstructing justice. The officers showed no warrants but acted with authority and impunity. Just a year earlier, police had told Mildred Pless that they had no jurisdiction over East Lake Meadows.[73]

Widespread outrage over the harm of East Lake Meadows residents and the threat of more police violence in Black working-class neighborhoods prompted a quick and tactical response. On April 11, 1973, fifty members of Black Citizens Against Police Repression (BCAPR), a coalition of Black radical community groups—including Ujamaa Society of Atlanta University, African Liberation Support Committee, the Black Workers Congress, the Committee for Independent Black Politics, Georgia Prisoners Observers Committee, the People's Committee to Insure Justice, and the Atlanta chapter of the Black Panther Party—stormed the Atlanta City Council's police aldermanic committee meeting to announce their goal to liberate Black Atlantans from police terror. BCAPR spokesperson Juanita Vaughn stated that the coalition sought to "expose and combat repression in the Black Community, expose and combat the repressive conditions which Black people are forced to live under ... and to organize and mobilize people against these forces."[74]

BCAPR's demands to the city council sought to redistribute power away from city hall and the police to the communities. "The present situation in the Atlanta Police Department clearly demonstrates that Black people have no power to do what is really necessary to protect the Black community from a racist police department," BCAPR said. "We see that Atlanta is a city with a Black majority and that in light of this Black people must control the Police Department." The coalition demanded "community control of the police" and the abolishment of "terror-type" police units, particularly the STAKE-OUT and SWAT squads. They also demanded a citizens' review board with the power to oversee investigations of complaints of police abuses. They opposed city officials, business owners, police, and even civil rights leaders to join the review board and explicitly sought members from their neighborhoods to volunteer as board representatives.[75]

In constructing an oversight body, BCAPR sought to neutralize municipal support for the wide range of recent anti-Black laws that allowed police abuses against community folks and social movement activists. A few years earlier, Atlanta had passed a law that resembled the Jim Crow–era Mississippi vagrancy Black code. City hall prohibited "loitering, spending time in idleness, lingering, sauntering idly, and lurking." According to the witnesses in city hall that day, it was rushed through the board of aldermen to be used

Black Atlantans swell downtown to protest the police murder of Andre Moore. The *Great Speckled Bird*, November 9, 1970. Courtesy of the Atlanta Progressive Media Foundation / Georgia State University Library Special Collections and Archives.

against the sanitation workers on strike. Two months later, Fulton County superior judge Luther Alverson approved a "no knock" rule for officers storming residences—stating that "if officers announced their presence before entering, it would endanger their lives and risk disposal of evidence." In September 1970, in response to the rebellion sparked by the murder of fourteen-year-old African American Andre Moore a month earlier, Atlanta police converted an old library bookmobile into a new mobile police precinct in Summerhill. The following year—after three Black men from the Edgewood community were beaten by police—Black Atlantans organized multiple protests so widespread that they culminated in city council hearings against the perpetrators.

In a shocking response, however, the police aldermanic committee declared that citizen police brutality reports would no longer be made public in Atlanta. Additionally, Atlanta residents were no longer permitted to address the police committee directly concerning any police violence complaint.[76] These attacks against the safety and organizing capacity of Black working-class Atlantans during the Black Power era laid a foundation for BURs to take Atlanta back from working-class militancy by force.

Atlanta police quickly used their newfound powers to systematically dismantle multiple fronts in working-class Black Atlanta. In fact, the targeted attack on social institutions and reputable neighborhood activists removed a sizable portion of the use value of low-income communities. On March 23, 1972, officers no-knocked the Atlanta chapter of the Black Panther Party (BPP) in Kirkwood. The police claimed they had a warrant for someone the Panthers had never heard of to justify the stripping of the headquarters. Dozens of Kirkwood residents swarmed the site and sat watch over the Panthers and their building during the search. Because of this vigil, no further incidents occurred that day.[77]

Police did not let this setback alter their planned assault on the Atlanta Panthers and their community resources. In August 1972, Black Republican Clayton Powell accused the Atlanta Panthers of making threatening phone calls to the Richard Nixon–Rodney Cook headquarters. Even though the Panthers noted that "it would be against the goals of the Black Panther Party to intimidate and run candidates out of the electoral arena of politics," Atlanta police used this allegation to spread another accusation that Panthers had threatened the lives of multiple store owners and extorted them for $50,000. Because the alleged payment was said to have gone to the Panthers community survival programs, the police used this as a pretense to shut down the free breakfast program. Unsurprisingly, when the Panthers attempted to get a solicitation license permit to override the charge, they had to answer to the fund appeal review—headed by known anti-Panthers Sam Massell and the police aldermanic committee. "We know this clique of corporate capitalist bandits who have been exploiting Black workers with low wages and robbing Black customers with soaring prices has escaped without returning any of their wealth to the Black communities."[78]

In November later that year, police arrested Panthers Ron Carter and Alton Deville on trumped-up charges of possessing a stolen shotgun and "numerous explosive items." Officers claimed that they found the weapons during a search raid at the English Avenue residence and that both Panther leaders lived there. Actually, neither of the Panthers lived there. Also, eyewitnesses claimed that the alleged explosives "couldn't blow up a paper bag," but the charges were enough to jail the activists and allow authorities to shut down another BPP community center in the city.[79]

Less than a month later, police sieged another BPP headquarters, at 620 Parkway, that was used to house their survival programs. Like the previous search, the police used a John Doe search warrant to turn the place upside down looking for marijuana. Law enforcement officers reported that they "confiscated about a pound of marijuana and a suitcase full of weapons and ammunition." To add more damage, police also charged the Panthers with contributing to the delinquency of a minor, because children were around the building when the raid occurred. Other charges included operating a dive and possession. Although the case went nowhere (the warrant was deficient), it added to the litany of charges and bad press against the Panthers. Also, it unraveled their survival programs, with multiple homes put under surveillance and raided.[80]

With the BPP body and organs on life support, law enforcement set its sights on the head. Atlanta police surveilled, questioned, and arrested Ron Carter numerous times in the 1970s, including on highly questionable charges in early 1973 of "creating a turmoil, violation of the safe streets and sidewalks act, and inciting a riot" while he sold a BPP newspaper on the street corner. Police reported that Carter was engaged in "aggressive acts towards the general public." However, multiple eyewitnesses told the *Great Speckled Bird* that Carter stood "peacefully on the street selling the paper and not bothering anyone.... At the moment he was [arrested] two white men in dungarees came running across the street and beat him up." This report seems valid because Carter did receive treatment for a swollen lip, lacerations on the arm, and a head bruise.[81] Police used these multiple incidents to tarnish the reputation of the Panthers and strengthen their public rationale for militarized police units.

BCAPR attempted to intercept the crime propaganda campaign headlined by city hall and the downtown business owners and redirect the narrative and funding toward alleviating poor social conditions in Atlanta neighborhoods. They specifically demanded membership on the High Impact Advisory Task Force, which made recommendations for a $20 million allocation for the High Impact Crime Fighting Program. The city earmarked these Nixon administration law enforcement assistance funds for the expansion of its "crime fighting capacity," including more parole and probation supervisors.[82] BCAPR sought the funds to establish preventative programs, job training, community centers, liberation schools, and community education. In other words, the two sides could not be further from each other's interests.

The second and most significant issue arose when city hall replaced the retiring Herbert Jenkins with new police chief John Inman in March 1972. A close friend to former mayor Sam Massell who held reported ties to organized crime, Inman worked as a beat cop for twenty-two years before skyrocketing up the ladder—from sergeant in 1966 to chief of police in 1972. Inman's philosophy aligned closely with Atlanta power brokers' in that he believed police should be a paramilitary occupying force. Inman's background made it clear why BCAPR demanded city hall remove him so early in his tenure. Yet Inman won the hearts of downtown developers and city hall. His "Crime Stopper Battle Plan" centered on the creation of "innovative," special, heavily armed plainclothes units and helicopter patrols, effectively containing the underground economy and intercommunal violence to designated, impoverished areas of Black Atlanta. This plan also included an initial grant of $80,000 to form an intelligence division that surveilled and controlled "subversive" individuals and organizations.[83]

Inman immediately targeted Atlanta's most recognizable radical activists in one of the most controversial police actions in Atlanta history. In September 1972, the police department issued a "Red List" in its newsletter, *Signal 39*. On the fourth page, under the headline "Survival Information," the department detailed the names, aliases, and addresses of Black neighborhood leaders. The statement read: "The following list of persons and addresses is furnished by the Intelligence Division in the hopes that it will enable the police officers of the Atlanta Police Department to stay alive. The following are some of the extremist militant individuals and addresses. Caution should be used when arresting these subjects or a call is received to these addresses. When approaching these addresses and individuals, request assistance and use extreme caution."[84]

The residents on the list included Ron Carter, Samuel Lundy, and many other local activists. Numerous neighborhood groups stormed the police aldermanic committee the following Wednesday protesting the criminalization of activists. "The people on this list are not criminals nor are they wanted for any crimes," Mary Joyce Johnson of the National Lawyers Guild exclaimed. "They are on it because they are Black or because of their exercise of rights under the first amendment to free expression of political ideas. . . . This shoot to kill mentality is reminiscent of the murders of Fred Hampton and Mark Clark by the Chicago police." Inman shouted directly back at Johnson, "Where, young lady, did you get the idea that shoot-to-kill orders have been given?!" Johnson responded, "What can be expected of these officers who are told to approach the people on this list with extreme caution and reinforcements, when they have been told the list has been furnished to help them stay alive?"[85]

The most impactful statements came from the top two names on the Red List, Sam Lundy of the All-African People's Party and Ron Carter, who both spoke at length. Carter detailed the difficulty he now faced in continuing the free breakfast program for poor Black Atlanta youth due to fear of violence to the children and neighborhood residents. Lundy's testimony revealed that Atlanta police had already committed to playing dirty when Lt. W. W. Holley infiltrated the Panther headquarters in Kirkwood again, posing as a building inspector. When confronted, Holley, visibly embarrassed, said, "Well, I just happened to look that building up, and it was due for inspection, so I just went along with the building inspector. Anyway, I was only there for about three or four minutes when they recognized me and asked me to leave." Toward the end of the confrontation, a family of three approached the police aldermanic committee and asked why their address was on the list when the only thing they did was host two anti–Vietnam War discussion sessions.[86]

With Black activist circles wounded in Atlanta, Inman set out next to siege poor Black neighborhoods and reduce their spatial and social access to downtown capital. In late 1973, the STAKE-OUT squad and SWAT team commenced operations to be, as the head of the Afro-American Patrolman's League stated, an "execution squad." STAKE-OUT—a plainclothes unit—was allotted $1 million in funding for fifty-nine officers in the summer of 1972, and less than two weeks later it had already killed two Black men, shooting them a total of twenty-nine times. SWAT placed squads across five different quadrants in the city. Like the STRESS unit deployed in Detroit at the time, the STAKE-OUT and SWAT teams received training from the FBI and employed decoy methods to target people, then lure them into criminal situations. Unlike STRESS, though, the Atlanta Police Department selected Black policemen for both units—seeking to delegitimize public accusations of racism in police forces and input members from the exploited racial class as state oppressors, fulfilling internal neocolonialism on the Black masses.[87]

SWAT and STAKE-OUT terrorized Black Atlanta throughout the 1970s. In early April 1973, STAKE-OUT detective E. F. White disguised himself as a homeless man passed out on the pavement; recent transplant Charles Jerome Oliver attempted to go through his pockets. After Oliver found a fake roll of money wrapped in three one-dollar bills, White identified himself as a policeman. Oliver and his two friends attempted to run but stopped when they heard warning shots. Oliver put his hands up and walked back to the police, and Officer H. F. Pharr put the barrel of his gun to the back of Oliver's neck, walked him to an empty parking lot, and squeezed the trigger without provocation.[88] STAKE-OUT officer Daniel P. Bowens killed twenty-nine-year-old African American Charles Henry Underwood, making Underwood the fifth Black man Bowens had killed in thirty months.[89] Killing with impunity was not only rampant in this unit but expected.

Not every police officer followed along with Inman's Crime Stopper Battle Plan, and a few sought to expose the department's corruption and disregard for life. On June 1, 1974, the *Atlanta Voice* published a damning testimony by two anonymous STAKE-OUT officers who had worked on the unit for ten months before leaving. According to their testimony, their unit leader, Captain Riley, insisted that all officers "shoot to kill" and "entrap people" to "make arrests at all costs." The testimony's most shocking revelation was that Sgt. H. F. Pharr falsified the police report on the shooting of nineteen-year-old African American David Jack, who was killed on April 20, 1974. Although he had no expertise in bullet trajectories or understanding of the incident, Pharr reported that one of the bullets Detective Durham had fired hit a fire alarm box, ricocheted backward, and struck Jack in his chest. The two anonymous officers concluded their statement by demanding that Captain Riley and other decorated officers be removed from STAKE-OUT and the affiliated DECOY squad and that "many of the tactics used by the [DECOY and STAKE-OUT] squad should be eliminated, and more humane methods be introduced."[90]

Inman's other "innovations" arrived in January 1974 in a program titled Target Hardening through Opportunity Reduction (THOR). The program consisted of six phases intended to "check such crimes as breaking and entering, burglary, and larceny of goods" from homes and businesses. The largest part included residential surveys where police officers looked through a person's home and demonstrated ways that the owner or renter could make it more difficult to break in. Also, THOR recruited fifty to 100 businessmen to give talks and lectures and accompany security officers on residential surveys. Next, these businessmen recruited "right-thinking" people for an auxiliary police force. Thus, as journalists for the *Great Speckled Bird* put it, this equated to right-wing "vigilantes being used to search people's house on whatever pretext."[91]

Maynard Jackson aligned with Inman to secure massive funds for police expansion—demonstrating to Atlanta capitalists that he was the right choice to demobilize working-class African Americans and criminalize their community.[92] As author Alec Karakatsanis posited, pathologizing and propagandizing crime expands state power over exploited groups in three specific ways. First, it redefines the public's notion of "safety," which seeks to promote condoning and, in many cases, *championing* apartheid. By launching million-dollar sponsored campaigns that identified poor Black people as the most likely criminals on a twenty-four-hour basis, the public focus remained largely on those depicted in all forms of media and publicity. Consequently, larger, long-term social crises like gentrification and revitalization appeared as nonthreatening and welcoming political solutions to crime.[93] Combined with emerging scholarship from cultural pathologists like William Julius Wilson in 1978, the public began to fear low-income Black people. Consequently, the public alienated itself and its empathy from the dire social conditions and blamed low-income Black people for their own shortcomings. This tactic also worked against the movement capacity of the Black working class. Safety became the overriding objective and supplanted autonomy, power, or even liberal reforms. As a result, community organizations shifted most of their resource capacity toward attacking the underground economy in their neighborhoods.

The second benefit for the bourgeoisie and petty bourgeoisie in pathologizing and propagandizing crime against poor people is that the manufactured crime surges—facilitated by the police containing, and not attempting to eliminate, the underground economy in specific nodes of poverty in Black urban spaces—fluctuate the value of land and property. As discussed in chapter 3, the combined forces of real estate, police, and city government worked in concert to lower or raise urban rent based on whether they wanted to gentrify an area (and displace poor people) and attract middle- and upper-income people to an "emerging" space. It also provided the municipal government with the leverage to sway public opinion about passing draconian anti-poor laws and inflated police budgets via mass hysteria over crime. Third, propagandizing crime redefines how the public rationalizes solutions to safety.[94] As class antagonisms fade from public critique of capitalism and poverty, collective social-movement-driven solutions like strikes, urban rebellion, and self-help violence against state-sponsored or private white terrorism appear irrational, while incarceration, rugged individualism, racial "uplift," and bureaucratic nonprofit management/supervision of poverty appear "rational." Thus, as the next pages will show, the Atlanta ruling class used crime as a unifying force for capital against the Black working poor during the worst economic recession since the Great Depression.

In August 1973, Atlanta's top Black and white business leaders sponsored research from the Metropolitan Atlanta Commission on Crime and Juvenile Delinquency—an ultra-right-wing organization headed by Atlanta market corporatist and private security force owner Dillard Munford and African American insurance giant and future ACOC president Jesse Hill Jr. Other affluent African American members of this group included Herman J. Russell, educator Horace Ward, and Lyndon Wade. The commission argued that

Atlanta must construct a "campaign to eliminate undesirable business locations," citing that Tenth Street was a "gathering point for disorderly elements." Thus, they equated crime with a significant Black residential corridor. The commission recommended a "thorough investigation and use of undercover operations to collect information to justify closing places that constitute a public nuisance by cancelling their business licenses." The paper concluded by urging "residents and operators and business located in the vicinity of these undesirable locations [to] report to the police the nature of the activities which occur making them unattractive to the general public but a gathering point for hoodlum elements."[95]

Once crime became the rallying cry for the bourgeois and petty bourgeois classes, it provided justification for increasingly brutal tactics to isolate the Black poor in enclaves away from areas of capital accumulation and disrupt their spatial and social interaction with areas outside of their neighborhoods. Munford continued his personal crusade to portray Black "collective" activity in Atlanta as "undesirable" and in need of an extreme response: "As of right now, if I could move every store, every office, and every warehouse my company has out of the city, I would do it, as I think we are sitting on a time bomb. . . . Frankly, I'm terrified at the future of Atlanta. . . . The city won't survive . . . if it is to become a) all Black; b) a welfare capitol [sic]; c) a crime haven; d) the crime capitol [sic] of the South."[96]

Atlanta's power structure attempted to scare the "crime crisis" into residents via the local media. In late August 1973, city elites sponsored a ninety-minute "community dialogue" called *Murder in Atlanta* on WSB-TV. The program featured several affluent panelists discussing the causes of crime —including Howard Stanback of the National Association of Black Social Workers; psychologist Dennis Jackson; Marvin Marcus, a white Georgia State University professor; and Rev. Joseph E. Boone of the Metropolitan Atlanta Summit Leadership Conference.[97]

Because most of the police units materialized through the crime commission's "crime-fighting" federal funds, they focused on protecting private businesses and eliminating perceived threats to consumer spaces. By late 1974, Inman reported that crime against business was down. The Atlanta Retail Merchants Association endorsed Inman, claiming he was doing an "outstanding job" in the Crusade Against Crime, a program founded by Jackson and championed by Munford.[98]

The other part of Inman's Crime Stopper Battle Plan involved tactical aerial deployment. Inman and city hall spent $1.5 million on four new helicopters equipped with infrared body-heat-detection technology that could identify an individual behind a thick wall. According to Inman, the helicopters "greatly increase patrol capabilities" because a patrol car covered 100 linear miles in an eight-hour shift while a helicopter covered over 300 miles in the same time. With his new weaponry, Inman expanded the Atlanta police's helicopter patrol to twenty-four-hour surveillance in April 1974. According to residents, the helicopters were not only sent out on specific assignments where a crime was alleged to have been committed; they also patrolled areas regularly, acting as aerial patrol cars. They also flew low near apartment windows, shone bright lights into rooms, and flew by neighborhoods three or four times a night. Black residents felt that the helicopter patrol was such an invasive operation that they did not feel comfortable holding meetings in their homes anymore. One resident let it be known that "I would rather put up with a few more burglaries in my neighborhood than feel that I was being spied upon by the police!"[99]

Inman's final subversion involved infiltrating and surveilling the local Black alternative media. On April 8, 1974, African American police officer Marion Lee applied for employment at the *Atlanta Voice* newspaper—four days before graduating from the Atlanta Police Training Academy. She was hired as a typesetter at the paper. Unbeknown to the *Voice*, Lee altered her police department record to reflect that she had been fired from the department. However, not only was she assigned to the Atlanta Intelligence Division right out of training, but she was also under the direct supervision of Inman himself. According to Lee, who confessed her deceit to the *Voice* after being confronted, her assignment entailed locating the *Voice*'s "source of information" regarding police corruption, STAKE-OUT brutality tactics, and "gestapo-style policing."[100] Less than a week after the *Voice* outed Lee as a spy, Inman justified his COINTELPRO-style tactics by accusing *Voice* guest contributor and Black political scientist Adolph Reed Jr. of being connected to the Symbionese Liberation Army. In a shocking confession, Inman openly admitted that he authorized Lee to illegally wiretap the *Atlanta Voice*.[101] Reed's response to Inman as well as the *Atlanta Constitution*'s propaganda against him are noteworthy in their condemnation of the City of Atlanta's internal neocolonial tactics against Black radicals:

> Inman's infiltration of one of his lackeys into the *Voice* is of course just another incident in the increasing battle between Black people and John Inman as the commander of the terrorist occupation army which subjugates the black community.... There is no question that Atlanta has been infiltrated by hard-core terrorists; they are Inman's blue shirted

Atlanta Anti-Repression Coalition protesting police chief John Inman. The *Great Speckled Bird*, July 22, 1974. Courtesy of the Atlanta Progressive Media Foundation / Georgia State University Library Special Collections and Archives.

thugs, and they are running all over the city. Their kill record speaks for itself. The only disappointment is with policewoman Lee, who decided to turn on her people for a shiny badge and a pat on the head from Inman.... I am not certain what Officer Lee plans to do with her badge, but I have at least one suggestion.[102]

By the end of 1975, Mayor Jackson's administration and the Atlanta Police Department had spent $20 million to create THOR, SWAT, and STAKEOUT, among other policing units and divisions. In May 1979, Jackson provided even more support for the police and approved tangential perks for officers, including one box of ammunition per month for target practice; preferential treatment at Grady Hospital to police officers injured on duty; and an ordinance that allowed the city to assume liability for officers injured while off duty, with complete health and hospital coverage (sanitation, water, and other public employees did not have this coverage). Instead of telling police officers no, as he told other municipal employees, Jackson assured police that he would find a way to obtain the approximately $13 million necessary to pay for the upgrades.[103]

While these forces brutalized Black Atlantans and disrupted their NSMC, white and Black affluent residents praised city hall's tactics. By mid-1974, Inman supporters—led by Dillard Munford—initiated a "Support Our Chief John Inman" campaign with automobile bumper stickers. According to *Atlanta Voice* editor J. Lowell Ware, Munford was instrumental in helping Inman falsify crime statistics to make his department appear efficient. For example, Ware noted that Inman juked burglary statistics by marking several unsolved burglaries as solved every time one burglar was caught. When Inman installed television cameras in downtown areas and low-income Black neighborhoods, the *Atlanta Voice* polled African Americans and found that most of the support for the surveillance derived from middle-aged, professional, and managerial-class Blacks. One woman stated that she was "200 percent" in favor and that "I think it's needed more in the communities than downtown." She went on to suggest surveillance in Adamsville and on Simpson Road—areas far from Black middle-class suburbs but also adjacent to popular shopping strips where affluent African Americans encountered their working-class counterparts. Atlanta activist Tyrone Brooks, however, offered a unique perspective: "The main purpose of the cameras is for surveillance. To keep an eye on certain individuals." Brooks concluded that the one way to deal with the problem of crime is to "open up the job market."[104]

Outside of police repression, other forces attacked social institutions and reputable neighborhood activists to depower strategic components of NSMC. In September 1970, the landlord for the Harambee Living Art Gallery in the Black Edgewood community chose to close the center unexpectedly. Although it specialized in helping Black youth create art, the center functioned as a liberation school and offered community members political education sessions, meditation courses for radical healing, writing lessons, and storage for housing neighborhood resources. African American artist Dan Danner, who ran the center, stated that the youth are taught "things about themselves that the system isn't doing. We are letting them know that we are an African people." At the end of the month, armed white marshals removed Danner, ensuring that Black children lost one of their enrichment areas. "Now the kids won't have any place to go," Danner told the *Atlanta Voice*. "The people in the community are very, very, upset."[105]

In January 1971, the Southern Center on Public Policy abruptly fired John Shabazz and ended his federally subsidized community project. According to Shabazz, pressure to remove him came from the ACOC, the AFL-CIO international union, and other corporations threatening to cut their support to the United Negro College Fund. The vice president of Clark College, Edward J. Brantly, subtly confirmed Shabazz's claims—without implicating himself, of course—that entities threatened to divest funds if Shabazz was not removed: "All OEO [Office of Economic Opportunity] Funds were frozen. . . . The administration of Clark did not fire Mr. Shabazz." For the year 1970, Shabazz was instrumental in securing local resources for community organizations. He also challenged the racism in the AFL-CIO's handling of Black workers in construction hiring and led a labor strike against Kessler's department store. Kessler immediately withdrew all donations to Clark College after the strike.[106] Shabazz and Black Belt communities lost a major resource base for their escalating social movements.

Additionally, the internal combustion of the Southern Christian Leadership Conference removed critical social movement resources from Black working-class Atlantans. The fluidity of class positions produced contradictory interests, goals, and visions for the SCLC members. It began in July 1973 when SCLC national president Ralph Abernathy abruptly resigned from the organization. In his farewell message, he lay the blame of the failure of SCLC on "the failure of middle-class Blacks to support the organization." Abernathy went further, attacking the Black bourgeoisie as well, many of whom made up the SCLC executive board: "Many Black people feel that they have 'arrived' simply because they now occupy high positions made possible through our past struggles and the struggles of other poor people, but they will not support SCLC financially."[107]

Apparently, this was a veiled shot at Coretta Scott King, who had secretly been at war with SCLC for an undisclosed amount of time. Allegedly, Abernathy and Atlanta SCLC president Hosea Williams disliked King "siphoning off money" into her organization, the Martin Luther King Center for Social Change—funds that SCLC believed should be theirs. In his public statement of support for Abernathy, Williams singled out King and argued that SCLC would not have faced financial ruin if she had shared her profits with them: "Mass support from the grassroots is the only thing that will force Mrs. King to do right by SCLC."[108]

The other major cause of the SCLC fallout involved a power struggle over class. A month after Abernathy resigned, he returned as president in what SCLC called "a new era."[109] This involved splitting SCLC into three units: one attuned to the needs of poor Black people and the other two in service of conservative nationalists. In other words, SCLC pooled a good portion of its resources to boost the profile and power of the Black bourgeoisie by creating a unit that invested in Black business growth and another unit to fight crime in Atlanta.[110] This perplexing structure was doomed to fail from the start. Hosea Williams, a longtime resource for Black working-class struggles, always held a complicated position regarding his class identity and ideology. When he fully embraced Black capitalism, he betrayed the Black worker; however, when he moved toward anticrime, he transferred previous working-class social movement resources to the defense of capital from those very Black workers. As African American Odell Bennett expressed in a letter to SCLC, there was no doubt with whom the organization's loyalty lay in the war over Atlanta: "When the prison doors open the real dragons will fly out. . . . Let that be a harbinger to the boulevard Toms . . . the bootlickers that collaborate with the oppressors of Black and other oppressed . . . minorities. . . . Continue as you might to sell our people's interest down the drain for a few tokens so you may live in leisure. The day is drawing nigh when you flee or be trampled by the very people that you are proclaiming to weld into a 'non-violent army.'"[111]

Unsurprisingly, SCLC ceased to function as a full-time organization one year later. The Black worker had outgrown the ideological limitation of the SCLC years ago and now had no reason to support the organization. Despite the ideological contradictions, the loss of SCLC in Black Atlanta wounded the grassroots struggle in the city. SCLC had offered funds, local, state, and national kinship networks, and most importantly, physical spaces like churches to operate as local movement centers. With the loss of SCLC's stability, the grip on the churches slipped away. Thus, it is safe to conclude that the death of SCLC played some role in the Black church's pivot away from its role providing local movement centers for grassroots organizing.

"As if They'd Dropped Off the Face of the Earth": The Atlanta Child Murders and Black Working Women's Resistance to Urban Neglect

No other episode in Black Atlanta's class warfare exposed the contradiction between increased police power and spending and the malignant neglect of the working classes better than the Atlanta child murders crisis. The Atlanta child murders demonstrated that the Jackson mayoralty, development of downtown Atlanta, expansion of the Atlanta Police Department, and overall future planning of Atlanta did not take into account the safety, health, or viability of the Black majority. As working-class Black mothers protested for protection from the murders, the Atlanta power structure's dismissal and attack against them as "bad parents" contributed to a growing pathological and misogynist culture against low-income Black women.

On July 28, 1979, fourteen-year-olds Edward Smith and Alfred Evans were found dead fifty yards apart on Niskey Lake Drive in southwest Atlanta. Both Black working-class children were dumped on the side of the road.[112] The *Atlanta Journal* and the *Constitution* ran hardly noticeable stories. Atlanta police did not dispatch detectives to investigate. Two weeks after the murders, Harvey Gates, a writer for the *Atlanta Voice*, published a three-part editorial—the only in-depth analysis of the tragedy at the time—with pointed critiques at city hall and the buffed-up police force: "Why were they killed? . . . The overriding question is, why don't we know any of these answers? . . . Particularly, when we have all the apparatuses to send messages, photographs, and fingerprints all over the world in a twinkling of the eye."[113] After a month, the two boys had not been identified, claimed by any parents (because police had not contacted Black parents with missing children), or buried. In his second editorial, Gates doubled down on his critique of city hall and the racism and classism within the BUR: "Now if these children were white, the state, the city, the community would show some concern. They would offer rewards. They would keep the issue before the public's eye. It took me an hour this morning just to ascertain whether or not they had been buried yet; from the police department no less."[114] Gates concluded his piece with an ominous prophecy for Atlanta's Black working class: "If these [two] children were not safe, then none of ours are safe . . . and some of us will live to rue this day!"[115]

By May 1980, six more children had disappeared from Black working-class neighborhoods. Three months later, another eight children had disappeared. All but two of the fourteen kidnappings occurred during daylight hours. The victims were predominantly boys between the ages of nine and eleven and members of either the YMCA or the Boy's Club.[116]

Nothing infuriated African American Alice Kent more than coming home from a grueling day of work in 1980 to learn that another young neighborhood child had disappeared down the street from her. Kent grew up in Atlanta and noted that she had never experienced such fear as during the child murder crisis. In fact, the daily stories of mutilated children stressed her to the point that she developed a nagging pain in her leg. Although she believed it could be because of the rat infestation in her one-story home on Lucille Avenue, she considered the pain to be anxiety related. After all, Kent noted, the stress derived from the lack of protection and determination by the city to resolve the issue. She noted that Mayor Maynard Jackson "did all that talking and nothing was getting done," while "it felt like the crazy times would never end." The community efforts by the mothers of the missing children gave her some solace, but she "was so disappointed in how authorities dealt with the kids."[117]

Kent, like most Atlantans, felt abandoned by city officials in a time of crisis. More tragic figures, like Camille Bell, recalibrated their trauma toward community resistance. Bell, whose nine-year-old son Yusuf was found dead and stuffed inside a crawl space of an abandoned school in late 1979, captured the people's disappointment in Jackson's refusal to help Black working-class Atlantans protect their children: "I just know that [those] type of people are not being hurt. I hope I'm wrong, but either he's surrounded by a bunch of incompetents, or he doesn't care about black people that's bad, but if black people don't care about black people, that's deplorable."[118]

Although Jackson reportedly sent Bell a telegraph that stated that "the Atlanta Department of Public Safety will do everything within its power to expeditiously resolve this tragedy," when she confronted Atlanta police and city hall about the lack of an investigation, she was dismissed and stereotyped as a "bad ghetto mother." Bell had had enough of city hall's indifference. In May 1980, she organized other Black mothers who had lost children—Willie Mae Mathis, Chi' Chi' McGraw, and Venus Taylor—into the Committee to Stop Children's Murders (STOP). They held their first community meeting on July 24 at Wheat Street Baptist Church, where they presented community safety guidelines, including suggestions that children walk in groups or pairs, parents teach children to memorize their name, address, and phone number, parents give children an emergency dime to carry, and people designate safe places at neighbors' homes for children to run to when fearing trouble.[119]

Five more mothers joined the organization over time. The Campbellton Plaza Hotel donated a small room free of charge for STOP to hold meetings. The organization had seven main goals that reached beyond the current episode and sought to establish a local movement center for the protection and empowerment of Black youth. The goals were to (1) document abuses against children citywide, (2) develop programs that inform and protect children as well as community residents, (3) work to prevent the physical, emotional, moral, and educational destruction of children, (4) identify societal problems that may contribute to the abuse of children, (5) counsel families affected by tragedy, (6) establish a computer identification network nationwide to help identify more than 50,000 missing children in America, and (7) address potential violators or victims of children's rights through public service announcements.[120] STOP recognized that it filled a significant gap in the NSMC of the Black Belt.

Elements of protonationalism underscored STOP's movement activity. First, the group emphasized what Black studies scholar Helen Neville termed "radical healing" to channel their tragedy and struggle as colonized Black women and to reaffirm one another and construct resistance. They accomplished this by seeking out and building kinship bonds with other Black parents who had tragic experiences involving their children. Consequently, these Black mothers focused on the development of the "total personality" while healing from trauma so as to "prevent future occurrences" of harm in their communities.[121] By pushing these bonds of conscious Black working women beyond the parameters of the Atlanta child murders and into the tragedies of capitalist exploitation and white supremacy, STOP centered healing on *people* instead of *victims*.

STOP worked mainly as an information and political education hub with other residents supplying them with data and updated news, such as descriptions or characteristics of individuals who had approached children who were not picked up or any strangers in neighborhoods. Additionally, since the police were of little direct help, a private detective volunteered to serve as a liaison to the Atlanta Police Department. Second, STOP made itself available to neighborhood organizations who requested aid. It sought to both solve the murders and return the agency and character of the victims.[122] Their first tactic was to bypass the local police and phone bank the Justice Department until federal investigators took the case. Like city hall, the federal government ignored STOP. Thus, STOP recognized that it had to expand its membership base and influence both regionally and nationally to leverage federal intervention in the problem. The group next hosted a citywide conference on safety precautions for children that attracted dozens of residents. As more children disappeared, STOP canvassed neighborhoods to recruit more members and to leaflet neighborhood watch guidelines. City hall further alienated Black working-class Atlanta when it refused to create an investigative task force and instead hired Dorothy Allyson, a famous psychic, to solve the crisis. Alice Kent said she never joined the STOP efforts, but she "appreciated the acts since it was the only help [she] could see."[123]

City hall's indifference to the growing crisis pointed to the inherent contradiction of BURs as representatives for their constituencies. Maynard Jackson's administration spent tens of millions of dollars to weaponize police, surveil low-income Black enclaves, empower downtown business expansion, and incarcerate loiterers, vagrants, truants, drug dealers, burglars, neighborhood activists, and radicals—because the Atlanta power structure deemed them detrimental to the restructuring of capital. The BUR concerned itself with protecting capitalists, not grassroots folk. If the underground economy expanded in a contained quadrant of the city like East Lake Meadows, the Atlanta police would have no interest in intervening. The directors of the police—the ACOC and city hall—clarified that they did not consider an attack on low-income Atlantans as an attack on their "Atlanta." Emma Darnell, former commissioner of the Department of Administrative Services of Atlanta, highlighted the class antagonisms at the heart of this malignant neglect of Black working-class families: "Atlanta officials didn't move to catch the killer for over a year because it wasn't my child, and it wasn't Julian Bond's child." "This [classism]," she continued, "this elitism ... is what has cost us the lives of our children."[124] "The mayor has been invited to everything we've had," Camille Bell added. "The big meeting at Wheat Street [July 24] and another conference [July 28] and he hasn't even taken the time to send a man to the meeting to say he's interested."[125]

The Atlanta leadership's lack of reaction also exposed a gendered characteristic in colonial domination in Black Atlanta. When Black mothers of murdered children confronted city hall about the problem, the administration not only shunned them but also demonized the victims' characters, thereby diminishing public concern for poor Black residents. City hall repeatedly told the press that the missing children were street hustlers who came from single-parent welfare households and skipped school. According to city hall, the young victims broke the city curfew, so they brought their grisly fates upon themselves. "Well, if you can't keep it quiet that these kids are dead," Bell stated, "then let's tell the world that it's their fault that they're dead."[126]

The Atlanta bourgeoisie and petty bourgeoisie were more concerned with how media attention to the murders would affect international investment, the booming convention trade business, and early gentrification efforts. As chapter 3 showcases, Maynard Jackson and members of the ACOC embarked on numerous international trips to Japan, China, African nations, and European countries to recruit foreign capital to invest in the central city—during the murder crisis. Additionally, when Jackson was in town, he mostly campaigned for Democratic governor Zell Miller. "I find it strange that he has found the time to campaign for Zell Miller, but he couldn't find the time to be concerned about the kids of Atlanta," Bell stated. "He's a city father and he's supposed to act like one."[127]

The Atlanta power structure's interests directly conflicted with the needs of the Black working class at that time.[128] When Bell approached Thirty-Fifth District representative Billy McKinney for help, he clearly demonstrated where his allegiances lay, telling her, "The mayor's trying to get me thrown out of office, after the election I'll help you."[129]

Low-income Black residents were not part of city hall's future plans—so the Jackson administration classified the victims as different from the "respectable citizenry" of the city too busy to hate. Poor Black children were forgotten until they could no longer be ignored. Then, power brokers vilified them and their families. The Jackson administration and chamber of commerce put more effort into propagandizing low-income Black people as "degenerates" than into investigating the murders and protecting the victimized spaces. City hall disproportionately neglected the voices of poor Black women calling for protection for their children. Thus, Black working-class mothers experienced classist and sexist treatment from Atlanta city hall.

By December 1980, the number of missing Black children reached sixteen, and city hall dodged responsibility.[130] STOP's efforts, however, mobilized African American Atlantans across class lines. The Coalition to Save Our Children and the SCLC coordinated with STOP to conduct a "prayer pilgrimage" across the city to publicize the terrorized poor. The march of over 800 Atlantans began in front of the SCLC national office on Auburn Avenue and stopped at the Central City Park Amphitheater. Along the way, the Atlanta Muslim community, the Black Caucus of the American Federation of Teachers, the Boy Scouts, and a children's choir joined in the marching and singing with religious leaders. Surprisingly, the SCLC's Rev. Joseph Lowery offered some criticism of his petty bourgeois class and of city hall's preoccupation with international investment during the child murder crisis, stating that "Atlanta must not only boast of having the biggest airport in the world. But must strive to be the community with the biggest heart in the world."[131]

Besides constructing neighborhood patrols, negotiating childcare watch parties, and expanding publicity of the crisis, STOP countered city hall's constant victim blaming of their missing and deceased children: "Those are absolutely false statements that were perpetrated by our administration, that were sent purposely to sort of blame the victim for what happened to the victim."[132]

STOP's organizing efforts served as the vital reason that the Atlanta child murders came to the attention of the federal government. Bell used her publicity campaign to connect with CBS records, which raised over $60,000 to fund the investigation. Working-class spaces across the nation demonstrated for justice and Black working-class Atlanta throughout 1981. One thousand supporters marched across Chattanooga chanting, "WE WANT IT STOPPED!" In Columbus, Ohio, the Columbus Cares campaign raised $37,000 for STOP. In Harlem, thirty community groups organized a candlelight vigil. The Coalition for Black Colleges and the National Black Child Development Institute called for black ribbons with the slogan "We Must Do More." When the pressure was too much to ignore, President Ronald Reagan solicited $1.5 million in federal funds to help finance an investigation. Finally, by April 1981, people across the United States wore green, black, and red ribbons to express sympathy and solidarity with working-class Black Atlanta.[133]

As STOP's prominence grew, the state and city increased their attacks against the Black mothers. Harvey Gates shockingly turned against the movement and used his *Atlanta Voice* column to lambast STOP for raising funds for low-income mothers of victims. "I am opposed to raising money for the parents of these murdered children," Gates wrote. "It does not make sense. It would make a little more sense if they had lost the breadwinners. But this is not the case.... It is bad enough for citizens to have to subsidize the investigation of these murders."[134] As African American sociologist and Atlanta University professor Bernard D. Headley argued, this was a hypocritical attempt by the Atlanta bourgeoisie and petty bourgeoisie to demean the Black working classes for supporting one another while the affluent generally collected on the life insurance policies that they could afford when loved ones passed away. Besides the loss of young life, the death of poor Black boys in Atlanta in many cases meant an immediate loss of income for families. As Headley explained, money brought in from some of the boys' part-time work, like delivering neighbors' groceries, selling water, or doing yard work had contributed to the family and neighborhood income when heads of households were unable to work or denied stable employment. More clearly, the city attempted to transform the historical communal practice of giving money in times of stress into an exploitative gimmick to turn public opinion against STOP.[135]

In line with Headley, the Atlanta power structure's series of attacks and harassment against the Black mothers and STOP was an attempt to destabilize an indigenous working-class movement by removing any attention to the plight of low-income Black urbanites.[136] City hall used more energy in its attempts to destroy STOP than it did stopping the murders or solving the economic crisis plaguing much of Black America at the time. Masking their attack on STOP by questioning their spending at a time when Black workers struggled to protect themselves demonstrated the anti-working-class interests of Atlanta decision-makers at the time. Even after local and federal officials created a special task force, the neglect did not wane. Bell noted that eleven-year-old Patrick Baltazar called the task force before his death to report an encounter with a man who chased him in a car. The police task force did not respond to the call until several weeks after Baltazar's body was found on February 13, 1981.[137]

The Atlanta child murders further exposed the BUR pursuit of class interests at the expense of Black working-class lives, children, and safety. The increased surveillance of working-class Black activists and neighborhoods juxtaposed with the handling of the investigation of the Atlanta child murders throws into stark relief the growing distance between the Black working class and Jackson's BUR. This intraracial bifurcation along class lines would continue to shape the lived experiences of Black working-class residents and the development of the city itself in the coming decades.

As a result of these dynamics, the resulting retrenchment and police repression weakened Black working-class power to the point that the power brokers' spoils of class warfare faced little to no resistance from the masses. Real estate, international business, and finance capital—combined with Reagan's New Federalism—besieged the Central Business District and further regressed the social conditions of the Black working class in Atlanta. As Black Atlantans lost more control of the future of Atlanta, the New Nadir was set in motion.

CHAPTER THREE

The Spoils of Class War
Neoliberalization and the Fragmentation of Black Working-Class Atlanta

This land is like gold. It's so cheap because this is still considered a low-income neighborhood. Anything Black in America is cheap in White America. As soon as they get everybody out, it becomes gold. The rules state that in order to obtain block grant money, ten percent must go to help low-income people. This community is one hundred percent low-income. So that gives them [the] right to kick ninety percent of us out.
—FLORENCE MCKINLEY, Auburn Avenue neighborhood resident and activist, 1986

If they do us like they did Summerhill, we're going to look like trash on top of trash. [Atlanta Falcons owner] Rankin Smith took all those people to Dallas last Sunday to show them that domed stadium. And everything where that domed stadium is sitting, in 1973, was Black neighborhoods.
—DOROTHY BOLDEN, Vine City neighborhood resident and activist, 1988

This is an example of what happens traditionally in Black neighborhoods where the people of the community are left out of the planning process. We are talking about a community that is one of the *oldest* Black communities in America. One of the crucial things they do to regentrify a community is to destroy its support services. The support services in our community are being eradicated. The concerns of the community, what the people want, is to stay here and control the destiny of their own lives. It's a shame for this neighborhood to be regentrified under the guise of preserving the neighborhood in the memory of Dr. Martin Luther King. It's a cardinal sin.
—ART CATO, Auburn Avenue neighborhood resident and activist, 1984

In late April 1979, Marian Green, the Black former president of the Northwest Techwood Homes Tenants Association, organized a minisquadron of her neighbors and stormed Atlanta Housing Authority (AHA) property manager David Maultsby's office. Techwood residents had grown tired of the falling plaster, water damage, moldy corners, gas leakage, inadequate heating, bad plumbing, and rat and roach swarms—and of city hall disregarding their complaints. "AHA has been getting away with too much," Green told the *Atlanta Voice*. "The[y] holler about what the tenants do to the housing, yet they don't do nothing about the housing for the tenant." After Maultsby refused to meet with the tenants, Green escalated the protest into a sit-in at the Techwood Homes office. Maultsby had Green arrested, which prompted the other residents to resume the sit-in. After a physical confrontation in which Maultsby pulled a chair out from under one of the protesting women and caused her to hit the floor, the police arrested and jailed the property manager for assault.[1]

Green and other Black housing tenants' growing disillusionment with their Black elected officials developed out of long-standing negligence for working-class living conditions in the redeveloping city. Many residents grew angry that officials gave more attention to corporations than neighborhood crises. "We helped every single one of them get elected," Green stated, "passed out leaflets, made phone calls, did everything ... and now that we need their help, they can't do anything for us. ... Tenants are crying out, but no one listens."[2] Instead, Mayor Maynard Jackson and his administration prioritized their courtship with the city's burgeoning international investment partners. Although Atlanta's hosting of the Organization of American States General Assembly served as the watershed moment in city hall's aggressive pivot toward internationalization in the early 1970s, the central city's established reputation across the globe as "foreign investor friendly" played a major role in Atlanta's globalization toward the end of the decade. According to the Southern Council on International and Public Affairs, the Organization of American States chose Atlanta to be the first American city to host the event outside Washington, DC, since 1962 because the city exhibited "very impressive ... international ambitions." With the Atlanta Chamber of Commerce's (ACOC) "leadership" and Coca-Cola's "lavish reception and international press" in the shopping center Underground Atlanta, Jackson's city hall assured investors of the city's unlimited potential as the convention trade, banking, and finance epicenter of the southern United States for decades to come.[3]

Consequently, Techwood residents alongside other low-income Black Atlantans begrudgingly faced the only logical outcome from encroaching privatization in their backyards. In fact, neoliberalization as urban policy in Black cities like Atlanta completely restructured the relationship between class, gender, labor, and power. This established a new racial formation—the New Nadir, discussed in depth in chapter 4—that retrenched the social conditions of working-class urbanites through the confiscation of public resources, specifically productive labor, social spaces, and affordable housing. More clearly, Atlanta Black leadership's targeted fragmentation of the Black Belt set the course for gentrification. Those Black residents who continued to fight the pro-growth direction of Atlanta faced brutal repression: surveillance, arrest, or eviction. Atlanta judge Grady Tittard accused Marian Green of "intimidating AHA employers with loud talk and cursing" for her leadership in the Techwood Homes movement. He sentenced Green to one year in prison and one year of probation.[4] Other Black antigentrification activists, such as Auburn Avenue residents, suffered a vicious misinformation campaign and subsequent displacement led by Coretta Scott King to transfer their land and homes to her burgeoning King Historic District area.

This chapter maps the extensive process that Atlanta elites undertook in the 1970s and 1980s to transfer the levers of power in the central city to international and domestic capital. Although previous scholars have discussed the internationalization of Atlanta from a cultural standpoint, most have overlooked the "sell" in neoliberalization—how the Black urban regime (BUR) collaborated with other state officials and the chamber of commerce, traveled domestically and overseas, and partitioned the spoils of class warfare to the highest bidder. Beginning with Maynard Jackson and culminating with Andrew Young, the BUR maintained a leading role in repurposing the land, labor, and social institutions necessary for working-class sustainability into new sites of financial and informational accumulation. With a well-funded and newly weaponized police force, the city's power brokers possessed a secure position to further destabilize the Black working-class sector of Atlanta without fear of the consistent rebellions at the point of production and beyond that plagued urban sites during the Black Power era. More clearly, the neoliberalization of Atlanta deregulated privatization of the public to further strain the Black worker's control of institutions.

Neoliberalization in urban America began with an assault on the worker by reducing the viability of the point of production. Once workers' bargaining power and subsequent purchasing power eroded over the late 1970s and 1980s, disproportionately disadvantaged blue-collar workers, like African Americans, gradually lost the capacity to challenge the destruction of productive labor that offered the best wage and job protection standards available. By replacing those spaces with financial, information, and nonunionized service-sector labor, capital shifted the power balance in Atlanta away from use value interests to maximize exchange value potential. By the end of Andrew Young's mayoralty, the power brokers never looked back as the central city became one of the most lucrative global spaces in a brief time span. By examining this hostile takeover of land and labor through a combination of macro- and microstructural analysis, this chapter sheds light on how gentrification, as a byproduct of neoliberalization, was initiated before the first bulldozer arrived in the neighborhood.

Where scholarly work often conceptualizes "neoliberalism" as a set of ideas severed from historical specificity, or at times as a label for a person or group who abides by these ideas, this chapter seeks to refocus how neoliberal political economy and its oppression of the working classes inform each other through a specific contestation over space, place, and power. In so doing, it points to the necessity of viewing gentrification as a historical process to properly account for its role in the racial oppression of African Americans in the history of the late twentieth and early twenty-first centuries.

A New Stage of Liberalism: Andrew Young and Neoliberalization

In September 1988, Atlanta mayor Andrew Young grandstanded in front of dozens of corporate executives at a National Press Club luncheon to celebrate Atlanta's fast climb to the top of the international market in less than a decade. His most notable claim was that his budding relationships with chairman of the US Federal Reserve Paul Volcker, Secretary of State George Schultz, and economist Arthur Burns—the chief theorists and engineers behind neoliberalization in the United States and the Augusto Pinochet coup in 1973 Chile—opened his eyes to the potential appeal of a privatized Atlanta to foreign capital. More clearly, Young languished about how a preoccupation with the "public" in Atlanta's political economy had exposed a weakness in early pro-growth efforts. "The failure is not the failure of the poor, but the failure of the rich," Young stated. "There is enormous wealth being generated, but there is no longer [a] disciplined framework."[5]

Young went on to scapegoat decreased federal spending to justify why he and other urban officials subsequently privatized vast amounts of land and institutions to international capital in the 1980s: "Look at what some of us have done as mayors. When money was pulled from us by the federal government and when state governments abandoned us, we had no choice but to find ways to give incentives to bring some of that money and apply it to our needs. . . . We brought in 200 Saudi businessmen who sit on the boards of major holding companies.... As a result, we have no problem selling bonds on the world money markets to almost any of our municipal projects."[6] In other words, the Andrew Young playbook aligned perfectly with a new phase of liberalism—one that alienated federal support and regulation and redistributed public space and resources to private interests for profit. According to Young, Atlanta generated over $52 billion from international capital over the previous five years, with $15 billion in 1987 alone. "The reason it [foreign capital] comes to Atlanta," Young noted, "is that we make it safe, and give the kind of governmental support . . . that gives [investors] . . . free of red tape."[7] The role of the BUR in this political economic transformation was to eliminate any potential regulation—legislative or grassroots resistance—that might be an impediment to privatization's conquest.

A brief investigation of neoliberalization as a *historical process* is necessary to understand how public and private forces (urban municipalities and business elites) form partnerships—informed by class interests—to determine the future of capital accumulation in urban redevelopment. First, neoliberalization derives from neoliberalism (*theory*)—the belief that the state must prioritize individual private property rights, the rule of law, and the institutions of freely functioning markets and free trade. What is crucial here is that proponents of neoliberalization legally regard corporations and businesses as "individuals." Thus, they contend that these same freedoms exercised by civilians must be extended to institutions and that their function within this framework of a free market is a fundamental "good" for society. Under this structure, urban power brokers believe that competition between individuals, firms, and territories (regions, nation-states, etc.) adheres to the "trickle-down theory"—the idea that the wealth and innovation of a few uplifts the entire population and eliminates poverty over time.[8]

In this structure, individual responsibility takes precedence. In so doing, neoliberalization is built on classic American narratives of individual bootstrapping as the way to success and moral failing as the root of anything that falls short. The deregulated market ensures freedom among its competing institutions, but individuals in society must be held responsible for their own welfare. Proponents of neoliberalization interpret individual loss or failure in capitalist virtues as personal weakness. In clearer terms, neoliberal theorists advocate that if individuals fail in a free market society, it is because of some intellectual or physical shortcoming, such as not investing enough in one's own human capital through education or having a fragile personality that keeps one from competing with a peer to move up in the corporate hierarchy.[9] As the BUR and its private investor partners in Atlanta championed poverty and inequality as personal weaknesses and failures, the power brokers normalized their belief in the *irrationality* of resistance and collective movements and the *rationality* of supervisory, individualized solutions to poverty such as nonprofit corporations and symbolic diversity.

Andrew Young's desire to move capital freely between sectors, regions, and nations demonstrated with vividness that neoliberals see global capital movement as a tool to simultaneously control problems (higher worker wages, power, and regulation because of social movements) and promote accumulation (low prices, monopolistic competition, higher productivity). Thus, the power structure of a neoliberal state surrenders sovereignty, state or popular, to the will of the global market. Noted economist Karl Polanyi pointed out the dialectics of "freedom" at the heart of neoliberal theory. Polanyi commented that two types of freedoms exist: the "good" freedoms—self-determination and democratic rights—and the "bad" freedoms—the freedom to exploit one's fellows, to make inordinate gains without commensurate service to the community, to keep technological innovations from being shared for public benefit, and to profit from public catastrophes engineered through private privilege. Also, Polanyi explained, "the market economy under which these freedoms throve also produced freedoms we prize highly. Freedom of conscience, freedom of association, freedom to choose one's own job." However, Polanyi concluded, the championing of private ownership as the essence of freedom counters these other potential freedoms. As a result, planning, control, and government are deemed the antithesis of freedom, and the freedoms the antithesis creates, such as welfare liberty and justice for all, are decried as "a camouflage of slavery." More specifically, the idea of freedom simply devolves into an advocacy for free enterprise for those whose material interests require no enhancement—and the good freedoms are lost under the authoritarianism that enforces the free market. Thus, the final component of neoliberalization, excess spending in military and police expansion, seeks to reinforce the futility in grassroots resistance and democracy and fear of violent state repression.[10]

The Golden Mile: The Atlanta Chamber of Commerce and the Early Push for International Capital

The archives tracing the historical process of neoliberalization in Atlanta are startlingly mundane, easily overlooked, but critical to the story of how power brokers consistently pillaged Black working-class communities for public resources. Scholars have generally disregarded chamber of commerce records and documents in investigating urban redevelopment and gentrification. These valuable sources provide succinct testimony to the predatory nature of the public-private partnership driving pro-growth reform. The ACOC, comprising executives from multinational corporations such as Coca-Cola and Marriott and real estate moguls like Tom Cousins (who developed much of the commercial real estate in the city, like the Omni International Hotel) and Herman J. Russell, played primary roles in fragmenting the Black working class by influencing and lobbying legislation, investing funds, conducting propaganda campaigns, and destabilizing working-class social movements.

Chamber of commerce records also allow us to reevaluate the scope of the city's disinterest in improving conditions for the African American majority. For example, many often credit Andrew Young with introducing international capital into the central city. However, chamber of commerce records, archival collections, and Black community sources like the *Atlanta Voice* and the *Great Speckled Bird* confirm that this process began much earlier. At a June 15, 1973, press conference, the ACOC laid out its pro-growth vision for Atlanta's future. The group sought rapid completion of the central city's tollway and expressway system, the construction of a second airport and the Georgia World Congress Center, and the consolidation of the Atlanta and Fulton County school systems. Although the ACOC had no comment on questions regarding neighborhoods or jobs, when pressed about community control of neighborhood services, it only recommended "new police precincts and jails." Maynard Jackson refused to critique the ACOC proposal and instead suggested that citizens provide input on the study and implementation of tollways and a new highway. However, this proved to be only lip service from Jackson, and as a result the ACOC locked out resident feedback. From this point on, it was clear that the ACOC held a monopoly on the direction of Atlanta.[11]

That same year, the ACOC launched its campaign to classify public housing as detrimental to the courtship of capital investment. In a June 15 press release the ACOC stated, "Low-income housing needs to be less concentrated in the central city." Additionally, Central Atlanta Progress (CAP)—the ACOC's regional planning and real estate development apparatus—sent a memorandum to James W. Henley, the AHA's director of development, titled "Atlanta's programs for public housing may be COUNTER PRODUCTIVE!" The memo expressed that public housing projects should be abandoned and Atlanta should "increase the supply of housing available to the low-income family within the City of Atlanta from the top down." In other words, the ACOC constructed a blueprint where more middle- and upper-income privatized housing gradually replaced public housing projects in Atlanta. This resulted in poor Black residents being pushed into poverty-stricken public housing "enclaves" strategically placed away from the Central Business District (CBD) or outside of city limits altogether. Thus, capital's goal of eradicating federally subsidized public housing from cities materialized as a decades-long process of destabilization at all levels of society.

Evidence suggests that the city's Black elite leadership cosigned and facilitated this early displacement. According to Research Atlanta, the US Department of Housing and Urban Development and the AHA built an estimated 2,000 subsidized public housing units to replace the 22,000 units torn down in the 1960s. Real estate developers built more middle- and upper-income housing, while the number of people on public housing waiting lists climbed into the thousands over the 1970s.[12]

The most powerful real estate tycoons in the ACOC headed CAP. John Portman, the architect who designed and built downtown Atlanta's Peachtree Center, served as president. Tom Cousins served as CAP's vice president. African American realtor William Calloway served as both the second vice president and the conduit between the white business community and the city's Black elite leadership. Harold Brockley, the chairman of Rich's and president of the ACOC, held CAP's third vice presidential position. The final officers, George S. Craft (treasurer) and Mills B. Lane (treasurer), controlled the largest Atlanta-area banks, Trust Company of Georgia and C&S Bank, respectively.[13]

The ACOC next influenced the creation of the aldermanic housing committee in the municipal government to "get to the low-income question from the top-down." Richard Fleming noted this strategy to the *Atlanta Voice* when he stated that "more and more business and government leaders ... are seeing the necessity of dispersing low-income housing throughout more affluent residential areas." The first targeted area, in the summer of 1973, was a seventy-eight-acre tract of Bedford Pine owned and operated by the AHA and bounded by Boulevard Drive on the east, Piedmont Avenue on the west, North Avenue on the north, and Stone Mountain Freeway on the south. Besides its access to multiple sectors of downtown, it also sat close to the Atlanta Civil Center—a new facility that had displaced the Black poor from the Buttermilk Bottoms neighborhood years earlier. The Bedford Pine neighborhood housed 4,000 residents, all working-class Black people, in 1,100 units.[14]

CAP partnered with the AHA and multiple private developers to set the guidelines for casting the Black worker off the land. They devised the stipulation for the land sale that included a guarantee of "500 moderate-, middle-,

Bedford Pine neighborhood, 1971. The *Great Speckled Bird*, September 6, 1971. Courtesy of the Atlanta Progressive Media Foundation / Georgia State University Library Special Collections and Archives.

and upper-income homes on 30 acres." The AHA also announced that rents for those units would start at $170 a month. Additionally, the AHA's requested sale price displayed how the agency's undermaintenance—combined with crime propaganda—had cheapened the Bedford Pine land and property to be given away. The AHA requested only $10 million, or $120,000 per acre. However, most estimates at that time valued Bedford Pine at $2 million per acre! The AHA initially sought to sell to Crow, Pope, and Land, one of the largest realtors in Atlanta at the time. The AHA claimed that Bedford Pine would double in value with a possible "World Trade Center" attraction, because it would be "a center for Atlanta and the rest of Georgia to show off products to foreign and national corporations at daily exhibitions and weekly conventions." The *Atlanta Journal* stated clearly that this World Trade Center would "make this area a focal point for international gatherings."[15] Although the planned center would become the Georgia World Congress Center soon, the planned pillaging of Bedford Pine on the cheap commenced the hunt for international capital in Black Atlanta.

CAP held little regard for the residents living in its targeted areas. In fact, Fleming said that CAP had already considered tearing down the other targeted sites, Techwood and Clark Howell public housing projects, before the area study was completed. CAP did not consider the projects to be in such disrepair at that point as to be condemned; rather, CAP felt that the affluent African Americans and whites it wanted to attract back to the central city would never live next to a public housing project—thus dooming Techwood and Clark Howell tenants. CAP dubbed this land "the Golden Mile," to mark the stretch of planned high-rise luxury housing that would ignite the takeover of Black Atlanta.[16]

Two months later, CAP's plans to tear down Techwood/Clark Howell leaked to the press. Subsidized by the federal government in 1935 as a by-product of New Deal funding, Techwood and Clark Howell originally housed white people. After the 1968 Fair Housing Act outlawed segregation in public housing, African Americans moved into the projects. The 600-acre Westside tract that housed the projects held a tremendous locational advantage for residents. It allowed residents to access each part of downtown effortlessly: it was bounded by North Avenue on the north, Spring Street on the east, I-20 on the south toward the metro suburbs, and Northside Drive on the west deeper into the cityscape. In short, residents had open, walking-distance access to downtown jobs and social life—a crucial component of the use value of the housing project.[17] Although the Techwood/Clark Howell demolition slowed until the Olympic era, capital maintained a voracious appetite for this area—when the timing was right.

As the public side of the pro-growth partnership, the Jackson administration expressed its allegiance to the ACOC's neoliberalization plan early. In December 1973, the board of aldermen approved a $45,000 contract for CAP to construct a housing plan for the region. CAP enlisted Philadelphia city planner Dan Crane—who held a notorious reputation for segregating Philadelphia neighborhoods—for its Bedford Pine redevelopment. According to Crane, CAP's private housing sought to entice middle- and upper-income whites by guaranteeing them a "safe enclave with buffers protecting them from Black Bedford Pine residents." This latest housing development contract demonstrated a clear conflict of interest as CAP privatized public lands while also acting as planners for the city. The lone alderman that objected to the purchases, white liberal Nick Lambros, argued that the deals compared to "my purchasing real property from the city and then, as alderman, voting to zone it for development." Lambros concluded that he opposed "developers working as planners for this city."[18]

CAP used petty bourgeois Black Atlantans to manipulate the locational advantage of Bedford Pine and leveraged pressure against the AHA. First, the organization "representing" the interests of Bedford Pine residents, the Policy Advisory Committee, consisted of four African American pastors and one white social worker. They initially refused to support the AHA plans. However, in July 1973, they did an about-face and signed a deal with the AHA to sell Bedford Pine to a developer who promised to build 100 low-income units alongside the other middle- and upper-income units. This deal amounted to nothing more than a sellout of the Black working class. First, the Policy Advisory Committee agreed to the rents for the "low"-income housing to range between $100 and $150 a month, making them unaffordable for virtually all working people. Second, the agreement greenlit the displacement of residents. Although the developer would construct 100 "low"-income units, 300 current low-income units still faced destruction to complete the renewal tract. On the books, this was illegal because laws prohibited developers from demolishing more low-income units than they constructed. Yet the Policy Advisory Committee still agreed to this. Finally, money for the petty bourgeois sealed the deal. The committee sold out the neighborhood residents for a $100,000 grant to oversee the design of the area.[19] Essentially, the AHA awarded the organization a large check to stand out of its way.

Although local officials stepped in to halt the deal, they only delayed it for a more favorable developer: CAP. CAP's winning bid for Bedford Pine was $3 million less than another competitor, Franklin L. Haney Company of Chattanooga. Haney sought to build the Georgia World Congress Center on the Bedford Pine land. However, CAP wanted to build the center on the west side with public funding near the Omni arena downtown. Thus, CAP's plan had the potential to reap more lucrative profits for the public-private partnership than the out-of-town Haney company, which did not possess the geographical strategy to maximize profits with its plan.[20]

The ACOC and CAP also implemented a spoils system to tighten their relationships with Black elected officials. First, CAP drafted Maynard Jackson's law firm partner, George Howell, to its board of directors. Next, AHA commissioner Michael Rich held the vice presidency of Rich's, the department store corporation chaired by CAP's president, Harold Brockley. CAP and the Atlanta Board of Education also struck a $200,000 deal in 1973 for the corporation to conduct a study of Atlanta Public Schools. Based on its findings, CAP expressed "deep concern with the image of Atlanta's public schools that exists in the minds of businesses and professional people who are thinking of moving to the city."[21] Additionally, all but four of the African American members of the Atlanta City Council received over $15,000 in cash contributions to their political campaigns from the ACOC.[22]

Never shying away from reciprocity, Atlanta city hall responded to its private partners accordingly. The city administration granted CAP the power to direct gentrification beyond the city limits into the surrounding metropolitan region. City hall funded $200,000 of the $250,000 needed for the Central Area Study, in which CAP and the US Department of Transportation outlined Atlanta's first phase of gentrification. While the study used abstract phrasing like "spiritually satisfactory milieu" to list objectives for redevelopment, the data clearly pointed to razing tens of thousands of poor residents out of the city. The report promoted adding an additional 160,000 parking spaces surrounding the central city and proposed spending $326.7 million over a twenty-five-year span to redevelop Atlanta's midtown and southeast areas. The study allocated $111.1 million for widening and extending existing streets and building new streets.[23]

Based on Atlanta's 1950s and 1960s urban renewal history—when the city destroyed 19,000 low-income housing units that left over 40,000 poor African Americans seeking shelter on housing waiting lists—many Black working-class residents recognized that their neighborhoods, schools, and social spaces lay in the path of bulldozers. One anonymous resident told the *Great Speckled Bird*, "Where will all the land for widening streets, building parking lots and freeways come from? People's homes mainly." When residents continued to challenge the Central Area Study at public hearings, the chamber of commerce soundly rejected public participation: "It's ridiculous for you people to ask us to change this plan or to call for a new study. This research cost us a quarter of a million dollars, and the only thing we can do now is hurry up and adopt it."[24]

What is revealing about this study, however, is that considering how the city promoted its "too busy to hate" racial harmony myth, extraordinarily little of the plan addressed the need to intervene in the spatial segregation that had enveloped Black working-class neighborhoods for decades. Expanded traffic capacity via the construction of more roads generally produced more traffic, because the more streets were widened, the more the local population was dispersed. Families needed more access to transportation to travel more and for longer distances to workplaces, stores, and schools. As a result, transportation reform linked with urban redevelopment threatened the use value of working-class neighborhoods, as more of a family's income was put into buying and maintaining automobiles and insurance and paying taxes for roads. Market failure also came into play. City hall disposed of pollution-inducing waste in poor Black neighborhoods like East Lake Meadows, Bedford Pine, and Vine City.

CAP also deployed its relationship with city hall to introduce tax increment financing (TIF) bonds to use public funds in bankrolling private investment.[25] Because TIF bonds are generally opaque, they usually reroute public funds to a different, more exploitative purpose and one that minimizes residents' decision-making power. In other words, the ACOC sought to implement TIF bonds as a long-term surplus-value-generating plan at the expense of the lowest-wage earners in the Atlanta metropolitan region.

Indeed, TIF bonds served as prime generators for the reconstruction of downtown Atlanta. In its June 1975 *Re/C.A.P.* newsletter, CAP targeted the poor neighborhoods south of Five Points (a white upper-income area) for its TIF plan. CAP outlined three major redevelopment goals for TIF: (1) a major revival of downtown retail (including the development of a major enclosed-mall regional shopping center along Alabama Street from Underground Atlanta to Omni International), (2) increased middle- and upper-income housing, and (3) a "downtown people mover" structure that connects major central business activity centers. CAP applied state constitutional power to exclude working-class residential opposition to TIF bonds. CAP's newsletter cited that section 2-5901 of the Georgia Constitution permitted "a city and/or county to contract to pay other public agencies and/or public corporations to provide services to the city and county where the parties to the contract have the power to do the function for which the services are being provided." In clearer terms, CAP disingenuously promoted its privatized redevelopment plan as "public services" so that the City of Atlanta would supply the power to both carry out revitalization and enforce a contract for repayment of the front-end debt for a fifty-year period. Additionally, CAP explicitly stated that its interpretation of the state constitution allowed it to bypass public consent in directing public funds to private interests. According to the group, the city, acting as the redevelopment agency, provided the investors with an assurance that they "can issue revenue bonds on the strength of Tax Increments without needing a referendum."[26] CAP's statements portrayed the ACOC as "benevolent pioneers" who righteously monopolized power because working-class input proved to be a nuisance. This element of TIF-directed gentrification allowed an endless money supply from public tax funds without the input or support of the residents whose living, working, and social spaces served as development sites.

The ACOC's public relations task was to sell Atlanta to international tourists, corporations, and entrepreneurs. In late 1975, newly elected chamber president Joel Goldberg, who also chaired Rich's, Inc., kick-started the "Talk Up, Atlanta" program, a multimedia advertising effort "designed to sell . . . Atlanta" and "remind people of the good things about Atlanta." The ACOC invested millions of dollars into the campaign with automobile bumper stickers, billboards, newspaper articles, television commercials, commissioned artwork, neighborhood canvassing, and radio spots. Nationally, chamber members spoke with Osbourne Elliot, editor of *Newsweek*, Jack White of *TIME* magazine, Austin Scott of the *Washington Post*, and Fred Powledge of the *Journal of American Institute of Architects*. To court the Black student population in the propaganda, the ACOC enlisted the Morehouse College Glee Club to do a special concert where the sixty-member group sang historically significant Georgia and Atlanta songs and a new "Talk Up, Atlanta" tune.[27]

These early pro-growth efforts expedited the desired results for Atlanta elites. The ACOC and Maynard Jackson's city hall reported that in 1975 they held extensive meetings with multiple international businesses interested in moving their headquarters to the central city. According to the ACOC's July 1975 briefing sheet, they negotiated with "a Swedish trade delegation, a group of British investors with potential $20 million to invest in Atlanta, another investor with $17 million potential investment in downtown, Arab consortium with $10 million to invest, and others." The mayor also met with a visiting French delegation and New York investors who invested $50 million in the city.[28]

International capital required a central hub that had locational advantage for the targeted revitalization sectors. Most important, the concourse needed to establish a base for the global finance economy to develop, expand, and circulate relationships, investments, and capital. Thus, Atlanta and Georgia leadership both introduced the idea of the Georgia World Congress Center (GWCC) in 1972 as a "too big to fail" investment. The state legislature appropriated $35 million for the project and designated it as tax exempt. Thus, much of the state footed the bill, which with added interest almost doubled the price of the center to $70 million. This added fuel to public outcry that the GWCC functioned as a private-use facility funded by public dollars. According to Atlanta attorney Frank Castellani, who sued the state over the development, not only would excess taxing burden Atlanta residents—typically through regressive options like sales taxes—but the GWCC had no legal requirement to invest its profits back into the communities. The center of Atlanta's global capital dreams emerged through a grifting of public goods.[29]

Additionally, the GWCC devastated the use value of Vine City and other low-income neighborhoods. Jackson's BUR closed off four downtown streets—Thurmond, Fuller, Foundry, and Hulsey—to construct the concourse. This closed off much of Vine City's and Regan Homes' access to the CBD and sealed the Black working class into an isolated enclave.[30]

When the GWCC opened its doors on September 9, 1976, it provided Atlanta elites their key justification for privatizing large swaths of the city for international investment. The ACOC endowed the facility with extravagant technology and space to stand out among other US international convention sites. The chamber viewed the $35 million plaza as the southeastern hub for the international market. According to CAP's 1975 GWCC opening press release, the center functioned simultaneously as a "convention, trade show, and international meeting facility." The center's 350,000-square-foot central room was the single largest exhibition room in the United States at the time. The ACOC equipped the additional twenty-two meeting rooms inside (70,000 square feet) and the 2,000-seat auditorium with "complete simultaneous interpretation/translation facilities," which enabled the center to accommodate large international meetings—making the GWCC the only space in the nation with such capabilities at the time.[31]

Atlanta's power structure regarded the GWCC's return potential for the metro region and Southeast as paradigm shifting. CAP estimated (and predicted correctly) that over 2 million visitors passed through the plaza each year. In its first two years, CAP expected the center to generate over $526 million for Atlanta's economy through attendance, state sales tax revenue, hotel-motel tax revenue, concessions, and international business migrating to the city. In its first year in operation, Atlanta hosted over 700 conventions and brought nearly 750,000 delegates to the metro region. This new revenue stream added $125 million to Atlanta's economy in 1976.[32]

As the GWCC exceeded expectations in not only profits and investors but also middle-class visitors seeking to build a new life in this new international city, only the Black working-class neighborhoods surrounding the CBD disrupted the pro-growth flow. In December 1976, CAP and Mayor Jackson held a special investors group gala, where they presented the top US companies—whose combined investment in the city by that time totaled $1.5 billion—with a sweeping neighborhood revitalization plan documenting the new market for growing professional- and managerial-class people moving into the central city. As a result of the construction of new middle- and upper-income housing in the northeast part of the city, the ACOC promoted new office parks and retail shops, dubbed "Peachtree Walk," that would be built adjacent to Virginia-Highlands, Ansley Park, and other gentrifying northeast neighborhoods. Other sites targeted for gentrification at that time included West End, where city officials took real estate appraisers from the Atlanta Mortgage Consortium on a residential bus tour and documented rehabilitation strategies.[33] West End's revitalization removed crucial resources from the area for working-class Blacks, particularly access to fresh-food grocery stores.

"Eating Uncle Niger": Atlanta's Overseas Recruitment of Capital

Although domestic recruitment of international investment reaped major results early, the Atlanta power structure sought more direct relationships with foreign capital by spending critical time and public funds overseas. The first known international trip by Atlanta's private-public partnership can be traced to Maynard Jackson's BUR in 1978. ACOC records show that the chamber's first Black president, Jesse Hill Jr., joined US president Jimmy Carter on a trade mission to Nigeria that year. While there, Hill established a business network with over a dozen Nigerian capitalists and worked with Jackson to coordinate a "major private sector economic mission from Nigeria to Atlanta" from Sunday, June 25, to Wednesday, June 28, that same year. Twenty-seven top Nigerian business leaders made the journey to Atlanta and held meetings with multiple local business executives focusing on the textile manufacturing, agriculture, maritime shipping, telecommunications, hotel management, beer and soft drink production, water treatment, hospital and medical supplies, food processing, legal services, and construction sectors of labor. Chief Dotun Okunbanjo, the president of the Lagos Nigerian-American Chamber of Commerce and mission leader, emphasized the desire to establish agriculture ventures because of the demand in his home country. "Instead of eating Uncle Ben's [rice]," Okunbanjo stated to over 100 Atlanta businesspeople, "we should be eating Uncle Niger."[34]

In November of the following year, Jackson and the ACOC upped the ante and hauled dozens of Atlanta metro capitalists, southeastern state governors, and various regional business executives to China and Japan for ten days of investor recruitment. The American group hosted an all-day "Georgia Investment Seminar" at the Okura Hotel in Tokyo on November 7, with over 100 Japanese capitalists in attendance. Both the ACOC and Kajima International, Tokyo's equivalent to a chamber of commerce, presented their respective political economies. The ACOC highlighted the antiunion right-to-work law in Georgia in its pitch to entice Japanese firms. The following day, Tokyo hosted the Japan-US Southeast Conference at the Imperial Hotel, where US state governors of Alabama, Georgia, Florida, North Carolina, South Carolina, Tennessee, and Virginia delivered pitches for Japanese investment in their respective states. Georgia governor George Busbee stood out among his peers in his international recruitment experience. He took numerous trips to multiple European and Asian nations to promote foreign investment in the Atlanta metro region and even formed a Japan–southeastern United States free trade association. He often promoted his goal that "Atlanta-area counties could work together to sell the urban region to out-of-state business executives."[35]

Jackson also recruited capital in West Germany during the final year of his second tenure. According to Jackson's personal records, between May 30 and June 2, 1980, he met with "Dr. Jordan, President of the German American Chamber of Commerce," and "various business interests in Germany." Jackson visited governments and capitalists in three cities—Frankfurt, Heidelberg, and Munich—to maximize German business profit for Atlanta's growing convention trade.[36]

It is safe to assume that Jackson and Atlanta elites wanted their international recruitment trips shrouded in secrecy. No local or national media outlet reported on this trip, and Atlanta city hall did not speak of the trip on returning to Atlanta. Additionally, these trips occurred during Atlanta's revenue crisis and the Atlanta child murders. It is possible to ascertain that Atlanta's ruling class traveled in secrecy because they sought to avoid the obvious contradiction of their expensive trips during an economic depression and social crisis in the city.

Andrew Young's election to the Atlanta mayoralty in 1981 amplified the neoliberal potential of Atlanta capital and the loss of public resources for Black working-class urbanites in two specific ways. First, Young's travels to 122 nations as US ambassador under President Jimmy Carter built lucrative corporate networks with multiple international businesses. In effect, Atlanta elites knew that they were getting a cache of international and private resources exponentially greater than Maynard Jackson's reach. Second, Young's mentor as ambassador and later mayor, George Schultz, had served as a key pioneer of Ronald Reagan's foreign policy of neoliberalization and anticommunist and antiunion repression in multiple nations. Therefore, Young not only knew how to accrue surplus profits but also understood how to discipline the worker under the guise of "progress."

Young's controversial history in the international oil business sheds light on his reputation as a "crony capitalist." Investigation by the *New York Times* and independent journalists discovered that when Young served as UN ambassador between 1977 and 1979, he met and built a business relationship with Nigerian president Olusegun Obasanjo, a CIA-installed operative who came to power with a US-backed military coup in February 1976. "Obasanjo and I kind of hit it off immediately," Young stated to the *New York Times*. "We were mainly interested in democracy." The truth is that the United States had attempted to annex Nigeria's oil reserves using Obasanjo and Young after the OPEC oil embargo damaged the American monopoly over global oil. The *International Herald Tribune* reported that Obasanjo "monopolized power the day he entered office," kept "the oil portfolio for himself," and used "Nigeria's vast oil wealth for political ends."[37]

When Andrew Young returned to the city where he had gained notoriety for his involvement with the Southern Christian Leadership Conference during the civil rights movement and his role as a community "liaison" with the Atlanta Community Relations Commission, he bombarded Black working-class Atlanta with foreign capital the likes of which had never been witnessed before. European and Kuwaiti dollars helped complete the two bastions of the new international character of the city: the Omni International (CNN Center) and the Atlanta Center (Hilton Hotel and Tower). The Netherlands and Saudi Arabia purchased two major downtown Atlanta institutions, Life of Georgia and the National Bank of Georgia, respectively. Atlanta real estate's long-term manipulation of urban land rents—through blight, city policies that expanded the underground economy in poor Black neighborhoods, and purposeful neglect of housing repairs—gave international financial institutions unregulated paths to build headquarters in the central city. In fact, the world's twenty largest banks at the time built branches in the CBD. By 1984, international capital had poured over $3 billion into private metro Atlanta companies. According to Charles Rutheiser, foreign capital in 1984 Atlanta broke down like this: one-third of all foreign investment derived from Canadian capitalists, $500 million from British and Dutch companies each, $400 million from Japanese companies, and $109 million from German businesses. By that same year, foreign companies in Atlanta totaled over 780, with 240 being the US headquarters for those firms. By 1990, that number had exploded to over 7,800 foreign companies in the Atlanta metro region![38]

Mayor Young continued the Atlanta power structure's practice of recruitment abroad to the extent that Atlanta residents nicknamed him the "absentee mayor." One such trip that captured notoriety occurred on April 17, 1985, when Young accompanied African American Fulton County commissioner Michael Lomax, African American Atlanta City Council president Marvin Arrington, and 100 ACOC members to Paris to "sell Atlanta," according to

ACOC vice president Gerald L. Bartels. "If Atlanta is truly to be all together better," Bartels continued, "it is vital we foster strong ties in the international marketplace." The weeklong trek attempted to lure close to fifty French businesses to the metro region to join the other sixty there at the time. Young also spearheaded the growth of Australian capital in the metro region. Between 1984 and 1988, Australian businesses doubled from eighteen to thirty-eight. There were 3,270 employees working in Australian Atlanta-based companies in 1988, with eight firms serving as US headquarters. Young participated in the signing of a treaty between the United States and Australia that established increased international flights between the nations. Young also opened negotiations with the US Department of Transportation to determine direct air service routes from Atlanta to Australia—creating more convenience for Australian capital to privatize the Atlanta metropolitan region leading up to the Olympics era.[39]

Young's deep connections with oil helped him maintain ties with South Africa during the anti-apartheid movement. As the *Great Speckled Bird* reported, the most alarming part is that many of the South African businesses that had headquarters in Atlanta at that time worked closely with the South African military and police forces "in supplying oil and oil products, in promoting and providing loans and assisting the racist regime in its plan to withstand sanctions." To understand the magnitude of this relationship, Atlanta graciously housed the following corporations in 1984: Barclay's Bank International, which controlled 25 percent of the South African banking sector; Control Data Corporation, one of the largest suppliers of computers for the South African police; and Brown Boveri Electric, which managed nuclear power and transport.[40] Simply put, Atlanta's revitalization, or the destruction of working-class Black urbanites, upheld a nefarious diaspora with its South African counterpart in circulating the machinations—profit, weapons, and repressive anti-Black-working-class policies—in the domination of an oppressed class.

By 1987, seventy major metro area commercial real estate properties were operated through international capital. Dutch, British, Canadian, and German businesses accounted for three-fourths of that total, while Korean, Indian, Saudi, and Taiwanese capital entered the market on a smaller scale. Japanese capitalists also made a splash in Atlanta real estate that year with the $300 million purchase of the One Atlantic Center in upper midtown, better known as the IBM Building. They also constructed multiple banks, insurance companies, and pension funds that generated nearly $1 billion for CBD real estate alone.[41]

Domestic capital also wanted a piece of Atlanta's newly privatized pie. US insurance companies like Equitable Life Assurance and Metropolitan Life Insurance set up offices across the northeast and northwest sections of the city. Real estate developers also took advantage of the cheapened land and the rebounding stock market with real estate investment trusts (REITs).[42] REITs especially thrived in Atlanta because, in the 1980s, the AHA and the Andrew Young administration filled the area with an array of cheap land and low-income housing stock for purchase. The AHA sold public housing properties while the bourgeoisie and petty bourgeoisie provided a demand for a boom in office parks, shopping centers, and middle- and upper-income housing in the region. With REITs, the lower the price for which shareholders buy land and property, the higher the dividend yield (dividends stay the same regardless of share price, so if shareholders can buy the shares cheaper, they obtain a higher percentage). Additionally, REITs expanded with stabilized, moderately low interest rates after the economic crises of the 1970s. Thus, corporations established REITs through the office space construction boom and middle- and upper-income housing boom at the time because they both provided stable rents for REIT shareholders. Because of this, Atlanta became one of the national leaders in REITs, with five trusts that ranked among the largest: Great American Mortgage Investors, Citizens and Southern Realty Investors, Cousins Mortgage and Equity Investments, Tri-South Mortgage Investors, and Atlanta National Real Estate Trust.[43]

The opening of the newly expanded $400 million Hartsfield International Airport on September 21, 1980, facilitated easy access and circulation of capital, consumers, and labor across the globe with Atlanta as a central hub. As the largest employer in the city with an estimated 35,000 employees, the airport easily managed the flow of over 60 million passengers in its first years of operation. Alongside passengers, the international airport shuttled an estimated 115,000 tons of mail and 220,000 tons of freight. The airport's primary architects emphasized that this airport relieved "the present rush-hour crowds, landing delays, taxiing to distant gates, waiting for gates to be free to accept planes or passengers . . . in spite of . . . 100% increase in traffic."[44] Hartsfield acts as the major hub of Atlanta-based Delta Air Lines and ensured that most international flyers changed planes at least once in Atlanta. Concourse E, as the largest terminal in the United States, is dedicated exclusively to international travel and scheduled twenty-four-hour nonstop service to Mexico City, London, Brussels, and Amsterdam. Upon its opening, the Hartsfield airport provided nonstop service to 110 cities and one-stop service to forty-four cities.[45]

Atlanta businesses took full advantage of the airport's expansion to maximize accumulation. In its first year, Concourse E had increased Hartsfield's international traveler base by 385 percent since 1973. This increase not only positioned Atlanta as number two in the nation for foreign travel, but it also sped up the region's tourism profits. Over three-fourths of the 700,000 convention goers in Atlanta arrived from foreign nations.[46]

Georgia businesses also organized multiple events to tap lucrative overseas markets. On February 11, 1983, the GWCC hosted Matchmaker '83, where statewide capitalists met with export management companies to strengthen trade ties between metro region business and global commodity markets. The University of Georgia's International Trade Development Center hosted the expo and emphasized "opening the free global market" through "simple promotion of products overseas or foreign exporters handling domestic products." The Atlanta-based M&M Products, an African American hair care company, offshored its production to Jamaica in 1983. M&M president Cornell McBride praised the move as "a giant leap in international marketing" during a trade and business recruitment trip in Kingston headed by Mayor Andrew Young and the ACOC.[47]

The Black Great Depression in Atlanta and the United States

This flourishing of international capital operated in a dialectic with the devastation of the socioeconomic conditions of most people living in the United States—a disproportionate number of them African Americans. As scholars Joseph Heathcott and Jefferson Cowie argued, "Neoliberalization and the resulting deindustrialization and displacement was not a story of a single emblematic place or a specific time period, such as the 1970s and 1980s." Rather, what scholars labeled *deindustrialization* was a much more "socially complicated, historically deep, geographically diverse and political perplexing phenomenon."[48] In other words, the social costs of processes like neoliberalization and the resulting displacement and gentrification are more accurately conceptualized as a structurally violent process against the productive forces within the working classes.[49] As colonized subjects, Black workers' extractive relationship to the dominant class shifted toward a much more fragile position. The fragmentation of the Black working class emerged, primarily, from the fragmentation and extermination of labor power of the Black worker. The dismantling of productive labor facilitated the precarity of the Black working class under gentrification.

Atlanta's position as the dominant wholesale and retail trade and distribution center in the Southeast meant that manufacturing was not dominant in the metro region. With only three major automobile manufacturing plants in the area, manufacturing accounted for only 14.5 percent of labor in 1980. Across Sun Belt cities, most manufacturers located their plants outside of urban spaces to take advantage of lower wage rates and lack of a union presence. Thus, the General Motors automobile plants located in Lakewood, Doraville, and Hapeville served as outliers and beneficial resources to poor Atlantans. Textile industrial work in the Southeast also dropped considerably at this time. The US Bureau of Labor Statistics reported that employment in the Southeast during the first quarter of 1986 averaged 481,500, down 1,600 jobs from the fourth quarter of 1985 and down 9,300 jobs from the first quarter of 1985. In fact, between 1973 and 1986, textile labor dropped 29 percent. Georgia outpaced other states in the region in textile jobs lost. The Labor Bureau concluded that overseas production and automation had displaced textile workers at a faster pace than normal.[50]

The declining political economy menaced autoworkers especially, one of the most powerful groups at the point of production for African American collective organizing. In March 1974, the big three automakers announced layoffs for 200,000 of their workforce across the United States. The Atlanta auto giants—which had produced their largest inventory in history (765,000 automobiles in 1973)—slashed production and jobs, closed multiple plants, and retooled mass production toward smaller vehicles that used marginally less gasoline. Although most highlight unemployment as the primary indicator of the devastation of the Black worker, labor instability and underemployment also hurt the viability of community stability and power. That year, the two General Motors plants in metro Atlanta, in Doraville and Lakewood—which manufactured large Chevrolet and Pontiac models—laid off an estimated 3,000 workers each. In an interview with the *Great Speckled Bird*, Ruth, an African American autoworker who had received her pink slip earlier that year, expressed the frustration that Black women workers felt at the instability of their jobs: "I was in the paint department on the passenger car side. I'd been there fifteen months. There were 749 people laid off. . . . They hired maybe sixty people back. That leave more than two hundred people before they get back to me." In fact, the layoffs hit Black women the hardest. Manufacturing companies only started hiring Black women workers and in small numbers in the early 1970s. "We don't have much seniority and we get laid off first. When they do start rehiring, if they ever do, they will rehire who they want to," said Nancy, a laid-off African American autoworker. "And I think it will be the minimum of Black and the minimum of women," she further claimed. Vicki, another Black autoworker added, "We are without work. We're not gonna have money, we're going to be forced into that situation without food and maybe without clothing. It's a bad situation." Nancy saw this devastation as a potential opportunity: "But this can also bring people together.... We have to do something, and I think it's going to cause unification of the laborer. It has to."[51] Nancy's astute analysis rang true as the correlation between the skyrocketing of Black unemployment and the loss of collective Black social movement organizing cannot be neglected.

The bleeding worsened as hundreds more Atlanta-area autoworkers found themselves stuck in a revolving door of layoffs, factory restructuring, downsizing, or market decline—all adding instability to their lives. After years of unstable production, the Doraville plant closed for most of 1981. The few hourly workers who remained in the plant brought in a meager $9.63 an hour plus a $1.79 cost-of-living adjustment for a total average of $456.80 a week ($23,753.60 a year before taxes). More layoffs followed throughout the 1980s, especially in 1989 when the Doraville plant fired 1,900 workers. While the Doraville plant did not officially close until 2008, the constant reshuffling of duties, layoffs, and closings severely disrupted the economic and social stability of Black working-class Atlantans. In 1990, though, the sixty-two-year-old Lakewood plant shut down, casting 3,200 workers into unemployment. General Motors questionably claimed that it fired thousands of workers and closed one of the only lucrative blue-collar union sites in metro Atlanta because it wanted to make those auto parts in a more modern factory.[52]

This severely undercut the capacity of Black workers to find equally good jobs in the metro area. By the end of 1991, the Doraville plant had spent about $750 million a year in Atlanta, contributing roughly 1.25 percent of the metro area's gross regional product.[53] Therefore, the loss of production and workers depleted the capacity for the creation of well-paying, productive jobs. Combined with neoliberalization, capital mounted countless obstacles against the Black worker.

The Devalorization Cycle and Gentrification

For the first five months of 1984, African American Mary Hill (a pseudonym) woke her five children up to no water or plumbing fixtures in their $360-per-month DeKalb County house in southeast Atlanta. The City of Atlanta cut off her water in late December because the inadequate plumbing had sent water spewing into the street. When a plumber finally arrived in early January, he removed the toilet, sink, bathtub, and all the pipes and never returned to replace them. By late January, rats and opossums entered Hill's apartment frequently through the gaping holes in the bathroom floor. Despite Hill's efforts through the proper channels, including frequent phone calls, a lawsuit, and a citation, the landlord refused to repair the apartment. Legal Aid filed a $20,000 lawsuit on Hill's behalf, while the Bureau of Buildings inspected and issued a citation directly to the landlord. Hill expressed frustration about the neglect and about how she had to rely on neighborhood resources to survive:

> It's unbelievable what's been happening to me ... living like this in the city of Atlanta. Since January ... me and my five children have been using a bucket and digging holes in the back yard to bury our waste. We've been bringing in jugs of water for cooling and bathing at relatives' houses. We've been getting sick all winter, especially me and the baby that's here all the time.... Then in December the sewage started coming back up in the bathtub and sink. My daughter went to wash up one morning and came back out crying.[54]

Hill, like so many other tenants renting from landlords, did not have access to better housing. Because she was a Section 8 recipient, many landlords refused to accept her subsidy certificate. Additionally, because of her five children, she had difficulty finding a four-bedroom house for the maximum $361 a month that the AHA was willing to spend for her voucher. In many cases like this, Section 8 terminated the assisted payment because of unfit housing conditions. However, this placed an even greater burden on poor tenants because it immediately evicted any occupants from the dwellings and forced them to seek shelter among the low housing stock available. This typically put them back on the 10,000-plus waiting list for housing.

Like most poor Black urbanites in her predicament, Hill leaned on her neighborhood kinship network for support. Neighbors shared water and plumbing with her family, carpooled with her, and exchanged services. Whenever Hill's pipes froze, her neighbor repaired them, and she returned the favor by cooking dinners for their families. Last, thanks to the *Great Speckled Bird*'s deep investigation and publicizing of Hill's crisis, it reached Interfaith, a fair housing organization in Atlanta. The group successfully found a house for Hill's family that met the Section 8 housing quality standards.[55] Thus, Hill's case demonstrated how poor Black urbanites used their informal kinship networks and other community resources to fight neoliberalization in housing.

Hill's case also demonstrates how land and property *devalorization* produced gentrification, which proved to be a more difficult consequence of internal neocolonialism to counter. Hill's landlord engaged in a widespread practice in which property owners in an area undergoing gentrification purposely devalorized their property. Many property owners during gentrification favored undermaintenance for two reasons. First, Georgia's "repair and deduct" statute gave tenants the right to deduct the cost of repairs from their rent payments if landlords did not rehabilitate within a reasonable period. However, urban landlords preyed on Section 8 residents because city housing authorities like the AHA continued to pay the rent for Section 8 residents under a housing assistance payment contract. In other words, landlords accrued profits by forgoing the cost of rehabilitation. Second, devalorization freed capital that could be invested in other properties in the city or suburbs. Additionally, under Neil Smith's devalorization cycle framework, if undermaintenance progresses throughout a neighborhood, landlords lose even more incentive to repair dilapidated housing, and the area experiences a net outflow of capital.[56]

Smith correctly noted that undermaintenance also leads to active disinvestment as capital depreciates and the landlord's stakes diminish further. This prompts financial institutions to also disinvest in the area through redlining. As a result, banks deny loans to Black and brown working-class people seeking home ownership in the devalorized area. The final group to disinvest, homeowner insurance companies, also redlines the neighborhood, ending all incentive for repair and maintenance. Next, real estate encourages local government to designate the neighborhood as blighted. To accomplish this, as discussed in chapter 2, urban municipalities manipulate the political economy of crime to simultaneously expand the underground economy in the neighborhood—by containing and allowing the distribution and competition for drug sales and the black market for stolen goods—and propagandize negative pathologies of the neighborhood residents. This causes the property value to plummet in a comparable way to undermaintenance, except that the former turns the public against the oppressed group and gives the pro-growth coalition the leverage to displace residents to "stop crime and poverty and make the city safer." An early example of this occurred in Bankhead Courts, a public housing project that sat on the very edge of the central city and bordered Cobb County. The predominantly low-income Black neighborhood's locational disadvantage made it one of the most vulnerable communities in the city. It contained only one entrance, through Bankhead Highway, and wooded areas and open fields separated the residents from every grocery store, school, and hospital in the city. In other words, Bankhead Courts resembled an archaic colony outside the wealth of modernizing Atlanta.[57]

In late summer and early fall of 1974, the Atlanta police and mainstream city newspapers concocted a flurry of stories regarding "roving bands" of "marauding youths" committing violence in "unprovoked incidents" like it was the inspiration for the film *The Warriors* (1979). Mayor Maynard Jackson exacerbated this crime mass hysteria by inviting his detailed security force to live with him in Bankhead Courts for a weekend to prove to the resource-deprived residents that the neighborhood was safe. Ironically, when the community organization Atlanta Anti-Repression Coalition investigated the incidents, they concluded that the police incited more violence than any residents. Some residents reported that they witnessed police attacking children when the officers set up blockades and cut off emergency services to the neighborhood.[58] Indeed, Jackson more than likely was genuinely appalled at the inhumane conditions of Bankhead Courts. However, his bourgeois liberal class interests determined that his solution lay in the hands of capital and revitalization instead of in building Black social institutions like fully funded schools, grocery stores, community centers, and hospitals in the neighborhood to increase the use value and power of Black Bankhead Courts residents.

In the Bankhead Courts episode, media and city officials focused on vandalism as a major problem. During most gentrification, landlords typically welcome vandalism because it further devalorizes property. After a brief period, landlords themselves disinvest totally from their properties, only paying the necessary costs that generate rents until they abandon the properties when they can longer collect enough rent to cover the necessary costs.[59]

As Neil Smith posited, landlords abandon properties in a neighborhood on a wide scale. The properties are generally structurally sound, but because they no longer yield surplus value, landlords deem them infeasible and, in many cases, destroy them. For example, landlords abandoned the Techwood and Clark Howell Homes housing projects in southeast Atlanta, co-opted their tenants organizations when they began protesting devalorization, then displaced the residents before demolishing the buildings.[60] Gentrification generally commences following such devalorization. However, as Smith concluded, devalorization is not an organic or inelastic process—meaning that gentrification does occur at times without devalorization.[61]

It is worth noting how the state's participation in devalorization affects poor urbanites. By assembling properties at a "fair market value" and returning them to developers at the lower assessed price, the state pays the costs of the last stages of devalorization, thereby ensuring that developers can reap the high returns.[62] For example, Atlanta's revenue crisis at the end of the 1970s resulted from city hall and Fulton County's appraisal of city real estate at lower assessed prices. Thus, the City of Atlanta and Fulton County lost millions in tax revenue, debt spiraled out of control, and Mayor Maynard Jackson sought to alleviate the negligence by taxing commodities that disproportionately affected the income of the working classes. In other words, devalorization both directly and indirectly regressed the social conditions of working-class Black Atlantans.

To understand why this benefits gentrification, it is appropriate to conceptualize how property is devalorized from use compared to its rate of *revalorization* when value is added during the gentrification process. In clearer terms, the sale price of a property represents not only the *value* of the house but also *rent* on the land. Karl Marx contended that *ground rent* is the claim made by landlords on tenants of their land. Thus, ground rent is a reduction from the profit created over and above cost. *Capitalized ground rent*, however, is the actual amount of ground rent that the landowner receives based on land use. For rental units, the landlord produces a service on land that he owns, and the landlord's capitalized ground rent returns mainly in the form of rent paid by tenants. For instance, landlords in Atlanta have typically added amenities like garbage collection or, more recently, physical fitness centers for their residents to use at an additional cost built into the rent payment. On the other hand, with homes, ground rent is capitalized only when property is sold and therefore appears as part of the sale price. This equation sums up Marx's conceptualization of sale price:

SALE PRICE = HOUSE VALUE + CAPITALIZED GROUND RENT

When we apply this framework to urban neighborhoods undergoing gentrification, we observe how landlords with property that holds locational advantage possess the ability to obtain higher capitalized ground rent if the land is used in a different, "better" manner. Specifically, this *potential ground rent* is the amount that could be capitalized under the land's highest or "best" use.[63]

Additionally, landlords manipulated urban rents to accrue greater profits based on a newly favorable locational advantage. By the 1980s, Atlanta real estate moguls recognized the effects of neoliberalization in the area: construction of luxury commercial properties, middle- and upper-income families moving to the redeveloped Southeast, and international capital buying land and revitalizing it into lucrative financial sector businesses. As a result, landlords accumulated higher extensive differential rent by raising rents on housing near the newly renovated GWCC, Georgia State University, and Underground Atlanta shopping center. Thus the neoliberal push in Atlanta facilitated the manipulation of urban rents by building extravagant beacons of international capital next to working-class neighborhoods—pushing low-income residents out of the area.

"Kicked Out with Nothing": Coretta Scott King and the Grand Larceny of Auburn Avenue

One glaring episode of how Atlanta elites gradually gentrified an area through rent manipulation and outright grand larceny occurred with Black Auburn Avenue residents in the 1980s. Unfortunately, these entities followed a disturbing trend of preying on the most viable Black spaces in Atlanta. Once dubbed the "richest Black street in the world," Auburn Avenue became the social and commercial epicenter of Black Atlanta by the 1920s. In fact, after the Atlanta pogrom of 1906, white Atlantans waged a violent assault on Black businesses and homes in downtown Atlanta and pushed all Black enterprise east of the white downtown business district. However, in the 1950s, the federal government built the Northeast Expressway and South Expressway through Georgia and elected to construct a highway connector, Georgia Route 295, through the city of Atlanta. This early urban renewal, known as "Negro removal" at the time, displaced two Black streets in the Sweet Auburn neighborhood—Techwood Drive and Williams Street. Most crucially, the project destroyed street grids east and south of downtown, which divided Auburn Avenue into two parts, and the interchange with I-20 leveled a sizable portion of the Washington-Rawson District.[64] This eliminated the Black business and residential base in the area. Combined with the malignant neglect and uneven development, Auburn Avenue transformed into a poverty enclave by the 1970s.

In 1980, Congress declared Auburn Avenue a historic district, which placed twenty-three acres of homes under eminent domain—all of the neighborhood except Ebenezer Church, the King Center, and all property owned by Coretta Scott King. Auburn Avenue activist Florence McKinley did not hold back her prophetic condemnation of the eminent domain scheme being used to throw Black workers out of the area: "It looks like this was done not to commemorate Dr. King, but to take some land," McKinley explained. "Take some land that in five, six, seven years is going to be very valuable. Everyone is going to make some money from tourism ... but the Black folks who had a part in making Dr. Martin Luther King who he was are going to be kicked out. Not only that, they are going to be kicked out with nothing. The King Center is leading this onslaught in this community."[65]

The secret plot against the Auburn Avenue residents was so vile that even some members of the Black petty bourgeoisie threatened to revolt against the revitalization. In a stunning revelation, Maynard Jackson—under the guidance of Coretta Scott King and without telling his city council—covertly flew to Washington, DC, in mid-1980 to deliver testimony to a US House subcommittee to propose turning Auburn Avenue into a Martin Luther King Jr. national park.[66] When the council called him out, Jackson urged his BUR to support his proposal, igniting a partnership with Coretta Scott King in exploiting Dr. King's legacy for new sites of accumulation in Atlanta.

The aggressive nature of the extraction of Black residents from their own Auburn Avenue neighborhood exposes how the bourgeoisie and petty bourgeoisie lacked respect for their working-class counterparts. After Georgia Power and Georgia Pacific sponsored a study of the property value, vacant lots, tax properties, and types of businesses that resided in the area, Jackson formed his gentrification squad: the Urban Design Commission, CAP, the National Park Service, Coretta Scott King and the King Center, and other major investors. According to a bombshell interview conducted by the *Great Speckled Bird* with Auburn Avenue activist Johnny Wilson, this pro-growth coalition, especially Coretta Scott King as ringleader, purposely misled residents regarding their potential role in a much more business-driven neighborhood. As a result, Black Auburn Avenue residents, who believed they would not only maintain power over their properties but also bring money into their community, followed King's instructions to go to the city council and request that the area be rezoned from residential to mixed commercial and residential. Black preachers who worked with King served as co-conspirators to this fraud when they supplied vans and buses to transport residents to the council meetings.[67]

Unbeknownst to the residents, after the Atlanta City Council unanimously approved the rezoning, King chose developers, architects, and other allies to collect money to do nothing other than oversee a study to build a hotel in the neighborhood. A year later, King herself received $3.2 million to develop the King Community Center. The most damning revelation from Wilson is that King took $85,000 of money from a housing community development grant for building low-income housing in Atlanta to instead build a swimming pool and auditorium for her center. Other Black elites—including Hosea Williams, who used his troubling endorsement of Ronald Reagan for president to attack

King—constantly berated her for "using government funds to build a monument to her husband instead of feeding the hungry."[68]

Additionally, King obtained the ownership of the neighborhood's homes, which gave her the power to displace residents when she saw fit. One elderly woman, seventy-nine-year-old Sally Glanton, had lived next door to Martin Luther King Jr.'s birth home since 1961. The owner of the home passed away, and Glanton's neighbors believed that the owner had left the house to her. However, as McKinley suggested, the transaction may not have been on paper and therefore ownership reverted to Coretta Scott King, who attempted to send Glanton out of Auburn Avenue into an apartment on Bradley Street. In an obvious attempt to coerce Glanton out of the house, King did not spend the $35,000 allocated to repairing the home on any much-needed maintenance. "What was put into this house?" Glanton said to McKinley. "They didn't put anything in here!" African American Auburn Avenue councilman and future mayor Bill Campbell refused to respond to McKinley's and Wilson's requests to investigate this process and halt the displacement.[69]

For forty-five years, eighty-one-year-old Alma Gibson worked at Scripto and collected a one-dollar-an-hour salary, participated in community activism, and raised one child and grandchildren at 491 Auburn Avenue. In September 1986, Coretta Scott King gathered her forces from the King Center, the National Park Service, and Andrew Young's BUR to displace Gibson and her Black working-class neighbors. Gibson resided in a locationally advantageous property behind the King Center—one of the most lucrative tourist attractions in the city. Additionally, the National Park Service owned five renovated houses near Gibson's residence. Her house, on the other hand, resembled a shanty. The owner, Mr. Bradberry, paid little for the dilapidated house and refused to maintain it. However, in August, he raised Gibson's rent from $130 to $330 per month, requiring her to pay it or face eviction. Other houses in her neighborhood received similar notices that month. Gibson's neighbors organized an investigation and discovered that Gibson's eviction carried profitable potential for Bradberry. According to the residents, the Martin Luther King Jr. birthplace site had just begun redevelopment, so the owner of Gibson's house could receive lucrative grants to restore the land and property for tours through the neighborhood.[70]

Strengthened laws protecting private property allowed landowners like Bradberry to exploit tenants. Because he owned the property, he had no responsibility to repair it while tenants resided there. However, Bradberry followed in the footsteps of the National Park Service—which had an all-Black administration in its Atlanta office. Years earlier, the service had blighted the houses it owned, evicted the tenants through rent manipulation, and refurbished the abandoned properties for higher extensive differential rent accumulation. As a result of the higher rents, working-class African Americans who had lived in a neighborhood for decades like Gibson no longer possessed the economic capacity to remain in the area. "What they are doing," Thomas Tyler, a lifelong friend of Gibson explained, "is buying them [houses] up and fixing them up but not letting people back in. The people don't know why they can't get housing. . . . People are robbing this community of its housing."[71]

Florence McKinley noted that Bradberry had worked with Coretta Scott King in the attack on Gibson. Gibson noted the hypocrisy in King's allegiance to the city power structure: "Martin Luther King didn't go to no rich neighborhood. . . . He wouldn't let no rich folks kick poor folks out." When McKinley, Tyler, and Gibson sent multiple letters to the King Center attempting to stop the eviction, Coretta Scott King never responded.[72]

Other Black civil rights leaders either shunned the Auburn Avenue residents' requests for aid or outright declared their allegiance to Bradberry and King. Southern Christian Leadership Conference president Rev. Joseph E. Lowery told McKinley that he "didn't want to do anything about it" and that they should abandon the neighborhood to those who want to redevelop it. According to Tyler, the Black churches supported gentrification because developers planned to build a new sanctuary behind the old one at Ebenezer Baptist Church. "[Ebenezer], they are waiting for the property value to go up," Tyler proclaimed.[73]

"I Define What We Have Experienced from the Dome as Rape": Vine City Struggles against the Georgia Dome Displacement

Black working-class urbanites engaged in the largest fight against displacement in the late 1980s when Atlanta and Fulton County officials voted to put a new domed stadium on thirty-two acres of the Vine City neighborhood. Without hesitation, the Georgia Stadium Corporation, the company that spearheaded the displacement and construction of the stadium, publicized that Vine City's locational advantage to the international convention center made Vine City residents superfluous: "We found that one option, one combination stood head and shoulders above all the rest, and that was an enclosed stadium of some sort located adjacent to the Georgia World Congress Center and managed as an extension of the World Congress Center. . . . We found that if we constructed an enclosed sports arena and operate it as a convention center . . . we could use that stadium literally year round . . . generate income, enough economic activity, enough jobs and enough tax benefits to justify its construction as a public investment."[74]

Residents reported that the Georgia Stadium Corporation rolled over their requests to talk about the Georgia Dome, despite a June 1986 study in which researchers spoke with dozens of Vine City people who stated they wanted affordable housing, not stadiums. "The only interest appears to come from the [Atlanta] Falcons and the Governor's office," the study read. The report concluded what residents already understood: "This project could be a tool to displace Blacks from the core of the city." The president of the Georgia Stadium Corporation, Lowell Evjen, reiterated his lack of care for residents when questioned about the quality of the neighborhood. "As I look out over the site . . . I see primarily empty land," he told a crowd of Black elites at the Hungry Club Forum. "I see [abandoned] warehouses an abandoned rail line, many, many acres of empty, unproductive property. I can't image that a $158 million investment on that land adversely affecting anyone." Residents had organized multiple protests and movements to either save jobs in those abandoned factories and warehouses or pressure the city to build affordable housing for Vine City's growing number of homeless.[75]

The protests ignited quickly. In late November 1987, forty-one Black children from Mount Vernon Baptist Academy—which sat on the designated site of the Georgia Dome—stormed a Hungry Club Forum at the Butler Street YMCA to protest the president of the Georgia Stadium Corporation's speech. Many of the children carried signs that read "Don't Take Our Future Away" and marched alongside Vine City residents and ministers in disrupting the event.[76] Protests mounted enough pressure that at-large city council person Carolyn Long Banks called for a public hearing and referendum before the city allocated 30 percent of the $158 million to start construction. In a strategic move to diminish the power of the working-class activists, capitalists argued that because they had invested 70 percent of the construction budget, they would take charge in a study of the area to determine public perception of a proposed dome. The Andrew Young BUR, ACOC, CAP, Fulton County Commission, Georgia governor's office, and state legislature supported Evjen and did not consider the voice of Vine City residents valuable in the decision-making about their own neighborhood. Black city council president Marvin Arrington best summed up the stakes at the heart of the Georgia Dome debate: the stadium represented the culmination of neoliberalization in Atlanta. "The long-term interests of our city and our state must drive this decision. The Georgia dome is an integral part of the future growth and expansion of

Atlanta's role as the regional leader in the Southeast, and of its emerging role as a national and international city."[77]

The 1988 session of the Georgia General Assembly approved $3.36 million for three parcels of land in Vine City for the Georgia Dome. Georgia also approved designing, engineering, and provision of additional parking spaces, which cost more residents their homes. Unsurprisingly, the Georgia General Assembly voted down any funds for relocation for displaced Vine City residents.[78] As construction plans began, 150 families and counting received eviction notices. Unfortunately, class warfare and petty bourgeois interests swallowed community solidarity. Vine City church leaders Rev. W. L. Cotrell of Beulah Baptist Church negotiated with Fulton County commissioner Michael Lomax, who proposed a $6 million trust fund to house displaced residents. Suddenly, Vine City ministers changed their tune on the stadium, shifting from opposition to ambiguity when Fulton County put money on the table. "We don't know what the development would be across the street," Cotrell stated. "But if there is to be a development and you are to support it, we hope that support will be conditioned to at least making sure that we have $6 million to go in a community development fund.... This would be a token in the right direction."[79] By summer 1988, relocation funds for displaced poor people transformed into "community development funds" and fractured the solidarity across class lines in Black Vine City.

Both sides of the movement addressed each other at a heated July 12 city council meeting. Many of the protesters attempted to appeal to the council's sense of historical legacy. One older resident, Dorothy Bolden, explained that "Dr. Martin Luther King, Jr. thought so well of Vine City that he indicated that he wanted to move there one day." Others argued that constructing the dome threatened to destroy one of Atlanta's oldest neighborhoods. In a surprising move, Bill Campbell announced his opposition to the stadium, citing that sporting arenas in the United States never turned a financial profit or enhanced the communities they resided in. In a statement that rallied cheers from Vine City protesters, Campbell suggested to councilman Buddy Fowlkes that anyone interested in building a domed stadium in his district—the white upper-class Buckhead area—would consult residents of Buckhead before going ahead with it. Dome supporters told the council that they must approve the resolution to finance their portion of the dome so that the construction lasts from September 1 to the summer of 1991.[80] Indeed, Campbell's politically savvy movement along class lines bolstered Black community support for his ascension to city leadership.

On August 1 of that year, the Atlanta City Council approved the resolution to provide money raised from the hotel-motel tax to pay for the debt service and any operating deficit to the Georgia Dome. According to the *Atlanta Voice*, the decision became a priority vote after a series of private meetings among city officials and Georgia Dome investors and supporters. Reporters for the *Voice* witnessed the following mini conferences in city hall that day: finance chairman Ira Jackson met with GWCC president John Aderhold; Aderhold also met with Evjen, city council human resources chairman Robb Pitts, and finance commissioner Pat Glisson. When the meeting began, many city council members denied a public hearing before the vote. Additionally, Vine City's other councilman, African American Jabari Simama, stated that he felt the public had had "enough input." "The city council needs to say what it's going to do," Simama exclaimed. "The community has spoken." Next, Bill Campbell flipped to Simama's side and silenced Vine City residents' uproar. He attempted to justify displacing residents by pointing to the housing crisis and the expanding and increasingly violent underground economy in Vine City. "Look at the dilapidation," Simama told the council. "Look at the drugs. Look at the teenage pregnancy. Look at the boarded housing. . . . We'll feel very proud of the decision we made today."[81] The increasing blight and loss of jobs throughout the 1980s provided the petty bourgeois leaders the justification to sell the violent removal of poor urbanites from the city.

By September 1988, the combined expansion of the GWCC and construction of the Georgia Dome sent hundreds of residents of the Black Lightning and Vine City neighborhoods seeking shelter and new lives. The Atlanta power structure did not instill confidence in the residents that they would ever find new homes. At a September 28 housing forum sponsored by the Economic Opportunity of Atlanta office, residents grew angry that their Vine City council representatives did not attend after voting in favor of dome construction and displacement. The residents' fear regarding relocation funds rang true. Council member Tom Cuffie told the attendees that the city could cut into their relocation housing trust fund. Residents noted that this resembled the 1966 Summerhill displacement, when the city evicted an estimated 10,000 poor Black people with no relocation plan. "If they do us like they did Summerhill, we're going to look like trash on top of trash," Vine City resident Dorothy Bolden stated. "[Atlanta Falcons owner] Rankin Smith took all those people to Dallas last Sunday to show them that domed stadium. And everything where that domed stadium is sitting, in 1973, was Black neighborhoods." When some residents suggested raising property taxes so affluent Atlantans could build a relocation fund, council members shut down that idea.[82]

The meeting ended with a resurgence in the movement against the stadium and another push for protonationalism at the grass roots. Lightning resident Sister Haniyfa Ali announced a new organization, Community Concern, and circulated a petition to attendees to move the dome to a public referendum. "If the people of the City of Atlanta want to have the onerous burden of a domed stadium to bear," Ali stated, "then it is only fair and right that that should be determined by them at the polls." "Representative government on this issue has obviously failed, we believe to express the real will of the people with what we believe are false claims of what is in the public good."[83]

On May 15, 1989, the Atlanta City Council passed a memorandum of understanding to pay for the relocation of Friendship Baptist Church and Mount Vernon Church out of Vine City. By summer of that year, the Atlanta power structure had decided every aspect of the Georgia Dome except who would fund the housing relocation for displaced residents. The ministers stated that the memorandum of understanding made them "happy" but had nothing to say in defense of the soon-to-be-displaced residents. Ministers were only concerned with "the timetable for relocating the churches."[84] To make it clear, the churches abandoned any responsibility in paying or pressing the city for relocation funds—thus abandoning the Black working class. "We are a Christian body, so we feel as though we will be treated fair," Mount Vernon Baptist Church's Deacon Harris expressed. "We have that much faith in our commissioners." To quiet antidome protesters, the Atlanta power structure propagandized its "sincere commitment to diversity" by hiring Sports Design Group, an African American contractor, to assist with designing the Georgia Dome. Additionally, the Fulton County Board of Commissioners unanimously passed a resolution in response to unanswered questions regarding displacement. The resolution stated, "This Board of Commissioners cares very deeply about the people who live, work, and worship in Vine City."[85] The empty affirmation rang hollow for the disillusioned Black working-class Atlantans.

Details of the relocation housing trust fund for displaced residents exposed it to have been an organized removal of poor Black people from the city. The trust fund did not provide real money. Rather, residents had to apply for mortgage loans to obtain housing. The trust fund paid the interest on bonds issued for constructing homes priced from $40,000 to $60,000 as well as for rehabilitation of existing homes. The problem, however, was that many of the displaced residents did not meet the income requirements to maintain middle-income housing. To qualify for the mortgage loans offered through the trust fund, residents had to make $17,000 a year. Some who did qualify based on income failed the credit check. As is detailed in chapter 6, many of the displaced left the city for cheaper suburban housing, added their names to the ever-increasing waiting list for public housing placement, or became housing insecure and moved from place to place. One former Vine City resident said of their eviction, "I define what we have experienced from the dome as rape."[86]

As neoliberalization accelerated in Atlanta, global private capital flowed into the city to discipline the Black worker in several ways. New capital influx did not result in increased investment in working-class communities but instead occurred alongside a decrease in manufacturing and other living-wage jobs. Neoliberalization also destabilized long-standing Black working-class neighborhoods with development projects that did not serve residents. Projects such as the King national park or the Georgia Dome jettisoned poor and working-class Black residents from the city, while providing few if any resources for relocation. The combined impact of these development decisions accumulated into a pogrom against Black working-class residents. Thus, early gentrification efforts in Atlanta served as an anti-Black-working-class process that left residents with minimal capacity to build social institutions and sustain protest movements for autonomy. Planned privatization conflicted with the interests of the Black worker, which would prove even more devastating during the city's Olympic period.

CHAPTER FOUR

Don't Work Yourself into a Shoot, Brother!
The New Nadir and New Tools of Class War in Olympic-Era Atlanta

> A nebulous process of displacement and dispossession has started, a protracted struggle for land and control over its use and by who, has clearly begun.
> —Atlanta Neighborhoods United for Fairness (A'NUFF),
>   August 16, 1991

> The list of projects which have destroyed our homes and neighborhoods is mindboggling: the Atlanta Civic Center, MARTA, the World Congress Center, Lenox Square, the Atlanta–Fulton County Stadium, and now the [Olympic Stadium]. Somehow the people who prey on the poor can always justify why our neighborhoods are the best place, the most feasible, and the only place for their new projects.
> —GENE FERGUSON, Summerhill resident and A'NUFF activist,
>   December 28, 1991

> What was the point of electing these various officials to office when they demonstrate a clear inability to support grassroots principles and interests when they possess no inner-directed collective vision of the good and just city, when they have expected outer-directed versions of growth and progress which, at best, only provide haphazard implications for the vast majority of Atlantans, especially its institutionalized poor.... This is a situation we in the "Other Atlanta" have tolerated for far too long and it must be addressed in words and deed of A'NUFF and others.
> —ETHEL MAE MATTHEWS, chairperson of A'NUFF the
>   Battle of Fair Street Bottom

On the morning of Thursday, April 30, 1992, students from Morehouse College, Clark Atlanta University, Spelman College, and Morris Brown College led a march through the Atlanta University Center and the Central Business District (CBD) protesting the acquittal of four white police officers in the Los Angeles Rodney King trial. However, by late afternoon, the march escalated to a rebellion as Georgia Bureau of Investigation and Atlanta police officers blocked the marchers' path when they attempted to organize the poor Black residents surrounding the campuses. After numerous physical altercations between the groups, riot-gear police erected a barricade, helicopters arrived and encircled the uprising, and hundreds of student activists—joined by many Atlanta residents at that point—fought through the barricade with fists, bricks, and bottles. Soon, they reorganized their protest at the corners of J. P. Brawley Drive and Fair Street—the street separating Morehouse and the University Homes housing project. From that point, the Black rebels spent the next twelve hours destroying Georgia Bureau of Investigation and Atlanta Police Department vehicles, fighting police officers, and burning and looting businesses, particularly targeting Black-owned businesses this time. By early the next morning, the police, with over sixty National Guard troops on standby, blocked multiple passageways throughout the area and fired so much tear gas that the rebels retreated. When the uprising officially ended in the early afternoon, the police had jailed 320 rebels, at least forty-one people had suffered injuries, and property damage totaled close to $1 million.[1]

Although the Rodney King trial served as a catalyst for multiple Black working-class rebellions in cities like Los Angeles, Detroit, and Oakland in 1992, these uprisings revealed a fiery bloc of African Americans frustrated by more than just the brutal combination of social instability and police violence and surveillance over the prior decade. They also loathed the calculated *depoliticization* of their struggle by petty bourgeois forces. Indeed, parasitic Reaganism at the national, state, and local level had sucked the blood out of the labor, housing, education, social safety net, and resource base for low-income Blacks. Additionally, Black urban regimes (BURs) had supervised the looting of public resources in low-income Black neighborhoods. The final piece, however, was their push for "rational" management of working-class crises, such as enterprise zones, antipoverty bureaucratic offices, community development corporations, business giants like Coca-Cola, and universities like Georgia Tech. The absence of a radical structural critique of racial oppression—typically produced through grassroots struggles and social movements at the point of production—created a void where bourgeois liberal and conservative voices reshaped the question of Black liberation around poverty management, cultural pathology, and self-improvement via crime intervention. This chapter demonstrates that by reconstituting interventions into inner-city crises in Atlanta and other Black cities outside the grass roots and within the capitalist structure, the Black petty bourgeoisie built their twenty-first-century city through violent gentrification and Black displacement, the silencing and ridiculing of radical working-class voices and organizations like Atlanta Neighborhoods United For Fairness (A'NUFF), and the rise of symbolic diversity initiatives by corporations, thus classifying social movements and grassroots resistance as "irrational" and "detrimental" to the Olympics and international progress. Additionally, municipal power brokers erased class from the critique by remaking the sociospatial debates on Black Atlanta cultural and pathological. More clearly, the Atlanta BUR shielded the economic dislocation and class-warfare consequences of the New Nadir from public scrutiny as it accelerated its international investments in time for the Olympic Games. As a result, grassroots movements that critiqued gentrification or fought outside of the immediate threats of the lumpenproletariat faced widespread scrutiny as "irrational" in a Black Mecca that was "too busy to hate."

Thus, this chapter examines how the Atlanta bourgeoisie and petty bourgeoisie worked their low-income counterparts into a shoot. As low-income urbanites marshaled their meager resources to challenge Olympic gentrification, pro-growth machines "worked" their public into discrediting grassroots struggles as "unreasonable" and against the "progress" of the central city. This work produced other intended consequences for the Black working class. For instance, they often depleted their movement capacity when mobilizing against the expanding underground economy. As the economic dislocation of the 1990s forced many African Americans out of the class structure and into the lumpenproletariat, the city publicized low-income Black spaces as crime infested but also allowed the underground economy to fester in controlled enclaves. As a result, Black working-class neighborhoods in 1990s Atlanta focused so much on the *symptom* (lumpenproletarianization) and not the *problem* (class warfare) that they struggled against the long-term threat of capital's predatory attack on colonized bodies and spaces. Atlanta's Olympic gentrification period exemplified the New Nadir era that ravaged Black workers across the nation; it deepened internal neocolonialism and initiated the subproletarianization of the Black poor.

A Case for the New Nadir in 1990s Atlanta

By the middle of the 1980s, federal, state, and local confiscation of productive labor and neighborhood resources expanded the needs of the Black working class with little relief in sight. The abandonment of the Black working class at the federal level spurred the New Nadir, because it eliminated the little material support for the majority of African Americans under racial oppression. With little to no opposition from liberal Democrats—and many Democrats aligning with regressive federal and state legislation—white and Black neoconservatives launched an anti-Black-working-class political strategy that reshaped racial oppression. As Black studies scholar Sundiata Cha-Jua conceptualized, this contemporary racial formation, the New Nadir, is a consequence of the political economic transformation into financialized global capitalism. Cha-Jua's New Nadir model succinctly exemplifies the last quarter of the twentieth-century African American sociohistorical experience because it characterizes the ineffectiveness of Black resistance and the "subsequent drastic devolution in African Americans' role in the political economy, position in the polity, social status, and cultural representation."[2] In other words, this racial formation must be defined as reactionary: it sought to scale back Black gains and resistance through the loss of resources and rights. The New Nadir severed most African Americans from the concern of the political structure and reshaped the social atmosphere into a backlash against the Black poor. To be clear, the New Nadir framework is not Afropessimism, because it centers on the dialectic of domination and subjugation. More clearly, it considers that Black collective resistance to capitalist exploitation is the primary rationale for the reshaping of the political economy against the political, economic, social, and cultural conditions of the Black worker.

The 1990–91 Great Recession—often overlooked by urban scholars—played a pivotal role in deepening apartheid in Atlanta and expanding the New Nadir. The US invasion of Kuwait in the summer of 1990 shocked oil prices and dropped aggregate consumption demand, but as urban scholar David Geltner pointed out, the Gulf War only acted as the "proximate catalyst." The antecedents that caused this proximate spark—the drop in aggregate consumption demand—were tied directly to ongoing struggles in Black America.[3]

As is the case with any major tax reduction, the working class carried the brunt of President Ronald Reagan's devastating corporate tax cuts. Income taxes by the mid-1980s claimed 7.5 to 8 percent of the gross domestic product, the same as in the 1960s and down from 9.2 percent in the late 1970s.[4] As the federal deficit continued to expand, Reagan gradually gutted social program spending across the board. Reagan and liberal Democrats followed with the Tax Reform Act of 1986. The bill increased the basic tax deduction in order to remove the poor from tax rolls and, most importantly, cut the number of income tax brackets to three. By 1989, tax receipts totaled 8.2 percent of the gross domestic product; the tax receipts generated more revenue, but they did not significantly reduce the deficit. Reagan's tax policy also cut real wage growth at the knees. The tax breaks did not command capital to increase productivity at a commensurate rate, so wages—and thus consumer demand—plummeted toward the end of the decade.[5] This hit African American workers especially, because they sat at the lower end of the wage gap and cycled in and out of the labor participation pool disproportionately more than white workers.

The Congressional Budget Office concluded that the wealthiest 1 percent of the population paid 36 percent less in taxes in 1990 than under the 1977 tax code. However, poor families paid as much as 14 percent more than they previously had under the same tax code.[6]

Reagan failed to reduce the federal deficit while his anti-working-class policies spiraled American debt out of control. During his tenure, the US deficit ballooned from $74 billion to $155 billion.[7] This impacted real estate prominently. The federal deficit kept interest rates high. Inflation hovered between 3 and 4 percent, so the cost of money skyrocketed. As historian Wyatt Wells suggested, Americans paid for these long-standing deficits with higher interest rates while under the illusion that tax cuts solved money woes. High interest rates, a leading factor in the size of mortgage payments, forced potential homeowners to take on high monthly payments or settle for cheaper housing.[8] On the supply side, real estate developers responded with a significant drop in housing construction in the late 1980s. From a peak rate of new housing at nearly 2 million units per year mid-decade, the rate had fallen to below 1.4 million units per year by the beginning of the 1990s. Consequently, this also meant a steep decline in construction jobs and in other affected areas—especially retail.[9] Construction and retail companies cut African Americans first, increasing the number of underemployed and stagnating their wages.

Commercial real estate also played a part in exacerbating Black economic crises. Inflation placed banking executives in an interesting position in the early 1980s. The commercial real estate asset market sent total commercial and multifamily mortgages from $315 million in 1978 to a shocking $1.1 trillion in 1990. To keep in front of the impending burst of this real estate bubble, banks extended increasingly risky and often predatory loans—many to African Americans who did not possess the income or job stability to pay exorbitant interest rates. When inflation subsided after 1987, investment demand for real estate followed, exacerbating the oversupply problem in commercial real estate and driving commercial real estate prices to their lowest level in 1992.[10] In sum, Reagan-era fiscal and monetary policy and the onset of the Gulf War contributed to the 1990–91 recession.

These factors intensified structural violence against Black Atlantans in many ways. Residential real estate volatility intensified housing insecurity in the metro region. As Black people's migration to the metro region exploded over the 1980s, they found less low-cost housing stock available. The Southern Center for Studies in Public Policy from Clark Atlanta University estimated that a new house in Atlanta in 1992 cost an average of $72,000, while rental rates averaged $525 a month for a two-bedroom apartment and $600 for a three-bedroom apartment. Thus, many Black Atlantans who made less than $20,000 a year were either paying close to 75 percent of their wages in rent or having to find cheaper, one-bedroom apartments, where multiple family members slept in the same room.[11]

With the Reagan administration slashing federal housing subsidies for the poor by 75 percent—the largest cuts to any domestic program—the number of Black Atlantans seeking shelter swelled at the end of the 1980s, prompting two long-term consequences: The Black poor competed over the low amount of affordable housing. And there was a sharp rise in the number of poor families spending upward of 60 percent of their income on rent. In fact, the Southern Center reported that more than 62 percent of Black Atlantans who earned less than $10,000 spent a disproportionate share (30 percent or more) of their income on gross rent.[12] As rents remained high, housing quality deteriorated. Atlanta metro region landlords "unsatisfactorily housed" more an alarming number of renters. This means that close to 40 percent of the city's rental units did not have adequate plumbing and close to 60 percent lacked heating. The City of Atlanta's own Comprehensive Housing Affordability Strategy for 1992 incorrectly reported that 78 percent of rental units and 73 percent of single-family residences were classified as being in "standard" condition. It is safe to assert that the fixation on commercial real estate both at the federal and local level shrank the availability of affordable housing.[13]

The 1990–91 recession also exposed the City of Atlanta and the Atlanta Housing Authority (AHA) as culpable in the housing crisis in the metro region. In examining the vacancy rates during this period, Atlanta's power structure displaced Black residents out of housing faster than it rehoused them. Between 1980 and 1992, the vacancy rate in the Atlanta metropolitan region increased from 6 to 10 percent. Additionally, the fifteen census tracts in metropolitan Atlanta in 1992 with vacancy rates above 25 percent were all located in the city of Atlanta. In other words, the number of vacant housing units rose during the recession while homelessness increased, meaning that over 14,000 units of federally subsidized housing stock were available for poor people.[14] However, the City of Atlanta chose to either demolish this housing or leave it vacant while the homeless filled the AHA waiting lists.

The recession disproportionately damaged Black wage growth. The decrease in aggregate consumer demand played a key role in the loss of construction and retail jobs. As a result, many Black workers picked up low-wage work that did not make up for that loss in income. In 1977, the poorest 20 percent of American families made 4.4 percent of the national income. By 1993, their share dropped to 3.6 percent. Thus, real earnings for the superexploited declined while the wealthiest 20 percent of families increased their share of total income from 43.6 percent to 48.9 percent. By the end of the 1980s, the top 10 percent of wealthy Americans controlled nearly 70 percent of the wealth in the United States. Particularly in low-income urban spaces, changes to the political economy played a crucial role in wage regression.[15]

The 1990–91 recession laid the foundation for a deepening housing crisis that was a major factor in poor Black urbanites losing major ground in their struggle for improved social conditions. It served to validate the African American aphorism that "when white people catch a cold, Black people get double pneumonia." The largest declines in average household income in 1990 Atlanta (when adjusted for inflation) occurred in the CBD and the Hartsfield International Airport area—the same spaces that experienced significant racial transitions from white to Black over the 1980s. In fact, the Black population of the airport area skyrocketed from 28 percent in 1980 to 68 percent in 1990. Concurrently, the three largest increases in average household income during this time occurred in northeast Atlanta, Buckhead, and most notably north Fulton County, east of Cascade Road—the Gold Coast.[16]

The decline in productive labor, such as in manufacturing jobs, reduced the number of livable-wage, skilled jobs. Concurrently, the rapid growth of the information, technology, and finance-based sector—nonproductive labor—restricted individuals without the appropriate education and training background to command premium wages. Last, federal and state legislatures opposed raising the minimum wage for close to a decade after 1982 despite rising costs of living.[17] Nonproductive labor jobs included those in banking institutions, the stock market, and most importantly, middle management and human resources.

Bill Clinton's emergence as a major player in a new Democratic Party helped blast the social conditions of poor urbanites into the New Nadir. He and a group of mostly moderate southern Democrats formed the Democratic Leadership Conference in 1985 to move the party toward middle-class whites. Clinton and the Democratic Leadership Conference followed Reagan and exacerbated a racial stratification in the working class and cast Black people as the symbol of American degradation. For example, while campaigning for president, when Clinton launched a public attack on hip-hop artist and political activist Sister Souljah for her critique of white supremacy following the 1992 Los Angeles rebellion, he jumped in the presidential polls from trailing by fifteen points to leading by thirty. In fact, many reports argued that Clinton's war against Sister Souljah won him the white vote and served as the catalyst for his upset presidential victory over incumbent George H. W. Bush.[18]

Clinton promoted a moderate-conservative Republican platform to the "forgotten white middle class" to win their support for the Democratic Party—a strategy that expelled the working class, especially low-income Blacks, from the party's public policy platforms. By 1991, Black working-class interests ranked so low on the list of Democratic Party priorities that African American delegate to the US House of Representatives Eleanor Holmes Norton stressed that the Civil Rights Act of 1991—an antidiscrimination measure that challenged President George H. W. Bush's veto of the Civil Rights Bill of 1990 was not meant to address Blacks but must benefit middle-class white women.[19]

It is safe to assert that Clinton's presidency inflicted more economic and social damage to the Black majority than either the Reagan or Bush administrations. As neoconservatives argued that affirmative action "oppressed" white males, Clinton worked to end what he called "abuses in federal government affirmative action programs." He bolstered his reelection campaign with his "Mend, it, don't end it" slogan—but he chose to cut affirmative action in the Department of Transportation, leaving thousands of African Americans without jobs. Clinton's crime and welfare legislation served as the most punitive and destructive bill in federal history against working-class African Americans. The programs gutted drug rehabilitation and prevention funding in the middle of the crack cocaine epidemic, reduced youth employment and job training programs, cut thousands of poor people from welfare rolls, and gave white-collar drug producers "slap on the wrist" punishments. Concurrently, the bill provided billions of dollars to militarize police and build prisons, strengthened the death penalty, and enacted "three strikes, you're out" rules against nonviolent offenders, predominantly Black and brown people. Conservative and liberal Clinton apologists point to his appointment of African Americans in his administration and his support of Black redistricting. However, much of Clinton's symbolic diversity served to offset his destruction of Black spaces and bodies and simultaneously weaken collective protest against his policies.

Clinton and liberal Democrats instilled confidence in the white and Black petty bourgeoisie by scaling back government spending. Elites under this new racial formation structured their ideology around two points. First, with corporate philanthropic efforts and symbolic diversity initiatives, corporate leaders not only subdued working-class resistance but also felt that they contributed enough capital to affirmative action to back away from support of race-based legislation.[20] Additionally, since liberal Democrats' revised ideology envisioned no role for the Black poor under financial capitalism, federal, state, and local officials promoted public policy to curtail the growth and upward mobility of the working class. This was carried out through the twin processes of deproletarianization—dismantling the manufacturing and industrial sector and moving remaining factories to the antiunion and more racially discriminatory rural South—and subproletarianization. The disciplining of the Black worker through the elimination of viable labor provided proponents of pro-growth, anti-working-class agendas the political, economic, social, and cultural capital to devalue the lives of the working class, propagandize them as "undesirable," and toss them out of revitalizing space without significant outcry from the public. Indeed, crushing indigenous resistance under neocolonial domination deregulates capital more than any legislation could ever hope.

In August 1990, twenty-two-year-old African American Jerry Clark joined 2,200 of his coworkers and walked out of the Lakewood General Motors automobile manufacturing plant for the final time. The sixty-four-year-old, 1.8 million-square-foot factory that produced the Buick Estate wagon and the Chevrolet Caprice sedan and wagon closed without relocation, leaving Clark and other Black and white working-class people without viable work. Clark saw his pay crash from $640 a week, or sixteen dollars an hour, to $350 a week. The loss in wages, labor, and time necessary to find supplemental employment destabilized Clark's daily routine. Located in southeast Atlanta, the plant had possessed a locational advantage for Black working-class residents who lacked access to consistent transportation. Many workers walked to and from the plant, using the time to discuss neighborhood issues, plan social events, and reciprocate resources for survival. In other words, the location of a productive, livable-wage source of labor provided a net advantage for the social viability of Black working-class people. As one of many illiterate workers, Clark was almost guaranteed not to find new work that would compensate for the social costs of worker disruption and displacement the plant closure had caused. "You're not prepared for them to shut down so quick," Clark stated.[21]

The rest of the Atlanta metro region reeled from this relatively small-scale deindustrialization as well because the manufacturing sector had provided some of the most stable work in the area. However, auto production across the city declined from 12,242 employees in June 1987 to 7,316 in June 1991. Mindis International, a newly arrived European business, bought the closed General Motors facility and land for $5 million and transformed it into a scrap metal recycling center.[22]

The locationally advantageous Bainbridge Filament Yarns Plant, fifteen minutes from the central city, was part of the Amoco Fabrics and Fibers Company. The facility manufactured nylon carpet fiber. When it closed in July 1991, it cost 600 people their jobs. Bainbridge lost two other factories soon after.[23]

More plant closures and layoffs followed across the region. Grumman Corporation's plant in Milledgeville, which produced parts for airplanes, laid off dozens of production line workers that same month to "reduce the company's work force."[24] In 1994, 170 workers lost their jobs at the McCord Payen gasket production plant in LeGrange. The president of the company, Ronald R. Comer, stated that the jobs and workers were expendable because the company did not need two gasket plants.[25] The Hapeville Keebler factory fired all its workers in 1996, citing that "the cookie and cracker market has softened."[26]

Productive labor, especially in manufacturing, fled the city limits. Between 1980 and 1990, the number of manufacturing jobs in the City of Atlanta declined from 48,986 to 36,054. Most of those jobs were either relocated to the northern suburbs or disappeared forever. Between 1970 and 1990, the total share of jobs in the suburbs almost doubled from 29 percent to 52 percent. Productive labor employers sought suburban advantages such as lower land and labor costs, lower property taxes, lower insurance premiums, and greater availability of outdoor amenities. The retail and services industries added the most jobs to the metro region, providing over 90,000 jobs each in the 1980s.[27] Atlanta's Black workers who did not possess the necessary skill sets to work in increasingly shrinking productive labor sectors found themselves confined to a restrictive selection of jobs mostly housed in retail and services after 1990.

By 1990, class boundaries demarcated Black Atlanta. To the east of Cascade Road in southwest Atlanta, Black workers resided in Carver Homes,

Vine City, Perry Homes, Auburn Avenue, Summerhill, Pittsburgh, Mechanicsville, Peoplestown, Capitol Homes, University Homes, and Techwood/Clark Howell Homes. Black women headed over three-fourths of poverty-stricken African American homes in the city. Dilapidated and abandoned homes plagued most neighborhoods, and many of them served as offices for illegal capitalists (drug dealers) in the crack cocaine trade. Police helicopters and cruisers surveilled these areas twenty-four hours a day.[28]

Most notably, Black workers to the east of Cascade faced a crisis of disappearing productive, livable-wage labor. Thirty-two-year-old Leroy Wilson and his thirty-four-year-old brother Lonnie Foster—a certified mechanic—served as two of the thousands of skilled, working-class African Americans who migrated from cities like New Orleans to Atlanta in the early 1990s in search of viable work. However, as was the case in many metropolitan areas at the time, the demand for skilled Black tradespeople like mechanics did not meet the supply in the City of Atlanta, as automobile repair shops moved to suburban spaces for cheaper costs and quicker access to more affluent car owners. Additionally, banks refused to issue loans to many Black workers like Wilson and Foster who wanted to start a business but did not possess the capital. Thus, for six days a week between 11:00 a.m. and 6:00 p.m., Wilson and Foster shined shoes on the corner of Poplar and Forsyth Streets in the CBD. "We've been here about a year now," stated Wilson, "and unless forced into working for someone, we will be here until we can get our [repair] shop or something." On their best days, the brothers made enough money to sleep at a motel, but on many occasions, they ended their days at the Salvation Army. Atlanta police arrested them multiple times for working on a public street without a permit. On each occasion, the judge sentenced them to jail time because they were too poor to afford the fine of seventy-five dollars per person. This cycle repeated because the brothers continued to shine shoes for their regular customers on that corner to make enough money to fund the permanent address and fee required for the work permit.[29] Many African Americans in poor Black urban enclaves found themselves in similar predicaments. Uneven development constructed colonial barricades between Black workers and access to viable work that builds sustainable wealth.

To the west of Cascade Road, however, sat Cascade Heights and Ben Hill, referred to as the "Gold Coast" because of an array of upscale houses owned by bourgeois African Americans. *Ebony, Black Enterprise,* and other Black publications that showcased the perceived "Black Mecca" of the United States often highlighted the Gold Coast as the premier destination for upper-class African Americans on the move. A who's who of Black elites resided on this side of Cascade: elected officials Maynard Jackson and Andrew Young, prominent capitalists like C. A. Scott and Jesse Hill Jr., and celebrated civil rights movement icons like Joseph Lowery and the King family. Additionally, Atlanta's burgeoning $300 million entertainment industry attracted African American celebrities such as actor Emmanuel Lewis, singer Bobby Brown, former Bowen Homes resident and heavyweight boxing champion Evander Holyfield, and music producer Kenneth "Babyface" Edmonds to the Gold Coast. To put the level of disparity between the west and east sides of Cascade in perspective, the Gold Coast's median household income was $48,333 in 1991. Within a five-mile radius, the median household income dropped to $32,816. In the poorer areas surrounding the CBD beyond the west side of Cascade Road, the medium household income did not top $22,000, with many households hovering around $10,000.[30]

Andrew Young's decimation of Black working-class neighborhoods launched a deer-hunt-like siege by real estate developers through the central city. Young issued several hundred permits to real estate companies to develop upscale residential and commercial built environments. Between 1987 and 1993, real estate constructed subdivisions, including Cascade Park, Mays Manor, McMurray Woods, and Cascade Glen, with homes ranging in property value from $96,000 to more than $180,000. Additionally, Quality Living Services, a development corporation specializing in extravagant senior citizen living, signed a $5.4 million deal in 1993 to build luxury retirement homes on Campbellton Road on top of Granada Park Apartments. According to Atlanta Economic Development Corporation vice president Keith Melton, city hall's direction over the past few decades had provided capital the impetus to reinvest within the city limits: "What you see happening throughout Southwest Atlanta is developers taking advantage of the pent-up demand for middle- and upper-income housing. You are seeing the culmination of efforts the city has marshaled to focus attention on the upscale market in Southwest Atlanta. Now developers are responding."[31] According to president of Urban Systems Realty Davey Gibson, "People from Los Angeles, Detroit, Chicago, and elsewhere are asking to specifically be relocated in southwest Atlanta. It is a new trend." Longtime city councilman Jim Maddox, known as the "global advocate" in Atlanta and heavily criticized for using public funds for international investment trips, expressed enthusiasm at city hall's efforts to gentrify southwest Atlanta. "I'm very excited about what's happening.... Clearly the pendulum has swung. We have been working for years to encourage more growth and development."[32]

After a rebound in commercial real estate in 1992–93, Mayor Maynard Jackson marked his return to the Atlanta mayoralty by ramping up revitalization in southwest Atlanta. Developers brought three new supermarkets, two major shopping centers, two banks, two upscale restaurants, and multiple fast-food outlets to accompany the influx of new bourgeois and petty bourgeois residents. Black city council members C. T. Martin and Sheila Brown also sponsored the Community Empowerment Conference at the African American Hoosier United Methodist Church that year to "explore why the southwest [Atlanta] is still underserved by retail establishments, compare the composition of retail establishments in Southwest Atlanta with those in northeast Atlanta, and make recommendations for improving the level of retail in the area."[33] With the "retail revolution," city hall and Fulton County sought to ensure Atlanta capitalists that the newly gentrified space possessed enough growing locational advantages to warrant continued private investment into the twenty-first century. In other words, as Jim Maddox stated, the region's pro-growth leadership believed that "you should go to Lenox Square if you want to, not because you have to. . . . We've been able to encourage businesses to give us what we need, where we live."[34]

Nonproductive labor—supervisory, financial, and information-sector labor that does not produce a finished product—gradually invaded Atlanta's inner city alongside the bourgeois and petty bourgeois classes. Research Atlanta documented that by the early 1990s, the expansion of white-collar managers transformed the inner city from a retail and transportation juggernaut to an agglomeration economy—meaning that a new class of middle-management professionals in sky-level office spaces allowed the power structure to focus labor growth on the flow of ideas and processes instead of on shop floors and distribution centers. In other words, the Atlanta metropolitan region's political economy became a processor of *ambiguous information*: the fragmented and technical negotiations and exchanges of ideas that occur in the offices of decision-makers in both the private and public sectors and at conferences and meetings with other white-collar specialists. The number of FIRE jobs—that is, those in finance, insurance, and real estate—grew by 50,000 in the 1980s, with most of them located in the metro area (Fulton and Dekalb Counties).[35]

Class stratification and aggressive private investment gave the majority of Black Atlantans little to show after twenty years of BUR rule. In 1993, Clark Atlanta University, a leading institute in the research of the political, economic, and social conditions of African Americans at the time, conducted the first comprehensive study of Black people living in the Atlanta metropolitan region through its Southern Center for Studies in Public Policy. The 126-page report not only revealed how Black social conditions in the city had regressed since Maynard Jackson's historic mayoral win in 1973 but also indicted Black elected officials for pushing class interests at the expense of Black suffering.[36]

Although the study reiterated many statistics that were publicized at the time—such as the fact that Black men and women were unemployed at three times the rate of white men and women—other findings uncovered a human rights crisis bubbling across the city. In the University Homes housing project, 94 percent of persons lived in poverty (with an annual income below $13,254 for a family of four), making it the poorest community in the state of Georgia by federal standards at the time. Additionally, under the Andrew Young regime, the number of African Americans living in poverty in metro Atlanta increased by more than 34,000, pushing the poverty rate to four times that of whites in the area. The Black-white income disparity gap widened as well. In Fulton County, 14,330 Black families possessed an annual income exceeding $50,000, compared to 58,493 white families with the same income. At the same time, 33,968 Black families had an income of less than $10,000, compared to only 12,878 white families with the same income.[37]

When the Clark Atlanta University researchers questioned anonymous Black elected officials on the findings, they reportedly "lacked consensus" on the issues and provided excuses like "Unless you put these things [statistics] down, people will not notice." Atlanta's Black urban regime placed so much of its focus on preparations for the 1994 Super Bowl, 1996 Olympic Games, and other neoliberal programs that the neocolonial conditions almost went unacknowledged. City councilman Bill Campbell, who succeeded Maynard Jackson as Atlanta mayor in 1993 after Jackson refused to run for a fourth term, scapegoated Black residents and defended city hall's pro-growth direction in his criticism of the report. "While there have been divisions, I am not aware that the business of the city was in any way hampered by those problems," Campbell stated. "[Researchers] would probably do better to look inward. ... It was a very disappointing and inaccurate portrayal."[38]

Most Black women in the Atlanta metropolitan region remained locked in a subproletarian position in 1993. According to *The Status of African American Women*, a study by the Metropolitan Atlanta Coalition of 100 Black Women, not only did Black women earn less than both Black and white men, but they also worked generally in the lower-paying industries and in the lowest-paying service and clerical jobs. "We are economically at the bottom," Miriam Chivers, a member of the coalition, stated. "Companies hire Black women to fill the hourly job without insurance, and when they offer insurance, it's not affordable. Many African American women are uninsured or underinsured."

Additionally, the coalition found that 60 percent of Black women had an annual income less than $25,000, with 50 percent falling below $10,000. The number of unemployed African American women in the region—47,373—was greater than the number of white women in the workforce! The report also noted that Black women outnumbered Black men in unemployment and underemployment.[39]

Last, Black Atlantan women's subproletarian position hindered their ability to live long lives. Black women comprised 93 percent and 90 percent of unwed mothers in Atlanta and Fulton County, respectively. When Black women were born, they had the same infant mortality rate as Black men. However, as they grew older, Black women's mortality rate increased as they struggled to survive and raise children on their low wages in the dirtiest jobs with limited outreach environments.[40]

The expansion of Black elected officials across the metro region meant that Black elites played a more active role in the fragmentation and subsequent destruction of Black working-class spaces heading into the twenty-first century. By 1990, African Americans controlled the city of Atlanta and held dominant majorities on the Atlanta City Council, the Fulton County Board of Commissioners, the Atlanta Board of Education, and the leadership of the Atlanta Police Department and increasing numbers in the Atlanta Chamber of Commerce. This fortified their neocolonial domination in a unique manner. As the larger BUR instituted racist and regressive policies against the Black worker, it made it much more difficult for the latter to critique the former. Consequently, white criticism of Black leaders forced oppressed Black people into a corner to defend their petty bourgeois counterparts. Thus, class fluidity worked both ways; the Black Mecca myth strengthened in the twenty-first century through this complex racial class relationship. Unfortunately, this helped mute the already dissipating class critique at the heart of Black working-class America during the New Nadir.

Under these structures, Atlanta expanded rapidly while ranking second in the United States in highest poverty rate, behind Newark, New Jersey.[41] The Atlanta metropolitan region had the third-largest percentage change in population in the United States—growing from 2.2 million in 1980 to 2.9 million in 1990, a change of more than 33 percent—trailing only Chicago and Phoenix. The Atlanta metropolitan region ranked twentieth nationally in population in 1970; by 1990, it was ranked thirteenth.[42] A considerable portion of the growth of the Atlanta region was due to the in-migration of residents from other parts of the country and abroad. Between 1985 and 1990, nearly half a million people moved to the region from other areas. Additionally, residential movement rates from city to suburb or suburb to city in the region accelerated in that time span as gentrification expanded. For example, 30 percent of inner-city residents moved to the DeKalb County suburbs, more than to any other metropolitan county in the region.[43] This data suggests that gentrification, and the displacement that resulted from it, during the end of the Andrew Young regime initiated a small suburbanization of working-class African American Atlantans. Last, Black urbanites driven away by the rising costs of living in the central city sought cheaper land and built environment in surrounding urban areas outside the central city. In 1970, nearly 80 percent of African Americans in the Atlanta metropolitan region lived in the city. By 1990, that total dropped to less than 40 percent. African Americans in the 1980s found cheaper housing and accessible transportation via the Metropolitan Atlanta Rapid Transit Authority (MARTA) development in surrounding urban areas. In fact, the number of African Americans living outside the city limits increased 313 percent in Clayton County, 91 percent in DeKalb County, and 76 percent in Fulton County during this decade. White flight helped drive this trend in these counties, except in affluent sections of the counties where bourgeois and petty bourgeois African Americans and whites lived among one another.[44] However, hypersegregation in the municipality continued into the final decade of the twentieth century. Ninety percent of Black people in the city of Atlanta resided on the south and west sides in the city limits—a trend that had continued from the late 1960s.[45]

"Get Lost!": Bourgeois and Petty Bourgeois Tools of Class Warfare in the "Rationality" of Management

Many Black elected officials funneled the relief for the oppressed through programs that addressed their own racial class insecurities—making themselves and their white counterparts richer. In fact, since the 1960s, as African American elites gained control of federal, state, and local public policy for the next thirty years, spending for the needs of the poor increased twenty-five-fold. Yet the number of children, particularly African Americans, living in poverty expanded during this same time. Much of the funding designed to alleviate social crises in poor Black communities bankrolled a new class of what scholar Larry Thompson dubbed the "Poverty Pentagon": counselors, bureaucrats, and social workers, or middle managers who command high salaries to simply *supervise* the poor and provide sparse, symbolic monies to diversity and poverty initiatives. This new tool in class warfare exploited the poor to create a new wave of professional-class individuals to manage the poor, not alleviate them.

Corporate philanthropy served as a potent co-optation weapon for working-class critiques of urban revitalization. In fact, philanthropy had long propped up urban power structures while acting against collective social movements in the United States and other capitalist nations. Steel robber baron and union buster Andrew Carnegie argued in his 1889 article "The Gospel of Wealth" that the wealthy possess the ability to undermine social protest by donating money to causes that directly impact the material conditions of the workers.[46] Friedrich Engels summarized the purpose and execution of philanthropy as a tool of class warfare for the bourgeoisie in his examination of the working class in England in the aftermath of the Industrial Revolution:

> The capitalist class is charitable out of self-interest; it gives nothing outright, but regards its gifts as a business matter, makes a bargain with the poor saying if I spend this much upon benevolent institutions, I thereby purchase the right not to be troubled any further, and you are bound thereby to stay in your dusky holes and not to irritate my tender nerves by exposing your misery. You shall despair as before, but you shall despair unseen. . . . It is infamous, this charity of a Christian capitalist! As though they rendered the workers a service in first sucking out their very life blood and then placing themselves before the world as mighty benefactors of humanity when they give back to the plundered victims the hundredth part of what belongs to them![47]

As the number of nonprofits expanded in urban spaces in the 1990s, Black elected officials gradually stopped fighting for social welfare spending, signaling dire consequences for the Black working classes. Black leaders tended to either shrink away from responsibility in defending their disadvantaged racial counterparts or fully support the dismantling of social programs and privatization of public resources. In late 1991, twenty-four members of the Georgia Legislative Black Caucus voted to cut $415 million from the state budget—the largest cuts in Georgia history at the time. According to African American state representative Tyrone Brooks, the legislature understood before the vote that the cuts involved programs and jobs that served Black workers. As expected, Governor Zell Miller cleared 3,000 jobs from the state payroll.[48]

Black leaders also redistributed funds among their own professionalized classes. According to reports, 350 African American middle-class organizations spent an estimated $16 billion in annual meetings in 1990. Additionally, Black elites spent an estimated $500 million at the annual Congressional Black Caucus event in Washington, DC.[49] At the local level, Black elected officials funded external firms to tell them how to best protect their class interests. In March 1991, the Black Fulton County Board of Commissioners, which included Martin Luther King III, Michael Hightower, Nancy Boxill, and chairperson Michael Lomax, hired Switzerland-based think tank Egon Zehner International to conduct a hiring search for a county manager. The county paid the firm over $300,000 for the search—but according to reports, the county had the ability to hire a manager through the personnel office for free. Egon Zehner selected a white former military general whom both Lomax and King favored because he acquiesced power to the board chairperson.[50]

Corporate diversity philanthropy not only fragmented grassroots resistance but redefined racial class relations in the Atlanta metropolitan region for the next two decades. Corporations crafted a role as benevolent benefactors in poor Black areas to mask their long-term investment in their neighborhoods and bolster the private/public partnership. This strategy decreased the protest actions against corporations in Black urban spaces in the 1980s and 1990s. In fact, Black working-class protests generally did not target corporations like Coca-Cola, which drove much of the gentrification efforts in urban spaces. For example, Coca-Cola and Georgia Tech University—both known for making philanthropic donations to Black public schools in Atlanta and employing Black individuals in high-ranking positions—initiated the destruction of the Techwood and Clark Howell housing projects in downtown Atlanta for almost a decade leading up to the Olympics. However, Black activists heaped the most criticism on city hall and the Atlanta Committee for the Olympic Games. For much of the twentieth century, Coca-Cola's diversity philanthropy allowed it to masquerade as a benefactor to Black community progress and an entity outside of the structural problem caused by Black elected officials.

In March 1991, Mayor Maynard Jackson joined the Atlanta Chamber of Commerce in hosting a "warm welcome" ceremony for 100 companies at the Ritz-Carlton Hotel Plaza. These businesses, including American Honda, Lockheed Aeronautical Systems, and WORLDSPAN, a 500-employee computerized reservations operation, either relocated to the city or established new operations in 1990. With these new additions, Atlanta's chamber of commerce grew to over 7,000 members, one of the largest in the United States.[51] This event broadcasted city hall's deep relationship with capital and attempted to blur the lines between public and private interests in the region. Around this period, as diversity and affirmative action seared in national debates, corporate press conferences emphasized a "commitment to minorities and underprivileged communities." When neoconservatives and Black urban regimes explicitly cut funds to low-income Black neighborhoods, corporations filled the void—albeit symbolically—to subdue resistance to their attack on Black urban residences.

Pepsi-Cola's diversity philanthropy competition against Coca-Cola in Atlanta set the bar for symbolic diversity gesturing in the 1990s. Pepsi's "Minority Entrepreneurship . . . A New Generation" campaign highlighted the company's funding of nearly $400 million to minority businesses owned by African Americans, Latinos/as, Asians, and Native Americans. African American Betty Darrell, director of supplier development for Pepsi, stated that "the featured suppliers are role models for us all. Not only have they accomplished a great deal in the business world, but they continue to use their influence to give something back to their communities . . . inspiring others to follow in their footsteps." Pepsi also donated $10,000 to the African American Panoramic Experience Museum, the Black history museum located on Auburn Avenue. The contribution came from a citywide promotion in which Pepsi donated five cents on the sale of every two-liter bottle of Pepsi during Black History Month. Pepsi also commissioned a free poster for all children who visited the museum. Last, Pepsi created a diversity position that same year: the vice president of corporate development and diversity. The company promoted African American Maurice Cox into that position from his role as chief lobbyist for Pepsi. Craig Weatherup, president and CEO of Pepsi-Cola North America, expressed that the new position demonstrated Pepsi's "commitment to a customer-focused, service-oriented company run by people of diverse backgrounds, skills, values, and gender."[52]

Coca-Cola vied for the same benefactor perception in Black Atlanta. With the World of Coca-Cola museum located in downtown Atlanta and neighboring the Olympic Centennial Park, Georgia Tech, and Techwood and Clark Howell Homes (the oldest public housing projects in the United States), the soda giant understood both its locational advantage as well as its profit potential in partnering with African American leadership. Together, both entities helped propagandize Coca-Cola as a part of the daily life of Atlantans. Their most publicized community grant, Share the Dream, divided $130,000 annually among ten students who drafted an essay on a theme usually centered on cultural diversity. The company chose popular African American comedian Sinbad to promote the initiative across multiple Black media platforms, including *Ebony*, *Jet*, and *Essence* magazines.[53] Between 1991 and 1995, Coca-Cola also pledged to buy $1 billion worth of goods and services from minority and women vendors. The beverage company sought to publicize that it wanted to donate even more funds to "diversity" than it had in the 1980s, which had been $680 million.[54] Last, Coca-Cola and the Atlanta Chamber of Commerce recruited boxing legend, Olympic gold medalist, and former Bowen Homes housing project resident Evander Holyfield for the "Real Deal" advertising package. By 1995, Holyfield appeared in countless television commercials, speaking engagements, and schools with the Olympic mascot, Izzy, to promote Coke's philanthropy in African American schools.[55] Coca-Cola presented a well-known African American Atlantan to bolster Coke's image in the Black working class.

As a result, evidence suggests that Coca-Cola escaped any widespread scrutiny or organized resistance from Black residents during the Olympic period. Behind the scenes of this philanthropy, though, Coke CEO Paul Austin disparaged poor Black people in memos and conversations, telling other executives that the more African Americans in one place, the higher the homicide rate. He also spent the 1970s and 1980s attempting to demolish Black public housing in the city to replace it with shopping malls and upper-income housing.[56]

Many corporations fought to subdue Black protest through symbolic diversity philanthropy with the goal of privatizing education. Telephone company Southern Bell gave a $25,000 grant to Georgia State University to support "the establishment of Benjamin E. Mays Chair of Urban Education Leadership." AT&T targeted Black education—where working-class Black people often protested lack of funding and support.[57]

Other corporations joined the multinational giants in growing their power through symbolic diversity initiatives, like Xerox, which gave Clark Atlanta University's School of Business Administration $20,000 in what it called "Xerox scholarships" for Black MBA students.[58] Burger King, which basketball legend Earvin "Magic" Johnson partnered with across Atlanta, allocated $100 million to draft African American men and women into franchise ownership. However, Burger King only established this diversity program after being sued in 1988 for $500 million by twelve Black franchise owners for racist practices by the corporate office.[59] Symbolic corporate philanthropy served as a crucial tool for the bourgeoisie in class war against the Black poor because it not only challenged the grassroots collectivization of protest action but also co-opted individual African Americans into professionalized supervisory positions in capitalist structures as diversity middle management.

A'NUFF and Class Struggles against Olympic Gentrification

In January 1991, Summerhill resident Mary Williams issued a stern warning to the Atlanta leadership after the chamber of commerce and city hall held a press conference announcing their plans to use Black businesses to redevelop land surrounding the CBD for the Olympics. Williams aimed her comments directly at white real estate lawyer Billy Payne—the individual most responsible for obtaining Atlanta's Olympic hosting berth. "If it takes our marching in the streets, carrying pickets, sitting in front of the Olympics Committee's office or holding this effort out to the world, you may rest assured that there are those among us who are willing to make such a statement."[60] Williams and her Summerhill, Peoplestown, and Mechanicsville kin understood that Payne's motivations for bringing the Olympics to Atlanta endangered the social viability of their neighborhoods.

Black Summerhill residents understood Atlanta's Olympic era as a death sentence because of city hall's long history of breaking promises to the people. However, when the International Olympic Committee chose Atlanta for the 1996 games, many people—particularly residents—objected to the Atlanta Committee for the Olympic Games (ACOG) building a new stadium right next to Fulton County Stadium.[61]

Mayor Jackson stacked the ACOG with Black bourgeois and petty bourgeois brokers: Andrew Young as cochairman; former Jackson campaign official Ray McClendon; AME bishop John Hurst Adams; Jackson's chief of staff, Cecilia Hunter; and Atlanta Life Insurance president, former president of the Atlanta Chamber of Commerce, and director of the King Center Jesse Hill Jr. President of Georgia Tech University John P. Crecine and president of the DeKalb County Chamber of Commerce James Miller (who also founded the Reynolds Plantation Golf Resort) completed the committee. Summerhill residents, keen on protecting their rights and seeking decision-making power at the Olympics, immediately protested their exclusion from the ACOG. Jackson not only neglected their protests but worked outside of them with private interests within the community looking to make individual profits.[62]

Petty bourgeois African Americans exploited this conflict and attempted to leverage city hall via nonprofits for profiteering. Douglas Dean, an African American former state representative who grew up in Summerhill, created Summerhill Neighborhood Incorporated (SNI), a nonprofit community development corporation, in 1988 to plan a revitalization "determined by the residents." Ironically, Dean, who no longer lived in the neighborhood, possessed no close ties to working-class Summerhill. Dean and SNI served as foils to the antistadium movement. According to longtime Summerhill activist Gene Ferguson, Dean and the other African Americans on the SNI executive board (who also did not live in Summerhill) exhibited hostility toward poor residents and often ignored their voices for input in SNI.[63]

Sensing the profit motive behind SNI, Ethel Mae Matthews called for the creation of an oppositional Black citywide neighborhood organization—transforming Tenants United for Fairness (TUFF) into Atlanta Neighborhoods United for Fairness (A'NUFF) in December 1990. The group functioned as a coalition with elected officers and democratic-process decision-making. The main neighborhoods—Summerhill, Mechanicsville, Peoplestown, Techwood/Clark Howell, and Pittsburgh—elected representatives from their respective communities and recruited from neighborhoods that were not immediately affected by the Olympic gentrification (Kirkwood, East Lake Meadows, etc.). The other leaders included Columbus Ward, Duane Stewart (vice chair), Terry Wilson (secretary), and Shuretha Primorose (treasurer). A'NUFF's initial positions read as follows:

> Our major position is that the proposed Olympic Stadium is totally unacceptable to us in our neighborhoods. We want plans presently adopted dropped, and another alternative site found. We demand that the self-created and self-determining development programs we have, or are creating, to be the centerpiece of any revitalization plans for our neighborhoods. We want a democratically informed and publicly sanctioned discussion of all policies regarding all Olympic and related developments in all neighborhoods affected.
>
> In the long run, we want to work with all neighborhoods to [affect] the planning, programs, and outcomes of all future major developments in Atlanta. To integrate these major developments to an agenda of human rights and fairness toward the further advancement of a more humane and just city in the 21st Century.[64]

When questioned about why she formed this opposition movement to the SNI, Matthews stated clearly, "As poor people, we've got to come together and say no, we do not want another stadium sitting in our backyard." She continued with a declaration of war against Billy Payne and Central Atlanta Progress, explaining that "Mr. Payne isn't any kind of an elected official, and he talks as if he was in charge of everything. We don't want to be told by somebody who will never answer to the electorate what we will and will not do, and what is and is not negotiable."[65]

A'NUFF's movement to stop stadium construction spread quickly. Within a week of forming, the group kicked off its first action with a statement to Juan Antoni Samaranch, the head of the International Olympic Committee. The letter dismantled the "city too busy to hate" myth by providing an alternative perspective on the city, as a site of struggle between the oppressed and the power structure:

> We are the other Atlanta.... It is unfortunate you did not meet us during your many trips to Atlanta. We were there, but it was the intent of others not to let you see us.... We are the poor within the underdeveloped neighborhoods.... We are the lied to for whom endless promises have been unkept.... We are the invisible people of Atlanta.... The situation surrounding the 1996 Olympics has served to energize and make us gather together to end our invisibility.... We are [serving] notice that we will use every legal, democratic, and nonviolent means at our disposal to move the Olympic Stadium venue to another site. It is totally unacceptable to our neighborhoods to contain two stadiums which will only help to cause further deterioration of our quality of life.... Also, these neighborhoods ... contain structures and resources that are ... significant.... We respectfully invite the AOC and IOC to engage in serious and direct dialogue with A'NUFF.... We hope the events of the next several years will lead to an improved quality of life for all involved.[66]

A'NUFF increased the pressure on the ACOG by diversifying its tactics. On February 3, 1991, A'NUFF picketed Billy Payne's home in Dunwoody, waving signs and singing loudly "We Shall Overcome." After a few minutes of singing, various members made speeches under a candlelight vigil urging Payne and the ACOG to move the stadium elsewhere. "We are intent of stopping this stadium from being built in our backyard," Matthews exclaimed. The following week, A'NUFF held a press conference and presented its 1,000-signature petition to city hall to stop the stadium. Additionally, the group spent the remainder of the press event reprimanding Atlanta city hall and the Fulton County Board of Commissioners for their "pathetic performance" as African American leaders "in their position on the Olympic Stadium in Summerhill." "We question if Olympic officials are giving full consideration to Summerhill's own development goals and aspirations without holding them hostage to private, nebulous negotiations," Matthews stated. "In any event, we know we have support in what we are saying and doing." Matthews then hinted that the SNI and other private interests in Summerhill were fragmenting the anti-stadium movement: "Could it [the ACOG community relations task force] be for the purpose of separating dissenters from collaborators? Could it be for the creation of a two-tier system of community inputs and manipulative outputs?" She concluded the press conference with a callback to Black radicalism, demanding the fostering of a "renewed intellectual rigor and acumen within Black Atlanta, a new dialogue which seeks pro-active correctives to the intellectual laziness and unclear political and economic direction Black elected leadership is taking us."[67]

After six months of operations, A'NUFF's antistadium movement grew considerably—in popularity and tactics. On April 29, 1991, numerous A'NUFF members descended on the downtown Ritz-Carlton, where city hall often held business meetings for the Olympics. Another faction seized Inforum, the ACOG headquarters in the city. Both groups swarmed the areas with signs like "No Stadium in Summerhill" and chanted "Billy Payne's got to go!" However, word reached ACOG before the protests started, so it was able to keep A'NUFF out of the sight of Samaranch.[68] A'NUFF followed up this action with another mass protest to defend Black landownership against the ACOG. On July 26, A'NUFF gathered on African American Otis Hunter's property—a parking lot that the Atlanta power structure threatened to annex for the Olympic Games. When Hunter refused to sell his property to the city, he received an intimidation letter from a company called Properties Acquisition, Inc.[69]

In response, A'NUFF called on Atlanta and Fulton County governments "to [cease] and desist from this avaricious and misapplied attempt to exploit small property owners out of their investments and livelihoods. We demand an immediate end to this practice, and we encourage all property owners who have received letters regarding properties in Summerhill not to sell their land now nor in the future." Furious at Black elected officials' attempts to seize land owned by African Americans in poor neighborhoods, A'NUFF then demanded a recall of all public officials involved: "We are tired of people coming from outside Atlanta, who don't know anything about Atlanta, coming in and disregarding us, what we need, and what we are asking for.... If our voices are not heard now, they will be heard on the ballot box in 1992.... We have got a hit list on all those politicians and we are going to target all of them starting with the mayor going on down to the least."[70]

As A'NUFF's strategy gradually gained traction, Atlanta's power brokers faced increasing pressure to counter and destroy the movement. Atlanta resident Oliver Parker stated in a letter to the *Atlanta Voice* that A'NUFF deserves support and commendation "for their steadfastness in its opposition to the stadium, despite ignorance and arrogance from the Olympic organizing committee." Parker concluded that A'NUFF exposed to many people that "Atlanta is not the city too busy to hate as its boosters claim.... It has been and still is the city too busy to listen to Black folks.... The city fathers deserve a penalty for ignoring its citizens."[71]

With more support pouring in daily, Atlanta elites steepened A'NUFF's uphill battle in the stadium crisis. Atlanta capitalists used their ownership of the media to brand A'NUFF as "antiprogress" and, therefore, not in the best interests of the public. *Atlanta Journal* columnist Tom Teepen's article "Atlanta's Olympic Sport: Singing NIMBY Blues" distorted the organization's position on the Olympics by painting A'NUFF as "swearing to keep the games from occurring at all."[72]

A'NUFF responded quickly in the *Atlanta Voice*, stating, "We have never advocate[d] as policy that there should be no Olympics in Atlanta." The group reemphasized the danger of gentrification, adding, "We have said displacement . . . another effect of the . . . stadium would amount to the death of these neighborhoods." Its most impactful point reorients the argument toward a sociohistorical struggle waged against poor Black people by wealthy elites: "Even more perplexing is the categorization of efforts to prevent the building of the Olympic Stadium as a 'not in my backyard' approach. This trivializes the intent of those who are against the building of a second stadium.... Twenty-five years of urban renewal, stadium building, and highway construction have served to maintain this area as an undeveloped enclave in the shadows of downtown."[73]

Atlanta elites next sought to damage A'NUFF's credibility by questioning the group's motivations for fighting the stadium. Both the Atlanta media and city hall claimed that A'NUFF pursued "financial concessions from the Atlanta Committee for the Olympic Games." The rebels responded immediately to the charges, demanding communal autonomy over pro-growth investment: "The Olympic Stadium, as plans are presently constituted, is totally unacceptable. Our intent is not to coerce but to determine the fate of our homes and communities for our own selves to achieve self-determination. The determination should not be made by Billy Payne . . . or downtown businessmen."[74] Thus, A'NUFF argued that a return to the protonationalist framework that provided a radical critique of urban revitalization and produced tangible, successful outcomes for Black working-class Atlantans served as the means to defeating stadium construction and overall gentrification in the central city.

Despite the searing critique in A'NUFF's response, Atlanta's media structure successfully muddled the rebels' position, partly because of SNI's continued role in Olympic gentrification. A'NUFF's fears rang true in 1991 when the Atlanta Olympic Committee appointed Douglas Dean to its team. Dean reiterated often to the public that SNI did not oppose the building of the Olympic Stadium but rather that it sought a "cooperative partnership" with ACOG to obtain concessions and special consideration for the neighborhood. As a community development corporation, SNI recognized the potential for individuals in the organization to reap major benefits from acquiring business deals with city hall under the guise of community development. Dean, claiming to speak on behalf of Summerhill residents, proposed to ACOG a cap on stadium parking construction, a portion of parking revenues set aside for Summerhill residents, and a street-level retail complex.[75] For Summerhill, SNI proposed a mixed-income redevelopment: one-third of new housing construction built in Summerhill would be middle income; one-third upper income; and one-third lower income. As A'NUFF activist Gene Ferguson noted, SNI's redevelopment plan displaced 66 percent of the current Summerhill residents from the neighborhood. The Summerhill residents who made less than $15,000 a year did not possess the capability to move to the middle- and upper-income housing being erected throughout the city. Also, real estate developers refused to tear down affluent housing for low-income housing. As Ferguson concluded, SNI's gentrification plan was a snake-oil scam to poor Black people and "embraced equal parts racism and classism."[76] In other words, SNI wanted a slice of the Olympic pie regardless of how many of its residents the Atlanta power structure tossed out the window.

Atlanta media continued to manipulate public opinion against A'NUFF—including instituting a de facto blackout of its protests. The other major Black Atlanta newspaper, the *Atlanta Daily World*, stopped covering A'NUFF protest actions altogether. Consequently, the *Atlanta Voice* became the last major news outlet covering A'NUFF's protests in 1992. Because the *Voice* was a weekly aimed at a more progressive Black audience, it published critical pieces that questioned the validity of the stadium. However, weekly publishing was not consistent enough to keep up with the daily press machine slamming A'NUFF. By 1993, the *Voice* ceased reporting on the stadium fight and A'NUFF struggled to get its message out on a timely basis to the people it wanted to educate and mobilize.

Because of these factors, the Atlanta press more consistently publicized critiques against A'NUFF, extinguishing its community support. Eldon Frazier wrote to the *Atlanta Voice* that he wondered why the "hell-raisers who oppose the Olympic Stadium" were not "doing anything to enhance their communities" instead of letting the "Atlanta Olympic Committee do it for us."

Joe Collins expressed support for SNI, stating that "property owners have the right to do what they want.... If they want to sell it to the Atlanta Olympic Organizing Committee, that's their business.... I personally have had enough with A'NUFF (get it?) raising hell."[77] Henry Leroy Thomas invoked "bootstrap economics" in his reprimand of Summerhill residents: "If Summerhill and the neighborhoods surrounding it are not willing to make the necessary sacrifices to improve their own lots, then I will not support any opposition to the Olympic Stadium."[78]

Meanwhile, city hall was planning for the Olympic Stadium to become the home of the Atlanta Braves after the Olympics ended. Thus, ACOG took SNI's proposal to Braves owner and Atlanta media corporatist Ted Turner, cutting A'NUFF out of the negotiations altogether. Turner at first refused to relinquish exclusive control over concessions, parking, and retail, rejecting SNI's offer. However, by February 1993, all negotiating parties came to an agreement that set forth the demolition of public housing and the final remnants of historic Black communities in Atlanta. Turner and the Atlanta Braves received the most lucrative portion of the deal. They secured free use of the stadium and sixty luxury boxes, total control of stadium operations, 10,000 parking spaces (3,500 more than originally planned), nearly all the parking revenue, and naming rights to the stadium after the Olympics. In a shocking concession by city hall, Turner also assumed no financial liability for the stadium, meaning that Atlanta and Fulton County taxpayers paid the bill for any cost overruns associated with building and converting the stadium. This represented a significant loss for working-class Atlantans because the ACOG underestimated the $209 million it needed for stadium construction. After Fulton County commissioners stepped in to iron out the final points, ACOG and the Braves relinquished only 2,000 parking spaces and capped taxpayer liability for capital improvements at $50 million.[79]

The deal stated that Atlanta designated Summerhill the primary stadium-area neighborhood, meaning that it received a major share of any redevelopment funds that Central Atlanta Progress—with the assistance of the Urban Land Institute—raised over time.[80] As a result, SNI received gentrification funds while Peoplestown and Mechanicsville suffered a more immediate loss. When Dean cut the deal with ACOG, he moved parking construction out of Summerhill into the adjacent neighborhoods, meaning that both Peoplestown and Mechanicsville lost land plots to parking and Olympic venues. Last, the co-optation of SNI into Olympic gentrification undermined the political leverage that Black working-class neighborhoods held against the Atlanta power structure.[81] BURs now recognized that they could undercut the power of any grassroots movement by using nonprofits, moving forward in their gentrification dreams.

The Final Phase: Criminalizing the Poor in Atlanta

Pro-growth coalitions also destabilize urban working-class social movements by securing interests through direct force. The most common tactic they exercise is to overfund and discharge police surveillance and harassment in local activist areas. In other words, as historian Simon Balto noted, the public side of the pro-growth partnership flexes its power to protect and serve: protect business interests and serve the power structure.[82] With international investors and real estate growing by the year and the Olympics on the horizon, the city wasted no time in criminalizing the poor. Immediately upon taking office for his third term, Mayor Maynard Jackson and his transition task force called for a massive increase in police forces in the interest of "public safety." In February 1991, Jackson announced that Central Atlanta Progress (CAP) had issued funding for a transmitter for Atlanta police to use for what it called its "security communications network." At the time, Atlanta School Board president Joe Martin headed CAP and Underground Atlanta, making this funding ethically problematic. The transmitter allowed the Atlanta Police Department to stretch its surveillance network beyond the CBD into Black neighborhoods. With CAP's reputation for seeking control over Atlanta, it is safe to assume that CAP gained unlimited surveillance of the city.[83]

Jackson succeeded the CAP deal with a tax increase to fund hiring and pay raises for police. The Atlanta City Council voted to increase the millage rate by 0.96 percent, resulting in an increase of a little more than thirty-three dollars per year for property valued at $100,000. The move received heavy criticism across Atlanta, with many commenters calling out Jackson for misrepresenting the intent of the tax increase. "Mayor Jackson said that the money will be used for public safety purposes," said Atlanta resident Robert Lee Smith. "However, if he is correct in claiming that crime has gone down since he has taken office this time, then I want to know why do we need to spend this additional money in public safety?" He concluded, "I believe the public safety argument was used because the citizens are outraged at the crime picture in the city."[84]

Fulton County followed suit in increasing police powers, aiding Atlanta city hall in transforming the area into a makeshift military state for the Olympics. The County Board of Commissioners hired Maj. Gen. John H. Stamford, a white career army officer who hailed from the US Transportation Command at Scott Air Force Base in Illinois, as the new county manager. What is most alarming about this appointment is that Stamford joined an emerging body of war veterans in Atlanta's power structure: Gen. Donald L. Scott, the former second-in-command to Gen. Norman Schwarzkopf, as Jackson's chief of staff; Col. Delmar Corbin at the AHA; and Lt. Col. Joel Hall at the Atlanta Taxicab Bureau.[85] Indeed, the Atlanta bourgeoisie understood its conflict with the Black working class over gentrification as a literal "war" and drafted career warmongers to conduct direct and indirect violence.

Draconian laws depowered groups organizing protest activity as well as seeking work and housing. To pass such laws, Atlanta's city hall needed to manipulate public sentiment on the perceived threat of crime. This strategy had three crucial ramifications for the capitalist class in gentrification. First, it simultaneously provided justification for increased police funding and surveillance and lessened critiques of police brutality in low-income Black areas. Second, it blighted the land and built environment. Atlanta officials often cried wolf about crime, demanding federal funding and tax increases to solve the crisis, but often allowed the underground economy to expand in size and power uninterrupted in Black enclaves throughout the city. This led property values to plummet, allowing for land entrepreneurs to sweep in and buy the land and manipulate rents to expel working-class Black residents from the area. Third, because public officials neglected the underground economy in poor Black areas, the struggle was left solely on the backs of the residents to protect themselves from the consequences of a growing lumpenproletariat.

The lumpenproletariat—as Karl Marx dubbed them—are "illegal capitalists" who must engage in the same exploitative practices as their legal counterparts to make a meaningful living for themselves, family, or neighborhood kin.[86] In social terms, French philosopher Jacques Ranciere provided an apt description to build a contemporary understanding of illegal capitalists who are displaced by global finance capital. "For the proletariat," Ranciere explained, "the lumpen [are] the workers renouncing their revolutionary vocation and resorting to self-preservation." However, Ranciere also alluded to the lumpenproletariat acting in an equivalent manner to the financial aristocracy by "snatching productive wealth" in the form of territorial monopolies in both urban centers and rural spaces.[87]

As downturns in the economy produce higher numbers of workers in the reserve army of labor, this in effect raises the potential for more people to fall out of the class structure, end their labor participation, and join the lumpenproletariat. Consequently, as the size of the lumpen expands, they threaten to reduce the size of earnings for previously established lumpen—resulting in conflict over territorial/monopolistic control that is often violent. In clearer terms, the instability of the capital and labor markets influences the size of the lumpenproletariat and subsequently the intensity of violence in the underground economy. Illegal capitalists must not only acquire and sustain a viable profit but, in many cases, also display a hypermasculine manner to remove the possibility of competition, expand a monopoly over territory, strengthen their brand or reputation, or risk losing that revenue source. Popular examples include the street sale of pirated movies and music and cigarette "loosies"; chop-shop automobile sales; rival gangs' wars over turf for their drug trade; or the illegal lottery wars in 1920s Harlem between Ellsworth "Bumpy" Johnson, Madame Queen Stephanie St. Clair, Charles "Lucky" Luciano, and Dutch Schultz. A more urban regional instance includes drug syndicates in major urban centers like Chicago expanding their distribution nodes in smaller, surrounding metropolitan areas like Champaign County. To uproot previously entrenched syndicates, illegal capitalists must engage in monopolistic competition through any of three means: (1) buying out the competition, (2) establishing brand rivalry, or (3) engaging in territorial war. All three generally result in violence. On the other hand, a loss in monopolistic competition could result in a "blackout," when the individual or group is barred from participation in the underground economy.[88]

Increasing subproletarianization produces a swelling of reserve laborers who sometimes engage in illegal capitalism with little to no other options. Many individuals that sit at the top of illegal empires are non-Black, but like vampires, they accrue surplus profits from the exploitation of a disproportionate number of Black working-class people subjugated by the racist labor market and seeking any form of income. Crime—for most working-class people unfortunate enough to fall out of the class structure and join the lumpenproletariat—serves as their only means to procure the needs for human survival.

Thus, it is safe to correlate the swelling of Atlanta's underemployed in the 1990s with the rise in violent warfare in the underground economy. Consequently, the class struggle at the heart of underground economy community violence fueled a reshaping of how Black urbanites defined the "use value" of their neighborhoods and social institutions. Black urban communities shifted their priority from seizing power and autonomy to neutralizing more immediate threats to their lives and neighborhoods, particularly the drug trade and violent crime. Anticrime social movements exhausted neighborhood social movement capacity. As a result, community activists lost the time and capacity to protest long-term threats like gentrification until the bulldozers were at the gate.

With its new war-ready body of administrators, Atlanta city hall militarized the city's police. Jackson reinstituted hollow-point bullets for the Atlanta Police Department, a telling statement to his constituency of the "law and order" Atlanta he desired. City hall also opened the door for many private security forces to open shop in the region. Jackson also adopted a George H. W. Bush administration program, Operation Weed and Seed, and Atlanta served as a demo site for the $1 million federal operation. City hall chose the southwest neighborhoods of Englewood Manor and Thomasville Heights to "weed" out illegal capitalists via increased police foot patrol and technology and "seed hope" in the residents.[89]

Deputizing vigilantes offered the BUR a new force against poor Atlantans. The city council passed legislation in 1992 to create an updated version of its auxiliary police force called Friends of the City. The group, comprising volunteer citizens, resembled the New York City– and Los Angeles–based Guardian Angels "crime prevention" groups. They wore white shirts with red-and-black epaulets, white pants with red and black stripes on the sides, and white bobby hats with an emblem. The 125-citizen brigade carried nightsticks and walkie-talkies, but city hall did not allow them to carry guns. The security force received 200 hours of police training, six dollars an hour in wages (more than many African Americans were making at this time, when the Georgia minimum wage was $5.15 an hour), and better insurance coverage than offered by many blue-collar jobs. City councilman Morris Finley acknowledged that the council had created Friends of the City to halt the spread of bad publicity about the city. "We cannot afford to continue to allow downtown Atlanta to get bad publicity," Finley stated.[90] This newly created police force not only confined low-income Black residents to an isolated enclave during the Olympics but also recruited community members to oppress and subvert any protest actions against Olympics gentrification.

Atlanta often publicized crime statistics—often questionable because of false reporting and police harassment—to rationalize the call for funding the police "in the interest of public safety." In the report *Crime in Metro Atlanta: 1989–1993*, the Metropolitan Crime Commission argued that the violent crime rate rose 5 percent in Atlanta during those years while dropping nationwide. Property crimes, the report noted, rose 2 percent.[91] City hall fanned the flames of the business class's fear by pathologizing the underground economy as an inherent characteristic of the Black inner city. Mayor Bill Campbell stated that Black people should be more concerned about their crime problems than about being racially profiled because they're Black. "Black people are killing, robbing, and raping each other at an alarming rate. . . . We need to deal with that."[92] Purposely neglecting the political economic problems of racial oppression in Black working-class America, Campbell utilized his first public state of the city address to issue empty platitudes for what he called "the curse of crime in Atlanta." "Somewhere, we've got to start talking to our young people about the basic values of morality; about what is right and what is wrong." Campbell then pleaded for residents to put on a presentation for the Olympic visitors, because "none of us wants the world to come in the shape we are in today."[93]

Campbell's hollow pleas worked. The state of Georgia received $300 million from President Bill Clinton's crime bill, and the Atlanta metropolitan region allocated the funds for hiring hundreds of additional police officers, buying new computers and surveillance equipment, and building a $56 million jail in downtown Atlanta. Dubbed "Hotel 254," the 882-bed jail opened amid dozens of protesters, prompting city hall and police to threaten the group with being "the first guests in Hotel 254." The Atlanta City Council let its feelings be known about the facility, with council member Michael Bond ecstatic that the jail is "humane for corrections officers."[94]

Atlanta's war on the poor and housing insecure served as the defining subjugation of the Olympic era. During this time, African Americans constituted no less than 85 percent of those seeking shelter. Thus, it is safe to assert that many African American Atlantans lacked stable housing in the 1990s. Additionally, Black women comprised most of the African Americans seeking shelter. As Black women are disproportionately positioned in the lowest-paid, lowest-sector, and nonunion labor, they are more likely to experience financial precarity and therefore lose their housing more than other groups. Consequently, there were significantly more beds available to house men (2,000) than women (500) in the state.[95] Thus, the housing crisis that the Atlanta power structure produced over the last decade served as the impetus for anti-poor laws—the political solution to the consequences of class warfare in Black Atlanta.

A sizable portion of Atlanta's homeless originated in Techwood Homes and Clark Howell public housing. When city hall announced that the Olympics would take place in Atlanta, CAP, the AHA, and the ACOG proposed to remove all Techwood Homes tenants, renovate the project, and house athletes there. Locational advantage played a pivotal role for city hall targeting Techwood for gentrification. In fact, between 1970 and 1990, African American residency in Techwood/Clark Howell jumped from 60 percent to

90 percent. When African Americans became the majority in Techwood, the CEO of Coca-Cola, Paul Austin—the "darling of diversity and philanthropy"—stated that the "the felony rate will triple."[96]

Techwood consisted of thirteen three-story apartment buildings and seven buildings of attached houses. Clark Howell comprised fifty-eight two-story buildings with 630 apartment units. The buildings sat directly across the street from the Georgia Tech campus and adjacent to Coca-Cola's headquarters to the west. In 1991, Mayor Jackson formed the Techwood Advisory Committee to negotiate the redevelopment of the projects. The committee consisted of representatives from ACOG, AHA, CAP, and the Techwood Residents Association. Jackson also appointed the presidents of Georgia State University, Georgia Tech University, Atlanta University, and three real estate developers, an investment banking firm, and other various consultants. When the committee notified Techwood residents that it planned to develop mixed-income housing there, many protested on the justified fear of mass displacement.[97] Additionally, the residents accused and sued Techwood Tenants Association president Margie Smith, who sat on the committee, for abusing her power and remaining president past the end of her term.[98]

Because of resident co-optation, questionable ethics on the committee related to a resident survey on redevelopment, and lack of protest resources, Techwood/Clark Howell residents suffered a devastating loss on March 17, 1995, when the US Department of Housing and Urban Development approved the gentrification plan, dubbed the Revised Revitalization Plan. The proposal pledged that the AHA would replace the 1,195 Techwood/Clark Howell units that the redevelopment would eliminate.

It must be noted how the AHA deliberately forced residential displacement in order to empty Techwood/Clark Howell and reduce the chance for protest movement among residents. Based on Larry Keating's findings, evidence suggests that not only did the AHA maintain a policy to reduce the projects' occupancy rate by 20 percent, but it used an individual the community supported in order to manipulate them. In June 1990, residents occupied 531 of the 571 apartments (a 92.8 percent occupancy rate). The AHA hired African American Earl Philips in March 1992 to great fanfare amid Black working-class Atlanta. He had a reputation for improving housing conditions in other urban spaces and often visited the residential organizations. However, by October of that year, the occupancy rate of Techwood/Clark Howell dropped to 60.2 percent. By April 1993, residents occupied only 105 units (a 22.9 percent occupancy rate). Thus, when the residents voted on the final plan to gentrify the projects, only twenty-six families remained. The AHA had accomplished this by denying applications to all new residents. Also, the AHA instituted and enforced strict lease regulations that proved too difficult for many residents. Last, Mayor Bill Campbell's police sweeps in 1995 enforced a strict eviction mandate for anyone suspected of involvement in the drug trade.[99]

Emptying Techwood/Clark Howell provided multiple advantages to the Atlanta power structure. First, it engineered a favorable vote for redevelopment. Second, it reduced the cost of relocating residents.[100] By the end of 1999, the AHA had built only 49.4 percent of the housing lost to Techwood gentrification, and by 2011 Atlanta had destroyed the remaining units. Thus, it is safe to assume that half of the Techwood residents became housing insecure, with many becoming homeless.

After expanding homelessness through municipal polices, Atlanta city hall followed the national wave in removing the Black poor from public view. In fact, the city council preyed on Atlantans' struggles with the underground economy to further criminalize the poor. In July 1992, the Atlanta City Council approved the nation's toughest anti-poor ordinance at the time. The bill read as follows: "It shall be unlawful for any person to enter and remain on any property which is used primarily as Parking Lot for Vehicles, unless such a person has a vehicle parked on the property." The power structure praised the region's "leadership" in passing such a strict antihomeless law: "It shall be unlawful for any person to enter and remain in a vacant or unoccupied building. ... It shall be unlawful for a person to solicit or beg for alms." "We're again taking the lead nationally on this issue," said police chief Eldrin Bell. "We intend to clean up Atlanta and this is another tool to correct undesirables' behavior." In a surprising move, city councilman C. T. Martin not only voted against the measure but spoke out on the oppressive nature of such legislation: "What we're doing criminalizing behavior that is class specific ... that's not right. It has a chilling effect."[101] Martin's critique remains succinct: by positioning any individual asking for money or assistance on the street as acting against the law, the Atlanta power structure further pathologized poor Black people to ensure their status as superfluous for future private investment and gentrification. Atlanta leadership—in line with the liberal ideology of the nation at the time—believed that once they displaced poor Blacks, there was a smaller chance that residents would identify with the "criminal" poor and therefore fight to protect them.

Combined with the neoliberalization of public spaces in Atlanta over the previous two decades, Black working-class Atlanta lost access to many spaces with this new "vagrant-free zone." Police arrested poor Black people who set foot on private property without the property owner's permission or after a complaint. This measure also proved to expand the underground economy. Restricting panhandling meant that poor people lost access to a specific type of aid. Once that final pathway to aid disappeared, some poor joined the lumpenproletariat to acquire food, clothing, and shelter. As Atlanta scholar-activist Ajamu-Muhammad told Mayor Jackson, "When you think about the terminology—Guess who's coming to Dinner?—The homeless may be visiting you soon."[102]

As the Olympics inched closer, poor Black Atlantans lost access to more space and resources. In late June 1994, the Atlanta City Council took its attack on the homeless even further and approved equipping seventy-square-foot rail boxcars with makeshift kitchens and items for using the bathroom. The city planned to concentrate even more poor Black residents in meager spaces by placing the boxcars in the Carver Homes neighborhood, one of the poorest spaces in Atlanta at time. According to Wade Rogers, the project's white architect, the boxcars met state requirements for housing and Atlanta requirements for the size of a single room. Also, Rogers was set to pocket over $6 million annually by turning boxcars into makeshift homes. One lone city councilperson, Gloria Tinubu, spoke critically of the measure, saying, "This is substandard housing for the homeless, while we have standard housing for everyone else."[103]

Atlanta next targeted Woodruff Park at Five Points in downtown to displace poor Blacks. The park served as an aid bureau where the homeless and other low-income residents slept on the park benches, met with free clinic nurses for medical care, and received meals from church organizations. The Woodruff Foundation funded a $5 million renovation project in October 1994 that closed the park for months, transforming a crucial resource space for poor African Americans into a profitable tourist venue for the Olympics. "It's obviously a rehearsal for the Olympics," said Anita Beaty, executive director of the Task Force for the Homeless. "They're desperate to get the homeless out of sight." The new park added multiple security guards to keep the poor out of the park. The foundation also built new armrests on every bench to prevent reclining and sleeping. Finally, a new Georgia State University police precinct was built facing the park.[104]

Two months before the Olympic Games, the power brokers cleared the airport of poor Black people for the incoming tourists, vendors, and athletes. The city council passed a proposal in June 1996 to jail anyone for six months or fine them $500 if they were "loitering" at Hartsfield International Airport —meaning that the police were able to decide whether someone was waiting for someone or a flight.[105] A few months later, Atlanta City Council president

Marvin Arrington proposed jailing the city's homeless in a concentration camp. Arrington pushed a bill to make an abandoned factory in southeast Atlanta into a prison farm to supply Atlanta capitalists with a cheap labor force that lived outside of the region's public sphere. "I do believe that our working together with the business community will move us forward in the right direction," stated Arrington.[106]

As Atlanta's international guests arrived in July 1996, Atlanta stepped up its desperate attempt to mold the city as a middle- and upper-class haven without racial animosity or poor people. This often reached cartoonish levels. The city council pushed a law that made it illegal to remove anything from trash cans. Additionally, anonymous philanthropists bought one-way bus tickets out of town for thousands of poor blacks—a strategy used by Birmingham, Alabama, mayor Richard Arrington's BUR as well.[107] Many received a small amount of money if they signed paperwork stating that they would not return to Atlanta. Those who did not leave Atlanta or follow the new laws faced intense police harassment and arrest. In fact, Anita Beaty claimed that she found piles of arrest citations pre-printed with the designations "homeless" and "African American." When she attempted to organize a movement against city hall for this violation of human rights, Atlanta elites silenced her and told her, "Ya'll over there just need to chill."[108]

As a result of these combined factors, the Atlanta power structure condoned and rationalized a wave of police brutality throughout pre-Olympic Atlanta. One early example occurred on November 13, 1991, when narcotics officer Mike Polvilitis shot and killed eight-year-old African American Xavier Bennett in East Lake Meadows during a raid on the neighborhood. When community members and reporters pressed African American police chief Eldrin Bell about Bennett's murder, Bell stated without hesitation, "There is no connection between Xavier Bennett and the gangs"—changing the subject and erasing Bennett's agency in the process. On New Year's Eve 1991, the police stopped fifteen-year-old Arkala Lee—an African American resident of Summerhill with Down's syndrome—from entering his house, dragged him downstairs by his collar, and threw him in the mud. Officer R. J. Scapani put his knee in Lee's back while the youth screamed, "Mama!" When Lee's mother, Lucille, came outside to stop the officer, Scapani told her to "shut up" or he would arrest her. When Scapani attempted to justify his behavior by accusing Lee of stealing a car, his neighbors stated that Lee did not possess the mental capacity to operate a bicycle, let alone an automobile.[109]

State violence against poor Black people ramped up as the Olympics drew closer. In December 1995, Atlanta police officer Wine L. Pinckney shot and killed twenty-three-year-old African American Jerry Jackson while he lay on the sidewalk with his hands in the air. The police burst into a motorcycle shop without properly identifying themselves, causing the shop owner to shoot at the police. Jackson, an innocent bystander in the middle of the shooting, dropped to the sidewalk and put his hands in the air, when, as four witnesses reported, Pinckney deliberately aimed his revolver at Jackson and pulled the trigger. "Can cops just go around . . . shooting people?" asked Sarah Jackson, Jerry's seventy-two-year-old grandmother. The mechanic in the shop, Tony Delly, exclaimed that Black residents need self-defense to survive against the police. "This is not right. If a person with a badge can come in and take pot-shots at me, I'm going to protect my life."[110]

Police sweeps terrorized Black working-class neighborhoods in early 1996 leading up to the games. On November 30, 1995, Atlanta police and the AHA had jointly initiated their first sixty-day series of sweeps on public housing projects, specifically targeting areas surrounding Olympic Stadium. The AHA financed daily walking patrols as well, arresting over 100 African Americans during that operation.[111] The following month, as international guests arrived in the city for pre-Olympic events, Mayor Bill Campbell intensified police sweeps in the area and gave orders to evict any public housing tenants suspected of "criminal" activity.[112] As promised, police raided poor Black areas almost daily the month before the Olympics. A sweep of neighborhoods adjacent to the Atlanta University Center arrested thirty-six people in early July. The sweeps continued over the next few weeks, angering residents at city hall's facade put up for the international visitors. "This is unacceptable," stated Linda Pittman-Cotton, former chairperson of Neighborhood Planning Unit T. "There's two Atlantas. It's evident. It's everywhere. When the Olympics are over, they're gone, and that is not right."[113]

Atlanta's brutal tactics against Black urbanites did not deter the underground economy in the region, because a considerable number of officers participated in the drug trade. In mid-1995, the FBI conducted a sting operation—Operation Dirty Three—on the Atlanta Police Department and charged fourteen officers with corruption. According to the indictment, Sgt. Dale Hendrix and officers Ronald Grimes Jr., Willie Jackson, Edgar Allen Jr., Michael Williams, and Williams Vaughn Jr. patrolled zone 3—the Peoplestown, Mechanicsville, and Summerhill neighborhoods surrounding the Olympic Stadium—and accepted payments of at least $1,000 a week from drug dealers to protect a massive narcotics enterprise in the city. They also stole drugs and threatened violence against street-level dealers if they did not pay the officers. "He'll go through your pockets and take whatever he want and let you go," an anonymous dealer told the *Atlanta Voice*. "That's the price of justice out here."[114]

The sting also uncovered that rogue white police officers had used Thomasville Heights as "their own private plantation for years, where they could go in and take whatever they wanted." The sting followed numerous attempts by working-class Black activists to expose corrupt police in Atlanta. However, one anonymous Summerhill woman stated when she gave her report to the *Atlanta Voice*: "If you print this story I'm afraid that me and my family will be killed. Don't you know that the people who are dealing the drugs over here are the police."[115] This reiterates that the Atlanta power structure never intended to decrease or eliminate the underground economy or any criminal activity. Rather, it sought to isolate that economy from capital interests, hide it from international Olympic view, and, in some instances, control it and profit from it.

The New Nadir eroded the Black working-class capacity for sustaining social movements against Olympic gentrification in the city. The combination of the federal government's anti-working-class platform, the rise of the nonprofit-industrial complex and "diversity" philanthropy, and increased police powers decreased the use value of Black working-class neighborhoods and initiated displacement out of the central city. Neighborhood leaders like Ethel Mae Matthews challenged these policies with organizations like A'NUFF. However, community development corporations like SNI fractured the anti–Olympic Stadium movement along neighborhood lines. SNI's backroom deal with the City of Atlanta and Ted Turner positioned Mechanicsville and Peoplestown against Summerhill over revitalization funds and the Olympic Stadium parking lot. A'NUFF's damaged working-class resistance throughout the city, with Techwood Homes residents unable to fight the combined threat of the ACOG, the City of Atlanta, Coca-Cola, and Georgia Tech University. As a result, the destruction of Techwood Homes initiated the planned demolition of all public housing in Atlanta over the next twenty years.

In May 1995, longtime Summerhill activist and the head of the Atlanta Citywide Advisory Council on Public Housing Louise Whatley accurately prophesized the oncoming catastrophe for the Black poor with Atlanta's fever rush toward full private gentrification. In a speech to the Concerned Black Clergy organization, she argued that "they're gonna tear them [public housing projects] down and not bring them back." Whatley pointed to how the AHA sold huge chunks of land to private developers, calling out Coca-Cola for trying to buy the Perry Homes property. She concluded by pointing out the harsh reality: If the federal government allocated millions in public housing funds for renovation, why did the AHA sell land holding public housing funds to the increasing number of real estate developers coming to the region?[116]

Within ten years, Whatley and her Black working-class kin witnessed their housing stock destroyed for good. Because the New Nadir worsened the social conditions of Black Atlantans into the twenty-first century, formerly strong neighborhoods lacked the stability and resources to fight their oncoming destruction. As the next chapter will explore, financial and information sector middle managers, entertainment moguls, and a growing number of college students replaced the Black working class in Atlanta as the dominant racial class in the city.

CHAPTER FIVE

The Final Bite of the Apple
Nonprofits and Petty Bourgeois "Activism" in Post-Olympic Atlanta

> What's so perplexing is ... to revitalize blighted communities where low-income, poor people lived and turn them into safe, decent livable communities with affordable housing ... caught the eyes of the everyday capitalist. So the quest to make money drove the housing market to its maximum. When that occurs, you have those same low-income residents unable to afford to live in the place where they grew up. So, the exact group we set out to help, we've now become their harm.
> —DWANDA FARMER, Mechanicsville resident and activist, October 2003

In April 1997, forty-five-year-old African American venture capitalist, writer, and self-prescribed "community activist" Harold Barnett led the Atlanta Neighborhood Planning Unit-M (NPU-M)—the residential nonprofit organization responsible for providing planning and zoning recommendations for downtown Atlanta, Grady Homes, the Old Fourth Ward, Auburn Avenue, and Bedford Pine—in gentrifying their own neighborhoods. Barnett and Gallman Development Group (a member of Central Atlanta Progress) targeted the Atlanta Brushworks Factory on Hilliard Street in the heart of Sweet Auburn. The 70,400-square-foot Victorian-style plant represented one of the last historic businesses that had survived Auburn Avenue's postwar urban renewal and subsequent displacement of poor Blacks: it was originally built in 1905 and housed one of the largest commercial laundries in the Southeast, Trio Steam Laundry. By the late 1940s, it employed hundreds of working-class African American Atlantans who resided in the Old Fourth Ward neighborhood.[1]

As a primary investor in the project, Barnett's duplicitous leadership of NPU-M manipulated the class dynamics of "activism" for poor Black urbanites. While he claimed that he was not "politically persuasive" as chair, Barnett guided the NPU-M—which allowed any resident or property or business owner who attended three out of eleven meetings to vote on a planning or development recommendation—toward the newly revitalized Martin Luther King Jr. Historical Neighborhood Site and the recently expanded Georgia State University campus, which sat less than one mile away and less than two miles away from the Brushworks, respectively, as the model for neighborhood "empowerment." "People don't understand ... wealth," Barnett stated. "Creating broad based prosperity for a range of people in a socioeconomic structure.... I know development.... I know the factors [that] go into making the creation of wealth possible."[2]

While Atlanta media heralded Barnett as a "breath of fresh air" and "a new neighborhood leader," hundreds of predominantly Black Auburn Avenue and Old Fourth Ward residents lost their relatively stable factory jobs when the NPU-M recommended to the Atlanta City Council that the Brushworks building be rezoned for residential real estate. Gallman Development Group soon bought and closed Brushworks that year. By 2003, Gallman had transformed the plant into twenty-two condominium lofts, which skyrocketed surrounding rents and displaced the remaining poor into various unstable housing positions: other poverty-stricken Black enclaves in the central city, the rural suburbs in the metro region, or housing insecurity and homelessness. When the Brushworks closed, it left very few jobs that paid wages high enough to remain in the gentrified area. "They're tearing down housing that people have been living in for years," remarked African American activist Gwen Grieber. "You can't afford housing in Atlanta for minimum wage.... Now it's being torn down for monetary gain." By 2015, the Brushworks' condos with exposed brick interior, load-bearing walls, and stone foundation boasted an average rent of $275,000–$300,000 and held a locational advantage for numerous visitor market developments, such as the recently constructed Old Fourth Ward Distillery, the Edgewood at Hilliard Streetcar, and the Martin Luther King Jr. Center.[3]

Barnett's petty bourgeois activism embodied the class war transforming post-Olympic Black Atlanta into a private fortress for the affluent and tourism market. By the end of the 1990s, working-class African Americans who had ascended the class structure took a more substantive role alongside the capitalist class in building pro-growth, anti-working-class movements in their former neighborhoods. More clearly, petty bourgeois African Americans under the guise of "building bridges," "saving the streets," and "breaking the underclass pathology" pushed pro-growth ideology as antipoverty, anticrime, and wealth generating in media, schools, and social organizations. As a result, their activism to maximize the exchange rate potential of space and place opposed the class interests of poor African American Atlantans.[4]

Scholars have yet to examine how the tumultuous political economy at the onset of the twenty-first century informed the power dynamics and warring activisms between the Black working class, the Black petty bourgeoisie, and the Black bourgeoisie in urban metropolitan regions. This chapter investigates how the combined forces of the New Nadir and the pro-growth movement in the metro region restructured the political, economic, social, and spatial conditions of the Black working-class experience in Atlanta. The Black petty bourgeoisie in post-Olympic Atlanta, as the subordinate allies of the capitalist class, led pro-growth gentrification and privatization as their brand of "activism," which I term "petty bourgeois activism," that removed resources and the Black worker from the city.

Petty bourgeois activism refers to the strategy and tactics that pro-growth advocates use to gain public support for liberal, anti-working-class reforms like gentrification and public resource privatization. Petty bourgeois activists seek to privatize urban spaces, and therefore they target state-funded resources like schools, hospitals, and public housing. Petty bourgeois activists also misappropriate antipoverty discourse to garner support among the public and sow division and confusion among social movement actors. Thus, I argue that petty bourgeois activism is the means by which the ruling and middle classes co-opt tactical elements of working-class resistance to bolster their own class agendas. As the Atlanta power structure privatized housing, health care, and public schools, it removed a substantial number of tools needed for grassroots resistance. However, this chapter also highlights and charts the origins of petty bourgeois activism through the role of the state. Indeed, the empowerment zone fiasco in Mayor Bill Campbell's Black urban regime set real estate on a turkey shoot to annex as much land as possible in the ensuing years. Additionally, the Great Recession simultaneously exacerbated working-class precariousness and strengthened the strategic propaganda for petty bourgeois activism. Understanding how racial classes construct distinct and warring activisms based on class interests in the twenty-first century provides deeper insight into how the New Nadir restructured the relationship between the global capitalist political economy, the Black working class, the

Black petty bourgeoisie, the Black and white ruling class, and the state. As a result, we obtain a ground-level view of the inner working of urbanization and racial oppression in contemporary US cities.

"The Wizard of Oz Has Touched Atlanta": The Empowerment Zone Fiasco

To grasp the framework of petty bourgeois activism, we must trace the roots of the process back to empowerment zones. The "empowerment zone" catastrophe was the first major petty bourgeois activism conducted by the City of Atlanta and real estate developers for post-Olympic Atlanta. Empowerment zones derived from the federal "enterprise zones" program of the 1980s. Washington, DC, declared that urban centers would be given special tax breaks to encourage business investment in the areas. Jack Kemp, the former secretary of housing and urban development in the administrations of Ronald Reagan and George H. W. Bush, was the most ardent supporter of enterprise zones, remarking that "ghettoes are akin to a third-world socialist economy and capitalism would make them blossom." The truth is that enterprise zones functioned as a bridge for state support for gentrification, complete with the same ideas, slogans, and tactics of the War on Poverty of the 1960s and 1970s. As one report stated, enterprise zones were only "a means of *redistributing* investment and employment," not a means of *increasing* either.[5]

Atlanta's enterprise zone deal with the federal government dated to December 1994, when Bill Clinton's administration granted the city $100 million for poor Black neighborhoods to be designated as "empowerment zones." According to reporters who attended Mayor Campbell's press conference, he "gushed unabashedly" and proclaimed that he would "rebuild thirty poverty-stricken neighborhoods, give hope and opportunity [to] some 50,000 people and provide some 5,000 new jobs." "It's like the Wizard of Oz has touched Atlanta. Hope and salvation is on the way," Campbell told the 300-plus crowd. The zone was originally a 9.2-square-mile vise around downtown, gripping the Central Business District on the east, west, and south. Campbell chose these coordinates because the area had nearly three times the city's unemployment rate at 17.5 percent and a median income of $8,910.[6]

Petty bourgeois and bourgeois African Americans descended on the funds. Sulaiman Mahdi, a Mechanicsville representative on the Atlanta Empowerment Zone Board, announced plans to start a "youth community development corporation" with $4 million "that will go towards . . . establishing more businesses in the community." Before long, the Empowerment Zone Board functioned as a supervisory administration that managed, transported, and profited off of managing poverty instead of resolving it. In May 1995, the Atlanta City Council granted Herman J. Russell, the most prominent African American real estate developer in Georgia, special enterprise zone status for his Peachtree Street minimall construction project—a status usually reserved for impoverished areas. This allowed one of the richest corporations in the area to escape paying over $33.3 million in property taxes for over a decade. After securing the enterprise zone status, Russell built a 200,000-square-foot shopping mall and theater where Peachtree Street passes over I-85. He justified why his firm deserved enterprise zone status by stating his willingness to increase the property values around Peachtree Street to bring the middle and upper classes to the city. "The designated site is in a commercial enterprise zone, which is a technique that cities and states use to create enterprise, jobs, and . . . high property values that spur additional development," Jerome Russell, Herman Russell's son and president of H. J. Russell and Company, explained. "Without it, you're not going to get any kind of development in that area."[7]

As the years went by, the Black working-class neighborhoods further deteriorated. The problem was that Atlanta sat on the empowerment zone funds so long that officials at every level took notice of the neglect. It is clear in the lack of effort and policy by Atlanta officials that there never was an "empowerment" plan for the enterprise zone funds. Indifference and indecision allowed the Atlanta working-class neighborhoods to collapse under defunding and dysfunction. The debacle could only last so long without widespread scrutiny. In January 2002, the federal government publicly acknowledged the fiasco and stripped Atlanta of its empowerment zone status. The city had squandered a record $100 million in federal grant money and another $150 million in tax credits, proving the older working-class residents right: with empowerment zones, as with urban renewal, model cities, the war on poverty, and community development corporations (CDCs), the racial class interests and voices of poor African Americans contradicted the interests of the petty bourgeois and bourgeois classes in urban power structures. "I do not think the money was well spent . . . just like many other social service programs in our community during the last 40 years," stated African American Marie Cowser, an activist and resident of the Old Fourth Ward. "I don't know if the community was ever totally knowledgeable of what the Empowerment Zone was supposed to do."[8]

To make matters worse, only $58 million of the $250 million empowerment funds remained after alleged misappropriation and embezzlement. Activist

Ruthie Garrett-Wells accused the chair of the board of stealing funds for her family and friends and paying for a personal attorney. Board members openly attacked one another in the media, which resulted in Mayor Shirley Franklin dissolving the Empowerment Zone Board and creating a new public-private partnership, Renewal Community. Similar to the empowerment zone program, Renewal Community was a federally subsidized program that employed tax credits to promote economic development and revitalization in poor neighborhoods. Franklin appointed the Atlanta Development Neighborhood Partnership (ADNP) to oversee Renewal Community and dispense the remaining $58 million.[9]

Once again, problems arose and the ADNP defrauded poor Black neighborhoods of the millions promised to them. In July 2004, Franklin fired ADNP for not completing any projects. ADNP responded by requesting that the Atlanta City Council pay the group $426,000 for its efforts. The city did not approve ADNP's expenses and the only work to show for its efforts were a couple of disorganized community meetings that resulted in no follow-up planning. "ADNP has engaged in complete discord," stated African American Atlanta activist Darren Smith. "That's why they've been given their pink slip. ... Their community meetings were a complete joke. Their strategic plan is laughable."[10] After another four years, the federal government requested that Atlanta return all the empowerment zone funds. By July 2009, less than $30 million remained from the initial $250 million, and the designated empowerment zone neighborhoods were in worse condition than before 1994. The empowerment zone fiasco showcased the best intentions of CDCs in regard to alleviating the ills of working-class people. Petty bourgeois efforts ranged from nonexistent to possibly fraudulent with virtually no funding appropriated to community social institutions.

The Black urban regime's push to privatize Atlanta through the empowerment zones set real estate on the hunt for land that held favorable locational advantage for future use. Because of the spatial dimensions of the central city—little space between major profit-generating spaces—pro-growth opportunists categorized much of Black working-class land as viable. Thus, nobody in nonaffluent areas was safe. In 1997, Green Pasture Ministries, a Decatur-based religious organization, purchased a $60 million parcel of land in the West End neighborhood from the Sears building that sat near the Metropolitan Atlanta Rapid Transit Authority's (MARTA) West End Station, one of the busiest locations for public transportation in the city and the Atlanta University Center. Although the organization stated that its purchase was "in the business of Jesus," West End neighborhood residents like Rae McCall discovered that Green Pasture had partnered with Atlanta development company Walker Jackson, former Atlanta mayor Maynard Jackson's real estate firm, to construct high-rise apartments in the area. McCall also brought to light that Carol Gould, a residential real estate developer who facilitated the West End land acquisition for Green Pasture, had razed another neighborhood in the area to build an upper-income town house development that also held a locational advantage with the MARTA West End Station.[11]

Despite McCall's attempt to galvanize neighborhood support against gentrification, these projects jump-started more interest by Atlanta capitalists. Within the next few years, the Bill Campbell administration joined developers in pouring $150 million into another fifteen acres that stretched along Martin Luther King Jr. Drive, from James P. Brawley Drive (where Morehouse College sits) west to Lowery Boulevard and then north to Thurmond Street. This new "Westside Village" included seventy three-story town houses priced from $95,000 to $175,000, one hundred loft units, and sixty-six three-story apartment units. Commercial real estate included a new grocery store, a pharmacy, restaurants, a movie theater, and a laundromat. The H. J. Russell real estate giant joined Green Pasture Ministries in purchasing and razing significant portions of the West End neighborhood as well. The Russell–Green Pastures LLC built Sky Lofts Phase II, an $18 million development for 102 residential units, at the corner of Lowery Boulevard (formerly Ashby Street) and Oak Street next to Sky Lofts Phase I, a commercial retail development. Both encompassed a full city block within reach of thousands of Atlanta University Center students and hundreds of downtown businesses.[12]

By the early 2000s, petty bourgeois activism had emerged as the rallying cry for revitalizing Atlanta. "This is what is known as the new urbanization," stated Kevin Hanna, president of the Atlanta Development Authority.[13] Indeed, the gentrification of the West End demonstrated that the Black worker had no place in the future of the central city. At the onset of the twenty-first century, working-class African Americans existed on the neocolonial fringes of this new urbanization, either in isolated poverty nodes in the city or thirty miles or more away in the rural suburban parts of the region.

Around the same period, pro-growth interests attacked the remaining nongentrified segments of working-class Auburn Avenue. In 1999, the partnership between Coretta Scott King and the National Park Service spent an additional $10 million to renovate two blocks of late-Victorian-era-style homes. They tapped the Historic District Development Corporation (HDDC) CDC to serve as the housing wing of their revitalization. HDDC aggressively razed both Auburn Avenue and Old Fourth Ward sections. It purchased a vacant lot for the twenty-home Rosa Edwards Commons development on Howell Street. These developments raised the property values in the Old Fourth Ward to over $500,000, some reaching as high as $900,000. After some criticism for housing unaffordability, HDDC committed to finding housing only for middle-income families. Neither HDDC nor the Shirley Franklin Black urban regime mentioned the low-income residents losing their homes or a plan to find housing for the displaced.[14]

Black residents continued to fight displacement. One resident refused to sell his home to the developers for anything less than $1 million. "We couldn't do it," said Frank Catroppa, the National Park Service developer who wanted to take the home from a family. "It's unfortunate. It's the only property we'd like to have because it's between the birth home and the King Center." Another Auburn Avenue resident, Johnnie Haughabrook, used the National Park Service's valorization tactics against them. After refusing to take a low offer for his home, Haughabrook spent the summer of 1996 painting it. He then skyrocketed the asking price for his home and justified it through the new paint job. Ninety-two-year old Annie Johnson, who had lived in her two-story beige house on the corner of Auburn Avenue almost her entire life, stated that no price would force her to leave her space. "I've been here a long, long time," she told the *Atlanta Voice*. "I don't want to move until I'm dead and gone. Can they make me move? Well, they'll have a fight trying." Despite displacing over three-quarters of the original working-class residents from Auburn Avenue, the National Park Service and the King family concluded that "you can't own everything." At the end of 1999, they purchased the final two homes they expected would come under their ownership. By the early 2000s, homes listed on Auburn Avenue ranged between $300,000 and $400,000. African American J. C. Thomas, who owned an eatery in the neighborhood, lamented how gentrification destroyed his Black neighbors and the resident-centric aspect of Atlanta: "The new houses being built next to us start at near $350,000.... That tells you that the people who are there now are not going to [be] living there very long. Black folks are getting uprooted, and they don't have the means to hang on."[15]

Tom Davis, an African American Auburn Avenue resident who operated Love Radio Internet Station, echoed similar sentiments, pointing to the racial class characteristic of displacement in the area: "Blacks are losing Auburn Avenue.... Gentrification is likely to be Auburn Avenue's death knell."[16] Despite this opposition to the violent displacement and housing instability that characterizes gentrification, Black elites considered the removal of the majority of the Black residents as the only way to save Auburn Avenue. "I'm very happy to see what's happening there," Coretta Scott King stated. "I think without it the neighborhood would have been destroyed."[17]

Neoliberalization and gentrification over the previous two decades had upended Atlanta's racial class demographics dramatically by the turn of the twenty-first century. In 2004, Clark Atlanta University's Southern Center for Studies in Public Policy reported that "while [Blacks] are moving outside the city into subdivisions and housing developments," whites had purchased 95 percent of the newly built condos and lofts in the central city that replaced torn-down public housing projects.[18] In fact, the Southern Center predicted correctly that the first decade of the twenty-first century would see a drastic demographic shift as more new housing, tourism, night life, and upscale businesses lured white middle- and upper-class families to the central city. Kathy Holland, the fifty-four-year-old white chief operating officer and president of the Mescon Group consulting firm, moved her six children away from their two-story Gwinnett County home in Duluth, Georgia, to buy a 1,250-square-foot loft overlooking downtown Atlanta in 1998. She traded in her ninety-minute daily car trip to her office for a ten-minute walk to work. News anchor Charles Shepherd left a three-bedroom, two-story house in suburban Cobb County to reside in a 1,600-square-foot, $1,400-a-month loft in a renovated office building downtown. According to Terry Morris, the executive vice president of Northside Realty, Holland's and Shepherd's experiences were exceptions to the rule because they were each married. Most middle- and upper-class whites that moved to the central city around the turn of the century were single, divorced, childless, or recently graduated from college.[19]

The Southern Center's prophecy proved true. Between 2000 and 2008, Atlanta and Washington, DC, posted the largest increases in white share of a city since 2000, each up five percentage points to 36 and 44 percent, respectively. Other significant reverse white flight occurred during the same time frame in New York City, Boston, and San Francisco, which demonstrates that Atlanta was only one part of a late capitalist push to privatize major metropolitan centers.[20] Collectively these gentrification efforts expelled the Black working class to those decreasingly white suburbs, distancing them from neighborhood networks, community resources, and employment opportunities. In 2003, the average cost of a home in the city of Atlanta approached $250,000, more than double the going price in 1988. Concurrently, Central Atlanta Progress reported that over 80 percent of Atlantans who resided in downtown Atlanta made less than $40,000 a year. In other words, 80 percent of Atlantans did not possess the capacity to buy a home in the city of Atlanta in 2003. What is most revealing about the neoliberal character of the city of

Atlanta is that the housing costs in the areas with the highest concentration of low-paying jobs were the highest in the city—averaging between an estimated $300,000 and $7 million.[21]

As African American Mechanicsville activist Dwanda Farmer eloquently expressed, much of the blame for the skyrocketing cost of living in the city went to the exploitative character of CDCs: "What's so perplexing is [that] the city's mission to revitalize blighted communities where low income, poor people lived and turn them into safe, decent livable communities with affordable housing was a great idea at the onset.... The implementation ... caught the eyes of the everyday capitalist. So, the quest to make money drove the housing market to its maximum. When that occurs, you have those same low-income residents unable to afford to live in the place where they grew up. So, the exact group we set out to help, we've now become their harm."[22]

Black Working-Class Struggles against Privatization in Atlanta

For five days a week between 1985 and 1997, African American Carl Waller, a twelve-year veteran of the Atlanta Public Works Division of the Atlanta Water and Sewer Department labored over eight hours a day in sewage muck, twenty to thirty feet underground inside the city's decrepit sewer pipes that measured nine feet in diameter. A 1983 graduate of Fisk University, Waller chose the public-sector labor force because it provided him with a way to return public goods to Atlanta residents. "What I do is help the public," Waller expressed. "It feels good." However, in February 1997, Waller organized over a dozen of his coworkers and stormed the Atlanta City Council chambers in protest of Mayor Bill Campbell's announcement to privatize the city water and sewer system. Waller argued that Campbell's decision was a clear lack of respect for city workers as well as a tactic to allot more power to capitalists in government decision-making: "Our concern is that privatization is just a political solution because the mayor can't really provide real leadership in managing these departments in an efficient and effective manner.... Mr. Campbell is appealing to the private sector to tell him how to manage the Water and Sewer Department. He won't come to the workers and talk to us. He won't eliminate his bad managers."[23]

Campbell's privatization proposal was a sudden about-face following a strong agreement with municipal workers to keep services public. Olympic-era Atlanta teased the ruling class with an urban space defined primarily through a twenty-four-hour visitor market: capital flowing freely uninterrupted; isolated and surveilled poor Black neighborhoods and residents; the concentration of the underground economy in poor Black enclaves like Vine City; newly constructed dormitories, athletic fields, and basketball gymnasiums for Morehouse College, Spelman College, Georgia State University, and Georgia Tech University that replaced public housing (Techwood/Clark Howell Homes); new private "mixed-income" housing (which was code for 70 percent middle income, 25 percent upper income, and 5 percent low income) and parking lots decorating the periphery of poor Black neighborhoods on the Olympic bus routes; and the $250 million beacon to corporate capitalism, the Turner Field/Olympic Stadium complex.[24]

Thus, the Atlanta power structure sought to deepen neoliberalization in post-Olympic Atlanta to re-create the lucrative tourist market on a permanent basis. Residency in Atlanta undercut the exchange value potential of unending visitors willing to pay extravagant prices for the city's reputable social and cultural hotspots. Therefore, the Bill Campbell Black urban regime emerged as the vanguard in petty bourgeois activism by reducing public control of resources and services through privatization. African American city council president and longtime Atlanta politician Marvin Arrington had championed full privatization for years and used his career to strengthen corporate power. Arrington had practiced law for decades up to this point, and his partnership with African American civil rights lawyer Donald Lee Hollowell in 1989 specialized in defending employer interests and acquiring corporate bonds. According to African American city councilman Robb Pitts, "President Arrington has been on record for a long-time supporting privatization." While Marie Robinson, executive director of the American Federation of State, County, and Municipal Employees (AFSCME) Local 1644, defined Campbell's policy reversal as "political," his chief operating officer, Byron Marshall, coded privatization in pro-growth discourse, stating, "We are faced with . . . trying to provide high quality service to the citizens in the face of state mandates and fines . . . so this gives us the opportunity to . . . make the system more efficient . . . at the lowest possible cost."[25]

The Atlanta and Fulton County governments ramped up attacks on working-class social conditions. In the first week of March 1998, the city council voted 14–1 to privatize the city water service. To subdue public outrage, Campbell engaged in a fearmongering speaking tour across the metro region, threatening to raise water rates over 50 percent if the city did not privatize. The lone opposing council voter, Felecia Moore, provided a succinct explanation as to how the city's privatization proposal had less to do with solving financial and infrastructural problems and more to do with exploiting a new source of revenue: "The first thing we are doing is privatizing the drinking water system, from administration down to billing. And that's our revenue generator, it's our cash cow. Our problem is with our wastewater and our sewer system. That's what we're being fined for. We're using our water system to subsidize those problems."[26]

Atlanta's eighty-year-old water and sewer infrastructure allowed untreated sewage to flow into the Chattahoochee River. According to Campbell, rehabilitating this system would cost $865 million, but privatization would save Atlanta over $600 million over twenty years. Even if the city adopted this proposal with a private corporation, Felecia Moore continued, it still expected to increase sewer rates by 29 percent over four years, placing an undue burden on the poor residents. Moore cited additional evidence that Campbell and the city council preferred profits over solutions. She stated that an outside consultant recommended eight options for revamping the outdated sewer system and the mayor selected the "most risky and most intense" of those options.[27]

Campbell signed the twenty-year contract with United Water Service, a company from the French corporation Lyonnaise des Eaux, for $21 million in November that year, which was hailed as "the largest and most closely watched privatization of a public water system in North America" at that time. However, city workers organized a movement to block implementation of the contract before its December 1 start date. In the week before Thanksgiving, the Fulton County Superior Court denied their lawsuit against the city, and by the beginning of 1999, United Water had cut over 300 city jobs.[28]

When the contract ended abruptly and the water services returned to the city's purview after four years of increasing public outcry over job losses, brown water, pipe leaks, and boil water advisories, Atlanta had lost an estimated $18 million in transition, hiring, and consultation costs. This did not include the millions Atlanta needed to rehabilitate the failing sewer system. Additionally, city auditor Leslie Ward reported that the $21.4 million annual contract with United Water cost Atlanta twice that amount—$42 million a year—when she included utilities, city monitoring staff, insurance, and other miscellaneous costs. That was about $10 million more than the city had spent on the water system in multiple years before selling it to the French corporation.[29] Thus, as with most transitions from public to private control, Atlanta lost over $125 million over four years and hundreds of working-class jobs in a business deal that had been expected to reap significant profits. At the end of its deal with United Water, the city was in much worse shape than before privatization. Its budget revenue shortfall skyrocketed as it failed to address the increasingly expensive waste management crisis.

As privatization led debt to spiral further out of control, Atlanta officials sought to privatize more public services for the working poor in cost-cutting efforts. Grady Memorial Hospital, the largest hospital in Georgia and the fifth largest public hospital in the United States, became a target after the city declared that it needed to be "saved from closure by privatization." Located in downtown Atlanta right next to the Georgia State University campus, the 124-year-old superstructure medical facility contained sixteen floors; six neighborhood health centers; over 5,300 doctors, nurses, and staff members; and 950 beds. At the time, it was the only primary care provider for low-income, uninsured, and underinsured Atlantans. Besides its "public safety-net status," it also housed the most advanced level 1 trauma center within a 100-mile radius of Atlanta as well as a nationally ranked burn unit and stroke care center. Despite serving all nineteen of the counties in the Atlanta metropolitan region, Grady received funding only from Fulton and DeKalb Counties, which contributed almost 20 percent of Grady's funding. For fiscal year 2007, those counties paid $86 million and $27 million, respectively.[30]

Years of blatant underfunding resulted in a $60 million deficit and the threat of closure in 2007. On Grady's 121st birthday, when asked "What were the most troubled years of Grady hospital?" Martin Moran, a retired Grady physician, answered, "The first 120." The hospital barely met payroll in 2007 and required over $360 million worth of upgrades. Additionally, capitalists recognized the loss of substantial profit across multiple sectors if they did not seize control of Grady. "It couldn't close," said Michael Frankel, the hospital's chief neurologist. "Shutting it down would've had a ripple effect on the health care community. Without Grady, profit margins at other hospitals are gone. It would be like shutting Hartsfield Airport and would have ramifications for decades."[31] Thus, the threat of destabilizing the health-care profit industry provided justification for the Atlanta power structure to develop a plan to privatize the hospital.

In March 2007, the Fulton-DeKalb Hospital Authority, a politically appointed board selected by the commissioners of each county, aligned with the Atlanta Chamber of Commerce to form the Greater Grady Task Force. Atlanta elites on the task force included African American Michael B. Russell, CEO of H. J. Russell and Company; Carl Patton, Georgia State University president; and African American Renee Glover, executive director of the Atlanta Housing Authority and nicknamed the Gentrification Queen by fair-housing activists. In September 2007, the group submitted a report that recommended that management turn the hospital over to a nonprofit corporation "in order to attract funding from banks, the State of Georgia, and other sources." On August 21, the hospital's governing board approved a multimillion-dollar plan to fiscally stabilize the Grady Health System. The ten-member Fulton-DeKalb Hospital Authority approved $125 million, with a $100 million line of credit from Citigroup and Morgan Kegan and Company with the guarantee that both counties cosign the loan. This new money proved crucial because it allowed Grady to pay its debt to both Emory University and Morehouse College, both of which had loaned staff to the hospital.[32]

The Greater Grady Task Force saw fit to exclude neighborhood residents from participating in any decision-making regarding their hospital. According to the New Grady Coalition, a protest organization whose goal was to put the control (and therefore the fate) of Grady in the hands of the public, meetings to determine how to privatize Grady occurred in secret closed-door meetings that prohibited "non–task force members" access. Therefore, the New Grady Coalition organized a series of sit-ins and community town halls to both educate residents on the dangers of privatizing public resources and broadcast how Atlanta's elites quietly assumed decision-making power over the hospital. The most publicized and violent of these protests occurred on November 27, the day the task force met to vote on privatization. Outside of the meeting room in Grady, hundreds of neighborhood residents, Black AFSCME union officials, hospital staff, doctors, and progressive Atlanta officials like African American state senator and Morehouse College professor Vincent K. Fort flooded the hallways with loud chants, singing, and speeches to the press.[33]

According to *Atlanta Voice* reporters on the scene, physical confrontations with the police and hospital security almost grew into a large melee. At 3:30 in the afternoon, Fort, former city councilman Derrick Boazman, and two unnamed community members attempted to storm the boardroom, when officers restrained them, handcuffing Fort and dragging the other three protesters outside the building, with other protesters screaming at the police, demanding that they stop. The crowd then alerted the police that they wouldn't leave the building until Governor Sonny Perdue "delivered the money necessary to maintain Grady's existence."[34]

By 4:00 p.m., the police released all four protesters, and they rejoined the occupation. The protesters' chants and songs had pressured the board members to include them in the final vote session without public comment. However, chants of "let the people speak" drowned out the board members, and witnesses stated that "numerous members of the crowd were serious and ready to go to jail if they weren't heard." Finally, the board conceded and allowed everyone two minutes to speak. The protesters' comments focused on the class warfare at the center of privatization in Atlanta. They accused the state of Georgia of scapegoating the poor after misappropriating state funds and tax revenue. They also blamed the chamber of commerce for corruption in forcing Grady to go private, as well as the Fulton-DeKalb Hospital Authority itself in taking away one of the most vital resources for the Black communities in the city. "In Houston, Boston, and in California, hospitals of comparable size as Grady all failed after switching to a private governance model," stated African American activist and chairperson of the New Grady Coalition, Ron Marshall. "When you start privatizing something, it goes bad. It affects the community as a whole. . . . We lose the benefit of well-trained doctors. Who's going to take in the indigent? There would be five thousand people out of a job at Grady."[35]

Despite the hours of public testimony, the board approved privatization on the following terms: increased state funding for the hospital of at least $30 million a year; assurance that both Fulton and DeKalb Counties would increase their funding from $86 million to over $200 million total; an expectation that Grady's trauma center, one of the largest and highly reputable in the United States, remain financially stable; assurance that both Morehouse School of Medicine and Emory University uphold their education programs at the hospital and that the debts be renegotiated; and more abstract "promises" that "certain" current Grady employees keep their jobs and a "commitment to treating those less fortunate."[36]

As Vincent Fort stated, "They did not save Grady, they took it over" to reap surplus profits. "What these business leaders adhere to is: never let a crisis go untaken advantage of," Fort contended. "They made that point [that] Grady's going to close and all that. But the fact is, they took advantage of that hysteria and unleashed the dogs. They were enlisted in the fight against the community in a shameful way." Immediately after the agreement and vowing to oppose corporate restructuring, the Fulton-DeKalb Hospital Authority, at the behest of the Atlanta Chamber of Commerce, reconfigured Grady's leadership and transferred its oversight to a new body, the Grady Memorial Hospital Corporation. Unsurprisingly, many of the new leadership included Greater Grady Task Force members from the Atlanta Chamber of Commerce. "This is about green, not Black or white," stated Grady hospital chairperson Pete Correll. "It's about money." Associate dean of the Morehouse School of Medicine Daniel Blumenthal contextualized this process as a corporate coup that exploited a public crisis: "So because of the alleged threat of the hospital closing, this new board was created. . . . The Fulton-Dekalb Hospital

Authority was disempowered and a new board was empowered, so that the people running the hospital were now in the hands of the business community rather than the people."[37]

Fort's prophecy rang true as Grady became one of the most profitable corporations of the 2010s. The Woodruff Foundation promised to shower Grady with $200 million only if it moved from being a public entity to having nonprofit corporate management. With the Woodruff donation, Grady upgraded its infrastructure around billing, including a surprising $40 million electronics records system that streamlined payment collections on patients. In other words, corporate management argued that transforming public health care into a business structure strengthened the profit potential. "In health care, just like any business, you've got to get the bill out the door and get it collected," said John Haupert, Grady's CEO. By 2016, Grady hospital had increased its net revenue by $106 million a year. However, it cost workers hundreds of jobs and patients millions of dollars in extra fees. Despite management's initial claim that it would find new funding (Woodruff's donation was an exception), the corporate restructuring amounted to only slashing jobs and services. "Their goal was to cut waste, what they considered waste, and get Grady ... to make a profit," stated Dorothy Leone-Glasser, a neighborhood health activist. "That was their goal, with all disregard for the patients and that's the part that, to me, was most upsetting."[38]

Grady's program slashing severely undercut health resources in Black working-class Atlanta. Grady reduced the number of neighborhood clinics from nine to six without public input. As a result, poor Atlantans no longer possessed preventive care (a lesser cost), and many only saw doctors when they were sick enough to go to the emergency room when the costs for treatment were exorbitant. The most disastrous move under the neoliberalization of Grady hospital occurred in September 2009 when it closed its dialysis clinic, a crucial resource for African Americans. Baani, a twenty-nine-year-old resident of Fulton County, was turned away from multiple hospitals for dialysis treatment because she was uninsured. Grady hospital did not treat her until after she made numerous trips to the emergency room. After a few years of regular biweekly treatment and relative stability in her life, Grady informed Baani and other dialysis patients that it had closed the treatment center. "They were going to close the ... clinic without giving us a place to go after that. My heart just broke," Baani responded. Baani explained that Grady offered dialysis patients three options: emergency room care; a move to another state, which most could not afford; and for undocumented individuals, expatriation. In fact, Leone-Glasser said that Grady hired an expatriation company, Mexcare, which offered a plane ticket, a small amount of money, and three months of dialysis care for any undocumented patient to move to their original country.[39] Cutting public resources for undocumented people eliminated another undesirable group from the city of Atlanta in one way or another for the pro-growth faction.

Baani and other residents affected by the clinic closure organized multiple rallies against Grady that captured the attention of both local media and legal representation. In less than a month, community pressure forced a court injunction that blocked the dialysis center's closure for over a year. Despite Grady's pleas of infeasibility, the court forced the hospital to locate and sign a funding agreement with three local dialysis providers to extend treatment to all Atlanta patients. As of 2013, Grady was paying for the kidney treatment of fourteen Atlantans, while others moved out of the area for better options.[40]

Michael Young, the Grady CEO at the time, expressed his contempt for poor Black Atlantans at social events with city elites. At an October 2010 breakfast with Atlanta Chamber of Commerce members in Buckhead, taking full credit for "saving" the hospital, Young told his peers that Fulton County residents "should want to shine my shoes." Residents and politicians were justifiably angered at this blatantly racist remark. Public pressure led to Young's resignation less than a year later.[41] His remarks to Atlanta capitalists undergird the mentality of Grady management's disregard for poor Blacks.

Hospitals served as a strategic privatization target for liberal growth machines because of their fragile infrastructure. State funding cuts made hospitals especially vulnerable to takeover or privatization. Consequently, this allowed petty bourgeois activists to swoop in as "heroes" that "saved" a public necessity. This played a pivotal role in the positive reputation of pro-growth interests at the turn of the century. When private interests publicized their "generous" donations to fund a public resource under their supervision, it created a complicated dynamic in low-income Black spaces where resources were limited. Capitalists followed the same strategy with privatizing education as they attempted to convince parents that their structure and money was the key to saving "failing" schools and their children from the underground economy.

Public School Privatization

Public schools in Atlanta faced countless assaults by petty bourgeois activists to privatize and thus move further away from their role as a public resource. In 1999, over 400 charter and private schools opened across the United States, resulting in a quarter of a million children enrolled in all charter and private schools, a 40 percent increase from 1998. The Clinton administration bolstered the private and charter school movement when it allotted a $30 million increase to the $175 million in federal funding for states to develop charter schools. Exclusion based on race and class increased in correlation with the rise of charter and private schools. Because both charter and private schools are free from state laws and regulations, they can set their admission standards without legal scrutiny. By early 2000, the federal government designated 25 percent of all charter schools to serve "specific populations." Small school districts in Lufkin, Texas, Oktibbeha County, Mississippi, and Georgetown County, South Carolina, all received nationwide criticism over their segregated charter school patterns. However, larger school districts in St. Louis, Cleveland, and especially Philadelphia, which each experienced declining property tax revenues, lost so much funding that they faced a difficult choice: get taken over by the state or adopt charter and private schools. For example, Philadelphia schools only employed four psychologists who served 12,000 students in fifteen schools for the 1999–2000 school year. Additionally, the system had $2,500 less to spend per student per year, or $75,000 less to spend on a class of thirty per year than did suburban Pennsylvania counterparts.[42]

As Black middle- and upper-class parents gradually gravitated toward private schools in the early 1990s, the Atlanta power structure took advantage of the vulnerability of public schools to destabilize them. More clearly, petty bourgeois activists and capitalists promoted "free choice" ideology, meaning that parents must possess the freedom to choose where their student received education. Pro-growth advocates argue that public schools are intellectually, economically, and culturally degenerative. In their minds, offering the exclusionary private and charter schools allows parents the opportunity to uplift their child's education with the added benefit of "freedom of choice." However, petty bourgeois activists worked behind the scenes to bankrupt public school funding and slash resources so that parents had no choice but to choose a private or charter school with plentiful resources over the defunded public school.

Black public-school workers fought against early attempts to privatize the Atlanta Public Schools (APS) system. On the first day of school in August 1997, 375 AFSCME Local 1644 food service, transportation, maintenance, and custodial APS workers picketed multiple schools and the APS downtown headquarters on Pryor Street. The workers demanded the removal of APS superintendent Ben Canada and new policies regarding budget cuts and asked for improved working conditions. Black workers like maintenance staffer Robert Stevens and custodian Jackie Johnson proclaimed that their struggle was for the benefit of their neighborhoods because their public schools are vital to the strength of their communities. "This is our thing!" Johnson exclaimed. "This is for our kids that we have to raise!"[43]

Black APS workers demanded the reclassification of employees, which would simultaneously raise the salaries of veteran workers and combat job cuts by hiring more custodians, cafeteria workers, landscapers, and bus drivers. For example, Johnson, who cleaned Pitts Elementary School for three years, was supposed to move from step 3 (with an average salary of $23,141.50 a year) to step 7 (with an average salary of $27, 851.50 a year) in November. "They're telling me that I've got to wait until November 1998," she explained. "They're only to give me $13 [a month]. Thirteen times twelve [months] is $156." Unfortunately, because APS designated custodians, bus drivers, cafeteria workers, landscapers, and maintenance workers as "operational," their salary ceiling was step 10 ($30, 501.50 a year). Workers also contended that school budget cuts resulted in overworked operational staff. According to African American Marie Robinson, a custodian and one of the lead negotiators for the AFSCME labor negotiations, the predominantly Black custodial staff plummeted from 407 to 307 in less than a year in 1997.[44]

The Atlanta City Council attempted to offset those budget cuts and school renovation costs by selling public education to the highest bidder. In January 1999, APS officials requested proposals from private for-profit education management firms. The New York–based Edison Project, a seven-year-old corporation that was the largest for-profit education management firm at the time, with fifty-one schools in eleven states, put forward a bid. In February, Edison held several closed-door meetings in which it assured the Atlanta Board of Education that it had invested over $40 million in research and would implement "the best teaching methods used in public and private schools." Edison proposed to operate three K–12 clusters of schools in various parts of the city, which amounted to about 6,000 Atlanta students.[45]

In keeping with the gentrification of working-class Black Atlanta, private and charter schools served as a primary catalyst for land rent manipulation in urban communities. The Edison Project chose Drew Elementary School in East Lake Meadows because it held proximity to the Villages of East Lake, the new middle- and upper-income housing development that had displaced the predominantly poor Black residents of the area in 1997. Tom Cousins, who had been responsible for a significant portion of the corporate takeover of Atlanta over the previous three decades, said of East Lake Meadows that "if I had been born there, I'd be in prison or dead." Consequently, Cousins revalorized the land and property to maximize its exchange value potential and price out the lower-income residents. The new apartments, which averaged $1,100 a month for rent, had a plantation facade with upscale interiors, built-in bookshelves, garden tubs, nine-foot ceilings, light oak kitchen cabinets, pantries, tray ceilings, private balconies, walk-in closets, and extra-wide doorways.[46]

Cousins stated that "if the new Villages at East Lake is to attract a solid core of middle-class residents, it has to have a top-notch public school." Thus, Greg Girnelli, executive director of the East Lake Community Foundation —the nonprofit in charge of gentrifying the neighborhood and owned by Cousins—and African American Shirley Franklin, city executive during Maynard Jackson's third mayoral term, negotiated with the Atlanta Board of Education and Edison Project to establish the Charles R. Drew charter school in East Lake Meadows. Edison's promise to "place a computer in front of every student and in every home" gained popularity in Black working-class and middle-class neighborhoods.[47]

Despite that, fierce resistance across the class stratum challenged Edison's takeover of public schools in Atlanta. In late March, Research Atlanta held a metro-region-wide debate among forty educators, community residents, and college students. The Cobb County teachers' union criticized Edison's record. They claimed its profit was accrued by overrunning inexperienced teachers with overcrowded classrooms. Other teachers' organizations like the Georgia Association of Educators argued that Atlanta's push to adopt the Edison Project demonstrated its decades-long mission to remove education as a resource for the working classes: "Instead of dedicating scarce resources to taxpayer-funded vouchers and tax credits that weaken public education for all in favor of . . . private instruction for a few, we should instead fund . . . class size reductions." Three Black petty bourgeois organizations—the 100 Black Men of Atlanta, Concerned Black Clergy, and the Atlanta chapter of the NAACP—sponsored protest rallies and media conferences that both condemned Atlanta officials and exposed the Edison Project's pursuit of school districts throughout the nation with predominantly low-income, "underperforming" students. They also reported that in each of the Edison Project's districts, students did not achieve higher grades than their public-school counterparts and the group failed to turn around low-performing schools. "Edison . . . [has] never delivered anything that would make you proud with respect to poor Black kids," stated African American urban education professor Asa Hilliard.[48] Therefore, privatization of public schools served as one pro-growth measure that both the Black working class and a portion of the Black petty bourgeoisie united against, in opposition to the Black and white bourgeoisie.

The challenge to privatization did not garner enough heat to halt the project. Thus, the 200,000-square-foot Drew Charter Junior and Senior Academy, with its 880 students from preschool to eighth grade, became the cornerstone of the $103 million revitalization of the East Lake neighborhoods. Funded predominantly through Home Depot and Atlanta Falcons owner Arthur Blank, Chick-fil-A, the Bill and Melinda Gates Foundation, Georgia Power, the Kendeda Fund, the Marcus Foundation, and the Robert W. Woodruff Foundation, the school campus cost $15 million. Drew also served as a hub for private school promotion in Atlanta. The school also holds a locational advantage with the East Lake Golf Course, which has hosted the PGA Tour since 2004. Edison and the East Lake Foundation funded the First Tee program that moonlights as a golf prep course but more clearly served as indoctrination for the youth into capitalist interests and culture. According to First Tee, "Students meet and play with business executives from all over Atlanta . . . because many businesspeople do business while playing golf." One former Drew Charter student told the *Atlanta Journal-Constitution* that because of his time spent with executives at the school, he could "speak to any high-level executive about golf and interact with them." Once students completed eighth grade, they were steered toward private high schools. Because of the profitability of both the pre-K–eighth grade program and the Villages of East Lake's success in luring middle- and upper-class white families to the emptied area, Drew Charter expanded over its first fifteen years. By 2015, Cousins had spent another $55 million to build a high school that resembled a modern airport terminal as a part of Drew Charter.[49]

One of the most publicized struggles against school privatization in Atlanta occurred in 2004, when forty-eight-year-old Garry Ogden, a teacher at APS's alternative school, Community Education Partnership (CEP), exposed his institution to the *Atlanta Voice* for acting as a profit-generating "dumping ground warehouse" for "disruptive" Black students that principals did not want. "Instead of addressing their [students'] deficiencies," Ogden explained, "principals and administrators would rather remove these children from the learning environment and send them to an alternative. . . . Most of them [students] have been tossed away. They are not educating children; it is not a safe place. CEP is destined for failure." As Ogden argued, CEP enforced its education motto in order of importance: "Be-here, so we can get paid; Behave, so that you don't break anything and we have to get it fixed; and then if you do those two things, and we have to get learning done, then Be-learning."[50]

CEP became the first private alternative school in the state of Georgia in 2002 when APS contracted it to "educate" students whom they designated as "too disruptive for the normal learning environment." CEP also generated profit based on the number of students. The alternative school received $9,300 to $9,700 per pupil per year. In the 2003–4 school year, an estimated 1,416 students, virtually all Black, spent time at CEP, with 722 students enrolled at the end of the term. Based on these figures, CEP generated $7.4 million in profit for what Atlanta Legal Aid attorney Craig Goodmark dubbed incarceration for poor Black students: "There is a trend in regular education environments to send children who are labeled as bad kids out of the regular education schools, and then couple that with how difficult they're making it to be returned to the regular education environment—it becomes almost like a prison without ever having a trial."[51]

In October 2004, proving that profit overruled student intervention, APS negotiated a five-year, multimillion-dollar extension for CEP to continue being the alternative school for the system. "It's a for-profit business. I wish I owned it!" exclaimed William Shepherd, the principal of CEP in 2004. "I'm not going to worry about how much money CEP is making. . . . Call CEP and me what you want to."[52]

CEP demonstrates how school privatization not only served to displace poor urbanites via gentrification but also provided pro-growth power brokers a tool of class war to further strip autonomy from marginalized groups. As Ogden claimed, "Most of the kids at CEP come from homes where the parents are already marginalized. . . . They don't have a voice, so there's no real clamor to do anything about it. There is no regard for what the public thought about it. It was just done because the kids and their parents don't have a voice." By suppressing the voice of the working-class masses, private school firms actively segregated disproportionately poor Black students from the dominant group. This allowed investors to generate revenue from the children's relative imprisonment. Also, the firms inflated testing scores by removing students most likely to perform poorly on state board exams. When children were isolated from quality educational environments, they fell behind on learning skills needed to survive in a capitalist society. Those students either stayed at CEP until they dropped out or they returned to their regular schools far behind their classroom peers. The American Civil Liberties Union (ACLU) reported that less than 23 percent of the students at the alternative school met or exceeded standards across all subjects. In 2006–7, not a single student made it to their senior year.[53]

In other words, privatization often decreases or outright eliminates public resources. According to multiple parents of students who attended CEP, the private firm simply imprisoned their children and refused to teach them. "No homework, no books, you sit and eat in class all day long, what kind of learning are you doing," one anonymous person told the *Atlanta Voice*. Another parent, who identified himself as Saleem and participated in the PTA at Brown Middle School for his son, charged that CEP "is nothing but one step before going to a juvenile jail. . . . They are just . . . criminalizing those kids." Tracy Ransom reported that after her son, Leroy, was sent to CEP for defending himself in a fight, "he's not being advanced in terms of schoolwork. He says he does nothing but play checkers on his computer. There is no actual education." Pat Walker contemplated filing a cruelty and defamation lawsuit against APS because her eighth-grade child, Archie, was misdiagnosed with a learning disability at Bunche Middle School and sentenced to CEP for a "special education curriculum." Walker told the *Voice* that when Archie complained about his lack of learning at CEP, the staff called him a "snitch nigger" and further isolated him in a separate wing of the facility.[54]

When CEP's principal William Shepherd blasted the *Atlanta Voice* coverage as an "exaggeration" and "unfair," the former principal who had resigned "in disgust," African American Irving Mitchell, escalated the protests against APS with a request for federal intervention: "There is enough information out there coming from a number of sources that makes it fairly critical to ask the state and the feds to investigate this for misrepresentation and misuse of funds. . . . This [CEP] contract is for $700,000 a month or more. Taxpayers are spending probably $10 million for this program and it [is] being misused. It warrants an investigation." Mitchell also accused APS of outright fraud and corruption because it used CEP to generate revenue while simultaneously juking the federal and state education requirement data:

> CEP became a means of circumventing "No Child Left Behind." The concept is simple. Once you remove eight hundred kids—and I had eight hundred kids at the beginning of last year—from the Atlanta Public Schools automatically things get better. Attendance, climate, behavior, test scores, because those kids are eliminated. . . . There were reports made to the [Atlanta School] board, and the board knew these reports were not accurate. They accepted it because of the improvements that were automatically made at the regular schools by eliminating these

kids. And they are not considered drop-out statistics because they are being counted on the regular APS school enrollment, and they are being paid for.[55]

Atlanta Voice reports flamed a citywide discussion, outrage, and social movement against CEP and the Atlanta Board of Education. In September 2004, Ogden organized CEP students, former juvenile probation officers who patrolled the halls, parents, and former teachers into the Greater Atlanta Ministerial Alliance (GAMA) to oppose the harsh conditions of the school, school privatization, and APS problems in general. The alliance filed a lawsuit against APS that accused the school system of "failure to follow procedures or policies pursuant to" the Individuals with Disabilities Act (IDEA). GAMA first toured the alternative school and conducted a three-month study of national, state, and local schooling to better understand the plight of poor Black children at CEP. It next constructed a report that it shared at a public town hall meeting in December. GAMA's report concluded that the private firm that imprisoned their children, most of whom were low-income African Americans, further reduced their access to resources they needed to survive. "According to a survey conducted by the Holistic Stress Control Institute," GAMA stated, "the kids in that school [CEP] have more needs for services than any other school in the nation—public, private, alternative, military, you name it.... GAMA is going to treat and get answers to CEP's disease."[56]

APS officials and CEP regional vice president Anthony Edwards attempted to defend CEP as a space that at the bare minimum kept truant children away from the streets. More clearly, CEP officials ignored the profit and education critiques and relied on criminalizing children and seeking reprieve for principals, teachers, and the general student population. "We are not successful with every student referred to CEP; however, every student referred to CEP has been unsuccessful in his or her traditional classroom.... We want to reduce disruption in the traditional classroom." Some parents echoed APS sentiments and argued that CEP's main purpose is to keep their children in a building, and off the streets, during school hours. One anonymous parent said she "had no problem with CEP.... If we didn't have CEP where would our children be? In jail or in the streets selling drugs or worse." Angela Lane claimed that CEP transformed her daughter, Angelica, from a "destructive, fighting" teenager into a studious, college-oriented adolescent. "When I got there, I realized I had to mature," Angelica told the *Voice*. "CEP is not like a prison, it's cool because you get one on one attention with a teacher because there are not that many kids in their classrooms." "I don't see it [CEP] as a prison," said Lu Shunder Barber, whose eighth-grade daughter attended the alternative school. "I see it as somewhere for your kids to go rather than being on the street.... A lot of the kids there just need love."[57] Thus, Black working-class Atlantans split over school privatization because they saw their children at risk of joining the underground economy. More succinctly, the concentration and relative expansion of illegal capitalism in Black working-class neighborhoods by the city leadership and police restructured the hierarchy of needs and resources for Black Atlantans. Autonomy took a back seat.

Over the next three years, GAMA expanded its movement to remove CEP from APS by aligning with the ACLU. In March 2008, ACLU executive director Debbie Seagraves issued a civil lawsuit against APS on that grounds that "when the state set up an alternative school system, the intention was not to create a pseudo prison." The ACLU suit described an environment where armed guards patrolled the hallways, students were routinely searched, and female students had to lift their shirts to show that they did not have anything on themselves. The lawsuit also detailed principals of schools who sent students to CEP without due process and who were denied education. The newly selected leader of GAMA in 2008, pastor Darryl Winston, summed up the community outrage at the ACLU's shocking report: "Like a dog that returns to its vomit, CEP has returned to the vile and vicious practice of warehousing and dehumanizing our children; treating them like prisoners. . . . Despite their many promises to improve, the ACLU lawsuit shows that CEP is merely continuing its profiteering and caging our children like animals."[58]

In December 2009, the ACLU and APS settled the lawsuit out of court; APS did not renew CEP's contract and took control of the alternative school. In a statement to the press, ACLU alleged that APS "pledged to treat students fairly and follow a curriculum similar to what is available at the system's other schools." GAMA's movement to retain public control over Atlanta schools was a success by exposing an anti-Black-poor colonial project within APS. However, privatization continued to threaten the system. During the 2012 standardized test cheating scandal in which state and federal authorities indicted dozens of APS teachers, principals, and officials, APS superintendent Beverly Hall announced the closure of ten schools, all located on the southwest and southeast sides of the city. Each school had close to 100 percent Black and low-income enrollment. Hall did not choose to close any schools on the north side of Atlanta, which enrolled mostly middle- and upper-class white students.[59]

Following the mass closures, APS brought in Superintendent Meria Carstarphen, a white administrator with a notorious reputation for slashing public-school budgets and closing schools in inner-city St. Paul, Minnesota, and Austin, Texas. Petty bourgeois activists secured her ascension. Republican Georgia governor Nathan Deal campaigned on privatizing public schools in Georgia. Also, Carstarphen's largest supporter, former mayor Shirley Franklin, had a multimillion-dollar contract with APS to operate privatized schools on the south side of the city through her firm, Purpose Built. Franklin also operated for-profit schools in Kansas City, Missouri, and concocted a similar model for a district in Omaha, Nebraska. Franklin and other Atlanta capitalists supplied Carstarphen's salary when she was hired in 2014, a move that was a conflict of interest—a public official received money from private interests—setting the stage for her to implement their neoliberal agenda in Atlanta schools.[60]

In the first two years of Carstarphen's tenure, she brought sweeping neoliberal reforms that devastated an already reeling public education system in Atlanta. She immediately sold Thomasville Heights Elementary School (the public housing in Thomas Heights had recently been demolished), Drew Elementary School, Slater Elementary School, Price Middle School, and Carver High School to Franklin's Purpose Built and Gideons Elementary School to the Kindezi Corporation. Thomasville Heights Elementary, which enrolled over 90 percent Black and poor children and ranked at the bottom of all Georgia schools in 2015, served as Carstarphen's testing ground for inexperienced charter schools, even though most parents polled ranked charter schools as their least preferred option. When Carstarphen brought in Franklin's Purpose Built as a front-runner to privatize the school, Thomasville Heights parents shouted Franklin down at a community meeting, telling her, "We didn't invite you!" These new charter school foundations refused to be held accountable to the public for student performance, even though their funding was largely through public tax revenue. As a result, a group of teachers filed another federal lawsuit against APS for pushing a charter school takeover across the board.[61]

Additionally, 128 veteran teachers filed a federal class-action lawsuit against APS for terminating higher-paid, tenured teachers without cause to replace them with relatively inexperienced teachers at entry-level salaries. According to court documents, the teachers accused the school district of conducting non-evidence-based witch hunts against teachers over age forty to justify not renewing their contracts at the end of the school year.[62]

Carstarphens's petty bourgeois activism did expand capital accumulation for private interests, but it did not produce the desired uptick in education quality for parents. She closed and merged several schools under the guise of "improving student performance." However, a Mathematica Policy Research report on the APS turnaround strategy demonstrated that science, reading, and social studies performance by students who attended newly privatized schools dropped. Only mathematics saw a slight uptick in performance. The Black-white achievement gap also widened under privatization. According to the Georgia Milestones Assessment System, "School choice, closing public schools, and opening charter schools must be considered negative contributing factors, as they promote bold, disruptive change; scripted teaching; instruction delivery; personalized mechanistic learning; and rigid academic performance." Additionally, the report noted that suspensions increased at schools that turned for-profit.[63]

Last, in true neoliberal strategy, Carstarphen destabilized the resource base of APS to justify the private takeover of schools. She randomly moved teachers around to various schools so that they did not establish stability or relationships with students. When Carstarphen closed schools, teachers, librarians, and support staff had to reapply for their jobs, with many not being rehired.[64]

By the end of 2015, APS had embraced its newfound neoliberal position as a "charter district." APS posted on its website a notice titled "Walton Family Foundation to Support Atlanta Public Schools Turnaround Efforts; $2.1 million investment will also expand access to student and school performance data."[65] Thus, the Atlanta power structure's demolition of both public schools and decision-making power in the city's neighborhoods over the early twenty-first century served as a model for how private schools facilitate gentrification and displacement in urban spaces. As with New Orleans, Oakland, Washington, DC, and Indianapolis school boards, capital here benefited from school privatization in two ways. First, it increased the land and property values around poor neighborhoods, which resulted in more working-class displacement. Second, it reduced government spending on public education, which forced people to pay out of pocket for funded but generally lower-quality schools. This resulted in surplus profits for private-school capitalists. These factors fueled gentrification and increased the hardship for working-class urbanites to resist displacement in twenty-first-century cities.

Privatization of public services ranged from sewage service to health care to public education. Decision-makers typically devised these privatization efforts behind closed doors, muting the opportunity for public input and protest. Such privatization undermined public input into the operation of long-standing public services, threatened decent-paying jobs held by Black workers, and undermined Black working-class communities. This privatization occurred alongside, and was indeed in part fueled by, an aggressive gentrification of Atlanta's remaining working-class Black neighborhoods.

Nonprofit "Activism": Community Development Corporations and the Supervision of Gentrification

The petty bourgeois assault on working-class Atlanta provided justification for the rise of the nonprofit-industrial complex as the "rational" solution to social crises in inner cities. Consequently, nonprofits sought to redistribute the legitimacy of grassroots resistance among the urban majority toward a bureaucratic, exploitative structure within capitalism. Italian Marxist Antonio Gramsci noted that for capitalist societies to maintain legitimacy, political society (state institutions that rule through force, including the carceral state, courts, and police) and civil society (those aspects of the state that rule through consent, particularly government bodies) work in tandem to reinforce and perpetuate ideology explicitly and implicitly. To maintain class stratification, both groups propagandize—through the three dominant cultural production institutions (education, church, and media)—that solutions to social crises rest in their hands. For example, a nonprofit may promote that the solution to large-scale political problems is to donate to an organization that uses those funds to hire a lobbyist, create a human resources position, or hire an outside firm to conduct a study, as opposed to giving the money directly to the affected group to hire a community organizer and build a social movement.[66]

Particularly in the late 1980s and early 1990s, nonprofits gained an immense level of power in governing neoliberalization in urban centers. Sociologist John Arena's succinct framework for understanding these structures helps us examine how nonprofits worked in tandem with liberal institutions to displace African Americans in the lead-up to the Olympics. As Arena demonstrated, nonprofits in the final years of the twentieth century "helped cultivate critical Black working class support, or at least acquiescence, to the pro-corporate neoliberal development agenda." More clearly, nonprofits—through sponsorship from the Black petty bourgeoisie—replaced the city leadership as the primary voice to translate the demands of the Black poor into a more "rational" management structure that upheld pro-growth politics. Thus, Arena argued, by "marrying free market ideas of privatization with those of self-determination and empowerment, the nonprofit leaders helped to sell support for privatization that was key to the regime's redevelopment agenda."[67]

This framework successfully ties the partnership between twin ideologies of neoliberalism and nonprofits. By framing the solutions to problems in a specific manner—as individual freedom—nonprofits, at the behest of the bourgeois and petty bourgeois classes, *define* where social problems come from in the first place. For one example, to address homelessness, organizations focus on finding a bed for each person on a day-by-day basis—an individualized solution, which in turn individualizes the problem. As a result, the hegemonic understanding of social problems spreads as individualization becomes the dominant ideology, making collective solutions like social movements against a structural problem seem irrational. Therefore, individuals with a desire to fight for social change are funneled into the nonprofit-industrial complex, which incentivizes them, as Arena posited, to conform to "a narrowly circumscribed form of political action . . . that set limits on human action by establishing codes of conduct which [organize] entire populations."[68]

After Summerhill Neighborhood Incorporated struck its record-setting deal with the Atlanta Braves and the City of Atlanta to gentrify its neighborhood and raze Mechanicsville and Peoplestown, other Black petty bourgeois activists determined that they could fund their pro-growth interests through business activity centered on "community uplift." In fact, CDCs, which operate under the assumption that they improve neighborhoods and living conditions for poor people in general, threaten to supervise the Black urban poor under the control of a petty bourgeois nonprofit industry or administrative office. In other words, CDCs represent a new form of neocolonial *soft power*, where indirect rulers usurp state resources, taking them away from the oppressed for their own bourgeois interests while they lock the poor into poverty and shift their bodies and spaces in the region.

By the 2010s, over 3,600 CDCs operated throughout the urban United States. Although they sprang up throughout Black neighborhoods during the Black Power movement as a vehicle for conservative nationalists, CDCs really came to dominate urban revitalization in the 1990s as the nonprofit-industrial complex cornered the poverty reform market. Most CDCs, like many nonprofits, are run by paid employees and directed by petty bourgeois residents who often do not live in the neighborhoods for which they make decisions.

With direct and indirect federal funding designated to alleviate conditions that create urban poverty, CDCs manipulated redevelopment initiatives, waged neighborhood-destroying campaigns, and created hundreds of high-salaried administrative supervisory positions, constructed thousands of high-rent housing units, and displaced millions of working-class people from US cities.[69] CDCs, while politically centrist in nature, prey on leftist, antipoverty sentiment to garner support among the working classes and activist organizations. Their recruitment discourse often cites their mission to "advance social and economic justice" and "promote community solidarity" in a "displacement-free zone." In some cases, they adopt and misuse anticapitalist critique—while operating as a capitalist venture—to produce the illusion that they "challenge inequality through struggle against the state." CDCs move into marginalized spaces and take funding from the government and banks for their own profit motives. The Community Reinvestment Act, which "encourages" banks to solicit funds for low-income areas at the threat of financial strain, influenced banks to form public-private partnerships with CDCs to gentrify poor urban spaces. Besides investment funds, CDCs raise other monies for redevelopment through low-interest mortgages made available to them by state housing finance agencies.[70]

Because CDCs ensure that their investments guarantee profitable returns, they are generally able to pay back those loans. Thus, displacing poor urbanites and manipulating land rents benefits CDCs. In fact, one Boston CDC director bragged about how the organization was able to persuade the Department of Housing and Urban Development to set the fair market rent for its CDC-owned apartments in a low-income neighborhood at no less than $2,300 a month. Additionally, CDCs use their "social justice" reputation and favorable relationship to the federal government to leverage funds away from other investments. In other words, CDCs "work" the political economy of poverty to accrue surplus profits and investments for their own means.[71]

At the turn of the century, Atlanta CDCs functioned as brokers for capital to displace low-income African Americans from the Central Business District. Young Hughley, executive director of the Reynoldstown Revitalization Corporation, and William McFarland, leader of the Peoplestown Revitalization Corporation, worked with investors who bought homes from residents whose rents and property taxes exceeded their budgets. For Reynoldstown, the price of existing homes rose more than 50 percent between 1997 and 2000 and averaged between $62,000 and $109,000. Instead of organizing a neighborhood movement to demand renovation without displacement, the best advice McFarland offered to the desperate Peoplestown homeowners pressured to sell was to "hold on a couple of years [to their homes] to cash out at a higher level." Peoplestown, which had a median income of $13,000 in 2000, witnessed developers buying houses and properties for cheap and renovating them with higher prices and relatively higher property values that forced neighboring residents to either sell or lose their homes. However, McFarland argued that his activism was the best means to neighborhood growth.

"Peoplestown is a great... place to live," McFarland stated. "There are lots of hills and trees, you can see the skyline of downtown Atlanta, it is a neighborhood that anyone would want to live in."[72]

HDDC, the oldest Atlanta CDC and the firm that displaced low-income Auburn Avenue residents in the late 1980s and early 1990s, adopted a block-by-block strategy for gentrification. By late 1999, HDDC had renovated only sixty low-income apartments, or 10 percent, as affordable housing. In the Old Fourth Ward, adjacent to Auburn Avenue, houses sold for $300,000 to affluent whites. HDDC also worked closely with two economic development programs, Studioplex on Auburn Avenue and the Herndon Plaza Expansion Project, which promoted the expansion of cultural tourism in revitalized Auburn Avenue as revenue-generating projects.[73]

Another CDC, the Atlanta Development Neighborhood Partnership (ADNP), which oversaw redevelopment across the central city and provided training and technical assistance to other metro-area CDCs, utilized its $6 million yearly budget to raze Lakewood Village for a new complex with 170 new single-family housing units on the south side of Atlanta. The organization also partnered with a private developer and razed residences on Pryor Road to build 115 new homes in Highland Estates that were listed from $125,000 to $225,000. The City of Atlanta also demolished the Joyland Plaza site for a new shopping center on Pryor Road as part of its Southside Redevelopment Initiative. The other sites that Mayor Bill Campbell targeted for redevelopment on the south side included Carver Homes, High Point Estates, Amal Heights, and Betmar La Villa.[74]

In 2001, Lakewood Partners, a public-private CDC comprising the Atlanta Development Authority and New Pryor Development Company, built a new thirty-eight-acre, $68 million housing development, Park Place South, along Pryor Street just south of downtown Atlanta. The land once held the Lakewood Village Apartments, which housed predominantly low-income people who worked at the Lakewood auto plant. According to New Pryor Development, the new housing catered to "people at various income levels." However, Ron Keller, the managing director of development and finance for the Atlanta Development Authority, stated that the price floor for the 434 town houses, condominiums, and single-family homes that encompassed Park Place South was $130,000. This automatically priced out any low-income urbanites and displaced virtually all the previous Lakewood Village Apartment tenants from Pryor Street. Additionally, Park Place South's locational advantage to Hartsfield International Airport, the HiFi Buys Amphitheater, and the revitalized downtown tourist scene offered little hope for any price or rent decrease.[75]

Summerhill, which gradually lost poor Black residents to Olympic-era gentrification, listed houses for $200,000 by the end of the twentieth century. The SUMMECH CDC, which had challenged Summerhill Neighborhood Incorporated during the Olympic era for control over development in the Black working-class neighborhoods surrounding the Olympic Stadium, displaced nearly 100 low-income Atlantans along Ralph Abernathy Boulevard for a sixteen-unit town house development called Ware Estates that charged between $96,000 and $125,000 per unit. "We were able to sell these units in a matter of 25 days," bragged Janis Ware, president of SUMMECH and publisher of the *Atlanta Voice*. "The appraised value of these units [is] $20,000 minimum higher than what we sold them for." Ironically, she named the development after her late father, J. Lowell Ware, the founder of the *Atlanta Voice* and an activist for working-class power. Atlanta resident Hattie Dorsey's summation of this new petty bourgeois and bourgeois activism in twenty-first-century Atlanta demonstrates how it represented the latest tactic in class war against Black working-class Atlantans: "This [is] one of the more successful community development activities in the whole of the city. . . . We have people moving back into this community who represent Who's Who of Atlanta. . . . The story is not often told about what happens in our neighborhoods that are seen as being off the radar screen."[76]

Gentrification through devalorization fueled much of the displacement against Black Atlantans in the 2000s. Petty bourgeois activists cheapened land and property values by exaggerating or outright fabricating crime in the working-class neighborhoods surrounding the Olympic Stadium (renamed Turner Field). In April 2000, the *Atlanta Journal-Constitution* published a report by the Crimes Against Persons Index, a Philadelphia-based "crime forecasting" firm, which identified Summerhill, Mechanicsville, and Peoplestown as neighborhoods where people were most likely to be robbed, raped, or murdered. Neighborhood leaders from all three areas quickly denounced the report as fraudulent for using police reports from a decade ago to make its case. Douglas Dean, the former state senator who had led Summerhill Neighborhood Incorporated in razing Summerhill, reduced the issue to simply racial identity politics: "I just believe it is just bias by the *Constitution* because we gotta black Mayor and Black people in power." Dean also exploited this issue to publicize his success in razing poor Black residents out of the very areas that the *Atlanta Journal-Constitution* criticized: "People who used to run away from these areas are now coming back to the area and paying top dollar for land in these neighborhoods and buying good homes in that area. The last house we sold in Summerhill was for $300,000."[77] These reports continued to cheapen property values. In 2002, Morgan Quitno Press, a national organization that uses FBI crime figures to rank urban centers based on danger, listed Atlanta as the third most dangerous city in the United States, behind St. Louis and Detroit.[78]

Young members of Atlanta's emerging Black bourgeoisie eagerly joined the war against the Black working class. Twenty-two-year-old Clarence Artis represented the Atlanta capitalists' twenty-four-hour visitor market vision. As a member of the DeKalb County Chamber of Commerce, he purchased his first property in 2002 and created his real estate venture, theartiscompany, to spearhead projects geared toward revitalization in East Atlanta. Between 2005 and 2006, Artis purchased at least six properties for over $150,000, with one valued at $630,000. He participated in razing East Lake Meadows neighborhoods for his development twentyfour ELV, located next to the East Lake golf course. According to Artis, this property "boasts both resident living and retail space boasting boutique coffee shops and business specializing in dining." Despite displacing poor African Americans for his developments, Artis couched his gentrification in petty bourgeois activist discourse, claiming that "although development is our profession, growing communities by nurturing people is our passion."[79]

Forty-eight-year-old Trenna Ross, the vice president of brokerage for Ackerman and Company, one of the largest full-service real estate firms in Atlanta, and twenty-nine-year-old Tarsa Hawkins, the co-owner of Cornerstone Finance Corporation, both led the charge in renovating the city's dilapidated spaces for expensive lofts and booming businesses. For Ross especially, she set her sights on building shopping centers for profit. "To develop a center that is 20[,000] to 30,000 square feet," Ross explained, "could cost $75 a square foot, which could easily be a million-dollar project. Before taxes and expenses, add in the average profit from renters over a five-year-term, I could make about $3 million."[80]

Leah Braxton, a developer with the W. C. Bradley Real Estate firm, converted a cotton mill into condominiums in the downtown area that were priced between $154,000 and $569,000 in 2009. She stated that she refused to lower the unit prices because "we want to uphold the values of the people who have already purchased." Courtney Dillard, whom the *Atlanta Voice* dubbed the "black Donald Trump," stated to *Atlanta Magazine* that acquiring property was like "finding a lost girlfriend and being overjoyed by her return."[81]

The Black petty bourgeoisie in post-Olympic Atlanta, as the junior partners of capital, waged petty bourgeois activism against the Black working class by implementing neoliberal reforms that privatized public resources.

Pro-growth power brokers targeted hospitals, schools, and public housing to reduce both the population of the Black working class and their class interests from the future direction of the city. Petty bourgeois activism refers to how investors implement pro-growth reforms and how they sway public opinion through a progressive, antipoverty, anticrime discourse. In other words, petty bourgeois activism is the capitalist class's strategy of appropriating tactics and discourse of the working class for their own class interests.

The Atlanta power structure's plan to transform the central city into a twenty-four-hour visitor market meant that they had to replace low-income and non-profit-generating public spaces and resources with new enterprises more attuned to middle- and upper-class individuals. Both state hospitals and public schools suffered from decreased funding and shoddy infrastructure. Therefore, petty bourgeois activists justified their privatization by highlighting their efforts to "save" these institutions for the people and upgrade them through private investment. As a result, middle- and upper-class residents exercised the freedom to choose what institutions they frequented—so they chose privately funded, exclusive schools over poorly funded schools.

CDCs facilitated the displacement of poor residents by helping capitalists manipulate urban rents for middle- and upper-income developments. These institutions, which operate under the assumption that they improve neighborhoods and conditions for the poor, act as a neocolonial soft power by taking state resources meant for poor people and converting them into administrative and supervisory positions with high salaries. These bureaucracies work with developers to purchase land that poor Black residents live on and market it to the public as "ending poverty." However, these forces only remove poor people and do not help them relocate or help them out of poverty. CDC investments generally guarantee profitable returns for themselves and developers, thus demonstrating that they achieve their capitalist objectives through anticapitalist and antipoverty discourse.

CHAPTER SIX

Robbing Peter to Pay Paul
Suburbanization and Subproletarianization of the Black Working Class

> Now they've taken the land away and have sent people to and fro on the earth. They put us out here with no lifeline.
> —DEMETRIOUS RICHARDSON, former Bowen Homes resident of twenty-five years, displaced June 2009

> There's no dispersal of poverty. It's the general plan of the Chamber of Commerce and others to drive poor people out of downtown Atlanta and to bring gentrification in. This is a war on Black people.
> —DIANNE MATHIOWETZ, former Bowen Homes resident and activist, displaced June 2009

When twenty-eight-year-old African American Denise Broward had her first child, Nakia, in 1981, she and her husband, Michael, were excited to move back to her hometown, Atlanta. Unfortunately, they found only unaffordable housing and little to no real job prospects. According to Broward, the search went so poorly that the three were forced to move into Denise's older sister Stephanie's one-story home on Lucille Avenue in southwest Atlanta. The housing on Lucille resembled most undermaintained property: collapsing infrastructure, poor plumbing and drainage, and worst of all, a significant rat infestation. Denise recalled that on some nights, "we heard traps going off all night long! We had to keep our feet off the floor to keep from touching the rats running all over the floor." When reported by Denise and her neighbors, the city and county both refused to alleviate the cause of rats, instead opting to give each resident a free bag of rat poison.[1]

The only affordable housing options in the late 1980s for the Broward family rested in a rural, desolate metro suburb twenty miles west of Atlanta: Lithia Springs. Alongside Broward, other working-class African Americans like Al Johnson, who became a Broward family friend, migrated to Lithia

Springs after being displaced from the city. However, Lithia Springs offered little prospects to the Black working class. Broward explained that when she first arrived at Lee Road, the closest grocery store was over five miles away, there were only two gas stations—Starvin' Marvin and Pete's Convenience Store—one restaurant, and few jobs that offered above minimum wage. By 2015, Lithia Springs still closely resembled the town it had been when the Browards were raising their family, except now there were a few more restaurants, a new elementary school, and other small businesses like dry cleaners and barbershops. "There was hardly anything beyond the Lee Road bridge," Denise stated. For jobs there, "there's a whole lot of warehouses, there is a grocery store now, but that's really it."[2]

Gentrification and racial oppression create significant consequences of structural violence against poor urbanites—how they are displaced, where they are displaced, and how they seek to provide some semblance of agency and power in rebuilding their lives, informal kinship networks, and incomes. This chapter explores how the twin assaults of gentrification and the Great Recession expedited the shutting of the Black working poor out of the central city and into suburban spaces, where they were subproletarianized into unstable, unskilled, minimum-wage dirty work. Thus, the intended consequence of neoliberalization and gentrification for Black working-class urbanites is often subproletarianization. Black working-class Atlantans forced out of the central city because of public housing demolition landed in metro counties that offered little more than Wal-Mart jobs. Therefore, some residents moved into extended-stay motels to save money, pool resources, and in many instances build informal kinship networks with other motel residents. This chapter also demonstrates that Black working-class Atlantans transferred protonationalist strategies to help them build community or simply survive the economic catastrophes of the New Nadir.

The Great Recession and Class Warfare

By the end of the 1990s, Atlanta's cataclysmic public housing policies were too glaring to hide anymore under antihomeless laws and criminalization of the poor. The city had twice as many public housing units per capita as New York City and more than 2.5 times per capita the public housing of Chicago or Philadelphia. Also, the consequences of the New Nadir strained the Black poverty enclaves in the city. Atlanta was ranked fifth in the nation in percentage of population living below the federal poverty line, at 27.3 percent, trailing only Detroit, New Orleans, Miami, and Cleveland. Seventy-eight percent of

Atlantans in the metro area who lived below the poverty line resided within the city limits, although the city contained only 13 percent of the metro region's population! An estimated 25 percent of Atlantans earned less than $10,000 a year, and 45 percent earned less than $25,000. More than 75 percent of children in Atlanta Public Schools or their families received government assistance, and tens of thousands lived in Section 8 housing.[3]

The Great Recession began much earlier for Black working-class Atlantans than most. In November 2006, 3,100 workers lost their jobs when the Hapeville Ford manufacturing plant in south Atlanta closed. Six other manufacturing plants followed suit over the next few years, which resulted in the disappearance of over 34,000 stable, livable-wage, working-class jobs from the Atlanta metropolitan region. Factory workers at Hapeville made an average of $56,000 a year plus overtime; more senior workers earned five dollars more an hour. Atlanta was one of many metropolitan regions devastated by the Ford Corporation's "Way Forward" program that closed multiple plants to consolidate production and cut costs.[4]

Thirty-five-year-old John Rape, who had worked for Ford's chassis department and motor line since January 1995, represented most Black workers who had no prospects after leaving such a stable job. "It hasn't sunk in yet," Rape told the *Atlanta Voice*. "Wait until Monday morning when I wake up and don't have anywhere to go." Unsurprisingly, the City of Atlanta set in motion plans to rezone the Hapeville plant, 127 acres that held locational advantage for the Hartsfield International Airport, for "a more diverse use."[5]

Georgia officials proved futile in protecting poor Atlantans from the worst effects of the recession. Georgians reduced their purchases of food, clothing, furniture, and cars to the point that all major revenue streams across Georgia decreased, including sales tax (6.5 percent decrease), income tax (6.5 percent decrease), and worst of all, corporate tax (33 percent decrease). Unsurprisingly, the only Georgia tax revenues that jumped during the recession were for alcohol. State revenues tumbled 7 percent, while tax collections plummeted 6.8 percent, or $180 million for the year 2008. The state also reported 50,090 new jobless claims, a 72 percent increase from August 2007 and the highest total since the stock market crisis in September 2001. In response, Republican governor Sonny Perdue cut 6 percent of the state budget to close the projected $1.6 billion shortfall that year. Perdue borrowed $600 million from the state's cash reserves to make payroll and demanded that all state agencies develop plans that slashed their budgets.[6]

Perdue also attempted to exploit the recession to privatize state resources. In 2009, when an increasing number of people sought mental health services to deal with the economic collapse, Georgia's Department of Human Resources announced plans to privatize much of its public mental health hospital network and close its mental health facilities. It also planned to consolidate the seven mental health hospitals into two and rely more heavily on "community-based services." Although community protests, mental health advocates, state legislators, and even members of Perdue's own mental health commission outlined unmistakable evidence that privatizing public services does not save taxpayers money or improve quality of service, Perdue sped up the process and expected to fully privatize by June 2011. In January 2011, Perdue closed the Northwest Georgia Hospital, which served 180 patients and employed 764 staff. He further restricted access to health care when he ordered state hospitals to refuse to admit developmentally disabled people and to discharge all remaining patients by July 2015.[7]

The class interests of the Georgia Legislative Black Caucus impeded their willingness to intervene on behalf of the state's Black poor. With fifty-three members, it was the nation's largest Black caucus, but "collectively the caucus is ineffective," stated Rita Samuels, a former staffer for the Jimmy Carter gubernatorial administration. "The reason for it is their [GLBC's] inability to mobilize the Black community around issues." Instead, Black lawmakers in the state spent their collective energy protesting symbolic slights against President Barack Obama. In March 2009, the entire Georgia Legislative Black Caucus staged a walkout after the Georgia House of Representatives decided to delay a vote on a resolution that "would have honored President Barack Obama as a politician with an unimpeachable reputation for integrity, vision, and passion." In a surprising defense of his symbolic bill that would have made Obama an honorary member of the Georgia Legislative Black Caucus, state representative Keith Heard argued that because the caucus often voted for other "privileged" resolutions, including a 2005 commendation for then-president George W. Bush's response to Hurricane Katrina and for President Ronald Reagan, the house should have supported his bill.[8]

Atlanta revenues at the onset of the recession fared much worse. Mayor Shirley Franklin continued to shield the bourgeoisie from tax collection and instead chose to destroy public resources for the working classes. Sales tax revenue dropped 14 percent while the city deficit ballooned to an estimated $60 million. Franklin responded by reducing an increase in property tax for a $100,000 home from $43 to $7.31. In fact, Franklin reduced the increase on property taxes so much that under her revised plan, the tax on property valued at $300,000 went up $41.71, less than the lowest tax increase on property valued at $100,000 ($43). The Fulton County Tax Commissioners reported that over 10,000 property owners still believed the reduced tax plan was too high and appealed city hall's decision. Upset at Franklin's appeasement of wealthy Atlantans during a financial crunch, African American city councilman C. T. Martin gave a candid interview to the *Atlanta Voice* in which he called out Franklin's partnership with real estate, finance, and tourism: "So the biggest struggle for Atlanta other than race is the private sector outmaneuvering the public sector, which is what I call the shadow government.... The shadow government is the real estate industry which covers the banks, developers, appraisers, the agents, and others."[9]

Martin continued to name the social organizations that orchestrated Atlanta's neoliberalization: "You ... have the ... Chamber of Commerce, Central Atlanta Progress, the Buckhead Coalition, the Buckhead Business Association, and the Midtown Alliance.... All of those organizations represent interests of Ellis Street north to the city." Martin's admissions pointed to the idea that Franklin, and the Atlanta Black petty bourgeoisie in general, served as the conduit for real estate to gentrify Black working-class areas in Atlanta. "I submit to you that about 20 years from now that southeast Atlanta and southwest Atlanta will look like Buckhead."[10] Martin only reinforced what the working-class Atlantans knew about the Black urban regime: city hall operated solely on the leash of the chamber of commerce.

In his most startling comments to the press, Martin revealed the details of how the bourgeoisie exploited tax increment financing bonds and devalued property to profit from the city's regressive tax structure:

> Tax Allocation Districts. Much of this growth that you see in Atlanta for the past 15 years hasn't been revenue producing. The real estate people have been driving this. To spur development in several blighted areas in the city, the City Council has approved several low tax districts for businesses and homeowners for mostly a ten-year period. The taxes would increase in increments each year after five years. It takes about ten houses valued at $100,000 or more to bring in what one commercial business should pay. Whether it's paying or not is another question. You have commercial buildings that sit on property in Atlanta, but the corporation is in another county. So we lose the business license renewal fees and some of the taxes. Most of the real estate deals are a losing proposition for [the residents].[11]

The state's lax tax collection exacerbated dwindling revenue for monies for the poor. By July 2009, Georgia had lost over $1.9 billion over the previous twelve months because of tax collections plummeting 15.7 percent. Corporate income tax receipts dropped over $248 million—more than 26 percent—between fiscal years 2008 and 2009. Individual tax receipts fell about $1 billion, or about 9 percent, over the same period.[12] With no cash reserves, a budget shortfall, job cuts, a state revenue crisis, and Franklin's refusal to raise taxes on the wealthy, city hall fed Black working-class Atlantans to the real estate wolves.

To pour salt in the working-class wounds, Franklin chose to fire over 1,000 city workers, cancel numerous concerts and festivals (costing workers hundreds of dollars in wages), and close ten recreational centers.[13] This destabilized neighborhood after-school and summer programs where community volunteers taught courses like health, reading, cooking, and computer literacy and tutored students. The recreational centers also provided intramural sporting leagues for children. Without rec centers, Black parents no longer possessed a resource to supervise and instruct their children while they worked or searched for additional labor. Last, social organizations like Black fraternities and sororities, neighborhood associations, and protest movements held planning meetings and training sessions at recreation centers. The destruction of public recreational centers in urban spaces severely destabilized multiple interlocking parts of working-class people's daily routines and local movement centers for social movement organizing.

Franklin's hardship cuts also stagnated wages for those who remained employed. She implemented a thirty-six-hour workweek maximum, which resulted in a 10 percent pay cut for 99 percent of all public workers. Although Franklin sought to position herself as suffering alongside blue-collar city workers by cutting her mayoral salary, it was widely known that Franklin owned some for-profit ventures both inside and outside Atlanta. As the Atlanta metro region sometimes totaled 10,000 foreclosures in a single month in 2008 and 2009, public housing waiting lists swelled and shelters reported that families stayed for months instead of the usual ten to fifteen days because of a lack of housing.[14]

The combined housing crisis and plummeting real wages worsened precariousness throughout the Black working class. While the Atlanta metro region averaged close to 10,000 foreclosures per week in July 2009, the Atlanta city council piled on a 12.5 percent increase on water and sewer rates. The Black labor participation rate did not top 62 percent. Thus, during the nadir of the Great Recession, close to 40 percent of Black Georgians were actively looking for work.[15]

The permanent loss of working-class jobs that paid real wages aggravated African American Atlantans' struggles to hold on to the little resources they had. In 2009, the federal minimum wage rose from $6.55 to $7.25 an hour, yielding $13,920 a year for an individual who worked forty hours per week. Sixty percent of Georgia households that year were led by women, while 43 percent of households with one child had an income below the minimum budget required to support a household. Sixty-one percent of single women with two children or more earned below that level. Twenty-five-year-old African American Heather (last name withheld) raised her two children alone and earned an annual income of $23,040 a year as a worker in the auto industry. To meet the bare minimum of her bills, she worked the maximum allotted hours, which caused her to miss considerable time with her children. According to the *Self-Sufficient Standard for Georgia 2008*, a publication that measures how much money is required for families of various compositions to adequately meet their basic needs without private or public assistance, Heather and her children required a minimum yearly salary of $39,007 to reside in DeKalb County and cover the rising costs of food and transportation. Despite the precariousness, Heather was determined not to take on more than one job like most workers who make sub-working-class wages must do. "I've never considered working two jobs," Heather stated. My time is much more valuable than money. And, in the long run, what they'll remember is me being home with them."[16]

The metropolitan region lost over 12,000 jobs in 2010 alone. The unemployment rate in the city was 10.4 percent for the first quarter of 2011. Black workers faced the harsh reality of precariousness—not just finding a job but also keeping a job. Thirty-seven-year-old Tonya Pinkston, a college graduate and single mother with an eight-year-old daughter, was laid off three times over the span of the Great Recession. "I never dreamed I'd be faced with no job security and wondering how I'm going to feed my family," Pinkston shared. Another anonymous individual stated that as a homeless man, he could not get employers to accept his job application because they refused to list the shelter as a permanent address. Dracy Blackwell explained that her husband, who had been out of work since he lost his job at the onset of the recession in 2007, was suicidal because he saw no end in sight. A seventeen-year-old high school student said she had to find a full-time job after her mother could no longer pay the electricity bill.[17]

Despite the lack of resources, working-class Black Atlantans pooled support for the unemployed and underemployed in their neighborhoods. In April 2011, the 9 to 5 National Association of Working Women and the Atlanta chapter of Jobs with Justice hosted the Speak for Jobs Forum at Trinity United Methodist Church. Speakers shared their struggles in finding work, recorded testimonials of those who found work and posted them on YouTube to encourage others, and conducted a Q&A with supportive state officials like Vincent Fort. After the forum, Jobs with Justice served free lunch and provided legal aid for those fighting home foreclosure and eviction, a résumé-writing workshop, food stamps and Medicaid applications, career counseling, childcare network sign-ups for parents to have the freedom to search for work, health screenings, and free massages and haircuts. Alvin McCordy told reporters that simply getting a haircut for a job interview brightened his outlook in his bleak situation. "The barbers treat people like me with compassion," he explained. "I'm going to feel better and look better."[18] McCordy alluded to the historical significance of the barber and barbershop in Black working-class neighborhoods as an institution that provides community socialization and pride. Thus, Black working people consistently relied on the resources available during the worst attacks on their humanity.

The recession also provided the Atlanta power structure capacity to further distance the poor from its future visitor market. More clearly, petty bourgeois activism took advantage of the disastrous political economy to isolate the Black poor from spaces of capital accumulation. Like Governor Sonny Perdue, they accomplished this by restricting access to public resources. For example, the Metropolitan Atlanta Rapid Transit Authority (MARTA) chose mid-2009, during the worst months of the recession, to announce a higher bus fare of two dollars for one-way rides, higher parking fees, reduced service, and layoffs to fill a $109.8 million shortfall. Because MARTA received most of its funding from a penny sales tax in Fulton and DeKalb Counties, a significant decrease in sales tax revenue meant reduced services.[19]

Black working-class Atlantans did not recover from the Great Recession—primarily because they no longer had access to stable, livable-wage labor. According to the Georgetown University Center on Education and the Workforce, blue-collar workers lost the most jobs in the recession, with little to no recovery of living-wage blue-collar jobs. In fact, an estimated 5.5 million jobs for blue-collar workers did not return, with signs pointing to those jobs being lost forever. Consequently, the livable-wage jobs that were created since the 2008 crash, as the report noted, required "increasing sophistication" with new technology that "raised the complexity of many tasks that workers must be able to perform today."[20] More clearly, such labor demands skills and resources developed in social institutions that have been uprooted from African American working-class spaces for decades. The capitalist class's devotion to this structural violence guarantees a reserve army of subproletarian labor with few labor options available.

TABLE 6.1 **Largest Employers in the Atlanta Metro Area, 2015**

COMPANY	NUMBER OF EMPLOYEES
Delta Air Lines	31,237
Emory University	29,937
Walmart Stores	20,532
Home Depot Inc.	20,000
AT&T	17,882
Kroger Co.	14,753
Wellstar Health System	13,500
Publix Super Markets	9,494
United States Postal Service	9,385
Northside Hospital	9,016
Coca-Cola	8,761
United Parcel Service (UPS)	8,727
Piedmont Healthcare	8,707
Centers for Disease Control	8,539

Source: "Atlanta's 25 Largest Employers," *Atlanta Business Chronicle*, July 22, 2016.

Atlanta leadership championed subproletarian labor because it deepened their manipulation and control over the precarious economy for poor Atlantans. In December 2010, Shirley Franklin's successor, African American Democratic mayor Kasim Reed, held a press conference to announce and celebrate the news that Walmart was constructing a new store in the poverty-stricken Westside Village section of Vine City. Reed attempted to sell Walmart's arrival in the community as a game changer for Black job growth in the recession. "Walmart is bringing more than jobs, goods, and services to the residents of the community and the 12,000 students of the Atlanta University Center," Reed told the crowd. "The company is providing the spark this community needs to continue its transformation and become a healthy, thriving place where people want to live and study."[21] Thus, Reed promised Vine City residents both the possibility of underemployment—minimum-wage, low-skill labor without benefits—and increasing development that would price them out of their homes over time. By 2015, the service sector dominated the available jobs in the city.

The petty bourgeois activists continued their campaign for public support for the Walmart acquisition by propagandizing it as the way to defeat poverty. "We recognize an opportunity to make an impact in Vine City and metro Atlanta by bringing jobs, convenience, fresh options, and everyday low prices to the community," stated Greg Sullivan, the Walmart executive who spoke with Reed at the press conference. Construction giant Jerome Russell told Vine City residents to be happy that they get a Walmart, even if the jobs created were low wage or temporary. "With Walmart's everyday low prices in general merchandise and groceries," Russell stated, "the company is the ideal fit for the residents of this community and the broader Westside community. I know the store . . . is going to generate over 150 jobs. As far as construction jobs go, they won't be permanent, but there should be about two hundred of them." The truth is that Atlanta city hall only cared about the increased tax revenue that Walmart brought to urban spaces. Their leaders also brought in other business owners to sell Walmart to the residents. The owners of Johnny's Pizza Bistro and Busy Bee Café, a soul food staple in Black working-class Atlanta, spoke at great length about the benefits of Walmart in Vine City. "The traffic and the jobs it will bring is a win-win for the whole corridor," said Mims, whose family owned a significant amount of land around Martin Luther King Jr. Drive. "So, seeing this happen is wonderful."[22]

In another questionable campaign, city hall resurrected McDonald's 1990s commercials that were racist toward African Americans and promoted underemployment at McDonald's restaurants to lift neighborhoods out of the recession. In April 2011, McDonald's announced that it would hire 1,000 people in metro Atlanta on National Hiring Day on April 19. Some Black Atlantans who had struggled to find work for over three years settled for McDonald's minimum wages. By the early 2010s, companies that offered real wages were not investing in Black working-class neighborhoods. Twenty-year-old Nana Amanquah, who could not find stable work at that point, eagerly applied to the restaurant because it "offered a wealth of opportunities for all employees from their teens to their sixties."[23] LeQuinta Snell, who had not found work in over two years, best summed up the rush of Black Atlantans competing for jobs at McDonald's: "I think there are so many people here because there are so many of us out of work. . . . I applied to several companies, including several McDonald's, and I'm determined to get a job." Nineteen-year-old Dwight Hanchard added, "I've been looking for work since I graduated last May." However, the $200 billion fast-food industry paid a median wage of $8.69 an hour for core frontline workers in 2011. Only 13 percent of fast-food jobs provided health-care benefits.[24]

Underemployment became the long-term consequence of the Great Recession for the working classes. Automation, outsourcing, and gentrification permanently eliminated productive blue-collar industrial and service labor from urban centers. After five years as a salesman for a tractor company, Tarik Kaintuck lost his job and only worked ten months over a two-year period. As a result, Kaintuck registered with a temporary employment agency to pay his bills. Besides temporary work, underemployed workers sought seasonal jobs during the Christmas holidays. With an abundance of shopping centers in the area, like Greenbriar Mall, Lenox Mall, Lenox Square, Cumberland Mall, and many others, Black workers, who had access to transportation, found seasonal retail work lucrative.[25]

Nevertheless, underemployment did not produce real wages to offset the skyrocketing cost of living in the 2010s. The Economic Policy Institute's 2014 report *Raising America's Pay* stated that over the previous thirty years, productivity growth far outpaced wage growth, with Black workers disproportionately affected. The study reported that the number of Black and white workers that made poverty wages increased between 2000 and 2014. However, the number of African Americans increased to 36 percent, compared to 23 percent of whites. The study also concluded that Black males earned less than fifteen dollars an hour working full-time, compared to their white male peers, who made more than twenty dollars, even with the same levels of education. Because Black men tend to be crowded into lower-paying occupations, the oversupply of workers in the newly crowded sub-working-class sector lowered wages for African American workers in retail, fast food, and minimum-wage service-sector jobs. Thus, as worker productivity had increased about 90 percent since 1979, wages for production and nonsupervisory workers, especially African Americans, had not budged. The dominance of the Great Recession over the Black working classes meant that Black workers received an even smaller slice of the pie over time.[26]

The most significant consequence of the Great Recession was the decline of the working class, the swelling of the sub–working class, and the expansion of the lumpenproletariat. While the working class and sub–working class differed by type of labor (stable, skilled, living wage versus unstable/temporary, unskilled, minimum wage), the lumpenproletariat is outside the class structure and the general political economy—making it an underground economy. The political economy of the recession supplied the conditions for the expansion of the underground economy in both Black and white working-class America. More clearly, the plummeting quality-of-life indicators for low-income people increased demand for drug use as a means of self-medicating.

However, poor Black people, especially in metropolitan urban regions, suffered disproportionate joblessness, underemployment, housing and food insecurity, surveillance and violence from the police, and wage stagnation —regression with little to no relief. At a peak in 2008, African Americans represented 13 percent of drug users in the United States, with 59 percent of those convicted for drug offenses. Particularly for Black men who were formerly blue-collar workers and remained unemployed or underemployed for significant periods of time, alcohol and drugs, especially marijuana, served as a coping mechanism.[27] Thus, it must be stated that rates of drug use correlate with the political economy and the theft from working-class people of the material resources they need to survive.

Concurrently, Black petty bourgeois leadership, which allowed the underground market to grow, condemned the violence of growing competition between underground markets without addressing the class struggle that fueled it. "Atlanta has become a very scary, dangerous and violent city," Derrick Boazman proclaimed. "We got some mean-spirited young people out here," stated Black city council person C. T. Martin. "We've got to get control of our streets."[28] Through their liberal understanding of crime and violence, Atlanta leadership held dozens of Summit Against Violence events, where petty bourgeois activists and politicians wagged their fingers at the youth and ignored the criticism against government cuts, job closures, displacement, and police violence. In other words, the Black petty bourgeoisie treated the expanding underground economy like they treated the recession: they exacerbated class struggle by deepening poverty in Black colonial enclaves throughout the city, extracted more capital, and did extraordinarily little to address the class struggle.

"The Atlanta Way": The End of Public Housing in Atlanta

With the Great Recession and the Atlanta Black urban regime's malignant neglect wreaking havoc on working-class urbanites, virtually no resources available possessed the power to stop the assault on Black public housing. In 2008, the Atlanta Housing Authority (AHA) launched its Qualify of Life Initiative for "servicing and providing families with the ability to access affordable housing and build ultimate communities." It then demolished a dozen public housing complexes, including Leila Valley Jonesboro North and South, U-Rescue Villa, Englewood Manor, Palmer House, Bowen Homes, Thomasville Heights, Bankhead Courts, Hollywood Courts, Roosevelt House, and Herndon Homes, all by the end of 2009. Over 9,000 individuals, many of them children who did not contribute income and senior citizens on meager fixed incomes, lost their homes and either used their meager housing vouchers to join the growing waitlist for the small quantity of public housing left or abandoned the city altogether.[29]

Thus, Atlanta's final phase of extinguishing subsidized public housing from its future visitor market commenced during a period when Black residents possessed little to no capacity to sustain social movement protests against impending displacement. The truth is that the Great Recession, through its extended joblessness, underemployment, and budget cuts to social welfare, accelerated this petty bourgeois war against Black working-class Atlantans. By 2010, little safety net or blue-collar, working-class labor that produced real wages existed in the city. As a result, Black working-class Atlantans no longer possessed the components—funding, time, agency-laden institutions, and leadership—necessary to construct and maintain a social movement. Although Black workers attempted to challenge this petty bourgeois activism, the Great Recession not only set in motion a deepening of neoliberal policies that removed public resources but also facilitated the final stages of gentrification.

To recruit pro-growth advocates into their petty bourgeois activism, the Black urban regime publicized its attack on Black public housing tenants as a progressive, "revolutionary change." They elicited African American Renee Glover to be the spokesperson for their public housing destruction because of her esteemed reputation nationwide for "revitalizing" neighborhoods. In fact, since her arrival in Atlanta in 1994, Glover had used her position as the executive director of the AHA to wage war against Black public housing tenants by undermining property values in low-income neighborhoods for private developers. "I am pleased with the progress we've made," Glover stated. "With our private partners, we have demolished more than a dozen obsolete and distressed public housing projects, offering their residents vouchers." However, Glover's dealings with real estate capitalists made her one of the most powerful policy makers in the Atlanta power structure. According to African American state representative "Able" Mabel Thomas, the Black petty bourgeois leadership at the city and county levels allowed Glover to exercise "unprecedented and unchecked political clout in the drive to dismantle public housing." Thomas concluded by pointing to the Black leadership's silence on displacement as evidence of the collusion. "There's a lot of whispering about the Atlanta Housing Authority but the Black power structure and political people must do something," Thomas explained. "Most of the people ... don't speak up."[30]

The AHA negotiated a "flexible timeline" of July 1, 2003–June 30, 2010, with the US Department of Housing and Urban Development (HUD) to raze all public housing structures within the city limits. The planned demolition was implemented in phases, with private "mixed-income" town houses, multifamily units, garden-style apartments, and high-rises to replace public housing. The AHA admitted during the process that it had no intention of finding new housing for tenants within the city and that this was a forced relocation. It claimed that "people don't always want to come back into the city" and that the AHA was "planning and relocating committees that will make decisions on a case-by-case basis regarding who is eligible to return and who won't." The AHA waffled on a "re-establishment" process, stating that "the criteria had not been set yet."[31]

The AHA vouchers provided to displaced residents revealed the insidious way the Black urban regime manipulated tenants' capacity to relocate in the city. According to the AHA, if residents received a tenant-based voucher, it provided incentives to move anywhere in the United States, with rent being adjusted to accommodate utilities. If residents received a private-based voucher, it tied the resident to that private development to which the AHA sold the land and property. If the resident ever attempted to move for any reason, whether it be increased rent, transportation issues, or proximity to a new job or school, the landlord could revoke the subsidy. Additionally, as explained by Shirley Hightower, treasurer of the Resident Advisory Board (RAB), which represented all Atlanta public housing residents across the city, the voucher system locked poor Black people into a "do or die" scenario, where financial hardship equaled eviction, no questions asked: "I want to make sure with this [voucher] thing there is enough affordable houses to move to and not be homeless two years from now. . . . If you lose your job, it's not like public housing. If you lose your job in public housing, you can ask for a hardship. [The voucher program] is not like that. You got to pay your utilities on time. You got to pay the rent. What happens when they get out there and they snatch it all away?"[32] The AHA gave out few private-based vouchers, to fulfill quotas for a select few low-income people to live in middle- and upper-income "mixed" properties. Regardless of the voucher residents received, they had little control over their future living space, especially if they remained in the Atlanta metropolitan region.

Despite the lack of resources and capacity for a social movement, Black tenants attempted their offensive against the AHA prior to the arrival of the bulldozers. In August 2007, the RAB filed a civil rights suit with HUD. African American Diane Wright, the president of the RAB for Hollywood Courts, and

Hightower, RAB treasurer and president of the Bowen Homes Tenant Association, issued the complaint, which argued that the AHA's plan to demolish or sell Atlanta's public housing stock violated the Fair Housing Act of 1968 by discriminating against the residents, an overwhelming majority of whom were Black. Further, the complaint read, AHA failed to comply with HUD regulations requiring consultation with residents about the plans to demolish their housing. For example, AHA reportedly refused to comply with public records requests made by RAB. "We wanted to look at the vouchers," RAB's attorney Lindsay Jones explained. "We want to see how they're funding them. How many units of housing are out there? Is this a real opportunity? Information is not being shared. And there's how this is being spun to the public." The RAB complaint read as follows: "Please consider this correspondence as a formal complaint of racial discrimination in housing opportunity in violation of the Fair Housing Act of 1968. . . . This complaint seeks your office's intervention by way of investigation, conciliation and, or litigation as required and necessary to enforce the legally protected rights of the African American tenants currently living in the affected public housing projects to be free from racial discrimination in housing and community development opportunities."[33]

In the most revealing portion of the complaint, RAB provided credence to the structural violence thesis: the AHA and Renee Glover consciously sought to permanently expel low-income African Americans from the city. "Public is nothing but Black people, number one," Hightower told the *Atlanta Voice*. "That's what public housing is all about. They have some Caucasians here. But they're a few, you can count them on your hand." The intentional elimination of useful public housing projects occupied almost exclusively by low-income African Americans would be a double insult to the civil rights of African Americans, insofar that it would displace low-income African American families who had attained affordable housing security while compounding the lack of fair-share housing opportunities for low-income African Americans in general in the city of Atlanta by increasing the already significant affordable housing deficiency.[34] Hightower revealed that their struggle was not aligned with pro-growth liberal idealism; in fact, she suggested that protonationalism undergirded their strategy against the City of Atlanta. More clearly, the tenants sought agency for the Black poor to decide where they would reside and where they would build their own social institutions. "The goal of the complaint is not to get into the judiciary, but to get power in the hands of the tenants," Jones relayed to the AHA. "We want you to be conciliatory."[35]

RAB escalated action after filing the complaint. On December 3 of that year, over 200 Black tenants from the soon-to-be-demolished Bowen Homes,

Palmer House, and Roosevelt House swarmed the second-floor main meeting room and disrupted a city council meeting. The goal of the occupation was to force the city council to pass a resolution to create a task force to review the implications of the AHA's mass demolition of public housing and its discrimination against poor Black people. During the public comments, one anonymous resident delivered an impassioned speech that outlined the true stakes of gentrification as pogrom—the transformation of Black Atlanta from a working-class space to a petty bourgeois private fortress:

> I want to encourage the council to stand in support of the many of thousands of people in this city who earn [low] wages or fixed income. I want them to support this resolution that investigates how it can be that thousands of units of affordable housing have been torn down over the last decade. What have been put in place are units that are not even affordable for middle-income workers. There are instead million-dollar penthouses being built all over town in the places where the working people have raised their families.... Take the time to find out how the shift of the housing is going to go to those with millions of dollars, and the people who make this city run—the sanitation workers, the nurses, the waitresses and others—are being put outside the perimeter.[36]

Numerous housing-insecure and homeless people also provided their own experiences to offer the council glimpses of the dire future for public housing tenants if they allowed demolition. District 2 councilman Kwanza Hall and District 3 councilman Ivory Lee Young proposed the resolution, but at the end of the meeting it was referred to the community development committee for further discussion. Thus, the council did not consider any concrete action, and the action only delayed what seemed inevitable.[37]

The Atlanta media played a pivotal role in portraying the rebel tenants as pathologically dependent on the welfare of the state. The *Atlanta-Journal Constitution* ran multiple articles that lambasted the residents and championed the AHA for "making the right decision years ago to phase out the projects and encourage public housing residents to take greater responsibility for their own lives." Jim Wooten, a conservative white journalist and critic of public housing, parroted the ideological line that public resources, whether they be housing, school, Social Security, or health care, reinforced Black cultural pathologies of irresponsibility for their own lives and dependency on the government. Of African Americans in public housing Wooten stated, "It took decades to cultivate dependency and after that, passivity, to train them out of the values and the behaviors that moved the next generation upward.

Simply moving them out of public housing projects, while essential, is only the beginning." Wooten praised Glover's push to disrupt those alleged pathologies, stating, "Glover has been steadfast in insisting . . . that residents 'buy' their way back into attractive mixed-use communities by changing their behaviors, by taking responsibility for maintaining decent, crime-free apartments."[38] Thus, while petty bourgeois activists promoted gentrification as a revolutionary, progressive transformation of space to win support, they also propagandized the Black "underclass" pathological argument to justify their "liberation" of poor African Americans from their "dependent relationship" to government assistance and their help in getting them to "grow up" and "be responsible for themselves."

Glover's lead in the city's war against the Black working class paid off for her—especially at a time when the recession gripped the Atlanta metro region. In 2010, as she destroyed the last of the public housing, Glover took home $644,000 in total compensation, which a national survey conducted by HUD showed to be the highest salary of a public housing director in the nation. Glover challenged the report, stating that she only made $312,000 in base salary plus a onetime payment of $126,000, which she explained "represented 12 years of accrued and unused earned vacation since 1998," $135,000 that covered the 2009–10 fiscal years, a onetime payment of $11,250 for accrued paid holidays during the year, and a onetime payment of $4,100 incentive for nonuse of sick leave. Based on these figures, Glover defended herself by suggesting in an unconvincing manner that she never took a vacation day or sick day in over fourteen years as the executive director of the AHA. Unsurprisingly, during the investigation into her income, Glover announced her departure from the position in 2012.[39] She left behind a reputation celebrated by pro-growth liberals but despised by the Black majority class for her callous attitude toward their precariousness and unwillingness to consider options other than gentrification.

Working-class activists celebrated Glover's long-awaited resignation. "Ding dong the witch is dead!" Diane Wright, former president of RAB, exclaimed. When Glover claimed to have ended "concentration camps of poverty" by demolishing all of Atlanta's public housing, Wright replied, "What concentration camps? No, she put them in poverty. Now they're on the street. It's a concentration of homelessness. I'm so happy, I'm ecstatic. Hitler is gone, Hitler has left the building, thank you." When asked what Glover's legacy was, Joe Beasley, a member of African Ascension, did not hold back. "I still call her the Gentrification Queen, to remove Blacks from downtown Atlanta," he stated. "She privatized all the units. The few that are left have got to be held on to for the people who need them." "Renee Glover presided over the destruction of public housing in Atlanta. It's a very good thing she's leaving. It's a bad thing that she was allowed to be there for so long," said Anita Beaty, executive director of the Metro Atlanta Task Force for the Homeless.[40]

Metro Atlanta outside the central city followed the AHA's lead and demolished its public housing without favorable relocation plans for its majority Black residents. The Marietta Housing Authority razed the last remaining project in Cobb County, Fort Hill Homes, in 2012. When pressed as to why it did not simply renovate the units, the Marietta Housing Authority cited "prohibitive costs" that made maintenance infeasible. The 120 families in Fort Hill received similar vouchers as those in Atlanta that moved them into private housing with rigid financial requirements. Many of the residents expressed fear that they would not be able to pay a larger share of utilities on their meager incomes. Soon after, the Marietta Housing Authority announced the sale of the land to Traton Homes to build about forty-five houses that "will sell from $250,000 to $280,000."[41]

Because the city did not replace multiple housing projects with the promised "renovated mixed-income housing," it is appropriate to conclude that the goal of demolishing public housing in Atlanta was to remove poor African Americans from the city. Thus, the Atlanta petty bourgeois activists served as junior partners of capital in systematically displacing a massive portion of a population from their living and social spaces. In other words, class warfare and an anti-Black-poor pogrom defined the "Black Mecca" in the twenty-first century.

Subproletarianization and the Political Economy of the Atlanta Metropolitan Region

When Denise Broward gave up searching for work closer to her new, cheaper home in Lithia Springs, she turned to the city and found an administrative assistant job at Spelman College, twenty-two miles from her neighborhood on Lee Road. In fact, everything that contributed to the stability of poor Black families in metro suburbs—livable-wage jobs, social organizations, and family and adult entertainment—existed elsewhere. Denise shared that because there has never been public transportation in Lithia Springs, those residents who did not own a vehicle were forced to carpool to the city with others daily or risk being stranded on a poor island in Douglas County. "There was not a thing do," she stated. Until the early 2000s, the closest movie theater to Lee Road was ten miles away, and with the exception of Six Flags, family spaces like pro wrestling venues, circuses, and the Fulton County Fair were all downtown.[42]

The desolation of Lithia Springs was nothing new when poor African Americans began to populate the town. Lithia Springs is marked by a history of economic dislocation and diminishing resources for residents. Founded in 1882, the town was technically abolished in 1933 when city leaders bartered its only assets—two chains, a shovel, and a bucket—for a gallon of corn liquor. Because Douglas County provided Lithia Springs' sixteen required municipal services, the city officials sought to provide them by raising taxes on the working classes. Throughout the twentieth century, wealthy people visited Lithia Springs on the rumor that its waters provided "therapeutic" properties. In June 2001, a lawsuit brought by resident Thelma Turley led to a referendum vote that dissolved Lithia Springs into Douglas County again. The taxes on the working classes never resulted in investment for productive labor spaces, and the area became synonymous with service-sector labor and poverty.[43]

Between 1990 and 2010, the number of poor Atlantans living outside the central city perimeter catapulted by 249 percent, far outpacing the 155 percent population growth in the suburbs. In 1990, 57 percent of the metro region's poor lived in the central city; by 2010, only 27 percent remained—concrete evidence of gentrification and displacement of low-income Black people to the resource-strapped suburbs. Black displacement did not hit just a couple of metro suburbs. Between 1999 and 2013, metro counties Gwinnett, Henry, Rockdale, Chatham, and Douglas shifted from majority white to non-majority white. This followed a national trend of Black working-class displacement, as seventy-eight counties nationwide saw similar shifts in the same period.[44]

These new suburban Black workers found little relief upon arrival. The metro region outside the city experienced a 30 percent increase in food stamp requests, compared to a 19 percent increase statewide. Of the ten counties with the highest increases in food stamp recipients from 1990 to 1991, the top four were Clayton, Cobb, DeKalb, and Gwinnett.[45] As a result, the US Census also reported that the US suburban poor grew by 25 percent between 2000 and 2008—five times the growth rate of the poor in cities. Thus, for the first time in decades, a higher share of suburban residents had incomes below the poverty line than residents living in the city. By 2011, almost 16.4 million suburban residents lived below the poverty line, a conservative estimate when considering the cost of living at the time.[46]

Atlanta power brokers developed a spatially defined apartheid structure in the metro region, where northern areas held the most social resources for residents. The northern metro region, with counties like Forsyth, saw its median

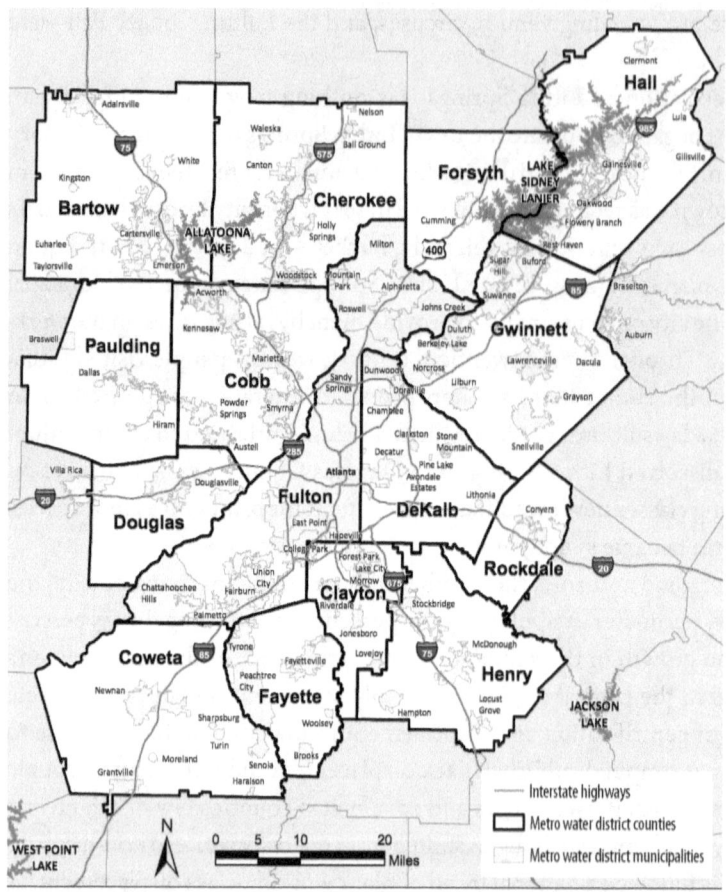

The Atlanta metropolitan region, 2015. Courtesy of Metro Water District.

income skyrocket more than 50 percent after 1990. Northern parts of Fulton, DeKalb, Fayette, and Henry Counties prospered with new homes, tech and distribution centers, golf courses, and high-rise apartments. In fact, affluent spaces like Alpharetta in the northernmost part of Fulton County saw a rise in tech jobs.

Fulton County south of the central city was so isolated from the affluent parts of the metro region that residents could not take buses to jobs north of I-20. Only about 5 percent of welfare recipients in Fulton and DeKalb Counties had access to a car. Yet more than half the Atlanta region's jobs sat outside those areas and beyond the reach of transportation. Between 1990 and 2000, the average time to travel to work increased by 67 percent in DeKalb County, from nineteen minutes to thirty-two minutes.[47]

TABLE 6.2 **Average Cost of Living Expenses by Category, Atlanta, 2015**

EXPENSE	COSTS
Housing	$10,752
Childcare	$6,072
Food	$7,418
Transportation	$6,991
Health care	$8,226
Clothes/personal care	$8,776
Taxes	$7,481
TOTAL:	$55,716

Source: "How Expensive Is It to Live in Metro Atlanta?," Regional Snapshot, Atlanta Regional Commission, 2016, www.documents.atlantaregional.com/snapshots/COLIJuneSnapshot2016.pdf.

Clayton County was the only county in the southern part of the metro region (which is predominantly African American) that expanded jobs. However, these jobs were mostly subproletarian—entry-level administrative, retail, and Hartsfield airport labor—which meant that low-wage, no-skill, unstable, no-benefits dirty work surrounded working-class Black neighborhoods. In fact, over 75 percent of all entry-level jobs were located at least ten miles from the central city, where most poverty-stricken Black people relocated in the 1990s and 2000s. Despite this growth of sub-working-class labor, the Black working-class population explosion in the suburban parts of DeKalb and Fulton Counties outpaced the economy. These areas experienced a net loss of nearly 1,000 jobs in the 1990s. By 2000, south DeKalb County, which was 83 percent nonwhite and working class, had a net gain of only 324 jobs![48]

Subproletarian labor crippled the growing mass of Black working-class people outside Atlanta. By 2015, Georgia had become the seventh poorest state in the nation, with an estimated 1.8 million people living below the poverty line. However, national census data does not account for cost of living to calculate its poverty line. For example, the poverty line for a family of two adults and one child was $18,850 in 2015. However, the cost of living in the Atlanta metropolitan region at that time was triple the poverty line—$55,716![49]

Thus, it is safe to assume that a large swath of metro Atlantans were not counted as being under the poverty line but hovered right above it, thus living in extreme duress as the amount of productive, living-wage labor opportunities shrunk across the state.

Neoliberal policies that stripped state resources from local budgets did not provide the necessary capital for these areas to develop more readily available social services for the migrating Black masses. Most suburban metro regions in the 1990s and 2000s were relatively rural; they lacked infrastructure, thriving economies, and geographical proximity to living-wage jobs. Additionally, working-class suburbs more frequently struggle with food insecurity for many reasons, all related to class position. First, many areas where poor Black people reside lack grocery stores that provide fresh meat, fruit, and vegetables within a five-mile radius. Pawn shops, check-cashing services, and fast-food restaurants replaced grocery stores that used to be located near the Extended Stay in Norcross, for example.[50] Alice and Richard Kent, retired African Americans who reside in predominantly Black southwest Atlanta suburbs on Eleanor Terrace, lost the only grocery supermarket within eight miles of their home when the Piggly Wiggly closed in the early 2000s.[51] In fact, the correlation between the disappearance of grocery stores that provide fresh food and the abundance of fast food, dialysis centers, and retail in suburban metro regions is problematic.

Under these conditions, where reliable personal transport is unaffordable and public transportation unstable, working-class suburbanites are more likely to socialize and spend money in the proximity of their homes, where nonessential consumer materials dominate social needs. As Ellen Gerstein, the executive director of the Gwinnett Coalition for Health and Human Services, stated, "The poverty keeps increasing, but the county tries to mask it. We have . . . the working poor, there's a lot of retail jobs because we have more shopping here than you ever imagine."[52] This intentional dialectic of plentiful consumerist commodities and a shortage of social needs in metro region suburbs is a crucial aspect of the political economy of the New Nadir. More clearly, Black working-class Atlantans displaced from the city and into the suburbs encountered a geographically different apartheid that trapped them in poverty-stricken rural neighborhoods surrounded by low-wage unstable jobs and unaffordable consumer products that took the place of grocery stores and public schools. As a result, Black working-class suburbanites lacked the capacity—resources like nutrition, livable-wage jobs, and time—to strengthen the use value of their neighborhoods and consequently sustain protest movements for social change.

Black suburbanites also struggled with nutrition because of the structural disinvestment and dismantling of physical and mental health services. School boards removed nutritional courses from public schools because neoliberal governments slashed home economics and health from physical education. Also, subproletarianization undercut the time for individuals to devote to healthy eating and meal preparation. Therefore, many low-income Black workers juggled multiple low-wage, unstable jobs that forced them to work fifteen to eighteen hours a day for minimum wage.[53]

Black working-class suburbs in the Atlanta metro region were at least thirty miles from Atlanta's Central Business District. This meant that displaced Black workers had to travel far for their jobs in the city or accept jobs in the emerging retail economy that enveloped their rural surroundings. To make matters worse, MARTA cut services across the board throughout the 2000s. In February 2004, MARTA dissolved or adjusted a record ninety-one of its 124 bus routes in the Atlanta metro region. To accompany the new route schedules, MARTA laid off 304 bus drivers and maintenance workers. The Amalgamated Transit Union told the *Atlanta Voice* that their general manager conceded to MARTA and allowed job cuts and hour reductions. This affected all 212,311 weekly MARTA riders, who had to alter their daily routines, especially those who lived in the metro suburbs around Fulton Industrial Boulevard in west Atlanta, Camp Creek Parkway in east Atlanta, Stone Mountain Freeway in north Atlanta, and Cleveland Avenue in south Atlanta.[54]

A breakdown of the political economy county by county showcases how subproletarianization decimated the use value of Black neighborhoods in the Atlanta metro suburbs. Between 2000 and 2010, Gwinnett County's Black population grew by 112,000, or 143 percent, while also losing $7,000 in per capita income during that same period. Thus, Gwinnett County increased its poor population by a double-digit percentage. Black workers in Gwinnett found mostly low-wage labor. By 2015, the second greatest number of African Americans in Gwinnett County were employed as cashiers (47,090) and earned an average of $10,743 in salary.[55] Over 90 percent of students in some Gwinnett schools were eligible for free and reduced lunch.[56] Although the county ceased being a white majority by this point (Gwinnett County was 90 percent white in the 1990 census), the county power structure remained fully white: the county board of commissioners, the school board, and all the county's state and superior court judges.

Douglas County, twenty miles west of the central city, transformed more than any other metro county because of gentrification. Between 2000 and 2010, Douglas County's Black population more than doubled, from 17,065 (19 percent) to 52,290 (40 percent). Displaced African Americans flocked to Douglasville, the major city in the county. Between 1995 and 2014, Douglasville grew from 15,000 residents, 15 percent of them Black, to over 32,000 residents, 56 percent Black and 33 percent white.[57]

In every common job category in the county, African Americans placed last in wages earned. In 2015, over 49,000 African Americans in Douglas County worked as cashiers and earned an average of $12,000 a year. Most jobs held by Douglas County residents included administrative support services, retail sales, and transportation. Only 25,029 Black people held jobs as full-time supervisors of retail sales workers and earned an average $35,000 a year or more. African Americans led all races in poverty in Douglas County, with over 41 percent.[58] The middle- and upper-class residents who owned cars traveled on I-20 East to the city to work. However, many of the displaced Black residents, who had little to no access to transportation, chose to work in proximity to their homes, mostly in retail and restaurants. By the end of the 1990s, retail jobs in Douglas County outweighed manufacturing jobs trifold, 7,540 to 2,331.[59] This trend would continue into the 2010s.

Much capital investment in Douglas County by the Republican regime rested on the construction of Arbor Place Mall, the first mall of its kind in the county's history. It measured 1.3 million square feet and employed over 3,000 people upon its opening in late 1999.[60] Unsurprisingly, most jobs available at Arbor Place offered minimum wage with no benefits, as did the restaurants surrounding the epicenter. Real estate developers constructed an apartheid living space in the area. The public-private partnership built the Bear Creek Golf and Country Club—a 500-home development on 2,000 acres. The neighborhood brought in a mostly affluent white clientele for the upstart mall, while most of the subproletariat resided in Lithia Springs or on Fairburn Road.[61]

The effects of the new political economy of Douglas County were clear. By 2001, Douglas joined Paulding and Coweta as the only metro region counties to register below the state average of 5 percent in per capita income growth. Like most other metro regions', Douglas's economy was mainly service sector, accounting for 30.4 percent of the jobs, while retail accounted for 24.8 percent.[62] In 2014, capital teased a manufacturing spike with the $337 million acquisition of a Keurig beverage plant in Lithia Springs. Unfortunately for residents, the deal stalled, and the promised 550 factory jobs never materialized. By that point, manufacturing jobs had plummeted 40 percent in the twenty-first century across the metro region.[63]

Fulton and DeKalb Counties, two of the main target areas for poor Black Atlantan flight, bore a disproportionate share of the Atlanta metro region's burden of poverty at the turn of the century. By 1995, these two counties held only 37 percent of the region's population but also 66 percent of the poor people. Cobb County had 11.1 percent of the region's poor but 18.2 percent of the region's total population. Cherokee County had 2.1 percent of the region's poor but 4 percent of the overall population. Additionally, higher-income families resided in the region's northern and far southern areas, while working families who earned less than the area's median income of $36,640 (the city of Atlanta's median household income was $22,275) were concentrated in poor enclaves in the central city and the DeKalb and Fulton County suburbs.[64]

DeKalb County had served as a landing spot for dispossessed African Americans since the 1990s, but their arrival prompted a shift in the political economy of the area. Between 1993 and 1998, 95 percent of all new DeKalb government jobs were in the public safety or criminal justice sectors.[65]

Following in the footsteps of the Lakewood General Motors plant that had closed in 1990, the massive loss of the Doraville General Motors auto plant in 2008 devastated the political economy of DeKalb County.[66] Opened in 1947, the 165-acre plant employed workers who installed everything from seats to carpet to windshield wipers in popular Chevrolet models for decades. Like the Lakewood plant, this factory held a locational advantage for Black Atlantans; it sat right inside I-285 (referred to as Spaghetti Junction), the highway that encircles a sizable portion of the metro region. The plant was also surrounded by Peachtree Road, Peachtree Industrial Boulevard, a MARTA station, and Buford Highway—all spaces that attracted dense populations daily.[67] Before its closure, the facility's average salary was fourteen dollars an hour for its 2,500 employees in 1991, one of the highest salaries in Georgia factories thanks to workers' union contract. By 2005, workers made an estimated thirty dollars an hour. As some workers noted, the union wage scale offered incomes sometimes better than middle-class professional jobs in the area. Additionally, workers maintained a top-tier health-care plan with no deductible or premium payment.[68]

The Doraville plant had escaped closure in the 1990s. In 1991, General Motors had classified the facility as one of the least productive plants in the company, ranked thirty-two out of fifty factories in the nation, and the worst midsized-car plant. Once it had announced its plan to close the plant in 2008, General Motors offered pennies on the dollar for its workers' jobs and lives. In 2006, the company offered almost 3,000 of the employees an insulting buyout deal of $21,470, less than half the yearly salary for full-time workers. These payments worked similarly to funds that real estate companies issued homeowners to take over a neighborhood; the payments were lower than the value of the workers' union contract and their labor. However, 52 percent—1,468 workers—took the buyout.[69]

Many of the workers grew disillusioned at the supposedly strong United Auto Workers union caving to, as well as benefiting from, the death of the Doraville factory. African American couple Carolyn Washington-Biggers and Charles Biggers, who both refused the buyout until the very end, noted that "the fire is gone" from the union to fight the plant closures. Reshonda Johnson, who worked at the plant for nine years, added that she "enjoyed working there, until I heard they were throwing us away like we were nothing."[70] When the factory closed in September 2008, it killed one-third of Doraville's 8,500-person employment base.[71]

Like most major manufacturing plants, the Doraville General Motors factory powered the entire community surrounding it. Like dominos, small businesses, supplier warehouses, entertainment spaces, and other crucial areas of community power collapsed after the plant. In fact, within four years of economic dislocation in the Black area, property values plummeted an estimated 30 percent.[72]

Additionally, General Motors' closure of multiple plants in the metro region left few options for displaced workers. Some, like third-generation autoworker Chris Crumbley, Judy Ashby, and Ryan Hill, moved to Texas, Kentucky, and Indiana, respectively, to chase General Motors jobs as more factories closed across the nation.[73] Most of the workers left before the final car passed through the assembly line were temporary workers. Fortunately for General Motors, they had less overhead costs with temp workers, because they did not have to give them severance packages or aid in transferring to other plants. Additionally, temporary workers received no benefits, vacation time, or union wage scale pay. One worker, Sam Alston, made only eighteen dollars an hour compared to the thirty dollars an hour full-time scale.

The decimation of public resources in Doraville and overall DeKalb County resembled the uneven development of Flint, Michigan, in the 1980s. DeKalb County, where a generous portion of African Americans settled outside of the city limits, saw its poverty rate jump from 10 percent in 1989 to 15.7 in 1995.[74]

Doraville's city officials wasted no time in attempting to sell the city to the highest bidder, but without taxing the increasing poor public, the factory cost millions of dollars in lost tax revenue. Instead of building union-scale productive jobs for the Black working class, DeKalb County officials sat on the property, and by 2015 land and property devalorization put Doraville on the radars of pro-growth interests. That year, MARTA leased land throughout the area for mixed-used development and private investment. As usual with gentrification, this development only provided the dirtiest work for low-income residents, particularly retail and restaurant labor.[75]

Displaced Black workers also migrated to Cobb County by the swaths. Around southwest Cobb County, including along Donald Lee Hollowell Parkway (formerly Bankhead Highway), Fulton Industrial Boulevard, Six Flags Drive, and Austell Road on the border with Douglas County, there was nothing more than used car dealerships, a row of auto body shops, fast-food restaurants, package stores, and an amusement park. Darlene Duke, the head of the Christian Aid Mission Partnership, noted the lack of any possible economic or social development in Cobb County: "I can't remember anything vibrant downtown in the last 20 years," Duke stated. "We're the red-headed stepchild. No one wants to come down here. They want to be where the money is."[76]

Factory closings removed livable-wage jobs from Cobb County too. In 2010, the National Envelope Corporation Plant moved from Austell to a much smaller facility in Smyrna, Georgia. With close to 240 people out of work, the Austell economic base deteriorated further. "The development now in Austell is gone," said Patricia Mewborn, a sixty-four-year-old veteran of the company for twenty-two years. "National Envelope closing is a bad hit for Austell. This is going to become a little dead town."[77] With a population around 7,000 in 2010, the town had little to no prospects for stable livable-wage labor.

Subproletarian labor ravaged other metro regions that are often forgotten when people think of the Atlanta metropolitan region. The London-owned Kysor-Warren plant, which manufactured grocery store refrigeration units, laid off its full employee base of 218 in Conyers in Rockdale County. Conyers especially was used to layoffs and mass unemployment. Every year of the 1990s except 1995 and 1999, at least one company in Conyers laid off workers.[78] In Carroll County, more than 380 workers lost their jobs when the fifteen-acre Sony Music manufacturing plant closed in March 2001. This was the final group of workers to leave after Sony had cut over 1,100 jobs over the past ten years. Opened in 1981, the factory attracted many people especially with menial, low-wage jobs in the area to instead manufacture records, cassette tapes, laser discs, and compact discs. Before its closure, workers took home between twelve and fifteen dollars an hour working on the production line and much more working in mechanics. Calling the Sony plant jobs the best in Carrollton at the time, Mary Lou Smith—hired by Sony in 1982 and forced into crisis after taking a large mortgage three years before the plant closed—stated that "these kids who came to Sony out of high school don't know how good they have it." However, those same workers faced a new political economy where most jobs available in Carroll County paid less than ten dollars an hour. "I'm scared," remarked Sheila Coker, an employee of the plant for over eighteen years. "Every time you listen to the news, some place is laying off. You wonder: Will there be enough jobs for all of us?"[79] Smith highlighted the disillusionment and loss of resources in Carrollton: "We're mostly sad.... There's an anger. We don't know what to do, where to go." To add insult to an already stressful situation, Sony ordered a police car to sit outside the company gates and armed guards to walk the plant in the final days of operation.[80] In its final "goodwill" gesture to quell the anger of the workers, Sony created "Hot Dog Day" for the employees but still charged a quarter per hot dog. Many of the workers walked out in defiance to eat elsewhere.[81]

Closing the Carrollton factory also disrupted the kinship networks and relationships between workers. "We've seen each other's babies born, grow up get married. We've seen people divorce, people retire," Smith said, describing workers in tears on their shifts. "We'll all lose touch. We won't be in the same place anymore. You just naturally drift apart." Thus, informal kinship networks were a primary characteristic of productive labor spaces like factories.

Clayton County also served as a destination for displaced African Americans seeking an option for housing that was cheaper than the central city. Between 1990 and 2003, the African American population in Clayton tripled from 43,403 to 121,927![82] That decade, Clayton County had the highest concentration of Black residents in the Atlanta metro region—surpassing previous record holder DeKalb County. Concurrently, the number of white Clayton residents dropped from 35 percent to 26 percent within one year. Displaced Black people fled to the area because of its much more affordable housing market and low taxes. This was reflected in the median age of new Black migrants to the county—thirty-one—which was far lower than in Cobb, DeKalb, Fulton, Gwinnett, and Douglas Counties. Additionally, displaced Black workers also made decisions on where to migrate based on protonationalist tendencies. In the early 2000s, Clayton County was noteworthy for its reputation that African Americans there would "participate in the political process" by joining local organizations such as the school board.[83]

Stranded at the Extended Stay: Consequences of Subproletarianization

Every weekday at 3:15 p.m. in 2015, the Norcross school bus dropped off dozens of children in front of the cluster of dilapidated, three-story, yellow motels where they lived. In front of each motel sat abandoned cars, discarded mattresses, and scattered debris. Stranded at the Norcross Extended Stay Motel for $169 a week, many of these individuals, like African American Rev. Harriet Bradley, did not possess access to stable transportation, especially since the public transit in Gwinnett County did not run on weekends. Instead, she planned her trips to her church in advance and remained at the motel for most days. At one point, Bradley, fed up with the county bus system, travelled to a Gwinnett County Board of Commissioners meeting to protest the lack of public transit. She spoke passionately about how this struggle contributed to deepening poverty in the county: "The bus schedules don't start early or run late enough. I've often heard people say, 'They don't realize I can't get to work.' Many have had to turn down jobs because they couldn't get there."[84] After she realized the commissioners ignored her pleas, Bradley stated, "They don't really want public transportation out here. . . . They wouldn't use it anyway."[85]

Extended-stay motels became a nationwide solution for many Black poor urbanites on the outside of an expensive, gentrifying city looking in. Because subproletarian jobs were so poorly compensated, members of the subproletariat could find themselves without housing, with the cheapest option being an extended-stay motel for a few dollars a day. Within Atlanta, extended stays served as the only viable option thanks to political maneuvering by petty bourgeois leaders. In 2013, Gateway Center, a nonprofit for homeless services, closed all its shelters for women and children. Despite the arrival of more displaced women and children, Gateway Center did not reopen its shelters dedicated to them or reallocate some of their spaces reserved for men. Instead, it herded homeless women and children into an empty office space with nothing more than chairs. When criticized for prioritizing homeless men's services and programs while shuttering those for women and children, Gateway chairman Jack Hardin launched into pathological bootstrap discourse to demean the work ethic, character, and values of homeless Black women and children: "The [women's] shelter operated outside of the Gateway philosophy because it was not advancing people along the path to independence. . . . In addition, [Gateway] provided a place for many consumers that enabled them not to take advantage of other housing opportunities or responsibility for their decisions and life."[86] In other words, Gateway, a supposed "progressive" nonprofit resource in the city, individualized the social problem and neglected the colonized position of poor Black urbanites under the neoliberalization and gentrification ravaging the working classes at the time. According to petty bourgeois activists like Hardin, poor Black people voluntarily chose to sleep in chairs in packs and on hard office floors because they were not motivated to do otherwise. This discourse is a primary characteristic of petty bourgeois activists, who seek to bureaucratize and supervise poverty and dispel the class argument at the heart of social dislocation in urban spaces.

Lacking a legitimate homeless shelter in Atlanta, poor Black women like thirty-five-year-old African American fast-food worker Ebony Wallace fought to obtain a room at an extended-stay motel whenever possible. When Wallace lost her job while eight months pregnant in 2011, she had no other choice than to move between the overcrowded homeless shelter and the thirty-four-dollar-a-night extended stay when she had the money. "I haven't been able to put a real roof over my head since when [my daughter] was born," Wallace stated. "I've been going shelter to shelter. Some people help. As soon as I get the $34.86 I need, I go to the motel." For women seeking shelter in Atlanta, homeless centers offered little safety and unsanitary conditions compared to the shelters for homeless men. Wallace and her newborn, Geneva, often encountered ninety-plus women and children huddled together and sleeping in chairs or on empty office floors, separated from the 400-plus men sleeping on rows of cots in the actual shelter building.

The political economy responded accordingly to the correlation of the social crisis of displacement and the use of extended-stay motels. Between 2007 and 2019, extended-stay hotels and motels achieved an average yield of 8.4 percent, 180 points higher than the industrial, retail, and office sectors. In fact, extended stays were the only US hotel subsector that exceeded demand in 2019, spurring billions in investment from corporate giants Blackstone Real Estate Partners and Starwood Capital Group. According to real estate giant Jones Lang LaSalle, investment volume in extended stays in 2021–22 exceeded that of the previous six years (2015–20) combined.[87] Thus, it is safe to assume that the catalyst for such expedited investment was the increasing number of poor people choosing extended stays over unaffordable housing or overflowing homeless shelters in the first fifteen years of the twenty-first century. More clearly, the consequences of neoliberalization and gentrification—displacement and subproletarianization—have radically restructured multiple investment sectors, particularly the hotel industry.

Unsurprisingly, extended stays have been resilient during economic collapses in comparison to the overall US hotel industry, mainly because demand for extended stays skyrockets as more people become housing insecure. Another reason for this trend is the cheaper cost to build and maintain such hotels; most extended-stay residents complain of the lack of furniture, fixtures, and repairs.

The boom in extended-stay investment in Atlanta is tied to the structural violence waged against Black working-class Atlantans. The combination of systematic gentrification since the 1980s and the Great Recession and its lingering effects provided large tech and banking companies in the city an opportunity to chase high-salaried employees who also flipped houses for profit in Atlanta's tumultuous real estate market. This investor frenzy priced out many working-class residents from affordable housing. Since the mid-2010s, the Atlanta metro region has had one of the largest concentrations of discount extended-stay motel chains in the nation. For example, in 2019, a survey of budget extended-stay hotels in Gwinnett County showed that 45 percent of the booked rooms were for stays of thirty days or more. By 2021, that number had jumped to 67 percent. Forty-three-year-old African American Shavetta Simmons, for example, rented a house in Lawrenceville, Georgia, for two years, but once the rent jumped to $2,000 a month plus utilities, she found her only option to be the Studio 6 extended-stay hotel in Duluth.[88]

Fulton Industrial Boulevard southwest of Atlanta housed one of the longest-running extended-stay motels for decades, the Mosley Motel, which charged families struggling to survive twenty-five dollars a night. Those who could not afford the rent often negotiated a lower payment, typically $450 a month with a $100 deposit. Those who could not afford lower payments or had debt-ridden or criminal backgrounds that disqualified them from the extended stay, found themselves couch surfing with kin, sleeping in abandoned cars on Fulton Industrial Boulevard, or fighting with other housing-insecure individuals for space in the decreasing number of homeless shelters.

The Mosley Motel became such a popular home for poor Black Atlantans that school buses for Randolph Elementary School, Sandtown Middle School, and Westlake High School made daily stops there. The Mosley was also notorious for being a base for sex workers and drug dealers. "I can't afford a U-Haul," fifty-two-year-old James Lott exclaimed as he carried his belongings outside the closed Mosley. "I'm just trying to hang on until I can find a job. I get an unemployment check and it's about to run out." The Mosley was the second extended-stay that Lott and his wife, Parolyn Walker, stayed in, after their last motel on Fulton Industrial closed that same year.[89]

Unfortunately for the 205 Mosley residents—some of whom had lived at the Mosley for over five years—the Fulton County Health Department closed the motel for health code violations. In fact, Fulton officials told the Mosley to close within twenty-four hours of its decision, leaving the residents homeless. Luckily, public outcry forced the county officials to negotiate an extension so residents could attempt to find alternative housing. For Black Mosley residents Stanley and Amanda Johnson, thirty-six and twenty-five years old, respectively, and other poor Black people, the closure removed another resource in metro Atlanta. The Johnsons had lived at the Mosley for six months because their household income totaled forty-seven dollars a day from a temp agency. When told the Mosley was closing, Stanley lost it: "Now I don't know what we're going to do. The other day, I started crying."[90]

Fulton County officials targeted extended-stay motels on Fulton Industrial Boulevard because of their reputation for sex work and drug dealing, but this neglects the resource that these motels provided for the Black subproletariat who could not afford other spaces in the metro region. County official Tony Phillips stated that the displacement "was for the best in the end," and that "the rooms are not designed for [people to live there in] that type of occupancy."[91]

However, the mostly Black residents at the Mosley had built a community of kinship, a collective struggle, and a resource base for their families. African American LaShanda Jones, the Mosley manager, described the Mosley as a kinship space for the residents. When one resident took a job as a forklift driver, he used his increased pay to cover the rents for his family, the Johnsons, and their extended families when necessary. Since many of the families there grew closer over the months they resided there, they participated in holiday celebrations, including buying each other's children Christmas presents that sat under the lobby's Christmas tree. Each night, parents gathered all the school-aged children in the meeting room to collectively complete their homework assignments. Community members like teachers often visited and sometimes paid monthly rents for some of the cash-strapped families. "The teachers adopted the kids for Christmas," Jones said. "They had food drives and clothing drives. It was awesome."[92]

These informal kinship networks, practiced more often when the Black working class lived in closer proximity to one another, demonstrated that elements of protonationalism survived the neoliberalization and gentrification of Black urbanites into the twenty-first century. Extended-stay motels, while a harsh consequence of displacement, offered Black residents some resources to build collective kinship networks in poor suburbs. In 2012, African

American Davida Baker, a longtime community leader in Gwinnett County, organized a nine-car caravan full of Christmas presents to deliver to four extended-stay motels. In fact, between 2002 and 2012, as more poor Black urbanites flooded Gwinnett County's extended-stay motels, she had organized community members into multiple programs that pooled resources for families. Each summer, Baker oversaw Project Kids Eat, a free breakfast and dinner program that delivered to the four major motels in her Norcross suburb. To fund the action, Baker pressed the original local movement center in Black working-class neighborhoods: the church. Like Black Power and labor organizers before her, Baker used Campus Christian Church as her local movement base—coordinating volunteers and drivers, educating them to the social crises plaguing the displacement and housing insecurity of poor Black suburbanites, arranging the delivery of food and toys, pooling cleaning supplies often absent from extended-stay motels, and drafting other community members to participate. Baker's system worked so efficiently that for every caravan of vehicles, she coordinated enough materials for close to eighty-five families. Although it was not happening as much on a grand scale because of the overall loss of resources, pockets of Black working-class communities fought subproletarianization via such kinship networks, demonstrating that there was a nationalist and class character to the struggle in the Atlanta metropolitan region. "Why are you doing this?" one motel resident asked Baker. "It's just love," Baker replied.[93]

As more poor Black urbanites chose extended-stay motels, more residents condemned them as "dangerous" spaces. For example, the city of Loganville in Gwinnett County organized opposition to the annexation and rezoning of 3.8 acres of land for the construction of a Hampton Inn extended-stay motel. More than seventy Loganville residents stormed a planning commission meeting and complained that extended stays "cause crime in neighborhoods."[94]

The New Atlanta and the Mercedes Conquest of Vine City

Once the Atlanta public-private partnership had flushed the Black masses away to those resource-deprived, rural suburban deserts in the metro area, it sold affluent whites a dream of retaking a newly financial and "modern" city. It worked incredibly quickly. For the third time in less than thirty years, the remaining Black workers in poor areas like Vine City faced impending stadium gentrification. In early March 2013, the city council approved a $1 billion funding bill to build a state-of-the art football stadium for the Atlanta Falcons in the Vine City and English Avenue neighborhoods. The Georgia World Congress Authority, which owned the bulk of the targeted land, approved of the plan under the conditions that the city did not levy new property taxes. The city's share of the construction was capped at $200 million using the city's hotel-motel tax. Arthur Blank, the owner of the Atlanta Falcons, contributed the remaining $800 million and would be responsible for any cost overruns. The city council also approved an annual contribution of 39.3 percent of the hotel-motel tax to the stadium through 2050 for operational costs—the same amount that was allocated to the Georgia Dome. The Falcons also contributed $70 million for infrastructure improvements around the stadium and $20 million for land acquisitions.[95] This set the stage for influencing land rent and property value fluctuation in surrounding areas. In a sense, the Mercedes-Benz Stadium was more than a new source for capital accumulation and a section of the new central Atlanta hub. Rather, it also provided the petty bourgeoisie an opportunity to price even more low-income African Americans out of their target investment areas.

The last three entities that had to give approval for construction to commence were Invest Atlanta, the city's economic real estate development agency; Friendship Baptist Church; and Mount Vernon Baptist Church, where Blank wanted the stadium located. The Vine City churches, both former agency-laden institutions for much social movement planning, training, and resource pooling over the decades, held the fate of Vine City neighborhood residents in their hands. If they voted not to sell their land to the city, the stadium more than likely would be built north of the Georgia Dome on Northside Drive, a previously gentrified area with expensive lofts, trendy coffee shops and shopping, and a large population of Georgia Tech and Georgia State University students.[96]

Mayor Kasim Reed did not raise the question of holding public forums for a community study before making sweeping, top-down decisions about their neighborhoods. The truth is that Reed, who had a reputation for being a close friend of the Atlanta Chamber of Commerce, considered the Vine City site as the only choice for his vision of neoliberal Atlanta. Reed stated that he wanted Mercedes-Benz Stadium to be connected to the Vine City MARTA station, the Georgia Dome, and the Philips Arena.[97] Ivory Young, who originally endorsed the military invasion of Vine City in 2002, joined Reed in championing the razing of the area again. He believed housing this stadium in his district on top of Vine City provided lucrative potential for private investment. Thus, he embarked on a publicity campaign that emphasized philanthropy and bourgeois diversity, more symbolic than functional, to win support for the stadium. Young negotiated an agreement with Blank and the Georgia World Congress Authority to develop an equal business opportunity plan that "would ensure at least 31 percent participation by women and minority business firms in design and construction of the stadium."[98] As is often the case with most construction companies and businesses, Black contractors were least likely to hire Black unionized labor and preferred out-of-town, cheap, nonunion labor. Therefore, these bourgeois diversity project labor agreements did not mandate standards for real diversity on job sites. As a result, area residents who sought livable-wage work were excluded, while external nonunion labor demolished their homes. Stadium construction contributed a net loss to neighborhoods because residents received little labor or other material benefit from the project.

Critics of the Atlanta City Council's string of empty promises warned Vine City residents to fight the stadium. African American James Sellers, a member of the Mount Vernon Baptist Church and owner of the Sellers Brothers Funeral Home on Martin Luther King Jr. Drive, cited the gentrification and subsequent displacement at Westside Village as an example of how the City of Atlanta operated: "At one particular time, that area was a prominent and thriving part of the Black business structure. All those businesses that had been there from the 1950s and 1960s were moved before the 1996 Summer Olympic Games and what was left was mostly vacated land. Now some 18 years later, they finally get a Wal-Mart over there."[99]

The August 1, 2013, deadline for Friendship Baptist and Mount Vernon Baptist approval passed with no decision made, but Mount Vernon's hesitation did not necessarily pertain to Sellers's sentiments of resistance against the city's gentrification efforts. Rather, evidence suggests that the churches were holding out for the right price to abandon their lands. In fact, the Mercedes-Benz Stadium episode closely resembled the Georgia Dome negotiation in 1988, when church leaders fractured the grassroots movement to stop the construction of the dome in Vine City. Instead, the churches gave the city and the developers permission once their pay and church relocation plans had been set. In the case of Mercedes-Benz Stadium, the churches held significant leverage to secure a substantial buyout. Lloyd Hawk, the chairperson of the Friendship Baptist Church executive board, told the *Atlanta Voice* that "we are definitely still negotiating. It's going well. We're waiting on some communication to come in. . . . I would say we're very close." When asked how far, monetarily, the two sides remained apart, Hawk said, "I won't say a dollar amount, but if you look at the grand scheme of the budget for the stadium project, it's a very, very tiny percentage of that." Reed, who more than likely was seeking to gain leverage from public outrage at the church, alerted press that he had offered Friendship Baptist Church $15.5 million and had been turned down.[100]

Friendship Baptist became the first church to officially abandon the Vine City residents. In the first week of August, Reed announced that he had purchased Friendship's land for $19.5 million, but the Mount Vernon purchase was in doubt at that point. Reed offered Hawk $6.2 million, which he rejected, setting Reed and Young on a path of more petty bourgeois activism. Reed informed the media that attempting to build Mercedes-Benz Stadium north of the Georgia Dome was "fiscal folly" because of the crippling cost (caused by their previous gentrification of the area) and environmental concerns about toxic soil, traffic gridlock, and many more "inconveniences to the public." At one press conference Hawk stood side by side with Reed, never mentioning the superfluous low-income Vine City residents, and stated, "We understand the potential benefits of the stadium being placed at the south site for the surrounding community."[101]

This undoubtedly put public pressure on Mount Vernon to "ease the burden on the Atlanta City Council" and take the deal, but Mount Vernon held firm until Atlanta upped the offer by an additional $8.3 million. In mid-September, Mount Vernon agreed to sell its land to the city for $14.5 million: $8.3 million from the city and $6.2 million from the Georgia World Congress Authority. The city paid a total of $37 million to historic Black churches to build a football stadium in Vine City. At this point, evidence suggests that Vine City residents' displacement had not been discussed as part of the deal, and the churches secured their funds and left. While Friendship Baptist Church only moved a mile away to Walnut Street, Mount Vernon moved over seven miles away to Lynhurst Drive near the I-285 exchange in southwest Atlanta. In the end, the middle class only tracked the progress of the bourgeois diversity initiative in constructing Mercedes-Benz Stadium. When celebrating the deal, Kasim Reed best summed up his petty bourgeois activism, the class interests of the Atlanta power structure, and the sociohistorical treatment of poor Black people: "We really think we've accomplished what we have accomplished today in the Atlanta way."[102]

The Atlanta power structure's petty bourgeois activism extended the superfluous character of Black working-class bodies and spaces in twenty-first-century Atlanta. Atlanta leadership used the Atlanta Chamber of Commerce and nonprofit capitalist organizations like the Edison Project and community development corporations to target state resources like hospitals, public schools, and housing for private investment. Although working-class resistance groups like the Greater Atlanta Ministerial Alliance attempted to protect low-income neighborhoods from further razing, petty bourgeois activism evoked a pathological discourse to recruit public support for pro-growth reforms. The section of Vine City with the most exchange value potential became the central hub for the twenty-four-hour visitor market in the central city.

The Great Recession increased the precariousness of the Black working class. Underemployment ravaged the already-diminished wage potential of Black workers. Minimum-wage, nonunion labor, like jobs at McDonald's and Walmart, replaced livable-wage jobs. As a result, Black workers did not possess the capacity to challenge Atlanta's gentrification efforts. With most of the Black working-class Atlantans now residing in suburban enclaves of poverty, the relationship between apartheid and resistance for the Black working class is transformed for the foreseeable future.

EPILOGUE

The Black Worker
What Is to Be Done?

> As I assess our work in the 1950's, one of our problems was that we moved to the defensive too quickly without contesting the terrain at every point. Too little attention was paid to developing limited offensives, for only in offensives can you raise new questions. ... In the midst of defending political and economic terrain that was important, the old left lost the capacity to project a vision of a viable alternative society. The only alternatives they put forth were cast in terms of the thirties and the Great Depression—revive the New Deal coalition. ... Are we menaced by a real fascist threat? When you take the racial realties of America into account, this situation requires a more complex analysis because the norms of bourgeois democracy have never been fully applied in the black community. For the black community, the major controls are still exercised through the traditional state and corporate methods.
> —HAROLD "HAL" BARON, March 5, 1981

The preceding chapters of this book will indeed anger many people—primarily at the notion and ample evidence that the callous disregard for the lives of African American workers built the opulent dreams of urban fortune for many wealthy African Americans. Others may object to the contextualization of noted community and celebrity figures as antagonists of the Black masses, driven by their class interests. Make no mistake about it: individuals made decisions to assist in the destruction of Black working-class Atlanta, but no specific decision over the last sixty years in Atlanta stands above the others in the system of domination. This book considers all decision-makers in the destruction of Black working-class Atlanta as well as other urban centers to be equally culpable in building and sustaining an inhumane, violent, bourgeois structure at the center of urbanization.

In fact, *Class Warfare in Black Atlanta* reiterates Malcolm X's poignant point that Black people have often been subjected to the American Dream of "democracy." Bourgeois in nature, American history is often written to emphasize the minor, temporary, and illusory reconciliations of African Americans with the state. Thus, Black workers—who by their capacity of resistance contradict the dominance of the state and submission of the masses—are often hidden in the historical and contemporary analysis of the United States and world. As radical scholar-activist Hal Baron alluded to in the letter excerpted at the beginning of this chapter, the sociohistorical experience of the Black worker in Atlanta encompasses the contradiction of the American Dream: ravaged by decades of capitalist restructuring and decimation of public resources; demonized and criminalized by bourgeois and petty bourgeois wars against poor urbanites; laid to waste by capital's technological revolutions and the hollowing out of the productive industrial and manufacturing sector; locked out of the international beacons of finance, education, downtown prosperity, and real estate affluence; locked down by mass incarceration; and devastated by the retreat from the urban core of the city.

Despite the fact that the Black worker has been the most critical component of the growth, expansion, sustainability, and transformation of the structure of the United States and global economy, scholars often position these forgotten protagonists in the following ways: as either (1) passive objects without the capacity to embody agency; (2) culturally broken over centuries of "social death"; (3) a simple monolithic community in which every member embodies the same political, economic, social, and cultural values; (4) politically and ideologically too superfluous to care for or defend; (5) politically and ideologically impotent and in need of external guidance or leadership; or (6) spontaneous and apolitical in their protests and "riots." More clearly, these narratives that restrict the Black worker to one or more of these categories contribute to the depoliticization of Black resistance and the decentralization of African Americans to US and world history. The revolutionary sentiment among the Black working class during Black Power was not a hidden, minor squabble in a few select locations. Rather, it tore the core of urban centers like Atlanta apart, thus reaffirming that a sizable portion of the Black population rejected the legitimacy of white authority and rule. In fact, the magnitude of the response by urban power brokers—who classified the Black working classes as an enemy of progress and tranquility—meant that the agency of local movement actors threatened the very restructuring of capital accumulation in the last quarter of the twentieth century.

Yet the troubling trend in scholarly narratives omits the linkage between the Black worker's philosophy of liberation and action in the political economy. More clearly, as scholar-activist Lou Turner theorized, the failure to conceptualize how Black workers intervene in social problems affecting their collective communities purports a crisis of historical forgetfulness.[1] Consequently, historical forgetfulness inherently produces mythmaking, typically with political motivations. As W. E. B. Du Bois prophesized over 100 years ago, this propaganda of history distorts the sociohistorical experience of African Americans across all class levels.[2] What purpose does mythmaking serve the Atlanta metropolitan region other than as a political solution to the crisis of the Black worker? Why soften the historically complicated relationship between the vying classes of African Americans?

The dialectic offers the most succinct means to build a critique of the political economy that addresses the social crisis of African American subproletarianization. Although this study sought to ground the subproletarianization thesis in a historical context, I argue that subproletarianization is the most pressing crisis in the African American majority today. In 2019, the Brookings Institute reported that at least 44 percent of all able-bodied individuals were working in low-wage, nonunion labor.[3] With the loss of affirmative action as a relatively weak, but still federally mandated, guideline for college admission for historically disadvantaged groups, white supremacists have barricaded another road for Black and brown working poor people to access the small number of "good" jobs that require skills obtained from a college education. Therefore, as I explain later in this epilogue, those same millions of locked-out Black people affected by this decision over the next decade will be restricted to the dirtiest and lowest-paid job types in the nation.

Class Warfare in Black Atlanta has traced the development of this crisis to the present day. However, our scholarship on the Black worker must reflect our understanding of this new political economic formation in which subproletarian labor will most likely be dominant in twenty years. The dismantling of livable-wage labor continues to accelerate at a disturbing rate. At this stage in labor market instability, construction remains one of the only job sectors that offer a living wage to working-class individuals who lack a college education. By 2022, thirty-two dollars an hour was the average salary for a construction worker in the United States. However, business unionism locks the Black worker out of gaining a sizable foothold in the industry. As of 2022, 88 percent of construction workers identified as white (some being Latinx) compared to only 8 percent as Black. Union stronghold cities like Boston, Philadelphia, and Chicago conspire against Black workers by monopolizing city contracts and project labor agreements. In Philadelphia, where 44 percent of the population is Black, the Equal Employment Opportunity Commission reported that among the forty Philadelphia unions who refer workers to contractors, 91 percent of the 39,000 workers were white compared to 5 percent Black. The nationwide data spells a much more harrowing crisis. Of the 843 US building trade unions that report their demographics to the Equal Employment Opportunity Commission, white workers make up about 75 percent of building trade workers, compared to only 16 percent African American![4]

These developments present dire consequences for the Black worker at a time when explicit white supremacy is no longer hidden from policy, practice, or interpersonal interactions in public. As Hal Baron contended, the labor market is intertwined with the education and housing markets. Thus, regression in one area disrupts the viability in the other areas for the Black working class. With white supremacists attacking local school boards to erase Black struggle from history textbooks and using antiquated, real-estate-friendly laws to purchase property cheaply and price poor urbanites out of housing, the New Nadir has been deepening for the Black working class. To make matters worse, a growing number of neoconservative and neoliberal African American policymakers have cleared the path for retrenchment in the Black working class. Public officials like Clarence Thomas, Ben Carson, Tim Scott, and Eric Adams and problematic social media "influencers" like Tariq Nasheed, Candace Owens, Jason Whitlock, and Larry Elder purposely shield any discussion about the grand larceny of resources from the African American majority. Instead, they work heartedly for white supremacist capitalists and swing the narrative back to pathological degeneracy in Black people. Their anti-Black narratives populate public policy, journalism, social media, and right-wing scholarship. Their mission is to erase the material realm of Black struggle and allow white supremacists to create, sustain, and transform the narrative.

To undertake racial oppression from the dialectical perspective, we must trace how self-understanding from a collective standpoint developed in unison with a consciousness of the material conditions that constrain self-determination. The Black worker's development of self is tied to the desire to transform those conditions that limit one's freedom. Under gentrification, multiple apparatuses of the state induce powerlessness in Black workers, forcing them to confront the legitimacy of struggle against the oppressive forces. However, as *Class Warfare in Black Atlanta* asserts, the materiality dictates the Black worker's strategy and tactics in resistance. Therefore, the loss of crucial community resources through the depletion of the use value of African

American neighborhoods changed the offensive mentality of revolutionary struggle to a defensive survival mode. Through subproletarianization, the Black worker is in constant precarity when it comes to material resources and therefore is in a constant search for the capacity to resist racial oppression, with diminishing results. If we are serious about US history and the structures of accumulation, we cannot neglect the centrality of the dialectic in the resistance and domination of the Black worker across time and space.

As a result, the dialectic framework removes much of the static nature of history often found in narratives that neglect the centrality of local actors in the social process of urbanization. Dialectics require hard, theoretical work to grasp the ideas that generate both movement action and the repressive response to revolt. Combined with a historical materialist framework, the dialectic sets crucial urban processes such as revitalization, neoliberalization, internationalization, financialization, gentrification, proletarianization, deproletarianization, and subproletarianization in motion so that we can recognize how the struggle for self-determination constructs the social forces for these processes to develop. History is the study of the method of this process, "even as philosophy is the recognition that to be humans means that these ideas are in us already by nature."[5]

Returning to Du Bois, if historical truth is the objective, then mythmaking —through the erasure of the centrality of the Black worker in urban space and the process of capital accumulation altogether or through the reduction of gentrification to nothing more than an unethical process of revitalizing a neighborhood—is a fantastical romance created by protected beneficiaries of internal neocolonialism. More clearly, the more we refuse to formalize critique in our analysis, the more we prop the propaganda of history and its consequences on the Black worker. As Du Bois argued, we will never have a history of reason or truth until we, as scholars, regard the truth as more significant than the defense of capitalism, white supremacy, or bourgeois nationalism.[6]

From a scholarly perspective, our undertaking must centralize history from below. Current and future scholars must collectively agree to negate the misinterpretations and political agreements among the dominant classes in distorting the sociohistorical realties of oppressed people. Our task is not merely to acknowledge and comment on the mythmaking aspect of gentrification and urban revitalization. Rather, we must critique it as the internal neocolony that it is and use our intellectual prowess to intervene and inform an equitable outcome for oppressed groups. Through the deep study of Black working-class communities, we can best represent this vision.

Several masterful works challenge the propaganda of history and move us in the proper direction. For the most serious studies of how proletarianization directs the struggles and social organization capacity of Black workers in urban space, one can look to Joe W. Trotter Jr.'s *Black Milwaukee: The Making of an Industrial Proletariat, 1915–1945* and *Workers on Arrival: Black Labor in the Making of America*; Sundiata Keita Cha-Jua's *America's First Black Town: Brooklyn Illinois, 1830–1915*; Tera W. Hunter's *To 'Joy My Freedom: Southern Black Women's Lives and Labors after the Civil War*; David Bates's *The Ordeal of the Jungle: Race and the Chicago Federation of Labor, 1903–1922*; Keona Erwin's *Gateway to Equality: Black Women and the Struggle for Economic Justice in St. Louis*; Simon Balto's *Occupied Territory: Policing Black Chicago from Red Summer to Black Power*; and Winston Grady-Willis's *Challenging US Apartheid: Atlanta and Black Struggles for Human Rights, 1960–1977*. Other works superbly dissect the intricacies of Black autonomy in fighting racial oppression, such as Rhonda Y. Williams's *The Politics of Public Housing: Black Women's Struggles against Urban Inequality*; Keeanga-Yamahtta Taylor's *Race for Profit: How Banks and the Real Estate Industry Undermined Black Homeownership*; and Edward Onaci's *Free the Land: The Republic of New Afrika and the Pursuit of a Black Nation-State*. Charisse Burden-Stelly's *Black Scare/Red Scare: Theorizing Capitalist Racism in the United States* successfully concretizes the political economy and the critique of capitalist exploitation at the heart of Black struggle. In fact, Burden-Stelly's noteworthy study illustrates the dialectic of resistance to domination in radical African American social movements. Historian Ashley Howard's "Whose Streets? Wielding Urban Revolts as Political Tools," as well as her work on the Black Midwest, lays pathbreaking ground on the intricacies of Black collective resistance and intraracial class conflict. These radical works situate historical materialism and the struggle over social conditions as primary determinants in the sociohistorical experience of African Americans.

The stakes for radical scholarship are high because gentrification and sub-proletarianization cannot be smoothed over or simplified under bourgeois liberal perspectives. Considering that both processes are central in metropolitan regions across the United States today, both require a rigorous theoretical framework to capture their insidiousness. One glaring omission in contemporary studies is the role of labor in the sociohistorical experience of the Black worker. Ironic as it is, very few analyses consider work and the conditions of work in the racial oppression or resistance of African American workers. Having said that, the labor studies discipline has not taken a serious approach to capturing the centrality of Black labor in national or global labor studies.

Because African American history is US history and the exploited labor of the Black worker created and has sustained the dominance of US hegemony in the global economy since slavery, labor history and labor studies can best be understood through the experiences of the Black worker. Thus, scholars must engage multiple disciplines that emphasize the material realities of Black workers to understand the political, economic, social, cultural, and spatial elements of society. Additionally, political science, political economy, sociology, history, and urban geography offer concepts that can address and critique detrimental structures against the Black worker appropriately. We cannot fear these disciplines; rather, as Burden-Stelly noted, these frameworks equip scholars and activists alike with resources necessary to build offensive fronts that challenge how abstract cultural diaspora studies "deterritorialized, relativized, and abstracted Blackness in a way that seriously hampered a structural critique of power."[7]

The current state of the subproletarian political economy in metro regions like Atlanta offers us the path forward for our work outside of academia. In fact, the forecast for poor workers in Georgia is grim as sweated, dirty work continues to replace livable-wage labor. According to Global Commercial Real Estate Services, Georgia led all other states in megawarehouse lease purchases, signing nineteen new megawarehouse leases in the first half of 2022. Companies especially targeted the Atlanta metropolitan region (where close to three-fourths of Atlanta's Black working class resides today) and purchased twelve leases, totaling a shocking 10.3 million square feet. For a clearer perspective, Global Commercial Real Estate Services reported that states only leased a total of nine megawarehouses of 1 million square feet in 2022—with five of them being in the Atlanta metro region alone.[8]

Capital is responding to the labor crisis that it created in disciplining the Black worker. By positioning sweated, sub-working-class warehouse labor in resource-starved areas, capital taps into a reserve army of labor desperately seeking work. As Stuart Pendly, the first vice president of Coldwell Banker Richard Ellis, stated in a press release from the company, the suburban metro neighborhoods in Atlanta offer capital "a growing population, [and] low barriers to entry (unskilled and high school education).... All of this combined has created [an] ... environment for developers to build speculative projects and large users to continue to lease space.... We don't expect to see demand for large warehouses subside soon."[9] Additionally, the higher tourism rates in the city led capital to invest in massive hotel construction in the Lithia Springs area—alongside Bob Arnold Blvd near Thornton Road, which, only fifteen minutes from the Atlanta airport, holds great locational advantage. Indeed, these hotels specialize in subproletarian labor for its overwhelming Black workforce, with low wages, unsanitary and unsafe conditions, and little to no opportunity for career development. This industry, along with home healthcare aid, also operates as a cesspool of exploitation against undocumented Black workers, who are threatened with deportation and loss of wages or labor on a consistent basis.

This is dire particularly for Black workers, considering that many are returning to southern urban centers. In fact, Georgia led all states or placed second in Black migration between 2008 and 2015. Between 2015 and 2020, the Atlanta metropolitan region gained 68,835 African American migrants, the highest number of all southern metro areas.[10] What is most interesting about this trend is that a disproportionate number were both young and held some type of postsecondary degree. Many claim that they were attracted to possible middle-class networking and social lifestyles. However, as this book demonstrates, many of these migrants find a very tight white-collar job supply that does not meet the demand. With tech and other white-collar jobs disappearing in correlation to the rise of subproletarian labor, many of these Black migrants will more than likely find better access to blue-collar and subproletarian labor like gig economy work. With the current recession-like economy crippling the working and living conditions for millions of people in the United States since 2020, sub-working-class labor is becoming a constant in daily life. Besides low-wage retail and warehouse labor, other sub-working-class jobs like gig economy and temp work have also ravaged the career prospects of millennials and Generation Z workers out of high school and college. Scholars must engage in more studies and theoretical frameworks to properly conceptualize the racial class warfare on Black workers.

The conditions continue to trend downward and, as Sundiata Keita Cha-Jua argued, this New Nadir has plunged us into the worst social conditions in the history of the African American experience. Capital and government continue to destabilize Black working-class resistance through resource deprivation, state-sanctioned and private violence, union busting, negation of social movements as a viable vehicle for addressing social crises, and anti-protest laws. The conditions of work and the conditions of employment are central to these historical problems and the sociohistorical experience of the Black worker.

Make no mistake about it: this propaganda of history has equipped capitalism in urban centers like Atlanta with a restructuring that requires more bourgeois African Americans at its command. It was not long before Atlanta caught the eye of Hollywood, which sought earning potential outside of California. By 2016, more feature movies were being filmed in Georgia than in California for the first time in history. In fact, blockbuster billion-dollar movies from the Marvel franchise like *Black Panther*, *Avengers: Infinity War*, and *Ant-Man and the Wasp* were all filmed in the Atlanta metro region.

It began in 2008, when then Georgia Republican governor Sonny Perdue enacted a huge tax break incentive for film productions in the state. The Georgia Department of Economic Development offered film producers a whopping 20 percent base transferable tax credit on all film and television projects budgeted at $500,000 or more—which eliminates smaller, independent filmmakers from receiving the tax break—and an additional 10 percent in tax breaks if the film includes an embedded Georgia peach logo on the project (typically in the credits).[11] The tax transformed the film industry. Film production costs in Atlanta skyrocketed from $93 million in 2007 to over $2 billion in 2016! Television hits such as *Stranger Things* and *The Real Housewives of Atlanta* and franchise giants like *The Hunger Games* and *The Fast and the Furious* took up substantial space for years at a time in the Atlanta metro region.[12]

Although Georgia officials estimated that film production boosted state revenue beyond $7 billion through job creation and tourism, virtually none of that money translated to improved social conditions among the Black working classes. In fact, virtually all the jobs that film productions created for metro Atlantans were subproletarian—they offered low wages and were typically temporary.[13] Additionally, the film industry purchased lands meant for affordable housing for poor Atlantans. Marvel's Pinewood Studios—opened in 2014—includes eighteen sound stages on 700 acres in Fayette County. The recently built 230-acre, 1,300-resident Pinewood Forest offers middle- and upper-income housing from $350,000 to $1.2 million.[14] In 2013, Tyler Perry's ETPC Company purchased 856 acres of land south of Sweetwater Creek State Park and I-20 originally meant to house 1,300 residents. This followed his 2008 purchase of land in southwest Atlanta, where he films many of his movies and television shows.[15]

These factors that allowed Hollywood to conquer Atlanta developed only through the disciplining of the Black worker. In New Orleans, sociologist John Arena vividly captured how the disciplining of the Black worker opened the city to nonprofit privatization. Across the nation, the disciplining of the Black worker has resulted in the loss of a radical critique of racial oppression and the subsequent resurgence of explicit anti-Black violence and neonativist fascism to be the counterpart to bourgeois liberalism. Thus, both sides have silenced intellectual radicalism in debates over reparations, with most national commentary focusing on the "detriment" of giving Black people money to waste or the lie that the United States has never given reparations to groups. Embracing the dialectic of the Black worker provides a study of the conditions of Black America to inform how to distribute reparations in a restitutive and, more important, rehabilitative manner. More clearly, a critique of the political economy can build a reparations proposal to repair the social institutions of Black America discussed in this book: housing, public education, transportation, jobs, health care, and community institutions. Thus, *Class Warfare in Black Atlanta* contributes a framework to chart a new path in both intellectual scholarship as well as public policy on reparations.

In other words, this study provides more than sufficient evidence that a historical theft—genocidal in nature—disrupted the material security and development of Black workers across US history. Therefore, the rehabilitation and reconciliation of social power—through a federal reparations program—is the key to reversing the retrenchment. While some opponents of reparations like Cedric Johnson point to it being an elite-driven demand that lacks the politics to fight oppression, this misinterprets a Marxist humanist understanding of reparations. From the point of alienation, there cannot be any denial that masses of African Americans have been robbed for centuries of land, labor, time, and lives. As scholar Brian Jones noted, the 2008 Great Recession was the largest destroyer of Black people's wealth in the United States. To Johnson's credit, though, he does highlight the potential failure of a reparations program if it does not consider a redistribution plan based on the disproportionality of oppression via class level—thus targeting the *legacy* of racial oppression.[16] In other words, the benefactors of capitalist exploitation —the Waltons (the owners of Walmart, which employs the largest number of African Americans in the United States besides the government), Jeff Bezos, and Elon Musk, among others—must be a major source of these reparations.

Thus, as Jones concludes, intraracial class struggle is at the heart of the reparations debate. The Black bourgeoisie and a sizable portion of the Black petty bourgeoisie wield immense power to oppose reparations to African Americans. *Class Warfare in Black Atlanta* provides the foundations for this betrayal of the Black working class in the Black leadership's allegiance to the benefactors of racial oppression: banks, insurance companies, global corporations, and the federal government. The reconstruction and rehabilitation of Black social space through a free housing and education program, a free prevailing-wage jobs program, and the redistribution of land to the Black working classes would blast a fatal wound to the neocolonial state in two ways. First, it would strengthen the social conditions of the African American masses. Second, it would open up critique from other oppressed groups, like Indigenous people, refugees, and others, to demand restitution for US imperialism and global theft at all levels. However, these objectives are only possible with the Black worker and the crisis of subproletarianization as the force in the narrative. More explicitly, *Class Warfare in Black Atlanta* serves as a justification for a Marxist humanist perspective for reparations.

What is to be done regarding the New Nadir? The answer lies in our willingness to engage in uncomfortable, rigorous discussion and debate. Class struggle is a historically uncomfortable analysis for African Americans because it invites an internal struggle—something that has not been the most dominant problem in the African American experience. However, scholars, activists, and residents must confront the crisis of intraracial class struggle as the most potent weapon for capitalism and white supremacy today.

In other words, we must embrace and then confront the dialectic in a genuine manner to construct a legitimate analysis and response to the contemporary racial formation. The New Nadir, like other racial formations of the past, can be successfully challenged and disrupted. The Black working class cannot shift from defensive to offensive any faster without difficult and uncomfortable analyses, debates, and confrontations. However, they cannot put the cart before the horse and diagnose the symptom outside of the larger problem. *Class Warfare in Black Atlanta* must function alongside other critiques of political economy as precedent-setting studies.

Notes

ABBREVIATIONS

MJMR-B Maynard Jackson Mayoral Records, Series B: First and Second Term Mayoral Records, Robert F. Woodruff Library of the Atlanta University Center, Inc., Atlanta, Georgia
RWLA Robert F. Woodruff Library of the Atlanta University Center, Inc., Atlanta, Georgia
SNCC Papers Student Nonviolent Coordinating Committee Papers, Subgroup A: 1959–1972, Vine City Project Records 1960–1971, University of Wisconsin-Madison, Madison, Wisconsin

INTRODUCTION

1. "National Guard to Raze Dilapidated Vine City Homes," *Atlanta Voice*, April 13, 2002, 4; "National Guard Raze Dilapidated Vine City Homes," *Atlanta Voice*, May 4, 2002, 1, 2; "Atlanta Launches Operation Crackdown," *Atlanta Voice*, May 4, 2002, 1, 2; "Vine City Residents Decry Plans to Bulldoze Their Homes," *Atlanta Voice*, November 30, 2002, 4.

2. "Vine City Residents Decry Plans"; "Where Is Our Leadership?," *Atlanta Voice*, December 7, 2002, 4; "Vine City Should Welcome Guard," *Atlanta Journal-Constitution*, April 17, 2002, A19; "Inner City Demolition Fails to Spur Progress," *Atlanta Journal-Constitution*, May 26, 2002, C1, C3.

3. "Where Is Our Leadership?"; "Vine City Residents Decry Plans."

4. "Where Is Our Leadership?"; "Vine City Residents Decry Plans."

5. "Where Is Our Leadership?"; "Vine City Residents Decry Plans."

6. "Where Is Our Leadership?"; "Vine City Residents Decry Plans"; "Get the Pharaohs Off the Community's Back," *Atlanta Voice*, April 12, 2003, 4.

7. Stephanie Garlock, "By 2011, Atlanta Had Demolished All of Its Public Housing Projects. Where Did All Those People Go?," *CityLab*, May 8, 2014, www.bloomberg.com/news/articles/2014-05-08/by-2011-atlanta-had-demolished-all-of-its-public-housing-projects-where-did-all-those-people-go.

8. Turner, "Los Angeles Rebellion '92."

9. "Young's Mouth Feeds Button Industry's Hunger for Slogans," *Atlanta Constitution*, July 23, 1986, p. 31.

10. Grady-Willis, *Challenging US Apartheid*.

11. Neil Smith, *New Urban Frontier*.

12. Cha-Jua, "C. L. R. James," 53–89.

13. Zasulich to Marx, February 16, 1881; and Marx to Zasulich, March 8, 1881, both in Shanin, *Late Marx*, 98–99, 104, 109, 121, 123–24.

14. Bacote, "William Finch"; Bacote, "Negro in Atlanta Politics"; Neary, *Julian Bond*; Hornsby, "Andrew Jackson Young"; Hornsby, *Black Power in Dixie*.

15. Kraus, "Significance of Race"; Reed, *Stirrings in the Jug*.

16. Keating, *Atlanta*; Kruse, *White Flight*; Rutheiser, *Imagineering Atlanta*; Sjoquist, *Atlanta Paradox*. Ghettoization frameworks are not relegated to Atlanta scholarship. See also Kenneth Clark, *Dark Ghetto*; Osofsky, *Harlem*; Spear, *Black Chicago*; Kusmer, *Ghetto Takes Shape*; Hirsch, *Making the Second Ghetto*; Sugrue, *Origins*; and Self, *American Babylon*.

17. Karl Marx described four types of alienation that are a consequence of workers laboring under capitalism, including *Gattungswesen* (species-essence, or "human nature"). He notes that it is related to humans' possession of the capacity to conceive of the ends of their actions as purposeful ideas; it also is connected to the other forms of alienation (from other workers, from the product, and from the act of production) that restrict their agency. Marx, *Economic and Philosophic Manuscripts*.

18. Wilson, *Declining Significance of Race*; Massey and Denton, *American Apartheid*.

19. Trotter, *Black Milwaukee*; Cha-Jua, *America's First Black Town*.

20. Oppenheimer, "Sub-proletariat."

21. Trotter, *Black Milwaukee*; Cha-Jua, *America's First Black Town*, 10.

22. Robert Allen, *Black Awakening*; Turner, "Toward a Black Radical Critique"; Sundiata Keita Cha-Jua, unpublished, untitled manuscript shared with the author.

23. Oppenheimer, "Sub-proletariat."

24. Oppenheimer, "Sub-proletariat."

25. Hobson, *Legend*.

26. Wright, *Class Counts*, 493–95; Thompson, *Making*, 9.

27. Wright, *Class Counts*, 493–95; Thompson, *Making*, 9.

28. Wright, *Class Counts*, 493–95.

29. Morris, *Origins*, 282–90.

30. Lipton, "Evidence"; Laska and Spain, *Back to the City*.

31. Berry, *Human Consequences of Urbanization*; Berry, "Inner City Futures," 1–2; Berry, "Islands of Renewal"; Sternlieb and Hughes, "Uncertain Future."

32. Neil Smith, "Toward a Theory"; Neil Smith, "Gentrification and Capital"; Zukin, *Loft Living*; Neil Smith, *Uneven Development*; Zukin, "Gentrification"; E. Clark, "On Gaps"; Lees, "Gentrification in London"; E. Clark, "Toward a Copenhagen Interpretation."

33. Lumpkins introduced the pogrom argument to US urban history by examining racial violence against African Americans in East St. Louis. See Lumpkins, *American Pogrom*.

34. For more on classic examples of European pogroms, see Vryonis, *Mechanism of Catastrophe*; Dekel-Chen et al., *Anti-Jewish Violence*; Klier and Lambroza, *Pogrom*; Khiterer, "October 1905 Pogroms"; Ioanid, *Iasi Pogrom*; and Zipperstein, *Pogrom*. For expanding concepts of violence, see Galtung, "Violence," 168–69; and Anglin, "Feminist Perspectives," 145.

35. Galtung, "Violence," 168–70.
36. Galtung, "Violence," 169.
37. Galtung, "Violence," 169–70.
38. Galtung, "Violence," 168–70, 171; Anglin, "Feminist Perspectives," 145.
39. Galtung, "Violence," 170–71, 187–88; Anglin, "Feminist Perspectives," 145; Ture and Hamilton, *Black Power*.
40. Cha-Jua, "New Nadir"; Arena, *Driven from New Orleans*, xxv–xxix.
41. Arena, *Driven from New Orleans*, xxviii–xxix.
42. See Marx, *Eighteenth Brumaire*; Marx, *Class Struggles in France*; and Marx and Engels, *Capital*, vol. 1.
43. Mack H. Jones, *Knowledge*.
44. Purple Ribbon All-Stars, *Big Boi Presents... Got Purp? Vol. 2*, Purple Ribbon and Virgin Records, 2005, compact disc.

CHAPTER ONE

1. "Garbage Updated in Disposal Style," *Atlanta Daily World*, January 23, 1970, 2; "City Workers Strike; Wage Demands Unmet," *Atlanta Voice*, March 22, 1970, 1, 11; "Garbage Power," *Great Speckled Bird*, March 23, 1970, 4; "What's behind Mail and Garbage Strikes?," *Atlanta Voice*, March 29, 1970, 3, 20.
2. "STRIKE!," *Great Speckled Bird*, March 23, 1970, 3.
3. "Strike... Marches On," *Great Speckled Bird*, April 13, 1970, 2–3. For more on community strike support, see "Atlanta Black Doctors Support Garbage Strikers," *Atlanta Voice*, April 26, 1970, 1. For a comparative perspective with the Memphis sanitation strike in 1968, see "Two Years Now... Some Thoughts on That Day in April, in Memphis," *Atlanta Voice*, April 5, 1970, 9.
4. "Union Men March Downtown," *Atlanta Voice*, April 12, 1970, 2; "5 Weeks Jobless Hurting Garbage Workers, Families," *Atlanta Voice*, April 19, 1970, 1, 11. For more takes on the effects of the strike, see "Rats Flourish in City," *Atlanta Voice*, May 3, 1970, 1, 13; "April 22, Earth Day Good Day to End Strike," *Atlanta Voice*, April 26, 1970, 1, 11; "Garbage Strike Over; but Wage Hike Slighted," *Atlanta Voice*, April 26, 1970, 1, 11; "Vice Mayor Jackson Asks Judge Panel on Increases," *Atlanta Voice*, April 26, 1970, 1; "Strike," *Great Speckled Bird*, May 4, 1970; and "Slim Victory," *Great Speckled Bird*, May 4, 1970, 5. For an alternative take on the strikes, see "What's behind Mail and Garbage Strikes?," 13; and "Look to the Needs of the Poor before Others," *Atlanta Voice*, April 19, 1970, 2. The *Atlanta Journal*'s and *Atlanta Constitution*'s coverage of the strike overwhelmingly supported Massell and questioned the "work ethic" of the majority Black strikers. See "City Strike Gains Support; Massell Issues Ultimatum," *Atlanta Constitution*, March 19, 1970, 1, 24-A; "Have We Lost the Will to Work?," *Atlanta Constitution*, March 26, 1970, 4; "Responsible Settlement," *Atlanta Constitution*, April 23, 1970, 4; "Strike Handling Praised," *Atlanta Constitution*, April 25, 1970, 21; and "After the Strike," *Atlanta Constitution*, April 27, 1970, 4.
5. Kidd to Jackson, March 27, 1970, box 5, folder 12, Maynard Jackson Mayoral Records, Series A, RWLA.
6. SNCC Atlanta Project position paper, 1966, box 1, folder 6, SNCC Papers.

7. SNCC Atlanta Project position paper, 1966, box 1, folder 6, SNCC Papers.
8. SNCC Atlanta Project position paper, 1966, box 1, folder 6, SNCC Papers.
9. SNCC Atlanta Project position paper, 1966, box 1, folder 6, SNCC Papers.
10. "Black Brothers and Sisters, Let's Get the Facts Straight," September 1966, box 1, folder 17, SNCC Papers. For a rich, detailed account of the 1966 Summerhill rebellion, see Grady-Willis, *Challenging US Apartheid*, 117–20. Atlanta's only newspaper catering to African Americans at the time, the *Atlanta Daily World*, did not cover the rebellion. For media coverage, see "Carmichael Arrested on Riots Charges in Raid on Snick Office," *Atlanta Constitution*, September 9, 1966, 1, 6.
11. Atlanta fact sheet, January 21, 1966, box 1, folder 17, SNCC Papers.
12. Atlanta fact sheet, January 21, 1966, box 1, folder 17, SNCC Papers. In 1970, Black Atlantans had a 51 percent majority to whites' 49 percent.
13. Emmaus House was formed in 1967 to fight slumlords in Atlanta and find adequate housing for those who needed it. For a detailed history and analysis of Emmaus House's work in African American Atlanta, see LeeAnn Lands, "Emmaus House and Atlanta's Anti-poverty Movements," *Atlanta Studies*, April 28, 2015, https://atlantastudies.org/2015/04/28/emmaus-house-and-atlantas-anti-poverty-movements.
14. Lands, "Emmaus House"; "15,000 Atlanta Families Income at Poverty Level," *Atlanta Daily World*, August 18, 1970, 2.
15. US Bureau of the Census, *1970 Census of the Population*, table 53, "Employment Status by Race, Sex, and Urban and Rural Residence: 1970," p. 249.
16. See "Minority and Hiring and Promotion Practices, City of Atlanta," August 1970, box 3, folder 11, Maynard Jackson Mayoral Records, Series A, RWLA.
17. Keating, *Atlanta*, 38–39.
18. According to the US Bureau of Labor Statistics, the wage regression was due in large part to a decline in the average workweek for Atlanta workers from 40.6 to 38.7 hours; a four-cent drop during the quarter in average hourly earnings; and a 1.5 percent rise in the Atlanta consumer price index. US Bureau of the Census, *1970 Census of the Population*, table 53, "Employment Status by Race, Sex, and Urban and Rural Residence: 1970," p. 249.
19. "17 Cents per Hour Is Pay for Elderly Workers Here," *Atlanta Voice*, July 31, 1971, 1, 7. See also Paul Cornely, "Health in Action," *Atlanta Voice*, February 8, 1970.
20. "Adillera Dollar," *Great Speckled Bird*, September 27, 1971, 5.
21. "Tax-Exempt Property in Atlanta," working paper, Research Atlanta, 1972, Research Atlanta Inc. Reports, Digital Collections, Georgia State University Library, https://digitalcollections.library.gsu.edu/digital/collection/researchATL/id/5613.
22. James v. Valtierra, 402 US 137 (1971).
23. Cabral, "Weapon of Theory."
24. Cabral, "Weapon of Theory."
25. Howard, "Whose Streets?," 240–41.
26. Statement by Stokely Carmichael, September 8, 1966, box 1, folder 17, SNCC Papers.
27. Grady-Willis, *Challenging US Apartheid*, 118.
28. Grady-Willis, *Challenging US Apartheid*, 120.

29. "King's Associate Bars Big Protest," *Atlanta Constitution*, September 13, 1966, 1, 10.

30. SNCC Atlanta Project position paper, 1966, box 1, folder 6, SNCC Papers.

31. SNCC Atlanta Project position paper, 1966, box 1, folder 6, SNCC Papers.

32. Winston Grady-Willis provides a rich, detailed analysis of SNCC's Vine City Atlanta Project organizing efforts. See Grady-Willis, *Challenging US Apartheid*, 83–113.

33. For further conceptualization of use value theory, see Marx and Engels, *Capital*, 1:42, 47–48, 52–53. Logan and Molotch expand on Marx's conceptualization in *Urban Fortunes*. See also Mendenhall, "Political Economy."

34. For more on the political economy of "home," see Cox, *Urbanization and Conflict*, 94–110.

35. Cox, *Urbanization and Conflict*, 94–110; Logan and Molotch, *Urban Fortunes*, 17–23, 103–10.

36. "Pittsburgh Rats Find Food Is Scarce Now," *Atlanta Voice*, July 26, 1970, 9.

37. "Atlanta Crisis in Southwest Atlanta," *Atlanta Voice*, February 1, 1970, 1, 3; "Bus Lines Cut Back," *Great Speckled Bird*, November 16, 1970, 3.

38. "Bus Lines Cut Back," 3; Logan and Molotch, *Urban Fortunes*, 103–10.

39. SNCC Atlanta Project position paper, 1966, box 1, folder 6, SNCC Papers.

40. "Atlanta Consumer Food Project," *Great Speckled Bird*, December 25, 1972, 8–9.

41. "Atlanta Consumer Food Project," 8–9.

42. Stack, *All Our Kin*, 9, 22, 129.

43. Denise Broward, interview by author, March 18, 2021.

44. Logan and Molotch, *Urban Fortunes*, 103–10.

45. Logan and Molotch, *Urban Fortunes*, 103–10.

46. Logan and Molotch, *Urban Fortunes*, 103–10.

47. Turner, "Notes on Henry Louis Taylor," 3–5.

48. Beverley A. Matthews, letter to the editor, *Atlanta Voice*, May 10, 1970, 9. The quotation in the heading above is from Boggs, *Racism*.

49. Carson, *In Struggle*, 215–28.

50. Hall, "Long Civil Rights Movement," 1233–63. Hall argued that the civil rights movement stretched from the 1940s to the 1980s. Black scholars Sundiata Keita Cha-Jua and Clarence Lang successfully challenged the long movement thesis in their award-winning article "Long Movement as Vampire."

51. Onaci, *Free the Land*.

52. See Austin, "Cultural Black Nationalism."

53. See Austin, "Cultural Black Nationalism."

54. "New World Developers to Break Ground January 3," *Atlanta Voice*, January 2, 1971, 1; "Children Break Ground for New Super Market," *Atlanta Daily World*, January 7, 1971, 1.

55. "Black Community-Owned Stores Called Lunacy," *Atlanta Voice*, March 15, 1970, 9.

56. For a more detailed breakdown of the core Black Power tenets, see Marable, *Race, Reform, and Rebellion*, 84–112; and F. C. C. Campbell, "The Senecan Rambler: Signs of Progress," *Atlanta Voice*, April 10, 1971, 4.

57. Rev. Isaac Richmond, "Politics of the Proletariat," *Atlanta Voice*, June 17, 1972, 8.
58. "Black Capitalism in the Red," *Great Speckled Bird*, July 3, 1975, 8.
59. "Black Capitalism in the Red," 8.
60. "Black Break-Fast," *Great Speckled Bird*, May 4, 1970, 10.
61. Georgia Black Liberation Front, "Black Challenge," reprinted in *Great Speckled Bird*, June 1, 1970, 2; Atlanta Revolutionary Youth Movement statement, reprinted in *Great Speckled Bird*, June 15, 1970, 5.
62. Georgia Black Liberation Front, "Black Challenge," 2; Atlanta Revolutionary Youth Movement statement, 5.
63. "Rally," *Great Speckled Bird*, June 1, 1970, 3; "Posted," *Great Speckled Bird*, June 15, 1970, 5.
64. "Integration: 400 Years of Patience," *Great Speckled Bird*, March 8, 1971; "School Board Meeting Ends with Walkout of 50 Blacks," *Atlanta Daily World*, May 16, 1971, 1; "Cobb County's Bi-racial Committee Agrees on Schools," *Atlanta Daily World*, June 4, 1971, 1.
65. "Black Control," *Great Speckled Bird*, September 22, 1969, 16.
66. "Integration," 2; Campbell, "Senecan Rambler," 5.
67. "Black Students Speak," *Great Speckled Bird*, June 2, 1969, 2–3.
68. "Atlanta Center for Black Art Opens," *Atlanta Voice*, April 26, 1970, 11.
69. "Mayson School Parents Pledge to 'Shut It Down,'" *Atlanta Voice*, July 12, 1970, 1, 11. For alternative coverage, see "Mabry Shift Gets Backing," *Atlanta Constitution*, July 23, 1970, 9.
70. "Dump Thornton Group Converges on Area IV," *Atlanta Voice*, July 19, 1970, 1, 6; "SW Schools Stir Protests," *Atlanta Constitution*, July 25, 1970, 11.
71. "Help Us, CRC Is Told, or Watch Out for Us," *Atlanta Voice*, July 19, 1970, 1, 6.
72. "Help Us, CRC Is Told," 1, 6.
73. "Help Us, CRC Is Told," 1, 6.
74. "Community Control Argued: Mayson Struggles Shift to Remove Thornton," *Atlanta Voice*, August 2, 1970, 1.
75. "School Board Meeting Ends with Walkout," 1; "Cobb County's Bi-racial Committee," 1.
76. "West Manor Boycott Dramatizes Crowding," *Atlanta Voice*, April 17, 1971, 1, 7; "PETA Votes Boycott at W. Manor," *Atlanta Constitution*, April 8, 1971, 10.
77. "BLACC at Dekalb, Jr.," *Great Speckled Bird*, March 29, 1971, 6; "Dekalb Students March April 2 for Studies," *Atlanta Voice*, March 27, 1971, 1.
78. "Azar Must Go!," *Great Speckled Bird*, January 26, 1970, 3; "Azar's Tricks," *Great Speckled Bird*, February 2, 1970, 2.
79. "Azar Must Go!," 3; "Azar's Tricks," 2.
80. "Azar's Tricks," 3; untitled article, *Great Speckled Bird*, September 14, 1970, 12; "Curbs Remain on Summerhill," *Atlanta Constitution*, August 26, 1970, 9; "Azar's Attorney and Mayor to Meet," *Atlanta Constitution*, September 1, 1970, 11; "Hearing Set on Picketing Azar Store," *Atlanta Constitution*, October 9, 1970, 14.
81. "Whitemans," *Great Speckled Bird*, February 15, 1971, 4; "Whiteman," *Great Speckled Bird*, February 22, 1971, 8; "Arlan's Oinks," *Great Speckled Bird*, March 15, 1971, 3; "Customer Intimidation Cause Store's Boycott," *Atlanta Voice*, April 24, 1971, 1.

82. "Whitemans," 4; "Whiteman," 8; "Arlan's Oinks," 3; "Customer Intimidation," 1.
83. "Whitemans," 4; "Whiteman," 8; "Arlan's Oinks," 3; "Customer Intimidation," 1.
84. For more on documented racial oppression by the American labor movement, see Herbert Hill, "Racism within Organized Labor"; Herbert Hill, "Black Protest"; Foner, "Organized Labor"; and Herbert Hill, "Myth-Making as Labor History."
85. "Black Fire," *Great Speckled Bird*, August 18, 1969, 7; "If They Say So, It Must Be True!," *Great Speckled Bird*, January 12, 1970, 16; "Jackson, Dodson Meet with Black Firemen," *Atlanta Voice*, January 25, 1970, 2.
86. F. C. C. Campbell, "Retroactions: Firemen Racism," *Atlanta Voice*, February 5, 1970, 2E.
87. "HoJo Walkout," *Great Speckled Bird*, June 29, 1970, 3.
88. "HoJo Walkout," 3.
89. "HoJo Walkout," 3.
90. "HoJo Walkout," 3.
91. "Off Our Backs, into the Street!," *Great Speckled Bird*, March 16, 1970, 2; "The People Speak," *Atlanta Voice*, May 1, 1971, E2, E8; "Atlanta Women Speak Out: Felicia Jeter," *Great Speckled Bird*, September 7, 1970, 10–12.
92. Farmer, *Remaking Black Power*, 2–4, 12.
93. "Just Git!," *Great Speckled Bird*, May 25, 1970, 5; "Kesslers Fires Six Year Black Department Manager," *Atlanta Voice*, May 17, 1970, 1, 9; John Shabazz, "Public Supporting Boycott against Kessler's Store," reprinted in *Atlanta Voice*, May 31, 1970, 1, back cover.
94. "Slums of the Future," *Great Speckled Bird*, April 24, 1972, 12–13.
95. "Chickenshit," *Great Speckled Bird*, May 8, 1972, 7.
96. "10 Stores to Close in Labor Dispute," *Atlanta Constitution*, May 9, 1972, 9.
97. "Church's Closes Stores, Negotiations Under Way," *Atlanta Voice*, May 13, 1972, 1, back cover.
98. "Church's Chicken Strikes Again!!," *Great Speckled Bird*, May 15, 1972, 6.
99. "Church's Settlement Hailed as Victory for Poor People," *Atlanta Voice*, June 10, 1972, 1, 2.
100. "Church's Settlement Hailed as Victory," 1, 2.
101. "SOS" to Maynard Jackson, memorandum regarding the meeting of the AHA Tenants Advisory Board, July 20, 1972, box 8, folder 3, Maynard Jackson Mayoral Records, Series A, RWLA; "Tenant Grievances Lead to Taking Over Ceremony," *Atlanta Voice*, July 8, 1972, 1.
102. "New Public Housing: Model Apartment, Model Hell," *Great Speckled Bird*, September 7, 1972, 14–17.
103. "Atlanta Housing Authority," *Great Speckled Bird*, August 14, 1972, 8–9.
104. "Atlanta Housing Authority," 8–9.
105. "SOS" to Jackson, memorandum, July 20, 1972; "Tenant Grievances," 1.
106. "SOS" to Jackson, memorandum, July 20, 1972; "Tenant Grievances," 1; "Tenants vs. AHA," *Great Speckled Bird*, July 24, 1972, 2–3.
107. "A.H.A. Tenants Protest," *Great Speckled Bird*, July 17, 1972, 11.
108. "A.H.A. Tenants Protest," 11.
109. "A.H.A. Tenants Protest," 11; "The Atlanta Housing Authority Rent Strike," *Great Speckled Bird*, October 16, 1972, 9.

110. October League, *Wildcat at Mead*; Waugh-Benton, "Strike Fever," 58–59.
111. "Workers Fight," *Great Speckled Bird*, June 8, 1970, 2; "Racism," *Great Speckled Bird*, June 8, 1970, 3; "STRIKE! MEAD," *Great Speckled Bird*, September 4, 1972, 2.
112. "Workers Fight," 2; "Racism," 3; "STRIKE! MEAD," 2; Waugh-Benton, "Strike Fever," 61–62.
113. October League, *Wildcat at Mead*; Waugh-Benton, "Strike Fever," 62–64.
114. October League, *Wildcat at Mead*; Waugh-Benton, "Strike Fever," 65–66.
115. October League, *Wildcat at Mead*; Waugh-Benton, "Strike Fever," 65–66, 68–69.
116. October League, *Wildcat at Mead*; Waugh-Benton, "Strike Fever," 68–69.
117. October League, *Wildcat at Mead*.
118. Waugh-Benton, "Strike Fever," 68–69.
119. October League, *Wildcat at Mead*.
120. October League, *Wildcat at Mead*; "Workers Fight," 2; "Racism," 3; "STRIKE! MEAD," 2.
121. October League, *Wildcat at Mead*; "Workers Fight," 2; "Racism," 3; "STRIKE! MEAD," 2.
122. October League, *Wildcat at Mead*; "Workers Fight," 2; "Racism," 3; "STRIKE! MEAD," 2.
123. October League, *Wildcat at Mead*; "Workers Fight," 2; "Racism," 3; "STRIKE! MEAD," 2.
124. "October League & Mead," *Great Speckled Bird*, October 16, 1972, 2; October League, *Wildcat at Mead*.
125. October League, *Wildcat at Mead*; "Red Activist Cell under Probe Here," *Atlanta Constitution*, September 29, 1972; Waugh-Benton, "Strike Fever," 77.
126. "Workers: Mead Workers Caucus Recognized," *Great Speckled Bird*, September 18, 1972, 11.
127. "Mead Settlement," *Great Speckled Bird*, October 16, 1972, 2; Waugh-Benton, "Strike Fever," 80–82.
128. October League, *Wildcat at Mead*.
129. "J. D. Roberts: Guilty," *Great Speckled Bird*, July 2, 1973, 9.

CHAPTER TWO

1. "Ain't No More Niggers in This World," *Great Speckled Bird*, February 22, 1971; "The Truth of Riot Should Be Told," *Atlanta Voice*, February 27, 1971, 4–5.
2. "Ain't No More," 4–5.
3. "Ain't No More," 4–5.
4. "Broad Street Crowd Erupts: Police Quell Flareup," *Atlanta Constitution*, February 16, 1971; "Downtown Fracas Draws 100 Police," *Atlanta Daily World*, February 18, 1971; "Panthers, Muslims Cause Rukus in Downtown Atlanta," *Atlanta Daily World*, August 11, 1972.
5. "Save Us from the Blacks," *Great Speckled Bird*, January 10, 1972, 3.
6. "After Battle: Mid-City Adds Police," *Atlanta Journal-Constitution*, August 9, 1972; "Muslims, Police Clash Mid-City," *Atlanta Journal-Constitution*, August 8, 1972.
7. Cabral, "Weapon of Theory."

8. Reed, *Stirrings in the Jug*, 79–119.

9. Joint Center for Political and Economic Studies, "The National Roster of Black Elected Officials," *Focus* magazine, July 1977; "Increase in Black Elected Officials," *Atlanta Voice*, March 19, 1978, 1.

10. For an extensive breakdown of BUR theory and its criticism of Clarence Stone's urban regime theory, see Reed, *Stirrings in the Jug*, 79–119; and Arena, "Bringing," 153–79.

11. Boston, *Race, Class, and Conservatism*, 35–36.

12. "Black Capitalism in the Red," *Great Speckled Bird*, July 3, 1975, 8.

13. "Take-Home Pay of Atlanta Workers Down," *Atlanta Voice*, September 9, 1978, 7.

14. "Black Capitalism in the Red," 8.

15. Quoted in "Black Capitalism in the Red," 8.

16. Wenger, "State Responses," 68–70; Boston, *Race, Class, and Conservatism*, 35–39.

17. "Yesterday's Shouts of 'Black Power' Are Today Replaced by 'Green Power,'" *Atlanta Voice*, August 9, 1980, 7.

18. "Yesterday's Shouts," 7.

19. Wenger, "State Responses," 68–70; Boston, *Race, Class, and Conservatism*, 35–39.

20. Turner, "Toward a Black Radical Critique," 7–13.

21. Turner, "Toward a Black Radical Critique," 7–13.

22. "Maynard Making Good (Friends)," *Great Speckled Bird*, July 9, 1973, 3.

23. "Politics Hurrah for the Red, Black, and Blue," *Great Speckled Bird*, May 12, 1969, 12.

24. "5250 Laid Off in Atlanta," *Great Speckled Bird*, March 25, 1974, 13.

25. "5250 Laid Off in Atlanta," 13.

26. "EOA Perry Area Studies Food Prices," *Atlanta Voice*, April 27, 1974, 9; "American Cost of Living Tied to World Food Crisis," *Atlanta Voice*, August 17, 1974, 2.

27. "EOA Perry Area Studies"; "American Cost of Living."

28. "EOA Perry Area Studies"; "American Cost of Living."

29. "EOA Perry Area Studies"; "American Cost of Living."

30. "Unfair Tax Collection: Why a Budget Crisis," *Great Speckled Bird*, January 2, 1975, 1.

31. Research Atlanta, *Other Side*; "Unfair Tax Collection," 1, 3; "Local Scene: The Rich Get Richer and the Poor . . . ," *Great Speckled Bird*, February 13, 1975, 4.

32. "Welfare Cuts for Christmas," *Great Speckled Bird*, December 18, 1975, 4.

33. "Poverty Figure Raised to $5,050," *Atlanta Voice*, May 31, 1975, 2.

34. Phil Hoffman to Bill Alexander, memorandum regarding the voting record on local option sales tax in Atlanta, July 16, 1979, box 65, folder 7, MJMR-B.

35. Coalition Against the Local Option Sales Tax position paper, undated, box 65, folder 8, MJMR-B.

36. Coalition Against the Local Option Sales Tax position paper.

37. Press release from Black Business Leaders endorsing the local option sales tax, October 1, 1979, box 65, folders 7–10, MJMR-B.

38. Press release from the Atlanta Board of Realtors endorsing the local option sales tax, August 31, 1979, box 3, folder 7, MJMR-B.

39. Press release from the Atlanta Board of Realtors; "Ministers Back Sales Tax Plan as Battle Shapes Up," *Atlanta Daily World*, July 19, 1979, 1.

40. "Vote against Sales Tax Surprises Supporters," *Atlanta Daily World*, October 4, 1979, 1.

41. "Revenue Shafting," *Great Speckled Bird*, July 9, 1973, 7; "New Federalism," *Great Speckled Bird*, November 5, 1973, 3; "Revenue Sharing Flops," *Atlanta Voice*, April 27, 1974, 3; "Revenue Sharing's Future," *Atlanta Voice*, February 1, 1975, 2.

42. "Neglect Hurts Cities, Says Coalition Head," *Baltimore African American*, December 2, 1972, 12; "Revenue Sharing for East End Police to Increase under Proposed Budget," *Suffolk Times*, September 21, 2015.

43. Finley Holmes, Marion Cullens, Wayne Moreau, Melvin Leeks, and Ron Reliford, interview, reprinted in "Bird Gets Inside Dirt from Garbage Workers," *Great Speckled Bird*, February 4, 1974, 4, 15.

44. Holmes et al. interview, 4, 15.

45. Holmes et al. interview, 4, 15.

46. Holmes et al. interview, 4, 15.

47. Marx, "Estranged Labor," 74.

48. Holmes et al. interview, 4, 15.

49. US Bureau of the Census, *Social and Economic Status*.

50. US Bureau of Labor Statistics report on the number of work stoppages in the city of Atlanta, April 1, 1977, box 114, folder 13, MJMR-B.

51. "City Workers Storm City Council More Demonstrations Planned," *Great Speckled Bird*, March 27, 1975, 1.

52. "City Workers Storm City Council," 1.

53. Maynard Jackson, statement on city employee wages and benefits, March 10, 1976, box 108, folder 2, MJMR-B.

54. Untitled document detailing a $2 million budget appropriation, undated, box 114, folder 16, MJMR-B.

55. AFSCME final points of the City of Atlanta 1976 budget, July 14, 1976, box 114, folder 10, MJMR-B.

56. Maynard Jackson, statement regarding docked pay for workers, February 7, 1977, box 114, folder 10, MJMR-B.

57. AFSCME Local 1644 union proposal, March 10, 1977, box 114, folder 12, MJMR-B.

58. AFSCME advertisement, *New York Times*, March 29, 1977, box 114, folder 13, MJMR-B.

59. Atlanta Chamber of Commerce to Legislative Action Committee, correspondence about the *New York Times* ad, March 30, 1977, box 114, folder 13, MJMR-B.

60. Sam A. Hider, letter regarding the effects of demonstration by sanitation employees, March 29, 1977, box 114, folder 12, MJMR-B; "City Workers Walkout," *Atlanta Voice*, April 2, 1977, 1, 13.

61. Termination letter sent to all striking public employee workers, April 1, 1977, box 108, folder 3, MJMR-B.

62. Sam A. Hider, letter regarding the effects of demonstration by sanitation employees, April 5, 1977, box 114, folder 14, MJMR-B.

63. Letter to terminated workers on strike, April 5, 1977, box 108, folder 3, MJMR-B.

64. Joint press release praising Mayor Maynard Jackson's actions during the strike, undated, box 116, folder 16, MJMR-B.
65. Statement from the *Atlanta Journal* executive board congratulating Jackson for firing striking workers, April 26, 1977, box 108, folder 4, MJMR-B.
66. Strike support flyer, March 19, 1977, box 114, folder 14, MJMR-B.
67. "In Solidarity with Striking City Workers," *Atlanta Voice*, April 9, 1977, 1. For more of Jones's critique of Atlanta's local government and economics, see Mack H. Jones, "Black Political Empowerment," 97–141.
68. Mack H. Jones, "Black Political Empowerment," 97–141.
69. Press release by undersigned faculty members of colleges and universities located in metropolitan Atlanta, April 19, 1977, box 114, folder 14, MJMR-B.
70. Press release by the Ad Hoc Committee in Support of Striking Sanitation Workers, April 12, 1977, box 114, folder 14, MJMR-B.
71. Lucy to Jackson, memorandum regarding retaliation against strikers, May 2, 1977, box 108, folder 4, MJMR-B.
72. Lucy to Jackson, May 2, 1977.
73. "Welfare Mothers Busted: Police Raid East Lake Meadows," *Great Speckled Bird*, March 26, 1973; "13 on Dekalb Welfare Charged with Fraud," *Atlanta Journal-Constitution*, March 13, 1973.
74. BCAPR statement printed in "Black Citizens vs. Police," *Great Speckled Bird*, May 14, 1973, 7.
75. "Black Citizens vs. Police," 7.
76. "Lurking with Intent to Loiter," *Great Speckled Bird*, May 4, 1970, 3; "Judge Approves No Knock Raid by Law Officers," *Atlanta Voice*, July 5, 1970, 1; "Police Committee Nixes Public Brutality Hearings," *Atlanta Voice*, April 10, 1971, 1, 7; "Police Brutality," *Great Speckled Bird*, May 3, 1971, 11.
77. "Police Beat," *Great Speckled Bird*, April 3, 1972, 2.
78. "Panthers," *Great Speckled Bird*, September 11, 1972, 11.
79. "The Black Panthers: Sufficient Evidence," *Great Speckled Bird*, November 27, 1972, 8–9.
80. "The Trumped Up Panther Case," *Great Speckled Bird*, December 11, 1972, 8–9; "Police Harassment of Panthers Continues," *Great Speckled Bird*, December 18, 1972, 6.
81. "Carter Busted Again," *Great Speckled Bird*, July 9, 1973, 6.
82. "Mayor Names Task Force to Find Uses for $20 Million in Crime-Fighting Grants," *Atlanta Voice*, May 20, 1972, 1.
83. "John Inman: Architect of a Police State," *Great Speckled Bird*, March 5, 1973; "The Continuing Saga of John Inman," *Great Speckled Bird*, April 23, 1973.
84. "Survival Information," *Signal 39*, reprinted in *Great Speckled Bird*, September 18, 1972, 4.
85. "License to Kill," *Great Speckled Bird*, September 25, 1972, 3.
86. "License to Kill," 3.
87. "Black Atlantans Fight Police State Tactics," *Great Speckled Bird*, April 2, 1973, 7.
88. "STAKE-OUT Murder," *Great Speckled Bird*, May 7, 1973, 3.
89. "Atlanta Cop Kills Blacks," *Great Speckled Bird*, August 13, 1973, 8; "Ernest Hilson," *Great Speckled Bird*, August 20, 1973, 6; "Police Review Fifth Slaying by Detective,"

Atlanta Constitution, August 5, 1973, 3; "City Officer Moved off Firing Line," *Atlanta Constitution*, August 9, 1973, 20A.

90. "Decoy Detectives Blast Riley," *Atlanta Voice*, June 1, 1974, 2.

91. "Crime," *Great Speckled Bird*, August 20, 1973, 4–5.

92. "Crime," 4–5.

93. Alec Karakatsanis, "Police Departments Spend Vast Sums of Money Creating 'Copaganda,'" *Black Agenda Report*, July 22, 2022, https://blackagendareport.com/police-departments-spend-vast-sums-money-creating-copaganda.

94. Karakatsanis, "Police Departments."

95. "Big Business Declares War on Crime," *Atlanta Voice*, August 25, 1973, 1, 10.

96. Munford to Joel Stokes, February 10, 1975, box 65, folder 5, MJMR-B.

97. "Community Dialogue Reveals Causes but Not Solutions," *Atlanta Voice*, August 25, 1973, 3.

98. "Community Dialogue Reveals Causes," 3; "Atlanta Cop Kills Blacks," 8; "Ernest Hilson," 6; "Police Review Fifth Slaying by Detective," 3; "City Officer Moved off Firing Line," 20A.

99. "Police Helicopters Exposed," *Great Speckled Bird*, April 1, 1974, 1, 3.

100. "Policewoman Planted on VOICE Staff," *Atlanta Voice*, May 11, 1974, 1, 4.

101. "Police Spying and the Black Press," *Atlanta Voice*, May 18, 1974, 1.

102. Adolph Reed Jr., "The Constitution, Chief Inman, and the White Power Structure," reprinted in *Atlanta Voice*, June 1, 1974, 2–3.

103. Correspondence between Jackson and the Fraternal Order of Police, May 24, 1979, box 55, folder 3, MJMR-B.

104. "Law Enforcement, Where?," *Atlanta Voice*, June 15, 1974, back cover, 6; "Black Community Favors Inman's 'Candid Camera,'" *Atlanta Voice*, August 4, 1973, 1.

105. "Landlord Refuses Rent Money, Edgewood Losing Liberation and Art Center," *Atlanta Voice*, September 13, 1970, 1, 9; "Edgewood Area Gallery Closed by Armed Marshals," *Atlanta Voice*, September 27, 1970, 1.

106. "College Denies 'Pressure' to Get Rid of Shabazz in Community Study," *Atlanta Voice*, January 30, 1971, 1.

107. "By Williams: Keep-Abernathy Effort Urged," *Atlanta Journal-Constitution*, July 13, 1973, 28; "Abernathy," *Great Speckled Bird*, July 23, 1973, 9.

108. "By Williams," 28; "Abernathy," 9; "Abernathy Quits Post at SCLC," *Atlanta Journal-Constitution*, July 10, 1973, 1, 16A.

109. "SCLC Begins New Era," *Great Speckled Bird*, August 27, 1973, 9.

110. "SCLC Begins New Era," 9; "A New Thrust," *Great Speckled Bird*, November 12, 1973, 4; "Atlanta SCLC Implements New Programs," *Great Speckled Bird*, December 10, 1973, 4.

111. "Atlanta SCLC Implements New Programs"; "Reply to the SCLC," *Great Speckled Bird*, November 26, 1973, 2.

112. "Who Are the Niskey Lake Two?," *Atlanta Voice*, August 11, 1979; "Ex–Atlanta Official Raps Atlanta Administration for Failure to Solve Child Cases," *Atlanta Voice*, May 30, 1981, 2.

113. "Ex–Atlanta Official," 2.

114. "Who Are the Niskey Lake Two?," *Atlanta Voice*, August 11, 1979; Harvey Gates, "Who Are the Niskey Lake Two: Second Editorial," *Atlanta Voice*, August 18, 1979.

115. "Who Are the Niskey Lake Two?"; Gates, "Who Are the Niskey Lake Two."

116. "Black Leaders Lashed for 'Lack of Interest' in Missing, Slain Youths," *Atlanta Daily World*, August 14, 1980, 1, 9.

117. Alice Kent, interview by author, August 23, 2020.

118. "Black Leaders Lashed for 'Lack of Interest,'" 1, 9.

119. J. Lowell Ware, "Try to Make [Your] Child Safe," *Atlanta Voice*, July 19, 1980.

120. Letter from the Committee to Stop Children's Murders, 1981, box 120, folder 3, MJMR-B.

121. Document involving the Committee to Stop Children's Murders, 1981, box 120, folder 2, MJMR-B.

122. "Child Murders," *Atlanta Constitution*, November 2, 1980, 2; "Black Community Distressed over Death of Yusef Bell," *Atlanta Voice*, November 17, 1979, 2.

123. Kent interview.

124. "Ex–Atlanta Official," 2.

125. "Ex–Atlanta Official," 2.

126. "The Atlanta Story," *Socialist Worker*, July 1981, 1, 6–7.

127. "Black Leaders Lashed for 'Lack of Interest,'" 1, 9.

128. Atlanta Chamber of Commerce *Forward Atlanta* newsletter, vol. 13, no. 5, February 25, 1980, box 3, folder 9, MJMR-B; "Black Leaders Lashed for 'Lack of Interest,'" 1, 9.

129. "Black Leaders Lashed for 'Lack of Interest,'" 1, 9.

130. "Missing Child Subject of Extensive Search," *Atlanta Constitution*, August 1, 1980, 2C; "Committee to Stop Murder of Children," *Atlanta Daily World*, September 14, 1980, 1.

131. "Marchers Rally in the 'Save the Children' Prayer Pilgrimage," *Atlanta Voice*, October 11, 1980, 21.

132. "Black Children: Can We Do More?," *Atlanta Voice*, April 4, 1981, 4.

133. "Black Children," 4.

134. "Children's Funds Need Strict Accountability," *Atlanta Voice*, March 21, 1981, 2.

135. "Actions to Stop STOP Unwarranted," *Atlanta Voice*, July 25, 1981, 4.

136. "Actions to Stop STOP," 4.

137. "Actions to Stop STOP," 4.

CHAPTER THREE

1. "Black Elected Official Abandoned AHA Tenants," *Atlanta Voice*, May 5, 1979, 2; "Harassment at Perry Homes," *Great Speckled Bird*, October 2, 1975, 2; "Conspiracy to Destroy AHA Tenant Leadership," *Atlanta Voice*, November 3, 1979, 2.

2. "Conspiracy to Destroy," 2.

3. "How the OAS Came to Atlanta," *Great Speckled Bird*, May 6, 1974, 4.

4. "How the OAS Came to Atlanta," 4; "Harassment at Perry Homes," 2; "Conspiracy to Destroy," 2.

5. "On the Hill: The New Andrew Young," *Atlanta Voice*, October 8, 1988, 4.

6. "On the Hill," 4.

7. "On the Hill," 4.

8. Chang, *Globalisation*; Jessop, "Liberalism"; Poulantzas, *State Power Socialism*; Harvey, *Brief History of Neoliberalism*, 64–65.

9. Harvey, *Brief History of Neoliberalism*, 66–67.

10. Polanyi, *Great Transformation*, 254–58.

11. "Jackson, Johnson Respond to Chamber's Platform Proposals," *Atlanta Voice*, June 23, 1973, 2.

12. "Low Income Housing," *Great Speckled Bird*, July 23, 1973, 4.

13. *Re/C.A.P.* newsletter, June 1975, box 16, folder 14, MJMR-B.

14. "Where Will the Poor Live? Atlanta Wants to House the Rich," *Atlanta Voice*, July 14, 1973, 2, back cover.

15. "Where Will the Poor Live?," 2, back cover; "Bedford-Pine: A Neighborhood Gives Way to High Rises," *Great Speckled Bird*, June 11, 1973, 3, 14; "Bedford Pine, Westside, and Low Rent Housing," *Great Speckled Bird*, July 16, 1973, 5.

16. "Bedford Pine, Westside," 5.

17. "Progress in Central Atlanta," *Great Speckled Bird*, August 27, 1973, 4; "Will Downtown Destroy Techwood Homes," *Great Speckled Bird*, July 1, 1974, 11.

18. "Chamber of Commerce Moves," *Atlanta Voice*, December 29, 1973, 1, 11.

19. "Bedford Pine, Westside," 5.

20. "Chamber of Commerce Moves," 1, 11.

21. "Chamber of Commerce Moves," 1, 11; "Downtown's Missing Link Proud of Accomplishments," *Atlanta Constitution*, February 13, 1974, 8.

22. "Four Council Members Not on Chamber's List," *Atlanta Voice*, September 17, 1977, 1. Those four unfunded African American council members were James Bond, Morris Finley, James Howard, and Arthur Langford.

23. "Appearing Soon in Your Local Neighborhood: Progress," *Great Speckled Bird*, January 10, 1972, 4.

24. Atlanta Central Area Study, "Central Atlanta Opportunities and Responses," Planning Atlanta—A New City in the Making, 1930s–1990s, Digital Collections, Georgia State University Library; "Central Area Study Says No!," *Great Speckled Bird*, September 11, 1972, 5; "CAS Plans Ignore City Dwellers," *Great Speckled Bird*, September 25, 1972, 12.

25. TIF bonds are public-funded trusts issued by local governments and backed by a percentage of projected future (and higher) tax collections. Tanvi Misra, "The Trouble with TIF," *CityLab*, September 12, 2018, www.bloomberg.com/news/articles/2018-09-12/does-tax-increment-financing-really-work-usually-no; Merriman, *Improving Tax Increment Financing*.

26. *Re/C.A.P.* newsletter, June 1975, box 16, folder 14, MJMR-B; Ga. Const. art. II, § 5901.

27. "Goldberg Elected Atlanta Chamber President; Unveils Talk Up Atlanta Campaign," Atlanta Chamber of Commerce press release, December 10, 1975, box 16, folder 13, MJMR-B.

28. Briefing sheet for CAP marketing the Central City Program, July 1975, box 15, folder 15, MJMR-B.

29. "World Congress Center and the State: Kissing Cousins," *Great Speckled Bird*, July 15, 1974, 5; "Design Team's Dismissal Upheld," *Atlanta Journal-Constitution*, July 9, 1974, 2; "Blast Heralds World Trade Center Beginning," *Atlanta Journal-Constitution*, October 31, 1974, 8.

30. "City Cuts Streets, Opens Way for WCC," *Atlanta Journal-Constitution*, September 4, 1974, 7.

31. *Re/C.A.P.* newsletter, June 1975, box 16, folder 14, MJMR-B.

32. *Re/C.A.P.* newsletter, June 1975, box 16, folder 14, MJMR-B.

33. *Re/C.A.P.* newsletter, December 1976, box 16, folder 14, MJMR-B.

34. Atlanta Chamber of Commerce, "Special Opportunity: Nigerian Trade Mission to Atlanta," June 1978, box 61, folder 23, MJMR-B; "Nigerian Delegation Emphasizes Investment by Small Businesses," *Atlanta Constitution*, June 28, 1978, 10.

35. ACOC memorandum on important travel information for Atlanta Far East Mission participants, September 21, 1979, box 3, folder 13, MJMR-B; "$1 Million Campaign Launched to Draw Business to Atlanta," *Atlanta Daily World*, May 3, 1983, 1, 6; ACOC's *Forward Atlanta* newsletter, February 25, 1980, box 3, folder 9, MJMR-B.

36. Memorandum detailing Maynard Jackson's trip to Germany, May 29, 1980, box 112, folder 10, MJMR-B.

37. "For U.S.-Nigeria Go-Between, Ties Yield Profits," *New York Times*, April 18, 2007; Lawrence Porter, "Andrew Young, Bagman for US Capitalism in Africa," *World Socialist Web Site*, April 30, 2007, www.wsws.org/en/articles/2007/04/youn-a30.html; "Worldwide Propaganda Network Built by the C.I.A.," *New York Times*, December 26, 1977; "Nike Appoints Andrew Young to Review Its Labor Practices," *New York Times*, March 25, 1997; "Nike's Asian Factories Pass Young's Muster," *New York Times*, June 25, 1997. For more on Young's reputation, see Bruce Dixon, "Andrew Young: Shameless Son," *Black Commentator*, March 7, 2006.

38. Rutheiser, *Imagineering Atlanta*, 181–85.

39. "Chamber and Mayor Intend to Sell Atlanta to France," *Atlanta Daily World*, April 9, 1985, 1, 6; "Atlanta Chamber Seeks Air Link to Australia," *Atlanta Daily World*, March 30, 1989, 7.

40. "Businesses in South Africa," *Great Speckled Bird*, September 1984, 15.

41. *National Real Estate Investor*, November 1987, 32; *National Real Estate Investor*, 1989.

42. See "Real Estate Trusts Offer High Yields," *Atlanta Constitution*, November 15, 1985, 1L; and "REIT's Popularity Building Again," *Los Angeles Times*, May 16, 1988, 26.

43. "The REITs Are Coming Back Strong," *Atlanta Constitution*, April 7, 1985, 1K.

44. Rutheiser, *Imagineering Atlanta*, 80–81; Hartsfield International Airport welcome guide and brochure, December 1978, box 60, folder 1, MJMR-B.

45. Hartsfield Atlanta International Airport welcome guide and brochure, December 1978, box 60, folder 1, MJMR-B; real estate and business clipping detailing the economic impact of Hartsfield International Airport, January/February 1978, box 59, folder 18, MJMR-B. For a more detailed description of the airport, see Rutheiser, *Imagineering Atlanta*.

46. Newspaper clipping from the *Atlanta Journal* regarding the airport's lure of international tourists, August 7, 1979, box 59, folder 17, MJMR-B.

47. "Export/Ga. Manufacturers to Meet," *Atlanta Voice*, January 8, 1983, 7; "M&M to Start Production in the Caribbean," *Atlanta Voice*, July 9, 1983, 2.

48. Cowie and Heathcott, *Beyond the Ruins*, 2; Russo and Linkon, "Social Costs of Deindustrialization."

49. The transfer of productive labor away from urban spaces also served to increase competition between low-wage workers, drive down wages, and bust union activity in US industries. See Bluestone, "Economic Inequality," 177.

50. "Regional Textile Employment Declines," *Atlanta Constitution*, June 5, 1986, 3B.

51. "5250 Laid Off in Atlanta," 13.

52. "Doraville Still Closed," *Great Speckled Bird*, July 22, 1974, 5; "GM Will Idle 1,900 More at Doraville," *Atlanta Journal-Constitution*, December 23, 1989, 33; "GM Expected to Close Lakewood Officially," *Atlanta Journal-Constitution*, October 30, 1990, 19.

53. "Repercussions in Atlanta," *Atlanta Journal-Constitution*, December 19, 1991, 72.

54. "Tenant Terror," *Great Speckled Bird*, June 1984, 5–6.

55. "Tenant Terror," 5–6; "Mary Hill Gets House at Last!," *Great Speckled Bird*, July 1984, 11.

56. Neil Smith, *New Urban Frontier*, 62–68.

57. "Trouble on Bankhead Highway," *Great Speckled Bird*, October 17, 1974, 1.

58. "Trouble on Bankhead Highway," 1; "Angry Mayor Sets Meeting on Housing," *Atlanta Journal-Constitution*, October 20, 1974, 2.

59. Neil Smith, *New Urban Frontier*, 67–75.

60. See chapter 4.

61. Neil Smith, *New Urban Frontier*, 67–75.

62. Neil Smith, *New Urban Frontier*, 67–75.

63. Marx and Engels, *Capital*, 1:497, 532, 561–62.

64. Rutheiser, *Imagineering Atlanta*, 115–16.

65. Florence McKinley and Johnny Wilson, interview, *Great Speckled Bird*, August 1984, 12–14.

66. "Council Members Angered by Mayor's Testimony before House Panel on Park," *Atlanta Journal-Constitution*, September 20, 1980, 50.

67. "Council Members Angered," 50; McKinley and Wilson interview; "Plan to Rescue Historic Houses to Be Considered," *Atlanta Journal-Constitution*, December 15, 1980, 1C, 2C.

68. McKinley and Wilson interview; "Williams Calls Carter 'Non-Responsive,'" *Atlanta Journal-Constitution*, October 18, 1980, 4; "Mrs. King to Launch New Fund Drive," *Atlanta Journal-Constitution*, October 15, 1981, 22; "Aid Eyed for King Church," *Atlanta Journal-Constitution*, September 12, 1980, 49; "Coretta King Kicks Off $5 Million Fund Drive," *Atlanta Journal-Constitution*, October 16, 1981, 19.

69. McKinley and Wilson interview.

70. "Threatened Eviction Part of Conspiracy," *Atlanta Voice*, September 20, 1986, 2, 4.

71. "Threatened Eviction," 2, 4.

72. "Threatened Eviction," 2, 4.

73. "Threatened Eviction," 2, 4.

74. "Georgia Dome's Effect on Vine City Questioned," *Atlanta Voice*, November 28, 1987, 1, 5.

75. The June 1986 report was reprinted in *Atlanta Voice*, November 28, 1987, 1, 5.

76. "Georgia Dome's Effect," 5, 21.

77. "Georgia Dome's Effect," 5, 21; "Council President Arrington Backs the Dome Stadium," *Atlanta Voice*, October 8, 1988, 4.

78. "1988 Session One of No State Flag Change, Domed Stadium Approval," *Atlanta Voice*, March 19, 1988, 1.

79. "No Housing for Vine City, No Domed Stadium, Says Lomax," *Atlanta Voice*, June 18, 1988, 2, 12.

80. "City of Atlanta Appears Not Ready for Domed Stadium," *Atlanta Voice*, July 16, 1988, 1.

81. "City Agrees to Georgia Dome, Now Up to Fulton County," *Atlanta Voice*, August 6, 1988, 1–2.

82. "Relocation Forum on Georgia Dome Results in Tension and Suspicion," *Atlanta Voice*, October 8, 1988, 1.

83. "Council Says Ye to Dome Stadium and Georgia 400," *Atlanta Voice*, May 27, 1989, 1, 3.

84. "Council Says Ye," 1, 3.

85. "Dome Jumps Two Obstacles," *Atlanta Voice*, June 17, 1989, 1; "Commission Sides with Vine City," *Atlanta Voice*, November 11, 1989, 12.

86. "Dome Housing Gives Vine City a Fresh Start," *Atlanta Constitution*, May 30, 1990, 28.

CHAPTER FOUR

1. "The Battle of Fair Street Bottom: No Justice, No Peace," *Atlanta Voice*, May 9, 1992, 1, 7; "What Happened Here Is No Surprise," *Atlanta Voice*, May 9, 1992, 3; "A Student's Account of AUC Disturbance," *Atlanta Daily World*, May 10, 1992, 8; "The Anger Spills into Atlanta," *Atlanta Constitution*, May 1, 1992, 1.

2. Cha-Jua notes that "New Nadir" is an appropriate term for this period because, like in the Nineteenth-Century Nadir, a term coined by historian Rayford C. Logan, racial oppression reversed the forward trajectory of the Black liberation movement and precipitated a sharp decline in "Black social conditions, their incorporation into the polity, and portrayal in the national discourse." Sundiata Keita Cha-Jua, unpublished, untitled manuscript shared with the author, 137–38.

3. Geltner, "Commercial Real Estate," 15–19; Wells, *American Capitalism*, 113–15; "The Budget Crisis: Reaping Bitter Harvest of Reagan Voodoo Economics," *Atlanta Voice*, November 3, 1990, 4.

4. Geltner, "Commercial Real Estate," 15–19; Wells, *American Capitalism*, 113–15; "Budget Crisis," 4.

5. Wells, *American Capitalism*, 135–38.

6. Geltner, "Commercial Real Estate," 15–19; Wells, *American Capitalism*, 113–15; "Budget Crisis," 4.

7. Wells, *American Capitalism*, 123; "Historical Tables," Office of Management and Budget, accessed September 1, 2024, whitehouse.gov/omb/budget/historical-tables/.

8. Wells, *American Capitalism*, 138.

9. Geltner, "Commercial Real Estate," 18–20.

10. Geltner, "Commercial Real Estate," 25–28.

11. Holmes, *Status of Black Atlanta 1993*, 90–91.

12. Avis C. Vidal, "A Community Based Approach to Affordable Housing," *New School Commentator*, Spring 1990, 1.

13. Hartshorn and Ihlanfeldt, *Dynamics of Change*, 51–57.

14. Holmes, *Status of Black Atlanta 1993*, 89–90.

15. Holmes, *Status of Black Atlanta 1993*, 89–90.

16. Atlanta Regional Commission, *Annual Report*; Holmes, *Status of Black Atlanta 1993*, 89–90.

17. Atlanta Regional Commission, *Annual Report*; Holmes, *Status of Black Atlanta 1993*, 89–90.

18. "Bill Clinton's Debt to Sister Souljah," *Chicago Tribune*, October 28, 1992; "There Are No Political Saviors," *Atlanta Voice*, August 8, 1992, 3.

19. "America Is Certifying African American Inferiority," *Atlanta Voice*, June 1, 1991, 4.

20. "Civil Rights Veto: What Does It Mean to Us?," *Atlanta Voice*, January 12, 1991, 1, 12.

21. "GM Negotiating to Sell Old Lakewood Plant," *Atlanta Constitution*, April 20, 1991, C3; "Atlanta-Area Workers Not Sure about the Future," *Atlanta Constitution*, August 4, 1991, F.

22. "GM Negotiating to Sell," C3; "Atlanta-Area Workers," F.

23. "Few Workers at Amoco Unit to Keep Jobs," *Atlanta Constitution*, June 15, 1991, 42; "Two Defense Contractors Laying Off 145 in Georgia," *Atlanta Constitution*, June 15, 1991, 42.

24. "Few Workers at Amoco," 42; "Two Defense Contractors," 42.

25. "LeGrange Gasket Plant to Close in '94," *Atlanta Constitution*, January 6, 1994, 56.

26. "Keebler to Shut Down Hapeville Bakery," *Atlanta Journal Constitution*, March 2, 1996, 25.

27. Atlanta Regional Commission, *Annual Report*.

28. Hartshorn and Ihlanfeldt, *Dynamics of Change*, i–v.

29. "All We Want to Do Is Work," *Atlanta Voice*, June 8, 1991, 8.

30. Hartshorn and Ihlanfeldt, *Dynamics of Change*, 10–11.

31. "Southwest Atlanta's Gold Coast Is Booming," *Atlanta Voice*, April 24, 1993, 1, 3.

32. "Atlanta's Global Advocate Jim Maddox to Retire," *Global Atlanta*, September 16, 2009.

33. "Southwest Atlanta's Gold Coast," 1, 3; "Retail Revival at Cascade and I-285," *Atlanta Voice*, May 1, 1993, 1, 3; Hartshorn and Ihlanfeldt, *Dynamics of Change*, 9–18.

34. Hartshorn and Ihlanfeldt, *Dynamics of Change*, 9–18.

35. Hartshorn and Ihlanfeldt, *Dynamics of Change*, 9–18.

36. Holmes, *Status of Black Atlanta 1993*; "The Status of Black Atlanta," *Atlanta Voice*, May 8, 1993, 1, 5; Metropolitan Atlanta Coalition of 100 Black Women, *Status of African American Women*.

37. Metropolitan Atlanta Coalition of 100 Black Women, *Status of African American Women*.

38. Holmes, *Status of Black Atlanta 1993*; "Status of Black Atlanta," *Atlanta Voice*, May 8, 1993, 1, 5.

39. Metropolitan Atlanta Coalition of 100 Black Women, *Status of African American Women*; "Metro Atlanta Coalition of 100 Black Women Release Their Status of Black Women Report," *Atlanta Daily World*, June 3, 1993, 3.

40. "Metro Atlanta Coalition," 3.

41. "Poverty Levels, Rates and Ranks: Places with Population Greater Than 50,000, 1990 Census," IPUMS USA, June 24, 1992, https://usa.ipums.org/usa/resources/voliii/pubdocs/1990/cph-l/cph-l-110.pdf; "A Real Tale of Two Cities," *Atlanta Voice*, March 16, 1991, 1, 7.

42. Population totals are based on revised census metropolitan area definitions, effective December 31, 1992. "Real Tale of Two Cities"; US Bureau of the Census, *1990 Census of Population: Social and Economic Characteristics*, table 24, "Labor Force Characteristics: 1990," p. 82.

43. "Real Tale of Two Cities."

44. Hartshorn and Ilhanfeldt, *Dynamics of Change*, v.

45. "Real Tale of Two Cities," 1, 7.

46. Carnegie, "Gospel of Wealth."

47. Engels, *Condition*, 205–10.

48. "Black Group Slow to React," *Atlanta Voice*, November 9, 1991, 1–2; "State Layoffs Not as High as Expected Here," *Atlanta Daily World*, December 17, 1991, 1, 6.

49. "What About Me? Is the Problem," *Atlanta Voice*, March 16, 1991, 4.

50. "Fractured Foolishness from Fulton County," *Atlanta Voice*, March 16, 1991, 1–2.

51. "100 New Atlanta Companies Recognized," *Atlanta Voice*, March 16, 1991, 3.

52. "Pepsi-Cola Salutes Economic Success in Minority Entrepreneurship," *Atlanta Voice*, January 5, 1991, 1, 2; "Pepsi-Cola Adds Position to Foster Diversity in Workforce," *Atlanta Voice*, July 27, 1991, 3; "Pepsi-Cola Raises Funds for APEX," *Atlanta Voice*, March 16, 1991, 1.

53. "Coca-Cola Offer Scholarships through 'Share the Dream,'" *Atlanta Voice*, January 19, 1991, 6.

54. "Coke Plans to Buy More from Women Businesses," *Atlanta Voice*, April 11, 1992, 2.

55. "World Heavyweight Boxing Champion Evander Holyfield Signs Coke Pact," *Pittsburgh Courier*, February 2, 1991, 7.

56. Austin to Robert Woodruff, memorandum, June 11, 1971, Woodruff Papers, Emory Special Collections, Emory University, Atlanta, Georgia.

57. "Georgia State Receives Grant," *Atlanta Voice*, January 5, 1991, 3; "AT&T Gives Four $1,000 Scholarships," *Atlanta Voice*, September 28, 1991, 4.

58. "Xerox Corporation Contributes to Clark's Program," *Atlanta Voice*, August 10, 1991, 6.

59. "Burger King Earmarks $100 Million for Minority Franchises," *Atlanta Voice*, December 18, 1993, 16.

60. "Holding On," *Atlanta Voice*, January 12, 1991, 4.

61. "Holding On," 4.

62. "Real Tale of Two Cities," 1, 7.

63. Gene Ferguson, "The Crisis of Accountability in Atlanta's Olympic Games," *Atlanta Voice*, December 28, 1991, 1, 8. Urban geographer Larry Keating offers a broad description of Summerhill Neighborhood Incorporated's subversion of the Summerhill protests. See Keating, *Atlanta*, 173–74.

64. A'NUFF position statement, reprinted in full in *Atlanta Voice*, December 22, 1990, 4.

65. "Summerhill About to Become Stadium Out," *Atlanta Voice*, December 8, 1990, 1, 3.

66. A'NUFF statement to the International Olympic Committee, printed in full in *Atlanta Voice*, December 22, 1990, 4.

67. "Thousand on Petition vs Olympic Stadium," *Atlanta Voice*, February 17, 1991, 4.

68. "A'NUFF Stepping Up Protests as Promised," *Atlanta Voice*, May 4, 1991, 1, 6.

69. Otis Hunter letter, reprinted in *Atlanta Voice*, August 10, 1991, 7.

70. Parts of A'NUFF's cease-and-desist letter printed in *Atlanta Voice*, August 10, 1991, 7.

71. Oliver Parker, letters to the editor, *Atlanta Voice*, February 9, 1991, 4.

72. Tom Teepen, "Atlanta's Olympic Sport: Singing the NIMBY Blues," *Atlanta Constitution*, December 9, 1990, 103.

73. "Teepen's Article Distorts A'NUFF Position," *Atlanta Voice*, December 22, 1990, 5.

74. "Teepen's Article," 5.

75. Rutheiser, *Imagineering Atlanta*, 250–51.

76. Ferguson, "Crisis of Accountability," 1.

77. Eldon Frazier, letter to the editor; and Joe Collins, letter to the editor, both in *Atlanta Voice*, January 12, 1991, 4.

78. Henry Leroy Thomas, letter to the editor, *Atlanta Voice*, February 9, 1991, 4.

79. Rutheiser, *Imagineering Atlanta*, 251–53.

80. Keating, *Atlanta*, 173–75.

81. Keating, *Atlanta*, 173–75.

82. Balto, *Occupied Territory*.

83. Summary report for the transition task force of Maynard Jackson administration, December 20 1989, box 12, folder 4, Maynard Jackson Mayoral Records, Series C, RWLA; "Was a Tax Increase Necessary in Atlanta?," *Atlanta Voice*, March 9, 1991, 4.

84. Summary report for the transition task force of Maynard Jackson administration, December 20, 1989; "Was a Tax Increase Necessary in Atlanta?," 4.

85. "New Fulton County Manager," *Atlanta Voice*, July 6, 1991, 1; "Atlanta Pre-Olympic Military State?," *Atlanta Voice*, July 6, 1991, 1–2.

86. Black studies scholar-activist Huey P. Newton first coined the term "illegal capitalists" when conceptualizing the lumpenproletariat.

87. For Marx's extensive conceptualization of the lumpenproletariat, see Marx, *Eighteenth Brumaire*; Marx, "Class Struggles in France"; and Marx and Engels, *Capital*, vol. 1. For Ranciere's analysis of the lumpenproletariat, see Ranciere, *Le philosophe*, 145.

88. Although not conceptualized as part of the lumpenproletariat, the drug trade and underground economy have been captured in striking detail in numerous works.

See Berger and Losier, *Rethinking*. For the manipulation of racial statistical data, see Zuberi, *Thicker Than Blood*.

89. "A Plan to Break the Cycle of Crime," *Atlanta Constitution*, April 27, 1992, 12; "Atlanta Makes Efforts to Weed Out Drugs, Seed in Hope," *Atlanta Voice*, April 11, 1992, 1, 8.

90. "Fighting the Perception of Downtown Atlanta Crime," *Atlanta Voice*, December 28, 1992, 4.

91. Metropolitan Crime Commission, *Crime in Metro Atlanta*.

92. "Unfair Targets," *Atlanta Voice*, September 2, 1994, 1.

93. "Campbell's State of the City: Decries Crime," *Atlanta Voice*, October 15, 1994, 3, 5.

94. "Georgia Expects $300 Million from Crime Bill," *Atlanta Voice*, August 13, 1994, 2; "Welcome to Hotel 254: New Atlanta Jail," *Atlanta Voice*, February 4, 1995, 1, 13.

95. Georgia Housing and Financial Authority, *Profiles of Homelessness*, 2; Wilkes, "Homelessness," 38.

96. Keating, *Atlanta*, 175–76.

97. "Olympic Village Part of Bit by Bit Destruction," *Atlanta Voice*, April 6, 1991, 10; "Housing Tenant Quits Olympic Development Group," *Atlanta Voice*, September 12, 1992, 2; "Housing/Funding," *Atlanta Voice*, September 14, 1996, 1, 6; Keating, *Atlanta*, 180–82.

98. Keating, *Atlanta*, 183–84.

99. Keating, *Atlanta*, 184; "Plan to Break the Cycle," 12; "Atlanta Makes Efforts," 1, 8.

100. "Atlanta Makes Efforts," 1, 8.

101. "Council Approves Controversial Anti-vagrancy Referendum," *Atlanta Voice*, July 20, 1991, 1, 2.

102. "Passing of the New Ordinance," *Atlanta Voice*, July 27, 1991, 4.

103. "Designer of Boxcars for Homeless Awaits OK on Lakewood Factory," *Atlanta Constitution*, September 8, 1994, 49; "Plan to Turn Boxcars into Residences for Homeless Is on Track," *Atlanta Constitution*, September 8, 1994, 35; "Boxcar Willies," *Atlanta Voice*, June 25, 1994, 1.

104. "Homeless Lose Woodruff Park to Renovation," *Atlanta Voice*, October 22, 1994, 2.

105. "No Airport Homeless," *Atlanta Voice*, June 22, 1996, 1.

106. "Why Prison Farm?," *Atlanta Voice*, November 23, 1996, 1.

107. "Local News: Managers of a Program," *Atlanta Constitution*, March 23, 1996, 2; Bill Littlefield, "The Olympic Juggernaut: Displacing the Poor from Atlanta to Rio," WBUR, August 5, 2016, www.wbur.org/onlyagame/2016/08/05/autodromo-rio-atlanta-olympics.

108. Littlefield, "Olympic Juggernaut."

109. "Don't Expect Justice if Brutalized by Police," *Atlanta Voice*, March 28, 1992, 1, 8.

110. "Police Shooting," *Atlanta Voice*, June 15, 1996, 2; "A Panel to Police Atlanta's Police," *Atlanta Constitution*, January 4, 1996, 14; "There Is No Justice for Shooting Victim's Family," *Atlanta Constitution*, February 9, 1996, 36.

111. "Police Sweeps of Projects Come and Go, but Do Little," *Atlanta Constitution*, April 7, 1996, 1.

112. "What Police Statistics Mean—Numbers Don't Tell Whole Story," *Atlanta Constitution*, May 7, 1996, 65.

113. "Police Sweeps Near Colleges Decried," *Atlanta Constitution*, July 17, 1996, 115.

114. "Corrupt Cops," *Atlanta Voice*, September 16, 1995, 5; "Atlanta Holds Six Policemen in Crackdown: F.B.I. Agents Help in Corruption Case," *New York Times*, September 7, 1995, A17. For an extensive detailing of the corruption and the testimony in the case, see "From Dream Team to Nightmare, Blurring the Blue Line," *Atlanta Constitution*, September 10, 1995, 84 (H6).

115. "Corrupt Cops," 5; "Atlanta Holds Six Policemen," A17; "From Dream Team to Nightmare," 84 (H6).

116. "Is Public Housing on the Extinction Blocks?," *Atlanta Voice*, May 13, 1995, 2.

CHAPTER FIVE

1. "A New Neighborhood Leader," *Atlanta Voice*, April 12, 1997, 4; "In Downtown's Shadow, Three-Level Industrial Loft at Brushworks Building Costs $300K," *Curbed Atlanta*, January 15, 2019, 1, https://atlanta.curbed.com/2019/1/15/18183960/downtown-loft-condo-for-sale-industrial.

2. "Councilwoman Threatens to Change NPU Voting Process," *Atlanta Voice*, January 9, 1999, 5.

3. "Councilwoman Threatens to Change," 5.

4. "The Ending of an Era: All Housing Projects to be Demolished by 2010," *Atlanta Voice*, June 12, 2009, 1, 15.

5. Nicholas Lemann, "The Myth of Community Development," *New York Times*, January 9, 1994, 27.

6. Lemann, "Myth of Community Development," 27; "Atlanta Wins Empowerment Zone," *Atlanta Voice*, December 1, 1994, 1.

7. "Atlanta Wins Empowerment Zone," 1; "A Sweetheart Deal? Or Is It Just Good Business Sense?," *Atlanta Voice*, May 20, 1995, 1, 25.

8. "Sweetheart Deal?," 1, 25.

9. "Atlanta's Empowerment Zone Mess," *Atlanta Voice*, September 21, 2002, 1, 8, 18; "Empowerment Zone Replacement," *Atlanta Voice*, March 15, 2003, 3.

10. "Atlanta's Empowerment Zone Mess," 1, 8, 18; "Empowerment Zone Replacement," 3; "More Problems, More Delays for Empowerment Zone Communities," *Atlanta Voice*, July 3, 2004, 2.

11. "West End Sears Site Pits Residents against Ministers," *Atlanta Voice*, February 22, 1997, 2.

12. "Citizens Trust Bank, H. J. Russell and Company Rebuild West End Atlanta," *Atlanta Voice*, March 29, 2007, 20.

13. "Multi-million Dollar Project for Westside Atlanta Breaks Ground," *Atlanta Voice*, March 20, 1999, 2, 11A.

14. "King's Neighborhood Restoration Almost Complete, Almost," *Atlanta Voice*, August 28, 1999, 1, 2; "HDDC's New Modular Home Effort," *Atlanta Voice*, May 24, 2003, 4.

15. "Sweet Auburn Now Attracting Everyone," *Atlanta Voice*, June 15, 2002, 1, 2.

16. "Sweet Auburn Now Attracting Everyone," 1, 2.

17. "King's Neighborhood Restoration," 1, 2.

18. "Is Atlanta Becoming the White Mecca?," *Atlanta Voice*, November 13, 2004, 1, 2, 3; "The Whitening of Black Neighborhoods," *Atlanta Voice*, July 26, 2003, 7, 17.

19. "Suburbanites Slowly Moving Back to Downtown Atlanta," *Atlanta Voice*, October 10, 1998, 1, 3A.

20. Kneebone and Garr, *Suburbanization of Poverty*.

21. "Affordable Housing in Atlanta—Forget It," *Atlanta Voice*, October 11, 2003, 2, 15.

22. "Affordable Housing in Atlanta," 2, 15.

23. "City Workers Protest Privatization Push," *Atlanta Voice*, February 22, 1997, 1, 5A, 9B; "Special Report: Remains of the Games," *Atlanta Journal Constitution*, July 13, 1997, sec. H, 75.

24. "City Workers Protest Privatization Push," 1, 5A, 9B; "Special Report: Remains of the Games," 75.

25. "City Workers Protest Privatization Push," 1, 5A, 9B; "Special Report: Remains of the Games," 75.

26. "Atlanta City Council Votes Yes for Privatization," *Atlanta Voice*, March 7, 1998, 1, 3A; "Mayor Privatizes Water System," *Atlanta Voice*, November 21, 1998, 1; "Atlanta Resumes Control of Water Department," *Atlanta Voice*, February 1, 2003, 1, 27; "Atlanta Water Contract Signed Today," *Atlanta Journal-Constitution*, November 10, 1998, 60; "Water Privatization Spurs Flood of Big Jobs," *Atlanta Journal-Constitution*, December 4, 1998, 65.

27. "Water Privatization Spurs Flood," 65.

28. "Water Privatization Spurs Flood," 65.

29. "Atlanta Braces for Water Transition," *Atlanta Journal-Constitution*, February 7, 2003, F3; "Water Contract Dissolution Set," *Atlanta Journal-Constitution*, February 28, 2003, C3; "City Vows Better Job on Water," *Atlanta Journal-Constitution*, February 14, 2003, D1, D2; "Atlanta Resumes Control of Water Department," *Atlanta Voice*, February 1, 2003, 1, 19.

30. "Report by the Greater Grady Task Force, 2007" excerpts reprinted in "Citizens Fight Privatization of Grady Hospital," *Atlanta Voice*, September 6, 2007, 1, 9.

31. "Report by the Greater Grady Task Force, 2007" excerpts, 1, 9.

32. "Report by the Greater Grady Task Force, 2007" excerpts, 1, 9.

33. "Grady Goes Non-profit," *Atlanta Voice*, November 29, 2007, 1, 5; Max Blau, "How Grady Memorial Hospital Skirted Death," *Creative Loafing*, February 28, 2013, https://creativeloafing.com/content-170678-how-grady-memorial-hospital-skirted.

34. "Grady Goes Non-profit," 1, 5; Blau, "How Grady Memorial Hospital."

35. "Grady Goes Non-profit," 1, 5.

36. Blau, "How Grady Memorial Hospital."

37. Blau, "How Grady Memorial Hospital."

38. Blau, "How Grady Memorial Hospital."

39. Blau, "How Grady Memorial Hospital."

40. Blau, "How Grady Memorial Hospital"; "Injunction Halts Grady Dialysis Closure after Board Approves It," *Atlanta Progressive News*, September 20, 2009, 1; "Grady Dialysis Deal Finalized," *Atlanta Journal-Constitution*, September 13, 2010.

41. "Grady CEO Apologizes for Shine My Shoes Remark," *Atlanta Journal-Constitution*, October 29, 2010, 1; Blau, "How Grady Memorial Hospital."

42. "CBC Report: Educator Assails Efforts to Privatize Public Education," *Atlanta Voice*, January 16, 1999, 17; "Public Choice School Movement Growing," *Atlanta Voice*, February 19, 2000, 15, 18; "Public Education in Crisis," *Atlanta Voice*, May 20, 2000, 5.

43. "Atlanta Public School Workers Picket Higher Wages," *Atlanta Voice*, August 30, 1997, 1, 5A.

44. "Atlanta Public School Workers Picket," 1, 5A.

45. "Atlanta Public School Workers Picket," 1, 5A.

46. "Public Schools Draw Criticism over Privatization," *Atlanta Voice*, January 2, 1999, 16; "Wanted; Tech-Minded Tutelage," *Atlanta Journal-Constitution*, January 7, 1999, 268; "Edison Project Is Bright Idea," *Atlanta Journal-Constitution*, January 26, 1999, 40; "East Lake Charter School on Hold," *Atlanta Journal-Constitution*, July 22, 1999, 185; "Villages of East Lake: Renewal at Its Best," *Atlanta Journal-Constitution*, October 30, 2005, HF14; "CBC Report," 17.

47. "CBC Report," 17.

48. "CBC Report," 17; "Privatization Consensus Still Elusive," *Atlanta Journal-Constitution*, April 1, 1999, 152; Engle and Scafidi, *Is It Better*; "Charter School Will Add to East Lake's Draw," *Atlanta Journal-Constitution*, October 17, 1999, 82.

49. "School Steers Students from Cradle to College," *Atlanta Journal-Constitution*, September 12, 2010, B1, B5; "Golf Suits East Lake Students," *Atlanta Journal-Constitution*, October 24, 2005, E10; "Charter," *Atlanta Journal-Constitution*, May 4, 2014, B1, B6.

50. "Atlanta's Alternative School Said to Be Privatized, Profit Driven Prison," *Atlanta Voice*, September 18, 2004, 1, 19.

51. "Atlanta's Alternative School," 1, 19.

52. "Atlanta's Alternative School," 1, 19; "Former Principal Calls for Federal Probe of APS' Alternative School," *Atlanta Voice*, November 6, 2004, 1, 7.

53. "ACLU Suit Claims Atlanta School Virtually a Prison," *Atlanta Voice*, March 27, 2008, 1, 15; "CEP Refutes ACLU Allegations," *Atlanta Voice*, April 3, 2008, 1, 2.

54. "ACLU Suit," 1, 15; "CEP Refutes ACLU Allegations," 1, 2; "Atlanta's Alternative School: Prison or School?," *Atlanta Voice*, October 2, 2004, 1, 5; "Prison or School—What's the Solution?," *Atlanta Voice*, October 30, 2004, 1, 5.

55. "Former Principal Calls for Federal Probe," 1, 7.

56. "Former Principal Calls for Federal Probe," 1, 7; "Community Voices Concerns to CEP Officials," *Atlanta Voice*, December 18, 2004, 5.

57. "Former Principal Calls for Federal Probe," 1, 7; "Community Voices Concerns," 5; "CEP: The Parents and Students' Perspective," *Atlanta Voice*, May 15, 2008, 5.

58. "ACLU Suit," 1, 15; "CEP Refutes ACLU Allegations," 1, 2.

59. "ACLU Suit," 1, 15; "CEP Refutes ACLU Allegations," 1, 2.

60. Vincent K. Fort, "Meria Carstarphen Believes She Has Divine Right to Position," *Jabari Simama Speaks* (blog), September 30, 2019, https://jabarisimama.com/2019/09/30/meria-carstarphen-believes-she-has-divine-right-to-position; Thomas Ultican, "A Rotten Peach Poisoning Atlanta Public Schools," *Tultican* (blog), April 17, 2018, https://tultican.com/2018/04/17/a-rotten-peach-poisoning-atlanta-public-schools.

61. Ultican, "Rotten Peach"; "Can Charter School Operators Save Sinking Atlanta Schools?," *Atlanta Journal-Constitution*, February 20, 2016, 1.

62. Ultican, "Rotten Peach"; "Can Charter School Operators," 1; "Carstarphen to Testify in Teachers' Age-Discrimination Suit," *Atlanta Journal-Constitution*, August 25, 2017, 1.

63. "Can Charter School Operators," 1; "Carstarphen to Testify," 1; Hallgren et al., *Year 2 Report*.

64. Anthropologist Karen J. Cook wrote a powerful master's thesis equating the redistricting and closing of Black schools in Atlanta to hypersegregation. See Cook, "Atlanta Public Schools." For more data on APS, see Eric Wearne, "Atlanta's Segregated Schools—in 2004," Cato Institute, May 17, 2004, www.cato.org/commentary/atlantas-segregated-schools-2004.

65. Wearne, "Atlanta's Segregated Schools"; Michelle Cohen Marill, "Resegregation," *Atlanta Magazine*, April 2008; Max Blau, "Picking Up the Pieces of Atlanta Public Schools," *Creative Loafing*, July 10, 2014, https://creativeloafing.com/content-185700-cover-story-picking-up-the-pieces-of-atlanta-public; Rachel Aviv, "Georgia's Separate and Unequal Special Education System," *New Yorker*, September 24, 2018.

66. Gramsci, *Selections*.

67. Arena, *Driven from New Orleans*, 82–83.

68. Medical scholar Susan Rosenthal detailed this phenomenon in more detail in her article "Philanthropy." She also argued that while the capitalist class only gives away money to stifle protest, the working class gives legitimate philanthropy to the wealthy in three ways: (1) workers produce a surplus for employers, (2) workers pay taxes that support the wealthy, and (3) workers donate to charities. Arena, *Driven from New Orleans*, 84.

69. Howard Husock, "Don't Let CDCs Fool You," *City Journal*, Summer 2001, www.city-journal.org/article/dont-let-cdcs-fool-you. For extensive detailing of the relationship between CDCs and private interests, see Myerson, *Community Development Corporations*. For an alternative perspective, see "CDCs Revitalized America's Poor Neighborhoods. What Is Their Role as a Community Gentrifies?," *Philadelphia Inquirer*, March 2, 2018.

70. Huscock, "Don't Let CDCs Fool You."

71. Huscock, "Don't Let CDCs Fool You."

72. "Managing Gentrification: Atlanta's Changing Landscape," *Atlanta Voice*, November 13, 1999, 1, 10; "The Resettling of Atlanta," *Atlanta Voice*, December 4, 1999, 1, 3.

73. "Managing Gentrification," 1, 10; "Resettling of Atlanta," 1, 3.

74. "Resettling of Atlanta," 1, 3; "Southside Renewal Project," *Atlanta Voice*, October 9, 1999, 1, 5A.

75. "Southside Renewal Project," 1, 5A.

76. "Southside Renewal Project," 1, 5A; "Ware Estates Adds to the Changing Face of Mechanicsville," *Atlanta Voice*, May 29, 1999, 5.

77. "Residents Blast Turner Field Crime Report," *Atlanta Voice*, April 15, 2000, 1, 10A.

78. "Atlanta Ranked Nation's Third Most Dangerous City," *Atlanta Voice*, December 14, 2002, 1, 17; "Despite Gains, City Ranks 3rd in Crime," *Atlanta Journal-Constitution*, December 28, 2002, E1.

79. "Clarence Artis: Real Estate's Rising Star," *Atlanta Voice*, August 23, 2007, 9. See home sales in *Atlanta Journal-Constitution* in the years 2005 and 2006 for Artis property purchases.

80. "African Americans Build Wealth in Commercial Real Estate," *Atlanta Voice*, September 20, 2007, 8.

81. "Courtney Dillard: The Black Donald Trump?," *Atlanta Voice*, July 26, 2007, 6; "Clarence Artis," 9; "Maybe Reinvent the Wheel—if You Want to Sell Condo Units," *Atlanta Voice*, February 20, 2009, 3.

CHAPTER SIX

1. Denise Broward, interview by author, March 18, 2021.
2. Broward interview.
3. "America's Public Housing Capital," *Atlanta Constitution*, April 20, 1997, R3.
4. "Ford to Close Hapeville Plant," *Atlanta Voice*, January 26, 2006, 1, 4; "Without Fanfare, Last Ford Taurus Rolls off Atlanta Assembly Line," *Atlanta Voice*, November 2, 2006, 12.
5. "Ford to Close Hapeville Plant"; "Without Fanfare, Last Ford Taurus," 12.
6. "The Great Recession Tightens Its Grip on Georgia," *Atlanta Voice*, July 10, 2009, 1, 5; "GA Revenues Continue to Slide, More Cuts Possible," *Atlanta Voice*, September 18, 2008, 3.
7. Lydia Senn, "Northwest Georgia Regional Hospital Set to Close," *Rome News-Tribune*, January 13, 2011, 1; "Georgia Proposes Privatization of Mental Health Services," *Atlanta Voice*, April 17, 2009, 3.
8. "Georgia's Legislative Black Caucus at a Crossroads," *Atlanta Voice*, February 27, 2009, 3; "Georgia: Black Lawmakers Walk Out of House after Obama Vote," *Atlanta Voice*, March 27, 2009, 3.
9. "Atlanta's Shadow Government," *Atlanta Voice*, June 6, 2008, 1, 15.
10. "Atlanta's Shadow Government," 1, 15.
11. "Atlanta's Shadow Government," 1, 15.
12. "Georgia Revenue Collections Continue to Fall," *Atlanta Voice*, July 17, 2009, 5; "GA Revenue Falls Again in September," *Atlanta Voice*, October 16, 2009, 3.
13. "No Federal Bailout for Cities Atlanta Makes Deeper Cuts," *Atlanta Voice*, December 11, 2008, 1, 18.
14. "GA's Public Housing Taxed amid Economic Downturn," *Atlanta Voice*, August 28, 2008, 4; "Great Recession Tightens Its Grip," 1, 5.
15. "Great Recession Tightens Its Grip," 1, 5.
16. "Robbing Peter to Pay Paul," *Atlanta Voice*, December 4, 2008, 1, 15.
17. "Residents Tell Riveting Tales of Unemployment," *Atlanta Voice*, April 8, 2011, 1, 13.
18. "Residents Tell Riveting Tales," 1, 13.
19. "MARTA Fees Raised—Services Reduced," *Atlanta Voice*, June 5, 2009, 8.
20. Carnevale, Jayasundera, and Gulish, *America's Divided Recovery*, 10–11.
21. "West Side Walmart to Spur Jobs, Growth," *Atlanta Voice*, December 17, 2010, 1, 3, 15.

22. "West Side Walmart," 1, 3, 15.

23. "McDonald's Set to Hire 50,000 Employees," *Atlanta Voice*, April 15, 2011, 1, 4.

24. "McDonald's Set to Hire," 1, 4; "Thousands Line Up for McDonald's Jobs," *Atlanta Voice*, April 22, 2011, 1, 2; "Study Shows Majority of Low Pay Workers on Public Assistance," *Atlanta Voice*, October 18, 2013, 5.

25. "Thousands of Job-Seekers Hoping to Land Season Work," *Atlanta Voice*, October 28, 2011, 5.

26. "Black Workers Stuck in Poverty Wages," *Atlanta Voice*, June 20, 2014, 1, 6.

27. "Just One More Hit," *Atlanta Voice*, July 3, 2008, 1, 14.

28. "Enough Is Enough: Are Atlanta's Streets Too Dangerous?," *Atlanta Voice*, July 31, 2009, 1, 10.

29. "Urban Renewal or Urban Removal?," *Atlanta Voice*, February 22, 2007, 1, 16.

30. "Atlanta Housing Authority: Are They the City's Savior for the Future?," *Atlanta Voice*, June 14, 2007, 1, 19.

31. "Urban Renewal or Urban Removal?," 1, 16.

32. "Urban Renewal or Urban Removal?," 1, 16; complaint made by RAB to HUD against the AHA, reprinted in full in *Atlanta Voice*, August 30, 2007, 10.

33. Complaint made by RAB, 10.

34. Complaint made by RAB, 10.

35. Complaint made by RAB, 10.

36. "AHA Demolitions: No Resolution Yet," *Atlanta Voice*, December 6, 2007, 1, 18.

37. "AHA Demolitions," 1, 18.

38. "Lewis' Help Will Be Right at Home," *Atlanta Journal-Constitution*, March 26, 2008, A18; "Atlanta's Public Housing Revamp Shows Real Hope for the Future," *Atlanta Journal-Constitution*, July 27, 2008, B6.

39. "Your Tax Dollars: Atlanta Salary Stings HUD," *Atlanta Journal-Constitution*, June 6, 2012, A1, A11.

40. "Activists React to Glover's Confirmed AHA Resignation," *Atlanta Progressive News*, October 10, 2011.

41. "Families Look to Relocate as End Nears for Projects," *Atlanta Voice*, September 13, 2010, B1, B4; "Activists Object to Public Housing Closing," *Atlanta Journal-Constitution*, August 10, 2012, B4; "Subdivision to Be Built on Public Housing Site," *Atlanta Journal-Constitution*, December 27, 2012, B4.

42. Denise Broward, interview by author, February 21, 2021.

43. "Dramatic Departure for Lithia Springs," *Atlanta Constitution*, May 4, 2005, 5.

44. US Census Bureau, *Georgia: 2000*; US Census Bureau, *Georgia: 2010*; "Metro Minorities Becoming a Majority," *Atlanta Journal-Constitution*, June 16, 2010, A1, A6; Karen Pooley, "Segregation's New Geography: The Atlanta Metro Region, Race, and the Declining Prospects for Upward Mobility," *Southern Spaces*, April 2015, https://southernspaces.org/2015/segregations-new-geography-atlanta-metro-region-race-and-declining-prospects-upward-mobility/.

45. "The Changing Face of Georgia's Poor," *Atlanta Voice*, August 10, 1991, 1.

46. US Census Bureau, *Georgia: 2000*; US Census Bureau, *Georgia: 2010*; "Metro Minorities"; Pooley, "Segregation's New Geography."

47. Brookings Institution Center on Urban and Metropolitan Policy, *Moving beyond*

Sprawl; "Work Drive Time Rises 67 Percent," *Atlanta Constitution*, September 19, 2002, JA1, JA6.

48. US Census Bureau; Brookings Institution Center on Urban and Metropolitan Policy, *Moving beyond Sprawl*, 18–19.

49. The US Census Bureau in 2015 reported that the poverty line for people living in the United States was as follows: $12,071 annual income for one person; $15,379 for two people; $18,850 for three people; $24,230 for four people; and $28,695 for five people.

50. Alana Samuels, "Suburbs and the New American Poverty," *Atlantic*, January 7, 2015.

51. Richard Kent and Alice Kent, interview by author, August 20, 2016.

52. "Regions' Suburbs See Rise in Poverty," *Atlanta Journal-Constitution*, December 23, 2012, A1, A13.

53. For more on food insecurity in urban spaces, see Mead, "Urban Issues"; Hillier and Chrisinger, "Reality of Urban Food Deserts," 74–86; Gundersen, Kreider, and Pepper, "Economics of Food Insecurity"; Mammen, Bauer, and Richards, "Understanding Persistent Food Insecurity"; and Stuff et al., "Prevalence of Food Insecurity."

54. Brookings Institution Center on Urban and Metropolitan Policy, *Moving beyond Sprawl*, 4; "MARTA's Day of Reckoning," *Atlanta Voice*, May 1, 2004, 1, 7; "MARTA Proposed Route Changes—What's Affected?," *Atlanta Voice*, May 1, 2004, 2.

55. In 2015, most Black people in Gwinnett County worked as drivers/sales workers or truck drivers. The third highest number of Black people worked as customer service representatives. "Region's Suburbs See Rise in Poverty," *Atlanta Constitution*, December 23, 2012, A1, A13.

56. "Region's Suburbs."

57. "Region's Suburbs."

58. "Region's Suburbs."

59. Construction jobs were also weak in Douglas County, with only 2,399. "Low Unemployment Made Hiring Difficult," *Atlanta Constitution*, October 10, 1999, 103.

60. "Development Squabbles Rise as Newcomers Change Character of Rural Area," *Atlanta Constitution*, July 6, 1998, 63.

61. "Low Unemployment Made Hiring Difficult," 103.

62. "Rapid Growth in West Georgia Refers to People, Not Paychecks," *Atlanta Constitution*, November 12, 2001, B6.

63. "550 Keurig Jobs for Region," *Atlanta Constitution*, June 20, 2014, A11; "Former Keurig Building Sold," *Douglas County Sentinel*, April 3, 2018.

64. US Census Bureau.

65. "You Must Work in Public Safety," *Atlanta Voice*, July 4, 1998, 9.

66. See chapter 4 of this book.

67. "Old GM Plant Site Faces Uncertainty," *Atlanta Constitution*, September 8, 2012, A1, A12.

68. "GM: For Many in Doraville, Plant a Member of the Family," *Atlanta Constitution*, November 25, 2005, A16.

69. "GM: For Many in Doraville," A16; "Doraville Called Vulnerable," *Atlanta Constitution*, December 20, 1991, 63.

70. "GM: Newlyweds Stick to Old Workplace—for Now," *Atlanta Constitution*, July 25, 2006, A6; "Card: Doraville About to Lose Its GM Plant, but Not Its Hope," *Atlanta Constitution*, September 21, 2008, A8.

71. "Deal Finally Closes on Doraville Plant," *Atlanta Constitution*, September 25, 2014, A14.

72. "GM's Doraville Plant Still Could Close," *Atlanta Constitution*, March 15, 1992, 29.

73. "GM Veterans Fear End of the Line," *Atlanta Constitution*, April 19, 2009, A1, A5.

74. US Census Bureau, 1999.

75. "Doraville Keeps Hopes Alive for Plan," *Atlanta Constitution*, September 8, 2012, A1, A12; "MARTA's Gold Line Beckons Growth," *Atlanta Constitution*, July 19, 2015, D1, D4.

76. "Doraville Keeps Hopes Alive," A1, A12; "MARTA's Gold Line," D1, D4.

77. "Plant's Closing Hits Austell Hard," *Atlanta Constitution*, November 13, 2010, B1, B8.

78. "Officials Optimistic Workers Can Find Jobs after Plant Closes," *Atlanta Constitution*, April 5, 2001, 271.

79. "The Closing of the Carrollton Sony Music Plant: When the Music Stops," *Atlanta Constitution*, March 11, 2001, A1, A10, A11.

80. "Closing of the Carrollton Sony Music Plant," A1, A10, A11.

81. "Workers Share Memories, Goodbyes as Carrollton Sony Plant Closes," *Atlanta Constitution*, March 31, 2001, F1, F4.

82. "Home Builder Helps Transform County," *Atlanta Constitution*, April 3, 2003, J1, J4.

83. "Blacks Flock to Clayton County," *Atlanta Constitution*, September 7, 2004, A1, A12.

84. Samuels, "Suburbs and the New American Poverty."

85. Samuels, "Suburbs and the New American Poverty."

86. "More Moms Homeless," *Atlanta Journal-Constitution*, October 19, 2013, A1, A14.

87. Dewey et al., *US Select Service*.

88. Michael Sasso, "Atlanta's Real Estate Boom Forces Locals to Live in Extended-Stay Hotels," *CityLab*, June 23, 2022, www.bloomberg.com/news/articles/2022-06-23/when-extended-stay-hotel-rooms-become-affordable-housing.

89. "As Mosley Motel Closes, Residents' Future in Limbo," *Atlanta Journal-Constitution*, January 29, 2010, B1.

90. "As Mosley Motel Closes," B1, B5.

91. "As Mosley Motel Closes," B1, B5.

92. "As Mosley Motel Closes," B1, B5.

93. "Help for Homeless Spreads to Suburbs," *Atlanta Journal-Constitution*, December 25, 2012, A1, A19.

94. "Residents Squash Loganville Motel," *Atlanta Journal-Constitution*, August 9, 2007, J2.

95. "Hope Reigns on West Side over Falcons Stadium Deal," *Atlanta Voice*, March 22, 2013, 1, 2, 4; "Mt. Vernon Sets Vote on Stadium Deal," *Atlanta Voice*, March 29, 2013, 1, 5.

96. "Mt. Vernon Sets Vote," 1, 5.

97. "Hope Reigns," 1, 2, 4; "Mt. Vernon Sets Vote," 1, 5.
98. "Mt. Vernon Sets Vote," 1, 5.
99. "Mt. Vernon Sets Vote," 1, 5.
100. "Deal or No Deal?," *Atlanta Voice*, August 2, 2013, 1, 4; "The Price Is Right?," *Atlanta Voice*, August 9, 2013, 1, 5.
101. "The Price Is Right?," 1, 5.
102. "Churches to Vote on New Stadium Deal," *Atlanta Voice*, September 20, 2013, 1, 5.

EPILOGUE

1. Turner, "Reason, Rebellion, and Revolution," 273–75.
2. See Du Bois, *Black Reconstruction in America*.
3. Ross and Bateman, *Meet the Low-Wage Workforce*.
4. "Why Are Philly's Construction Unions So White?," *Philadelphia Inquirer*, September 1, 2022.
5. "Why Are Philly's Construction Unions."
6. Du Bois, *Black Reconstruction in America*, 725.
7. Burden-Stelly, *Black Scare/Red Scare*, 83.
8. Sebastian Obando, "Warehouse, Distribution Center Demand Accelerates as E-Commerce Grows," *Supply Chain Dive*, January 31, 2022, www.supplychaindive.com/news/distribution-centers-warehouses-growth-2022/617804; "Georgia Leads Nation in Large Warehouse Leases for 1H 2022," press release, CBRE, August 23, 2022, https://www.cbre.com/press-releases/georgia-leads-nation-in-large-warehouse-leases-for-1h-2022.
9. "Georgia Leads Nation."
10. William H. Frey, "A 'New Great Migration' Is Bringing Black Americans Back to the South," Brookings, September 12, 2022, www.brookings.edu/articles/a-new-great-migration-is-bringing-black-americans-back-to-the-south.
11. "Incentives and Applications," Georgia Department of Economic Development, accessed March 13, 2022, https://georgia.org/industries/film-entertainment/georgia-film-tv-production/production-incentives.
12. "How Georgia Became the Hollywood of the South: *Time* Goes behind the Scenes," *Time*, July 26, 2018; "Hollywood of the South: Atlanta's Film Industry Is Building Its Own Mini City," *Guardian*, October 26, 2018.
13. "Hollywood of the South: Atlanta's Film Industry."
14. "Hollywood of the South: Atlanta's Film Industry."
15. "Tyler Perry May Be Buyer of Large Tract," *Atlanta Constitution*, March 22, 2013, A9, A10.
16. Brian Jones, "Socialist Case for Reparations."

Bibliography

ARCHIVAL COLLECTIONS

Archives, University of Wisconsin–Madison, Madison, Wisconsin
    Vine City Project Records, 1960–1971
        Student Nonviolent Coordinating Committee Papers, Subgroup A: 1959–1972
Auburn Avenue Research Library on African-American Culture and History
        Repository, Atlanta-Fulton County Library System, Atlanta, Georgia
    Andrew J. Young Papers, Subseries 5B: Administrative Records
    Dr. Robert "Bob" Holmes Papers, Writing and Publication Series
Digital Collections, Georgia State University Library
    Planning Atlanta—A New City in the Making, 1930s–1990s
    Research Atlanta Reports
Emory Libraries, Emory University, Atlanta, Georgia
    Archives and Special Collections
        Robert Woodruff Papers
Robert W. Woodruff Library of the Atlanta University Center, Inc., Atlanta, Georgia
    Grace Towns Hamilton Papers, Maps, 1960, 1963–1975, 1981, undated
    Maynard Jackson Mayoral Records, Series A: Vice Mayoral Records
    Maynard Jackson Mayoral Records, Series B: First and Second Term Mayoral
        Records
    Maynard Jackson Mayoral Records, Series C: Third Term Mayoral Records

INTERVIEWS BY AUTHOR

Denise Broward, February 21, 2021, March 18, 2021
Alice Kent, August 20, 2016, August 23, 2020
Richard Kent, August 20, 2016

GOVERNMENT DOCUMENTS

Atlanta Regional Commission. *Annual Report of the Atlanta Regional Commission, 1990.* Atlanta: Atlanta Regional Commission, 1990.
———. *State of the Region Report.* Atlanta: Atlanta Regional Commission, 2014.
———. *State of the Region Report.* Atlanta: Atlanta Regional Commission, 2016.
Current Population Survey from the Bureau of Labor Statistics, 1980–2018. Atlanta: Center for Human Capital Studies of the Federal Reserve Bank, 2019.

US Bureau of the Census. *Georgia: 2000*. Population and Housing Unit Counts series. 2000 Census of Population and Housing, August 2003. Report PHC-3-12. https://www2.census.gov/library/publications/2003/dec/phc-3-12.pdf.

———. *Georgia: 2010*. Population and Housing Unit Counts series. 2010 Census of Population and Housing, August 2012. Report CPH-2-12. https://www2.census.gov/library/publications/decennial/2010/cph-2/cph-2-12.pdf.

———. *1970 Census of Population and Housing: Census Tracts*. Atlanta, Ga., Standard Metropolitan Statistical Area. Final Report PHC(1)-14. Washington, DC: US Government Printing Office, 1972. Table P-3, "Labor Force Characteristics of the Population: 1970."

———. *1970 Census of the Population*. Vol. 1, *Characteristics of the Population*, part 12, *Georgia*. Washington, DC: US Government Printing Office, March 1973. Table "Employment Status by Race, Sex, and Urban and Rural Residence: 1970."

———. *1980 Census of the Population*. Washington, DC: US Government Printing Office, March 1983. Table "Employment Status by Race, Sex, and Urban and Rural Residence: 1980."

———. *1990 Census of Population*. Washington, DC: US Government Printing Office, March 1993. Table "Employment Status by Race, Sex, and Urban and Rural Residence: 1990."

———. *1990 Census of Population: Social and Economic Characteristics; Georgia*. 1990 CP-2-12. https://www2.census.gov/library/publications/decennial/1990/cp-2/cp-2-12-1.pdf.

———. *1990 Census of the Population: Detailed Occupation and Other Characteristics from the EEO File for the United States*. 1990 CP-S-1-1. Washington, DC: Government Printing Office, 1992.

———. *The Social and Economic Status of the Black Population in the United States: An Historical View, 1790–1978*. Current Population Reports, Special Studies Series P-23, No. 80. Washington, DC: US Government Printing Office, 1978.

———. *US Censuses of Population and Housing: 1960; Census Tracts*. Atlanta, Ga., Standard Metropolitan Statistical Area. Final Report PHC(1)-8. Washington, DC: US Government Printing Office, 1962.

NEWSPAPERS AND PERIODICALS

Atlanta Constitution
Atlanta Business Chronicle
Atlanta Daily World
Atlanta Journal-Constitution
Atlanta Magazine
Atlanta Progressive News
Atlanta Voice
Atlantic
Baltimore African American
Black Commentator
Chicago Tribune

Douglas County Sentinel (Douglasville, GA)
Global Atlanta
Great Speckled Bird (Atlanta)
Guardian
Los Angeles Free Press
Los Angeles Times
National Real Estate Investor
New School Commentator (New York)
New Yorker
New York Times
Philadelphia Inquirer
Pittsburgh (PA) Courier
Rome (GA) News-Tribune
Socialist Worker
Suffolk (NY) Times
Time

PUBLISHED PRIMARY SOURCES

Annie E. Casey Foundation. *Changing the Odds: The Race for Results in Atlanta*. Baltimore: Annie E. Casey Foundation, 2015.

Boggs, James. *Racism and the Class Struggle: Further Pages from a Black Worker's Notebook*. New ed. New York: Monthly Review Press, 1970.

Fredes, Ricardo, and Pilar Aguilera, eds. *Chile: The Other September 11; An Anthology of Reflections on the 1973 Coup*. 2nd ed. Melbourne: Ocean, 2016.

October League. *Wildcat at Mead*. Documentary, 1972. 50 minutes.

SECONDARY SOURCES

Books, Chapters, and Reports

Allen, Robert L. *Black Awakening in Capitalist America: An Analytic History*. Trenton, NJ: Africa World, 1990.

Arena, John. *Driven from New Orleans: How Nonprofits Betray Public Housing and Promote Privatization*. Minneapolis: University of Minnesota Press, 2012.

Balto, Simon. *Occupied Territory: Policing Black Chicago from Red Summer to Black Power*. Chapel Hill: University of North Carolina Press, 2019.

Berger, Dan, and Toussaint Losier. *Rethinking the American Prison Movement*. New York: Routledge, 2018.

Berry, B. *The Human Consequences of Urbanization*. London: Macmillan, 1973.

———. "Islands of Renewal in Seas of Decay." In *The New Urban Reality*, edited by P. Paterson, 69–99. Washington, DC: Brookings Institution, 1985.

Bluestone, Barry. "Economic Inequality and the Macrostructuralist Debate." In *Political Economy for the 21st Century: Contemporary Views on the Trend of Economics*, edited by Charles J. Whalen, 171–94. New York: Routledge, 1996.

Boston, Thomas D. *Race, Class, and Conservatism*. London: Unwin Hyman, 1988.

Brookings Institution Center on Urban and Metropolitan Policy. *Moving beyond Sprawl: The Challenge for Metropolitan Atlanta*. Washington, DC: Brookings Institution, 2000.

Brown, Scot. *Fighting for US: Maulana Karenga, the US Organization, and Black Cultural Nationalism*. New York: New York University Press, 2003.

Burden-Stelly, Charisse. *Black Scare/Red Scare: Theorizing Capitalist Racism in the United States*. Chicago: University of Chicago Press, 2023.

Burns, Rebecca. *Rage in the Gate City: The Story of the 1906 Atlanta Race Riot*. Athens: University of Georgia Press, 2011.

Carnevale, Anthony P., Tamara Jayasundera, and Artem Gulish. *America's Divided Recovery: College Haves and Have-Nots, 2016*. Washington, DC: Georgetown University Center on Education and the Workforce, 2016.

Carson, Clayborne. *In Struggle: SNCC and the Black Awakening of the 1960s*. Cambridge, MA: Harvard University Press, 1995.

Cecelski, David S., and Timothy B. Tyson. *Democracy Betrayed: The Wilmington Race Riot of 1898 and Its Legacy*. Chapel Hill: University of North Carolina Press, 2000.

Cha-Jua, Sundiata K. *America's First Black Town: Brooklyn, Illinois, 1830–1915*. Urbana: University of Illinois Press, 2000.

Cha-Jua, Sundiata K., Mary Frances Berry, and V. P. Franklin, eds. *Reparations and Reparatory Justice: Past, Present, and Future*. Urbana: University of Illinois Press, 2024.

Chang, Ha-Joon. *Globalisation, Economic Development, and the Role of the State*. London: Zed Books, 2003.

Clark, Kenneth. *Dark Ghetto: Dilemmas of Social Power*. Middletown, CT: Wesleyan University Press, 1989.

Cowie, Jefferson. *Staying Alive: The 1970s and the Last Days of the Working Class*. New York: New Press, 2010.

Cowie, Jefferson, and Joseph Heathcott, eds. *Beyond the Ruins: The Meanings of Deindustrialization*. Ithaca, NY: Cornell University Press, 2003.

Cox, Kevin R. *Urbanization and Conflict in Market Societies*. Chicago: Maaroufa, 1978.

Dekel-Chen, Jonathan, David Gaunt, Natan M. Meir, and Israel Bartal, eds. *Anti-Jewish Violence: Rethinking the Pogrom in East European History*. Indianapolis: Indiana University Press, 2010.

Dewey, Chris, Stephen M. Leslie, Katy Reynolds, Zach Demuth, and Ophelia Makis. *US Select-Service and Extended-Stay Hotel Investment Trends*. Chicago: JLL, 2023.

Dittmer, John. *Black Georgia in the Progressive Era, 1900–1920*. Urbana: University of Illinois Press, 1980.

Dorsey, Allison. *To Build Our Lives Together: Community Formation in Black Atlanta, 1875–1906*. Athens: University of Georgia Press, 2004.

Du Bois, W. E. B. *Black Reconstruction in America, 1860–1880*. New York: Free Press, 1998.

Dunayevskaya, Raya. *Marxism and Freedom: From 1776 to Today*. New York: Bookman, 1958.

Ellsworth, Scott. *Death in a Promised Land: The Tulsa Race Riot of 1921*. Baton Rouge: Louisiana State University, 1992.

Engels, Friedrich. *The Condition of the Working Class in England in 1844*. Translated by Florence Kelley. 1845. Oxford, UK: Oxford University Press, 2009.
Engle, Sam Marie, and Benjamin P. Scafidi Jr. *Is It Better for Michael and Maya: Contracting for the Management of Public Schools*. Atlanta: Research Atlanta, 1999.
Farmer, Ashley D. *Remaking Black Power: How Black Women Transformed an Era*. Chapel Hill: University of North Carolina Press, 2018.
Fulilove, Mindy Thompson. *Rootshock: How Tearing Up Neighborhoods Hurts America and What We Can Do about It*. 2nd ed. New York: New York University Press, 2016.
Garrow, David. *Bearing the Cross: Martin Luther King Jr. and the Southern Christian Leadership Conference*. 1986. Reprint, New York: William Morrow Paperbacks, 2015.
Georgia Housing and Financial Authority. *Profiles of Homelessness in Georgia*. Atlanta: Georgia Housing and Financial Authority, 1994.
Godshalk, David Fort. *Veiled Visions: The 1906 Atlanta Race Riot and the Reshaping of American Race Relations*. Chapel Hill: University of North Carolina Press, 2006.
Goings, Kenneth, and Raymond A. Mohl, eds. *The New African American Urban History*. Thousand Oaks, CA: Sage, 1996.
Grady-Willis, Winston. *Challenging US Apartheid: Atlanta and Black Struggles for Human Rights, 1960–1977*. Durham, NC: Duke University Press, 2006.
Gramsci, Antonio. *Selections from the Prison Notebooks of Antonio Gramsci*. Edited and translated by Quinton Hoare and Geoffrey Nowell Smith. 1971. New York: International, 2014.
Hallgren, Kristin, Naihobe Gonzalez, Kevin Kelly, Alicia Demers, and Brian Gill. *Year 2 Report of the Atlanta Public Schools Turnaround Strategy*. Princeton, NJ: Mathematica Policy Research, 2019.
Hartshorn, Truman, and Keith Ihlanfeldt. *The Dynamics of Change: An Analysis of Growth in Metropolitan Atlanta over the Past Two Decades*. Atlanta: Research Atlanta, 1993.
Harvey, David. *A Brief History of Neoliberalism*. New York: Oxford University Press, 2005.
Hill, Karlos K. *Beyond the Rope: The Impact of Lynching on Black Culture and Memory*. Cambridge: Cambridge University Press, 2016.
Hill, Lauren Warren, and Julia Rabig, eds. *The Business of Black Power: Community Development, Capitalism, and Corporate Responsibility in Postwar America*. Rochester, NY: University of Rochester Press, 2012.
Hillier, Amy, and Benjamin Chrisinger. "The Reality of Urban Food Deserts and What Low-Income Food Shoppers Need." In *Social Policy and Social Justice*, edited by John L. Jackson, 74–86. Philadelphia: University of Pennsylvania Press, 2017.
———. *Social Policy and Social Justice*. Philadelphia: University of Pennsylvania Press, 2017.
Hirsch, Arnold R. *Making the Second Ghetto: Race and Housing in Chicago 1940–1960*. Historical Studies of Urban America. Chicago: University of Chicago Press, 2009.
Hobson, Maurice J. *The Legend of the Black Mecca: Politics and Class in the Making of Modern Atlanta*. Chapel Hill: University of North Carolina Press, 2017.

Holmes, Robert. *Maynard Jackson*. Miami: Barnhardt and Ashe, 2011.

———. *The Status of Black Atlanta 1993*. Atlanta: Southern Center for Studies in Public Policy at Clark Atlanta University, 1993.

Hornsby, Alton P., Jr. *Black Power in Dixie: A Political History of African Americans in Atlanta*. Gainesville: University Press of Florida, 2009.

———. *A Short History of Black Atlanta, 1847–1993*. E-Booktime, 2015.

Hunter, Tera J. *To 'Joy My Freedom: Southern Black Women's Lives and Labors after the Civil War*. Cambridge, MA: Harvard University Press, 1997.

Ioanid, Radu. *The Iasi Pogrom, June–July 1941: A Photo Documentary from the Holocaust in Romania*. Indianapolis: Indiana University Press, 2017.

Jenkins, Herbert. *Keeping the Peace: A Police Chief Looks at His Job*. New York: Harper and Row, 1970.

Johnson, Cedric. *Revolutionaries to Race Leaders: Black Power and the Making of African American Politics*. Minneapolis: University of Minnesota Press, 2007.

Jones, Brian. "The Socialist Case for Reparations." In Cha-Jua, Berry, and Franklin, *Reparations and Reparatory Justice*, 178–89.

Jones, Mack H. *Knowledge, Power and Black Politics: Collected Essays*. Albany: State University of New York Press, 2014.

Keating, Larry. *Atlanta: Race, Class, and Urban Expansion*. Philadelphia: Temple University Press, 2001.

Keith, M., and A. Rogers, eds. *Hollow Promises? Rhetoric and Reality in the Inner City*. London: Mansell, 1991.

Klier, John D., and Shlomo Lambroza, eds. *Pogrom: Anti-Jewish Violence in Modern Russian History*. New York: Cambridge University Press, 2004.

Kneebone, Elizabeth, and Emily Garr. *The Suburbanization of Poverty: Trends in Metropolitan America, 2000–2008*. Brookings Institution, January 20, 2010. www.brookings.edu/articles/the-suburbanization-of-poverty-trends-in-metropolitan-america-2000-to-2008/.

Koditschek, Theodore, Sundiata K. Cha-Jua, and Helen Neville, eds. *Race Struggles*. Urbana: University of Illinois Press, 2009.

Kornbluh, Peter. *The Pinochet File: A Declassified Dossier on Atrocity and Accountability*. 2nd ed. New York: New Press, 2013.

Kotz, David M., Terrence McDonough, and Michael Reich. *Social Structures of Accumulation: The Political Economy of Growth and Crisis*. Cambridge: Cambridge University Press, 1994.

Kruse, Kevin. *White Flight: Atlanta and the Making of Modern Conservatism*. Princeton, NJ: Princeton University Press, 2013.

Kusmer, Kenneth. *A Ghetto Takes Shape: Black Cleveland, 1870–1930*. Urbana: University of Illinois Press, 1978.

Laska, S., and D. Spain, eds. *Back to the City: Issues in Neighborhood Renovation*. Elmsford, NY: Pergamon, 1980.

Logan, John R., and Harvey L. Molotch. *Urban Fortunes: The Political Economy of Place*. Berkeley: University of California Press, 1989.

Logan, Rayford C. *The Betrayal of the Negro: From Rutherford B. Hayes to Woodrow Wilson*. Cambridge, MA: Da Capo, 1997.

Lumpkins, Charles L. *American Pogrom: The East St. Louis Race Riot and Black Politics*. Athens: Ohio University Press, 2008.
MacLean, Nancy. *Democracy in Chains: The Deep History of the Radical Right's Stealth Plan for America*. New York: Penguin Books, 2018.
Marable, Manning. *Race, Reform, and Rebellion: The Second Reconstruction and Beyond in Black America, 1945–2006*. 3rd ed. Jackson: University Press of Mississippi, 2007.
Marx, Karl. *The Class Struggles in France (1848–1850)*. New York: International, 1964.
———. *The Economic and Philosophic Manuscripts of 1844*. Mineola, NY: Dover Publications, 2007.
———. *The Eighteenth Brumaire of Louis Bonaparte*. Translated by Daniel De Leon. New York: International, 1994.
———. "Estranged Labor." In *The Marx and Engels Reader*, 2nd ed., edited by Robert C. Tucker. New York: W. W. Norton, 1978.
Marx, Karl, and Friedrich Engels. *Capital: A Critique of Political Economy*. Vol. 1. New York: Random House, 1906.
———. *Capital: A Critique of Political Economy*. Vol. 2. Translated by David Fernbach. New York: Penguin Books, 1992.
———. *Collected Works*. Vol. 19, *Marx and Engels: 1861–1864*. New York: International, 1984.
Massey, Douglas S., and Nancy A. Denton. *American Apartheid: Segregation and the Making of the Underclass*. Cambridge, MA: Harvard University Press, 1993.
McAdam, Doug. *Political Process and the Development of Black Insurgency*. Chicago: University of Chicago Press, 1982.
McCormack, Richard, ed. *Manufacturing a Better Future for America*. Washington, DC: Alliance for American Manufacturing, 2009.
Merriman, David. *Improving Tax Increment Financing (TIF) for Economic Development*. Lincoln Institute of Land Policy, September 2018. www.lincolninst.edu/publications/policy-focus-reports/improving-tax-increment-financing-tif-economic-development/.
Metropolitan Atlanta Coalition of 100 Black Women. *The Status of African American Women*. Atlanta: Metropolitan Atlanta Coalition of 100 Black Women, 1992.
Metropolitan Crime Commission. *Crime in Metro Atlanta: 1989–1993*. Atlanta: Metropolitan Crime Commission, 1993.
Mixon, Gregory. *The Atlanta Riot: Race, Class, and Violence in a New South City*. Gainesville: University Press of Florida, 2005.
Morris, Aldon. *The Origins of the Civil Rights Movement: Black Communities Organizing for Change*. New York: Free Press, 1986.
Moses, Wilson J. *The Golden Age of Black Nationalism, 1850–1925*. New York: Oxford University Press, 1978.
Myerson, Deborah L. *Community Development Corporations Working with For-Profit Developers*. Washington, DC: Urban Land Institute, 2002.
Neary, John. *Julian Bond: Black Rebel*. New York: William Morrow, 1971.
Onaci, Edward. *Free the Land: The Republic of New Afrika and the Pursuit of a Black Nation-State*. Chapel Hill: University of North Carolina Press, 2021.

Osofsky, Gilbert. *Harlem: The Making of a Ghetto; Negro New York, 1890–1930*. New York: Harper and Row, 1966.

Payne, Charles M. *I've Got the Light of Freedom: The Organizing Tradition and the Mississippi Freedom Struggle*. Berkeley: University of California Press, 1995.

Peterson, Paul E., ed. *The New Urban Reality*. Washington, DC: Brookings Institute, 1985.

Polanyi, Karl Paul. *The Great Transformation: The Political and Economic Origins of Our Time*. Boston: Beacon, 2001.

Poulantzas, Nicos. *State Power Socialism*. Translated by P. Camiller. London: Macmillan Books, 1991.

Prather, Leon H. *We Have Taken a City: Wilmington Racial Massacre and Coup in 1898*. Cranbury, NJ: Dram Tree Books, 2006.

Ranciere, Jacques. *Le philosophe et se pauvres*. Paris: Flammarion, 2007.

Reed, Adolph, Jr. *Stirrings in the Jug: Black Politics in the Post-segregation Era*. Minneapolis: University of Minnesota Press, 1999.

Reich, Robert. *The Work of Nations: Preparing Ourselves for 21st Century Capitalism*. New York: Vintage Books, 1992.

Research Atlanta. *The Other Side of the Tax Problem*. Atlanta: Research Atlanta, 1974.

Rivlin, Gary. *Broke, USA: How the Working Poor Became Big Business*. New York: HarperCollins, 2010.

Ross, Martha, and Nicole Bateman. *Meet the Low-Wage Workforce*. Washington, DC: Metropolitan Policy Program at Brookings, 2019.

Russo, John, and Sherry Lee Linkon. "The Social Costs of Deindustrialization." In *Manufacturing a Better Future for America*, edited by Richard McCormack, 183–215. New York: Alliance for American Manufacturing, 2009.

Rutheiser, Charles. *Imagineering Atlanta: The Politics of Place in the City of Dreams*. London: Verso Books, 1996.

Ryan-Collins, Josh, Toby Lloyd, and Laurie MacFarlane. *Rethinking the Economics of Land and Housing*. London: Zed Books, 2017.

Self, Robert O. *American Babylon: Race and Struggle in Postwar Oakland*. Princeton, NJ: Princeton University Press, 2005.

Shanin, Teodor, ed. *Late Marx and the Russian Road: Marx and the Peripheries of Capitalism*. New York: Monthly Review Press, 1983.

Sjoquist, David L., ed. *The Atlanta Paradox: A Volume in the Multi-city Study of Urban Inequality*. New York: Russell Sage Foundation, 2000.

Smith, David M. *Geography, Inequality, and Society*. New York: Cambridge University Press, 1987.

Smith, Neil. *The New Urban Frontier: Gentrification and the Revanchist City*. London: Routledge, 1996.

———. *Uneven Development: Nature, Capital, and the Production of Space*. Oxford: Oxford University Press, 1984.

Spear, Allan. *Black Chicago: The Making of a Negro Ghetto, 1890–1920*. Chicago: University of Chicago Press, 1969.

Stack, Carol. *All Our Kin: Strategies for Survival in the Black Community*. 7th ed. New York: Basic Books, 2008.

Stanford, Karin, Akinyele Umoja, and Jasmin Young, eds. *Black Power Encyclopedia: From "Black Is Beautiful" to "Urban Uprisings."* Santa Barbara, CA: ABC-CLIO Books, 2018.

Stone, Clarence N. *Economic Growth and Neighborhood Discontent: System Bias in the Urban Renewal Program of Atlanta.* Chapel Hill: University of North Carolina Press, 1976.

Stone, Clarence N., and Robert P. Stoker, eds. *Urban Neighborhoods in a New Era: Revitalization Politics in the Postindustrial City.* Chicago: University of Chicago Press, 2015.

Sugrue, Thomas. *Origins of the Urban Crisis: Race and Inequality in Postwar Detroit.* Princeton, NJ: Princeton University Press, 2014.

Tarrow, Sidney. *Power in Movement: Social Movements, Collective Action, and Politics.* New York: Cambridge University Press, 1994.

Thompson, E. P. *The Making of the English Working Class.* Harmondsworth, UK: Penguin Books, 1968.

Touraine, Alain. *Beyond Neoliberalism.* Cambridge, UK: Polity, 2001.

Trotter, Joe William. *Black Milwaukee: The Making of an Industrial Proletariat, 1915–1945.* Urbana: University of Illinois Press, 1985.

Tucker, Robert C., ed. *The Marx and Engels Reader.* 2nd revised and enlarged ed. New York: W. W. Norton, 1978.

Ture, Kwame, and Charles Hamilton. *Black Power: The Politics of Liberation.* 1967. Reprint, New York: Vintage Books, 1992.

Turner, Lou. "Toward a Black Radical Critique of Political Economy." *Black Scholar* 40, no. 1 (2010): 7–19.

Tuttle, William M. *Race Riot: Chicago in the Red Summer of 1919.* Urbana: University of Illinois Press, 1970.

Van der Pijl, Kees, and Assassi D. Wigan. *Global Regulation: Managing Crises after the Imperial Turn.* London: Palgrave Macmillan, 2004.

Vryonis, Speros. *The Mechanism of Catastrophe: The Turkish Pogrom of September 6–7, 1955, and Destruction of the Greek Community of Istanbul.* Ann Arbor: University of Michigan Press, 2005. Digitized July 14, 2008.

Weiss, Peter. *The Persecution and Assassination of Jean-Paul Marat as Performed by the Inmates of the Asylum Charenton under the Direction of the Marquis de Sade.* Woodstock, IL: Dramatic, 1964.

Wells, Wyatt. *American Capitalism, 1945–2000: Continuity and Change from Mass Production to the Information Society.* American Way Series. Chicago: Ivan R. Dee, 2003.

Whalen, Charles J., ed. *Political Economy for the 21st Century: Contemporary Views on the Trend of Economics.* Armonk, NY: M. E. Sharpe, 1995.

Wilson, William Julius. *The Declining Significance of Race.* Chicago: University of Chicago Press, 1978.

———. *The Truly Disadvantaged: The Inner City, the Underclass, and Public Policy.* Chicago: University of Chicago Press, 1987.

Woodward, Komozi. *A Nation within a Nation: Amiri Baraka (Leroi Jones) and Black Power Politics.* Chapel Hill: University of North Carolina Press, 1999.

Wright, Erik Olin. *Class Counts: Comparative Studies in Class Analysis*. Studies in Marxism Series. New York: Cambridge University Press, 1997.
Yette, Samuel F. *The Choice: The Issue of Black Survival in America*. Silver Spring, MD: Cottage Books, 1971.
Zipperstein, Steven J. *Pogrom: Kishinev and the Tilt of History*. New York: W. W. Norton, 2019.
Zuberi, Tukufu. *Thicker Than Blood: How Racial Statistics Lie*. Minneapolis: University of Minnesota Press, 2003.
Zukin, Sharon. *Loft Living: Culture and Capital in Urban Change*. Baltimore: Johns Hopkins University Press, 1982.

Dissertations and Theses

Cook, Karen J. "Atlanta Public Schools Case Study: A Tale of Two Schools." Master's thesis, Georgia State University, 2013.
Howard, Ashley M. "Prairie Fires: Urban Rebellions as Black Working Class Politics in Three Midwestern Cities." PhD diss., University of Illinois at Urbana-Champaign, 2012.
Waugh-Benton, Monica. "Strike Fever: Labor Unrest, Civil Rights, and the Left in Atlanta, 1972." Master's thesis, Georgia State University, 2006.

Journal Articles

Abney, F. Glenn, and John D. Hutcheson. "Race, Representation, and Trust: Changes in Attitude after the Election of a Black Mayor." *Public Opinion Quarterly* 45, no. 1 (Spring 1981): 91–101.
Allen-Taylor, J. Douglas. "Black Political Power: Mayors, Municipalities, and Money." 20th anniversary issue, *Race, Poverty, and the Environment* 17, no. 1 (Spring 2010): 70–74.
Anglin, Mary K. "Feminist Perspectives on Structural Violence." *Identities* 5, no. 2 (2010): 145–51.
Arena, John. "Bringing in the Black Working Class: The Black Urban Regime Strategy." *Science and Society* 75, no. 2 (April 2011): 153–79.
Bacote, Clarence A. "The Negro in Atlanta Politics." *Phylon (1940–1956)* 16, no. 4 (1955): 333–50.
———. "William Finch, Negro Councilman and Political Activities in Atlanta during Early Reconstruction." *Journal of Negro History* 40, no. 4 (October 1955): 341–64.
Berry, B. "Inner City Futures: An American Dilemma Revisited." *Transactions of the Institute of British Geographers* 5, no. 1 (1980): 1–28.
Bondi, L. "Gender Divisions and Gentrification: A Critique." *Transactions of the Institute of British Geographers*, n.s., 16 (1991a): 290–98.
Boyle, M. "Still Top Our Agenda? Neil Smith and the Reconciliation of Capital and Consumer Approaches to the Explanation of Gentrification." *Scottish Geographical Magazine*, no. 111 (1995): 120–23.
Bryce, Harrington J., Gloria J. Cousar, and William McCoy. "Housing Problems of Black Mayor Cities." *Annals of the American Academy of Political and Social Science*, no. 439 (September 1978): 80–89.

Bullock, Charles S., III. "The Election of Blacks in the South: Preconditions and Consequences." *American Journal of Political Science* 19, no. 4 (November 1975): 727–39.

———. "Racial Crossover Voting and the Election of Black Officials." *Journal of Politics* 46, no. 1 (February 1984): 238–51.

Carnegie, Andrew. "The Gospel of Wealth." *North American Review*, no. 391 (June 1889): 653–64.

Cha-Jua, Sundiata K. "C. L. R. James, Blackness, and the Making of a Neo-Marxist Diasporan Historiography." *Nature, Society, and Thought*, no. 11 (Spring 1998): 53–89.

———. "The New Nadir: The Contemporary Black Racial Formation." *Black Scholar* 40, no. 1 (2010): 38–58.

Cha-Jua, Sundiata K., and Clarence Lang. "The Long Movement as Vampire: Temporal Spatial Fallacies in Recent Black Freedom Studies." *Journal of African American History* 92, no. 2 (Spring 2007): 265–88.

Clark, E. "On Gaps in Gentrification Theory." *Housing Studies*, no. 7 (1991): 16–26.

———. "Toward a Copenhagen Interpretation of Gentrification." *Urban Studies* 31, no. 7 (1994): 1033–42.

Eisinger, Peter K. "Black Employment in Municipal Jobs: The Impact of Black Political Power." *American Political Science Review* 76, no. 2 (June 1982): 380–92.

Foner, Philip S. "Organized Labor and the Black Worker in the 1970's." *Insurgent Sociologist* 8, no. 2 and 3 (Fall 1978): 87–95.

Franklin, Vincent P. "The Philadelphia Race Riot of 1918." *Pennsylvania Magazine of History and Biography* 99, no. 3 (July 1975): 336–50.

Galtung, Johan. "Violence, Peace, and Peace Research." *Journal of Peace Research* 6, no. 3 (1969): 167–91.

Gundersen, Craig, Brent Kreider, and John Pepper. "The Economics of Food Insecurity in the United States." *Applied Economic Perspectives and Policy* 33, no. 3 (Autumn 2011): 281–303.

Hall, Jacquelyn Dowd. "The Long Civil Rights Movement and the Political Uses of the Past." *Journal of American History* 91, no. 4 (March 2005): 1233–63.

Hamnett, C. "The Blind Men and the Elephant: The Explanation of Gentrification." *Transactions of the Institute of British Geographers*, n.s., 16 (1991): 173–89.

Hein, Virginia H. "The Image of 'a City Too Busy to Hate': Atlanta in the 1960s." *Phylon (1960–)* 33, no. 3 (1972): 205–21.

Hill, Herbert. "Black Protest and the Struggle for Union Democracy." *Issues in Industrial Society* 1, no. 1 (1969): 20–48.

———. "Myth-Making as Labor History: Herbert Gutman and the United Mine Workers of America." *International Journal of Politics, Culture, and Society* 2, no. 2 (Winter 1988): 132–200.

———. "Racism within Organized Labor: A Report of Five Years of the AFL-CIO, 1955–1960." *Journal of Negro Education* 30, no. 2 (Spring 1961): 109–18.

Hornsby, Alton P., Jr. "Andrew Jackson Young: Mayor of Atlanta, 1982–1990." *Journal of Negro History* 77, no. 3 (Summer 1992): 159–82.

Howard, Ashley. "Whose Streets? Wielding Urban Revolts as Political Tools." *Journal of African American History* 107, no. 2 (Spring 2022): 238–65.

Jennings, Keith. "The Politics of Race, Class, and Gentrification in the ATL." *Trotter Review* 23, no. 1 (2016): 1–38.

Jessop, B. "Liberalism, Neoliberalism, and Urban Governance: A State-Theoretical Perspective." *Antipode* 34, no. 3 (2002): 452–72.

Jones, Mack H. "Black Political Empowerment in Atlanta: Myth and Reality." *Annals of the American Academy of Political and Social Science*, no. 439 (September 1978): 90–117.

———. "Political Philosophy and Public Assistance in Liberal Society." *Review of Black Political Economy* 2, no. 1 (April 1980): 9–17.

Khiterer, Victoria. "The October 1905 Pogroms and the Russian Authorities." *Nationalities Papers* 43, no. 5 (September 2015): 788–803.

Kraus, Neil. "The Significance of Race in Urban Politics: The Limitations of Regime Theory." *Race and Society*, no. 7 (2004): 95–111.

Lands, LeeAnn. "Emmaus House and Atlanta's Anti-Poverty Movements." *Atlanta Studies*, April 2, 2015. https://atlantastudies.org/2015/04/28/emmaus-house-and-atlantas-anti-poverty-movements/.

Leaver, Erik, and Jenny Shin. "Iraq Quagmire: Costs of War." *Institute for Policy Studies*, March 27, 2008.

Lees, L. "Gentrification in London and New York: An Atlantic Gap?" *Housing Studies* 9, no. 2 (1994): 199–217.

Ley, D. "Liberal Ideology and the Postindustrial City." *Annals of the Association of American Geographers*, no. 70 (1980): 238–58.

Lipton, S. G. "Evidence of a Central City Revival." *Journal of the American Institute of Planners*, no. 43 (1977): 136–47.

Mammen, Sheila, Jean W. Bauer, and Leslie Richards. "Understanding Persistent Food Insecurity: A Paradox of Place and Circumstance." *Social Indicators Research* 92, no. 1 (May 2009): 151–68.

McGrath, Susan M. "From Tokenism to Community Control: Political Symbolism in the Desegregation of Atlanta's Public Schools, 1961–1973." *Georgia Historical Quarterly* 79, no. 4 (Winter 1995): 842–72.

Mead, M. Nathaniel. "Urban Issues: The Sprawl of Food Deserts." *Environmental Health Perspectives* 116, no. 8 (August 2008): A335.

Mendenhall, Ruby. "The Political Economy of Black Housing: From the Housing Crisis of the Great Migrations to the Subprime Mortgage Crisis." *Black Scholar* 40, no. 1 (2010): 20–37.

Morris, Aldon. "Reflections of Social Movement Theory: Criticisms and Proposals." *Contemporary Sociology* 29, no. 3 (May 2000): 445–54.

Oppenheimer, Martin. "The Sub-proletariat: Dark Skins and Dirty Work." *Critical Sociology* 4, no. 7 (1974): 7–22.

Rosenthal, Susan. "Philanthropy: The Capitalist Art of Deception." *Socialist Review* no. 402 (2015). https://socialistworker.co.uk/socialist-review-archive/philanthropy-capitalist-art-deception/.

Rothwell, Jonathan, and Douglas S. Massey. "The Effect of Density Zoning on Racial Segregation in U.S. Urban Areas." *Urban Affairs Review* 44, no. 6 (2009): 779–806.

Smith, Neil. "Blind Man's Bluff, or Hamnett's Philosophical Individualism in Search of Gentrification." *Transactions of the Institute of British Geographers*, n.s., 17 (1992): 110–15.

———. "Gentrification and Capital: Theory, Practice, and Ideology in Society Hill." *Antipode* 11, no. 3 (1979): 24–35.

———. "Gentrifying Theory." *Scottish Geographical Magazine*, no. 111 (1995): 124–26.

———. "Toward a Theory of Gentrification: A Back to the City Movement by Capital, Not People." *Journal of the American Planning Association*, no. 45 (1979): 538–48.

Sternlieb, G., and J. Hughes. "The Uncertain Future of the Central City." *Urban Affairs Quarterly* 18, no. 4 (1983): 455–72.

Stuff, Janice E., Michelle LaCour, Xianglin Du, Frank Franklin, Yan Liu, Sheryl Hughes, Ron Peters, and Theresa A. Nicklas. "The Prevalence of Food Insecurity and Associated Factors among Households with Children in Head Start Programs in Houston, Texas and Birmingham, Alabama." *Race, Gender and Class* 16, no. 3/4 (2009): 31–47.

Wenger, Morton G. "State Responses to Afro-American Rebellion: Internal Neocolonialism and the Rise of a New Black Petit Bourgeoisie." In "Race and Class in Twentieth Century Capitalist Development," special issue, *Insurgent Sociologist* 10, no. 2 (1980): 61–72.

Wilkes, Robert. "Examining President Clinton's Response to Welfare." *Endarch* 1997, no. 1 (Spring 1997): 14–35.

———. "Homelessness in the City of Atlanta." *Endarch* 1997, no. 2 (Summer 1997): 28–45.

Williams, Jennifer A. "The End of an Era: The Case of Public Housing in Atlanta, Georgia." *Agora Journal of Urban Planning and Design*, no. 2010 (2010): 60–63.

Zukin, Sharon. "Gentrification: Culture and Capital in the Urban Core." *American Review of Sociology*, no. 13 (1987): 129–47.

Unpublished Sources

Austin, Algernon. "Cultural Black Nationalism and the Meaning of Black Power." Paper presented at the annual meeting of the American Sociological Association, Atlanta, GA, August 16, 2003.

Cabral, Amilcar. "The Weapon of Theory." Address delivered to the Tricontinental Conference of the Peoples of Asia, Africa, and Latin America, Havana, Cuba, 1966.

Davis, Morris A., and Michael G. Palumbo. "The Price of Land in Large US Cities." Working paper, received November 2006, revised 2007.

Geltner, David. "Commercial Real Estate and the 1990–91 Recession in the United States." First draft, prepared for the Korean Development Institute, January 2013. Microsoft Word file.

Turner, Lou. "Los Angeles Rebellion '92: Whither Black Radicalism?" Paper presented at the Association of the Study of African American Life and History Annual Conference, Montgomery, AL, 2022.

———. "Notes on Henry Louis Taylor and Sam Cole, 'Structural Racism and Efforts to Radically Reconstruct the Inner-City Built Environment.'" Working paper, June 3, 2014.

———. "Reason, Rebellion, and Revolution: A Marxist Humanist Statement on the Black Dimension." Unpublished manuscript, August 2000. Microsoft Word file.

Index

Page numbers in italics refer to illustrations.

Abernathy, Ralph, 123–24
Abney, Michael, 1, 86
ACLU (American Civil Liberties Union), 228, 231
ACOC. *See* Atlanta Chamber of Commerce
ACOG (Atlanta Committee for the Olympic Games), 228, 231
ADNP (Atlanta Development Neighborhood Partnership), 212, 237
affirmative action, 175
AFSCME (American Federation of State, County, and Municipal Employees), 101–6, 108, 110, 217, 224–25
agency-laden institutions, 21–22. *See also* local movement centers
AHA. *See* Atlanta Housing Authority
Allen, Ivan, Jr., 39, 44, 45
American Civil Liberties Union (ACLU), 228, 231
American Federation of State, County, and Municipal Employees (AFSCME), 101–6, 108, 110, 217, 224–25
Anglin, Mary, 24
anti-Black laws, 111–12
anti-Black violence, by Atlanta police, 13, 21, 64, 85, 86–87; killings of Black males, 112, *112*, 116–17
anti-working-class policies/actions, 30–31, 97, 106, 131, 176, 182, 208–9
A'NUFF (Atlanta Neighborhoods United for Fairness), 31, 168, 189–94, 205
APS. *See* Atlanta Public Schools

Arena, John, 17, 25, 234–35, 286
Arrington, Marvin, 203, 217
Arrington, Richard, 92–93
Atlanta, 15, 173–74, 177, 244–58, 249, 261, *261*: apartheid structure of, 11, 13, 16; central neighborhoods, 40; community eligibility provision areas, 41; film production in, 285–86; inner-city, 180, 183; militarization of downtown, 89; murders of children, 9, 90, 125–31; population growth, 182–83; revenue crisis of 1974–1979, 95–101, 104
Atlanta Black leadership, 35–36, 134, 139–42, 160–62, 186, 253, 287
Atlanta bourgeoisie, 38–39, 88–89, 170
Atlanta capitalists, 12, 117, 147, 148, 163, 212–13; Black Atlantan capitalists, 9, 17, 27
Atlanta Chamber of Commerce (ACOC), 1, 88, 89, 106, 185, 245; Central Atlanta Progress, 31, 138–44, 146, 195; international capital and, 138, 145–47, 150, 152
Atlanta city council, 160, 161, 199, 201, 202; Atlanta city employees and, 105–6; Georgia Dome, Vine City displacement and, 163–66
Atlanta city employees, 34–36, 101–10
Atlanta city hall, 96, 133, 141, 143–44, 198, 201, 203; anti-Black laws and, 111–12; Atlanta child murders and, 125, 126, 128–31; BCAPR and, 114, 115; Black Atlanta workers vs., 88, 89, 103–7, 109; gentrification in Atlanta and, 143–44,

333

Atlanta city hall (continued)
    185; international investment and, 133, 145, 148
Atlanta Committee for the Olympic Games (ACOG), 188, 190–94
Atlanta Constitution, 28, 82, 120
Atlanta Daily World, 28, 89, 93, 193, 292n10
Atlanta Development Neighborhood Partnership (ADNP), 212, 237
Atlanta elites, 7–14, 134, 146, 148, 159
Atlanta Housing Authority (AHA), 41, 133, 173–74; displacement of low-income Black Atlantans by, 200–201; public housing and, 75–77, 138–42, 151, 204–6, 252–58
Atlanta Journal, 28, 76, 89, 108, 192
Atlanta Journal-Constitution, 238, 256
Atlanta leadership, 1–2, 3, 9, 30, 117–19, 128–31; anti-working-class policies/actions of, 106, 182; Black Atlantan autonomy and, 89; gentrification and, 31–32, 179, 188, 196; international capital and, 12, 31, 129, 134–38, 149–50. *See also* Atlanta Black leadership
Atlanta media, 89, 120, 122, 191–94, 256; propagandizing crime against poor Blacks, 118, 119, 157
Atlanta metro, 259–60, 260. *See also* working-class Black Atlanta metro suburbs
Atlanta Neighborhoods United for Fairness (A'NUFF), 31, 168, 189–94, 205
Atlanta officials. *See* Black elected officials
Atlanta petty bourgeoisie, 27, 82–85, 88–89, 170
Atlanta police, 30, 110, 123–28, 131, 198, 199, 204–5; BCAPR and, 111, 114; Black alternative media and, 120, 122; Black Atlanta neighborhoods and, 31, 72, 85, 89, 90, 195; Black Atlantan uprisings and, 86–89; BPP and, 113–14; BUR and, 90, 128; protests by Black Atlantans against, 112, 112, 115–16; STAKE-OUT squad, 111, 116, 117, 122; strikes and, 74, 75, 76, 82, 83; Summerhill rebellion and, 38–39, 44–45. *See also* anti-Black violence, by Atlanta police
Atlanta power brokers, 8, 85, 147, 166, 170, 259–60: ACOG and, 188; Atlanta child murders and, 129–31; Great Recession and, 248; homeless Atlantans and, 202; housing crisis caused by, 199; Jackson, Maynard, and, 108, 110; neoliberalization and, 217; Olympic Games and, 31, 203, 205; Olympic gentrification and, 191–93; underground economy and, 205; war veterans and, 196; working-class Black Atlantans vs., 6, 31, 90, 93, 108–10, 129–31, 240
Atlanta Public Schools (APS), 60, 62, 62, 223–34; Board of Education, 61, 63, 142, 225, 226, 230. *See also* Black Atlanta public schools
Atlanta universities, 63. *See also names of specific universities*
Atlanta University Center, 56, 57, 109
Atlanta Voice, 28, 52, 55, 61, 130, 139, 165, 238; A'NUFF and, 191–93; Atlanta police and, 120, 122, 123, 125–26, 205; privatization of Atlanta schools and, 227, 229
Auburn Avenue, 159–62, 213–15, 237
auto manufacturing, 153–54, 243, 265–66
Azar, Donald, 63–64

Bankhead Courts, 60–62, 156–57
Barnett, Harold, 207–8
Baron, Harold "Hal," 278, 279, 281
BCAPR. *See* Black Citizens Against Police Repression
Beckham, Harold, 2
Bedford Pine neighborhood, 139–42, *140*
Bell, Camille, 86, 126–30
Bell, Eldrin, 203
BEOs. *See* Black elected officials
Bird. See Great Speckled Bird

334 Index

Black Atlanta communities. *See* working-class Black Atlanta neighborhoods
Black Atlanta intraracial class conflict, 6, 8, 9, 12, 13, 14; Black Power and, 36–37, 45, 46; in Mead wildcat strike, 22, 78–79, 81, 85
Black Atlantan capitalist class, 9, 17, 27
Black Atlanta neighborhoods, 58–59; Atlanta police and, 31, 72, 85, 89, 90, 116–20, 122, 195. *See also* working-class Black Atlanta neighborhoods
Black Atlantan elites, 9–15, 20, 100–101, 108; gentrification and, 94, 178–79, 214–15
Black Atlantans, 112, *112*, 116–17, 199–200, 252–58; Atlanta elites vs., 7–12; Black majority of Atlanta, 39, 89, 292n12; BUR and, 93, 180–81; city worker sanitation strike (1970), 34–36; daily round of, 47–48, 51; exodus from inner-city Atlanta by, 183; Great Recession and, 173–74, 242–43, 246–58; inflation and, 42, 95, 96, 292n18; middle-class, 122, 224; New Nadir and, 205, 206; weakening of organizing capacity of, 90, 106–7, 110
Black Atlantan students, 59, 62, 63, 228–31
Black Atlantan unions, 71, 106. *See also* strikes
Black Atlantan working class. *See* working-class Black Atlantans
Black Atlanta public schools, 60–63, *62*, 142, 223–26, 230
Black Atlanta workers, 9, 20, 37–38, 167, 261–68, 316n55; Atlanta city hall vs., 88, 89, 103–6, 109; city employees, 42; jobs during Great Recession, 246–52; recession of 1970s and, 43. *See also* working-class Black Atlantans
Black Belt, 4, 49, 59, 67, 123, 127, 134; working-class Black Atlantan activists in, 2, 35, 56, 61, 63, 71, 75, 85
Black bourgeoisie, 54, 92, 100, 210–11, 239
Black businesses, 55–56, 91, 92

Black capitalism, 36, 54–56, 91–92. *See also* conservative nationalism
Black capitalist class, 9, 17, 27, 90, 91
Black Citizens Against Police Repression (BCAPR), 111, 114, 115
Black communality, 54
Black elected officials (BEOs), 90–91, 100, 108, 182, 183–85; ACOC and, 142; housing of working-class Black Atlantans and, 133. *See also* Black urban regime
Black firefighters movement, 67–68
Black history, 13, 17, 18, 279–80, 284, 287
Black leadership. *See* Atlanta Black leadership
Black neighborhoods. *See* Black Atlanta neighborhoods
Black Panther Party (BPP), 113–14, 116
Black petty bourgeoisie, 53, 73, 92, 93, 170, 252; activism and, 207–9, 239; empowerment zones and, 210–11, 212; sales tax and, 100–101; strikes and, 74, 83–85
Black policymakers, 281
Black political economy, 13, 28, 32, 56
Black Power, 8–9, 36–37, 45, 46, 59, 62; BUR and, 88, 91, 92, 112; conflict in Atlanta over, 52–57, 279; proto-nationalism and, 87; strikes and, 85; working-class Black Atlantan women and, 71, 72
Black Power movement, of Atlanta, 30, 45
Black radicals, Atlanta neocolonialism and, 120
Black restaurant workers strikes, 68, 69, 70, 73–75
Black urban regime (BUR), 92, 107, 136, 170, 212, 253–55; Atlanta city employees and, 104; Black Atlantans and, 93, 180–81; Jackson, Maynard, and, 94, 101, 106, 108, 128, 134, 147; low-income Black Atlantans vs., 88, 100, 128, 169, 198; Reed's conception of, 90, 91; working-class Black Atlantans and, 31, 88, 93, 97, 101, 106, 112, 128, 131, 182

Index   335

Black wages, 27, 43, 174, 178, 246–47, 251–52, 262–67
Black workers, 34, 153–54, 170–71, 182, 243, 285; American history and, 279–80, 284, 287; Black capitalism and, 54–56, 91–92; conservative nationalism and, 54–55; disciplining of, 286; labor studies on, 283–84; political economy and, 280; proletarianization of, 283; unions and, 280–81; in urban history, 18; wealthy Blacks and disregard for, 278
Bolden, Dorothy, 132
Bond, Julian, 45, 53
Boston, Thomas, 91
bourgeoisie, 27, 54, 92, 100, 210–11, 239; Atlanta bourgeoisie, 38–39, 88–89, 170; petty bourgeoisie and, 84. *See also* petty bourgeoisie
BPP. *See* Black Panther Party
Broad Street rebellion (1971), 86–89
Broward, Denise, 51, 241–42, 258
Brushworks Factory, 207, 208
BUR. *See* Black urban regime
Busbee, Georgia, 148

Cabral, Amilcar, 44
Campbell, Bill, 31, 161, 164, 181, 198, 199, 204, 210, 213, 216–18
Campbell, F. C. C., 55
CAP. *See* Central Atlanta Progress
capital, 3, 16, 93, 119, 264, 284; Atlanta city hall and, 185; domestic, 134, 151; gentrification and, 22, 23; subproletarianization of Black worker and, 10. *See also* international capital
capitalism, 6, 10, 15, 17, 46, 51–52, 170; Black Atlanta communities and, 93; Black capitalism, 36, 54–56, 91–92; corporate philanthropy and, 184; New Nadir and global, 171; nonprofits and, 25–26, 234; white capitalism, 55, 56, 92, 94
capitalist class, 9, 17, 27, 92; of Atlanta, 12, 117, 147, 148, 163, 212–13

capitalists, 55, 56, 92, 94, 196–98, 313n68
Carmichael, Stokely, 25, 45
Carson, Clayborne, 52
Carstarphen, Meria, 231–33
Carter, Ron, 113, 114, 115
Cato, Art, 132
CBD. *See* Central Business District
CDCs. *See* community development corporations
Central Atlanta Progress (CAP), 31, 138–44, 146, 195
Central Business District (CBD), 139, 146
CEP. *See* Community Education Partnership
Cha-Jua, Sundiata, 16, 17, 18–19, 293n50; New Nadir framework of, 27, 171, 285, 305n2
Church's Chicken restaurant strikes, 73–75
civil rights movement, 52–53, 293n50
Clark, Richard, 54–55
Clark Atlanta University, 28, 123, 169, 173, 180, 181, 215
Clark Howell, 141, 157, 185, 199–201
class, 13, 15, 16, 17, 18, 20–21, 27, 53; and anti-poor laws, 199, 201–3; Atlanta child murders and, 125, 128, 129; in Black Atlanta, 27, 87, 124, 177–79, 208, 209, 239. *See also* Black Atlanta intraracial class conflict
class warfare, 22, 32, 87, 170, 184–85, 242–58; of Atlanta power brokers, 93, 131; BEO management of funding for poor as, 183–85
Clayton, Ed, 28
Clayton County, 268
Clinton, Bill, 175–76, 210, 224
Cobb County, 267
Committee to Stop Children's Murders (STOP), 9, 126–31
communality, 54
community development corporations (CDCs), 211, 212, 213–14, 216, 236–38, 240

336   Index

Community Education Partnership (CEP), 227–31
Community Relations Commission (CRC), 60–61, 83
conservative nationalism, 36, 52, 53, 54–55. *See also* Black capitalism
corporate diversity philanthropy, 186–87
Cousins, Tom, 225–26
Cox, Kevin R., 47
CRC. *See* Community Relations Commission
crime, pathologizing and propagandizing, 117–19, 156–57, 196, 198–99, 238
crime in Atlanta, lumpenproletariat and violent, 196–98
criminalization of poor Atlantans, 195, 199, 201–3
cultural nationalism, 52, 53

daily round, 47–48, 51
Davis, Eva, 71, 72–75
Dean, Douglas, 193, 194, 238
deindustrialization, 95, 152, 177
DeKalb County, 264–66
Department of Housing and Urban Development, US (HUD), 254–55, 257
deproletarianization, 176
devalorization of property, 156–58, 238–39
displacement of low-income Black Atlantans, 139–42, 160–62, 200–201, 236–38, 240, 253–58; A'NUFF and, 168, 193, 205; by Black bourgeoisie, 239; by Black petty bourgeoisie, 170; Olympic Games and, 202; resident resistance to, 214. *See also* suburbanization of working-class Black Atlantans; urban removal of working-class Black Atlantans
displacement of working-class people, 236–38, 242, 270, 272
domestic capital, 134, 151
Dorsey, Hattie, 238
Douglas County, 258–59, 263–64

drugs, 201, 204–5, 252
Du Bois, W. E. B., 280, 282
Dunayevskaya, Raya, 1, 18

East Lake Meadows, 72–75, 110–11, 225–26, 227, 239
Edison Project, 225–26
Emmaus House, 41, 292n13
Emory University Black Student Alliance, 59
Empowerment Zone Board, 210–12
empowerment zones, 209–12
Engels, Friedrich, 184
enterprise zones, 210, 211. *See also* empowerment zones

Farmer, Dwanda, 1, 207
Federal Bureau of Investigation (FBI), 204–5
Ferguson, Gene, 168, 193
film production, in Atlanta, 285–86
Franklin, Shirley, 1, 31, 212, 232, 244–46
freedom, 1, 137
Friendship Baptist Church, 275–76
Friends of the City, 198
Fulton County stadium, 29, 188

Galtung, Johan, 24
GAMA (Greater Atlanta Ministerial Alliance), 230, 231
Gates, Harvey, 125, 126, 130
GBLF (Georgia Black Liberation Front), 56–57
gentrification, 7–8, 15, 22–23, 152, 281, 283; enterprise zones and, 210; myth-making about, 282; private/charter schools and, 233; structural violence of, 11–12, 24–25, 242; subproletarianization and, 13, 24, 32
gentrification in Atlanta, 2, 4, 5, 6, 147, 156–58, 239; Atlanta capitalists and, 212–13; Atlanta city hall and, 143–44; Atlanta leadership and, 31–32, 179, 196; Black Atlantan elites and, 94, 214–15; and Black petty

Index 337

gentrification in Atlanta (*continued*)
  bourgeoisie, 170, 207–8; corporate diversity philanthropy and, 185; historical materialist perspective on, 7–8; Jackson, Maynard, and, 160; low-income Black Atlantans and, 205, 241; neocolonialism in Black urban centers and, 11; neoliberalization in Atlanta and, 135, 159, 163, 167, 215–16; pathologizing and propagandizing crime and, 196, 238; privatization and, 233–34; public housing and, 205–6; repression of working-class Black Atlantans and, 88; sub-proletarianization of Black Atlanta workers and, 13, 242; suburbanization of working-class Black Atlantans and, 242, 263–64; working-class Black Atlantans and, 31–32, 88, 134, 167, 196, 214–16, 234, 242, 277. *See also* displacement of low-income Black Atlantans; Olympic gentrification
Georgia, 95–97, 98, 152, 243–44, 285; poverty in, 261, 284
Georgia Black Liberation Front (GBLF), 56–57
Georgia Dome stadium, 3, 162–67
Georgia Legislative Black Caucus, 244
Georgia Stadium Corporation, 3, 162–63
Georgia World Congress Center (GWCC), 138, 140, 145, 146, 152, 162, 165
ghettoization, 16, 17, 23
Gibson, Alma, 161, 162
Gipp, Big, 29
Glover, Renee, 253, 255, 257–58
Gold Coast, 178–79
Goodie Mob, 29
Grady Memorial Hospital, 219–23
Grady-Willis, Winston, 11, 45
Gramsci, Antonio, 234
grassroots revolutionary nationalism, 44, 46
Greater Atlanta Ministerial Alliance (GAMA), 230, 231

Great Recession, 171, 173–74, 242–43, 244–58, 277, 287
Great Speckled Bird, 28–29, 63, 81, 114, 155
Green, Marian, 133, 134
grocery store movement, 63–64, 65, 66
GWCC (Georgia World Congress Center), 138, 140, 145–46, 152, 162, 165

Hamilton, Charles, 25
Hartsfield International Airport, 151–52
Hayes, Tim, 56, 57
Hightower, Shirley, 254, 255
Hill, Jesse, Jr., 147
historical materialism, 7–8, 13–15, 22, 283
history, 1, 282; Black, 13, 17, 18, 279–80, 284, 287
Hobson, Maurice, 20
Holmes, Finley, 86, 101–2
homeless Atlantans, 199, 201–3, 269–72
Hornsby, Alton, Jr., 15
housing in Atlanta, 146, 173–74, 179, 199, 246. *See also* Atlanta Housing Authority; housing of working-class Black Atlantans; public housing in Atlanta
housing of working-class Black Atlantans, 72–75, 110, 133, 154–56, 173, 241; Atlanta city hall and, 133, 141, 143–44; Great Recession and, 173–74, 246; Jackson, Maynard, and, 133, 141, 142, 157, 160, 200; Olympic era lack of, 199; property abandonment and, 157; slum clearance, 41; Supreme Court and, 44. *See also* gentrification in Atlanta; urban removal of working-class Black Atlantans
Howard, Ashley, 44
HUD (Department of Housing and Urban Development, US), 254–55, 257

income of Atlantans. *See* low-income Atlantans
inflation, 42, 95, 96, 292n18
informal support networks, 49–51

338   Index

infrapolitics, 22
Inman, John, 114–17, 119–20, 122
international capital, 12, 31, 129, 134–38, 149–50, 167; ACOC and, 145–47, 152
international investment in Atlanta, 19, 129, 130; overseas recruitment of, 147–52; privatization in Atlanta and, 135–36, 146
internationalization of Atlanta, 2, 9, 11, 37, 134
international markets, Georgia businesses and, 152
interventions, capitalist, 170
intraracial class conflict, 17, 287. *See also* Black Atlanta intraracial class conflict

Jackson, Jesse, 57
Jackson, Maynard Holbrook, 13, 20, 21, 31, 36, 53, 185; Atlanta child murders and, 125, 126, 128, 129; Atlanta Police Department, 117, 122, 195, 198; Atlanta power brokers and, 108, 110; BUR and, 94, 101, 106, 108, 134, 147; housing of working-class Black Atlantans and, 133, 141, 142, 157, 160, 200; international investment and, 133, 147, 148; repression of working-class Black Atlantans and, 88, 89, 104, 110; revitalization of southwest Atlanta by, 180; sanitation strike (1977) and, 107–10; taxes and, 97–98, 100, 101, 104, 105; white capitalists and, 94; working-class Black Atlantans and, 88, 89, 94, 100, 101, 104–10, 117, 188
James, C. L. R., 18
Jenkins, Herbert, 89, 114
jobs in Atlanta, 246–52, 261–68, 316n55
Johnson, Cedric, 287
Jones, Mack H., 15, 28, 109

Kelley, Robin D. G., 22
King, Coretta Scott, 20, 21, 124, 134, 160–62, 215
King, Martin Luther, Jr., 108, 109, 159–62, 164

King, Martin Luther, Sr., 108
King, Rodney, 169
kinship networks, 50, 155, 272–73

labor, 14–15, 67–68, 180, 283–84; subproletarian, 249, 261, 267, 280, 285. *See also* strikes
Lakewood General Motors plant, 176–77
Lakewood Village, 237
Lewis, Boyd, 42
liberal pluralism, 36, 52, 53
Lithia Springs, 241–42, 258–59, 284–85
local movement centers, 21–22, 61
Logan, John, 46, 47
low-income Atlantans, 170, 189–94, 195, 198–203, 249, 261–62; poverty rate of, 182, 242–43; taxes and, 96–101, 99, 245
low-income Black Atlantans, 117–19, 139–42, 156–57, 160–62, 198–99, 238; areas of capital accumulation and isolation of, 3, 16, 93, 119; Atlanta bourgeoisie and, 38–39, 88; BUR vs., 88, 100, 128, 169, 198; disappearance of livable-wage labor for, 178; gentrification and, 205, 241; Young, Andrew, and, 181. *See also* working-class Black Atlantans
low-income Black neighborhoods. *See* working-class Black Atlanta neighborhoods
lumpenproletarianization, 170
lumpenproletariat, 196–98, 251, 308n88
Lumpkins, Charles, 23, 290n33
Lundy, Sam, 115–16

Mabry, Otie, 60, 61, 62
Malcolm X, 279
manufacturing, 153–54, 176–77, 243, 265–68
Marshall, Joel West, 54
MARTA (Metropolitan Atlanta Rapid Transit Authority), 103, 183, 212, 248, 263
Martin, C. T., 245
Marx, Karl, 14, 46, 102, 158, 196, 290n17

Massell, Sam, 57, 77, 89, 94
Mathiowetz, Dianne, 241
Matthews, Ethel Mae, 168, 189
Mayson Elementary School, 60
McFarland, William, 236–37
McKinley, Florence, 132, 159, 161, 162
Mead Caucus of Rank-and-File Workers (MCRFW), 22, 79–85
Mead wildcat strike (1972), 22, 78–85
Mechanicsville Community Freedom Center, 49, 50
Mendenhall, Ruby, 46
Mercedes-Benz Stadium, 3, 273–77
Metropolitan Atlanta Rapid Transit Authority (MARTA), 103, 183, 212, 248, 263
middle-class Black Atlantans, 122, 224
Miller, Sherman, 34, 79–81, 83, 85
mir (Russian peasantry), 14
Molotch, Harvey, 46, 47
Morath, David, 41
Morehouse College, 57
Morris, Aldon, 21
motels, extended-stay, 269–73
Mount Vernon Baptist Church, 275, 276
Munford, Dillard, 118, 119, 122

National Park Service, 161–62, 214
Neighborhood Planning Unit-M (NPU-M), 207–8
neighborhoods. *See* Black Atlanta neighborhoods
neighborhood social movement capacity (NSMC), 47, 51, 88, 122, 123
neocolonialism, 11, 120, 122, 235
neoliberalism, 134, 136
neoliberalization:, 134, 135, 136–37, 152, 234–35, 304n49; structural violence of, 23, 24–25, 152
neoliberalization in Atlanta, 135–37, 148, 217, 245, 262–63; gentrification and, 159, 163, 167, 215–16; working-class Black Atlantans and, 30–31, 133–34, 154–56, 159, 167, 215–16

New Nadir, 27, 134, 171, 175, 288, 305n2; Black Atlantans and, 205, 206; Black workers and, 170–71, 182, 285
New World Developers, 54
Nigeria, 147, 149
Nixon, Richard, 95
nonprofit-industrial complex, 25, 234, 235
nonprofits, 25–26, 234–35
NPU-M (Neighborhood Planning Unit-M), 207–8
NSMC (neighborhood social movement capacity), 47, 51, 88, 122, 123

October League, 79, 82–83
Ogden, Garry, 227–28, 230
Olympic Games (1996), 170, 194, 195, 202, 203; post-Olympic Black Atlanta, 208, 209; public housing in Atlanta and, 199–201, 204; working-class Black Atlantans and, 10, 31
Olympic gentrification, 170, 188, 189–94, 198–201, 202, 205
Olympic Stadium, 31, 189–94, 205, 238
Oppenheimer, Martin, 18, 19

Patillo, Mary, 91
Payne, Billy, 188–92
Peoplestown, 236–37
Perdue, Sonny, 243–44, 286
Persells, Lester, 75, 77
petty bourgeois activism, 209, 213, 223, 224, 232–33, 240; empowerment zones and, 210; against working-class Black Atlantans, 253, 256, 257, 258, 276–77
petty bourgeoisie, 26–27, 84, 91, 235. *See also* Atlanta petty bourgeoisie; Black petty bourgeoisie
philanthropy, 184–87, 313n68
Polanyi, Karl, 137
political economy, 13, 28, 32, 56, 280, 284
poor Atlantans. *See* low-income Atlantans
poor Black people, 97, 196, 251–58, 262

poor urbanites, 175, 242
poverty, 42–43, 182, 242–43, 261–62, 316n49; Black poverty wages, 251; CDCs and poverty reform market, 235–36
Prather, Harold, 38, 39
private and charter schools, 223–24, 225–27, 228–31
privatization, Georgia and, 243–44
privatization in Atlanta, 135–36, 146, 150, 212, 216–44; Black Atlanta workers and, 167; domestic capital and, 151
pro-growth, anti-working-class movements, 208–9
pro-growth interests, 195, 213–14
pro-growth revitalization of Atlanta, 32
proletarianization, 17–18, 170, 176, 283. *See also* subproletarianization
property in Atlanta, 96–101, 99, 104, 105, 195, 244–45; devalorization of, 156–58, 238–39. *See also* housing in Atlanta
protests by Black Atlantans, 1, 2, 57, 112, *112*, 115–16; Black Atlanta public schools and, 60–63; against Vine City displacement, 163, 164, 166
protonationalism, 58, 64, 66, 85, 87; revolutionary, 36, 37; of working-class Black Atlantan women, 70–77
public housing in Atlanta, 138–44, 199, 204, 242; AHA and, 75–77, 151, 200–201, 205–6, 252–58; Black Atlantans and, 199–200, 252–58;; destruction of, 205, 206, 252–58; end of, 252–58
public schools, 58. *See also* Atlanta Public Schools

RAB (Resident Advisory Board), 254–55, 257
race, 15–16 , 17, 175–76
racial class, 26–27, 51, 91, 185. *See also* intraracial class conflict
racial class, in Atlanta, 4, 29, 36, 215. *See also* Black Atlanta intraracial class conflict

racial class struggle, 20, 25, 252
racial oppression, 32, 48, 171, 281–82, 287, 305n2
racist violence, 56–57, 64. *See also* anti-Black violence, by Atlanta police
Ranciere, Jacques, 196
Reagan, Ronald, 171–73
real estate in Atlanta, 150, 158, 172, 179, 245–46. *See also* gentrification in Atlanta
real estate investment trusts (REITs), 151
Reed, Adolph, Jr., 90, 91, 93, 120
Reed, Kasim, 249–50, 274, 275–76
REITs (real estate investment trusts), 151
Renewal Community, 212
reparations for Black Americans, 286–88
repression of working-class Black Atlantans, 121, 124–25, 131; and activists, 113–16, 120, 122–23, 134; by Atlanta power brokers, 90, 109, 110; Jackson, Maynard, and, 88, 89, 104, 110
Resident Advisory Board (RAB), 254–55, 257
resistance by Atlantans, to privatization of Atlanta schools, 224–27
resistance by working class, to gentrification, 23
resistance by working-class Black Atlantans, 90, 185, 187, 224–25
revitalization of Atlanta, 7, 32, 145, 147, 150, 180
revolutionary nationalism/radicalism, 52, 53, 55, 56, 85; working-class Black Atlanta neighborhoods and, 57–59; working-class Black Atlantans and grassroots, 44, 46
revolutionary protonationalism, 36, 37
Richardson, Demetrious, 241
Richmond, Isaac, 55
Russell, Herman J., 211

sanitation strikes, 34–36, 101–10
SCLC. *See* Southern Christian Leadership Conference
Shabazz, John, 60, 61, 123

Index   341

Shaffer, Joe, 38, 46
Smith, Neil, 23, 156, 157
SNCC (Student Nonviolent Coordinating Committee), 45–46, 52
SNI (Summerhill Neighborhood Incorporated), 188–90, 192–94, 235, 238
social movements: nonprofits and, 26, 234, 235; NSMC, 47, 51, 88, 122, 123. *See also* working-class social movements
social services, in Atlanta metro suburbs, 262–63
social welfare divestment, 97, 256–57, 262
Southern Center for the Study of Public Policy, 28, 123, 173, 180, 215
Southern Christian Leadership Conference (SCLC), 45, 57, 73–74, 81, 83, 123–25, 129
Stack, Carol, 50
stadium construction, working-class Black Atlantans and, 3, 29, 32
Stamford, John H., 195–96
Stone, Clarence, 15–16
STOP. *See* Committee to Stop Children's Murders
strikes: AHA public housing rent strike, 75–77; Atlanta petty bourgeoisie and, 82, 83–85; Atlanta police and, 74, 75, 76, 82, 83; Black petty bourgeoisie and, 74, 83–85; by Black restaurant workers, 68, 69, 70, 73–75; Church's Chicken restaurants strike, 73–75; in East Lake Meadows, 72–75; Mead wildcat strike, 22, 78–85; Miller and, 79–81, 83, 85; 1967–1977 strikes, 37, 103; sanitation strike (1970), 34–36; sanitation strike (1977), 101–10; Williams, Hosea, 73–74, 82–85; Young, Andrew, and, 83, 84–85
structural violence, 4, 11–12, 20, 23–25, 173, 242
Student Nonviolent Coordinating Committee (SNCC), 45–46, 52
subproletarianization, 17, 176, 197, 283; gentrification and, 13, 24, 32; of Black

Atlanta workers, 6, 8, 11, 13, 39, 41, 72, 85, 88, 170, 181–82, 242, 263; of Black workers, 7, 8, 10, 13, 18–20, 29, 32, 39, 170, 280, 282, 284
subproletarian labor, 280; Atlanta leadership and, 249; of suburban working-class Black Atlantans, 261, 267, 285
suburban Black Atlantan poor, 183, 241–42, 258–61, 264–66; extended-stay motels and, 269; neoliberalization and, 262–63
suburbanization of working-class Black Atlantans, 183, 241, 259, 262; gentrification in Atlanta and, 242, 263–64; subproletarianization and, 242, 263
suburban working-class Black Atlantans, 183, 241–42, 258–60; problems of, 262–63; subproletarian labor of, 261, 267, 285. *See also* working-class Black Atlanta metro suburbs
Sum-Mec buying club, 50
Summerhill, 50, 63–64, 165, 188–94, 235, 238
Summerhill Neighborhood Incorporated (SNI), 188–90, 192–94, 235, 238
Summerhill rebellion (1966), 29, 30, 36, 38–39, 44–45, 292n10

taxes, working class and Reagan policy on, 171–72
taxes in Atlanta, 96–101, 99, 104, 105, 195, 244–45
tax increment financing bonds (TIF bonds), 144, 302n25
Techwood Advisory Committee, 200
Techwood Homes, 133, 141, 199–201, 205
Thompson, E. P., 20
Thornton, Cecil, 60, 61
TIF bonds (tax increment financing bonds), 144, 302n25
transportation in Atlanta: in Black suburbs, 262–64; MARTA, 103, 183, 212, 248, 263
Trotter, Joe W., 16, 17, 18

Ture, Kwame, 25, 45
Turner, Lou, 6, 51, 93, 280
Turner, Ted, 194

underclass, as concept, 17
underground economy, 196–97, 204–5, 251–52
unions, 103–7, 109, 280–81. *See also* Black Atlantan unions; strikes
United States (US), 18–20, 134, 153, 316n49
urbanization of Atlanta, 6, 20, 278
urban removal of working-class Black Atlantans, 4, 6, 15, 132; from Auburn Avenue, 160–62, 237; in Vine City, 1–3, 162–67
urban revitalization, 7, 32, 145, 147, 150, 180
urban studies, 12, 18
use value, of working-class Black Atlanta neighborhoods, 46–52, 57, 75

Vine City, 1–3, 56, 162–67, 249, 273–77
Vine City Atlanta Project, SNCC, 45–46
violence. *See* racist violence; structural violence; violent crime in Atlanta
violent crime in Atlanta, 196–98

Walmart, 249–50
Ward, Colette, 1
Ware, J. Lowell, 28, 122
Weiss, Peter, 34
West End neighborhood, 212–13
Whatley, Louise, 60, 61, 71, 72, 75, 77, 205–6
white capitalism, 55, 56, 92, 94
white supremacy, 13, 281
Williams, Hosea, 45, 57, 73–74, 82–85, 124
Wooten, Jim, 256–57
workers: neoliberalization's assault on, 134, 135, 152, 304n49; philanthropy by capitalists and, 313n68
working class, 26; gentrification as structural violence against, 11–12, 23–24, 242; Reagan tax policy and, 171–72; underemployment after Great Recession for, 251–52

working-class Atlantans, 2–3. *See also* working-class Black Atlantans
working-class Black Atlanta: destruction of, 278; fragmentation of, 134; international capital and, 149, 167
working-class Black Atlanta communities. *See* working-class Black Atlanta neighborhoods
working-class Black Atlanta metro suburbs, 262–68, 284, 316n55. *See also* suburban working-class Black Atlantans
working-class Black Atlantan activists, 20, 21–22, 32–33, *121*, 205; in Black Belt, 2, 35, 56, 61, 63, 71, 75, 85; repression of, 113–16, 120, 122–23, 134
working-class Black Atlanta neighborhoods, 46–52, 57–59, 75, 211, 212; Atlanta child murders in, 90, 125–31; BUR and, 169; CBD and, 146; class warfare and, 170; informal support networks of, 49–51; kinship networks in, 50, 155; loss of public resources in, 10; movements of, 56, 63–64, *65*, *66*; redlining of, 156; sanitation strike (1977) and, 108; Young, Andrew, and, 179. *See also* Black Belt; urban removal of working-class Black Atlantans
working-class Black Atlantan movement actors, 58, 61, 62, 64, 66, 85
working-class Black Atlantan rebellions: Broad Street rebellion, 86–89; King, Rodney, and, 169; Summerhill rebellion, 29, 30, 36, 38–39, 44–45, 292n10
working-class Black Atlantans, 44, 101, 153, 224–25, 230–31, 239; anti-working-class policies and, 30–31, 97, 106, 131, 182; Atlanta leadership and, 1–2, 3, 9, 30, 117–19; Atlanta power brokers vs., 6, 8, 31, 90, 108–10, 129–31, 240; Black Atlantan elites vs., 9–15, 100, 108; BUR and, 31, 88, 93, 97, 106, 112, 128, 131, 182; capitalism and, 6, 10, 15, 46; class warfare against, 170, 253, 257, 258; as community heroes, 25;

working-class Black Atlantans (*continued*)
film production in Atlanta and, 286; gentrification and, 31–32, 88, 167, 196, 214–16, 234, 242, 277; Great Recession and, 242–43, 246–58, 277; as internal colony, 59; Jackson, Maynard, and, 88, 89, 94, 100, 104–10, 117, 188; neoliberalization and, 30–31, 133–34, 154–56, 159, 167, 215–16; Olympic Games and, 10, 31; petty bourgeois activism against, 253, 256, 257, 258, 276–77; poverty of, 42–43; real estate industry and, 245–46; revitalization of Atlanta and, 147, 150; SNCC Vine City Atlanta Project and, 45–46; stadium construction and, 3, 29, 32; structural violence against, 4, 20, 173; struggles against privatization in Atlanta by, 216–23; urbanization and, 6, 20. *See also* low-income Black Atlantans

working-class Black Atlantan social movements, 56, 59–64, 65, 66, 72–77, 197–98; infrapolitics and, 22; movement actors, 85; New Nadir and, 205; NSMC and, 47, 51; SCLC and, 123–25. *See also specific social movements*

working-class Black Atlantan women, 9, 68, 69, 70–71, 73–77, 125–31; autoworkers, 153–54; and extended-stay motels, 269–70; Great Recession and, 247; lack of housing for, 199; subproletarianization of, 72, 181–82

working-class Black Atlanta social institutions, 16; Atlanta police and, 113, 123; control of, 4, 8, 36, 46, 57, 66; other attacks on, 123

working-class Black mothers, STOP and, 9, 126–31

working-class Black people, 26; Black Atlanta class warfare and, 27; Clinton's damage to, 175–76; gentrification and, 152, 281; nonprofits and, 25, 234. *See also* working-class Black Atlantans

working-class social movements. *See* working-class Black Atlantan social movements

working-class social movements and pro-growth interests, 195

Wright, Diane, 257

Wright, Erik Olin, 20, 21

Young, Andrew, 10, 31, 54, 135–36, 148–50, 152; low-income Black Atlantans and, 181; neoliberalization in Atlanta and, 135–37, 148; real estate in Atlanta and, 179; strikes and, 83, 84–85

Young, Ivory, 2, 274–75

Zasulich, Vera, 14

www.ingramcontent.com/pod-product-compliance
Lightning Source LLC
Chambersburg PA
CBHW020635230426
43665CB00008B/187